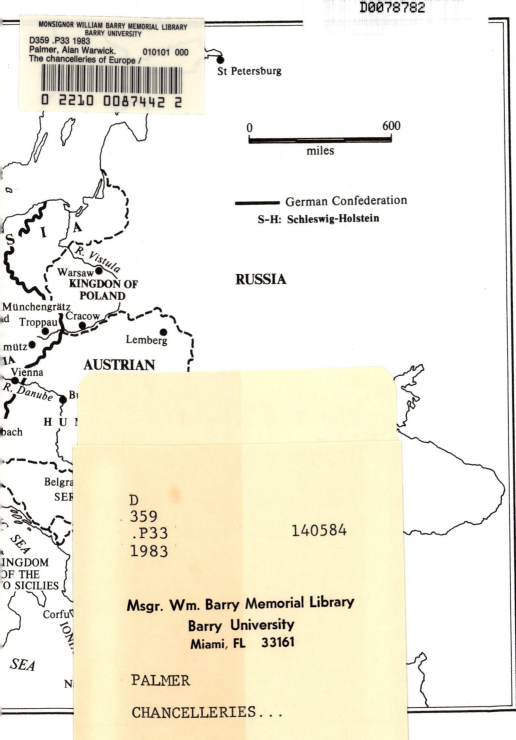

St Petersburg

0   600
miles

———— German Confederation
S-H: Schleswig-Holstein

RUSSIA

R. Vistula
Warsaw
KINGDON OF
POLAND
Münchengrätz
d Troppau Cracow
mütz
Lemberg
IA
Vienna
AUSTRIAN
R. Danube Bu
H U N
bach

Belgra
SER

SEA
INGDOM
OF THE
O SICILIES
Corfu
SEA
N

The Chancelleries of Europe

The Chancelleries of Europe

ALAN PALMER

London
GEORGE ALLEN & UNWIN
Boston   Sydney

George Allen & Unwin (Publishers) Ltd,
40 Museum Street, London WC1A 1LU, UK

George Allen & Unwin (Publishers) Ltd,
Park Lane, Hemel Hempstead, Herts HP2 4TE, UK

Allen & Unwin, Inc.,
9 Winchester Terrace, Winchester, Mass. 01890, USA

George Allen & Unwin Australia Pty Ltd,
8 Napier Street, North Sydney, NSW 2060, Australia

First published in 1983.

British Library Cataloguing in Publication Data

Palmer, Alan
    The chancelleries of Europe.
1. Europe – Foreign relations   2. Europe –
History – 19th century
I. Title
327'.094   D363
ISBN 0–04–940071–1

Library of Congress Cataloging in Publication Data

Palmer, Alan Warwick.
    The chancelleries of Europe.
Includes index.
1. Europe – Foreign relations – 1815–1871.
2. Europe – Foreign relations – 1871–1918. 3. Europe –
Politics and government – 1815–1871. 4. Europe –
Politics and government – 1871–1918. 5. World
politics – 19th century. 6. World politics –
1900–1918. 7. Diplomacy. I. Title.
D359.P33   1983   327.4   83–6442
ISBN 0–04–940071–1

Set in 10 on 11 point Bembo by Nene Phototypesetters Ltd, Northampton
and printed in Great Britain
by Mackays of Chatham

Contents

D
359
. P33
1983

140584

Preface

The hundred years which separate the downfall of Napoleon from the Sarajevo assassinations saw the perfection and ultimate failure of a unique diplomatic system. For the first time in modern history the conduct of relations between independent states was regulated by codes of procedure established by the five Great Powers of Europe. In 1814 Austria, France, Great Britain, Prussia and Russia began to assume a collective responsibility for maintaining peace or plunging the continent into war. Over the following hundred years Europe enjoyed longer periods of general stability than ever before. There was only one armed conflict which lasted for more than seven months, and that was fought out almost entirely on the west coast of a distant peninsula in the Black Sea, ravaging a comparatively small area of a vast empire. Three traditional campaigning cockpits of earlier wars – the Netherlands, the Baltic littoral, Poland – were spared the devastation of invading armies throughout the hundred years. Yet the diplomatic system of the nineteenth century stirred many contemporaries to righteous indignation and became a particular butt of American liberal idealists during and after the First World War. The system, so its critics said, perpetuated the dominance of three great autocracies and two colonial empires over both Europe and a Europeanised world. It allegedly encouraged governments to conclude secret treaties, the terms of which were cynically concealed from the newspapers and from Parliament. Above all, it completed the conversion of statecraft, by nature a primitive political science, into a sophisticated discipline of artifice practised by professional diplomats who gradually came more and more to formulate policy.

Already by 1814 there were specialised ministries of foreign affairs in almost every country of Europe. They were created during the eighteenth century so as to give coherence to diplomatic practices which had developed with the establishment of permanent ambassadorial representation and reporting in the later years of the Italian Renaissance. Russia under Peter the Great and the Empress Catherine, Austria under Maria Theresa, Prussia under Frederick William I and Frederick II, Sweden under Gustavus III accepted and amended the so-called 'French system' of cabinet diplomacy which was associated in the first instance with Richelieu and Mazarin but was elaborated and expanded throughout the reign of Louis XV. Administratively only Great Britain lagged behind. Charles James Fox became the first 'Secretary of State for Foreign Affairs' as late as March 1782 and it was not until the close of the Napoleonic Wars that Castlereagh as Foreign Secretary gained an ascendancy within the Cabinet comparable to the prestige held by Chancellors of the great continental powers.

It was, too, in the later years of the Napoleonic Wars that respected public figures began to be accredited as ambassadors in foreign capitals. At first they were mainly soldiers. Gradually, however, a diplomatic corps, small by twentieth-century standards but proud of its distinctive rights and privileges, came to play an important role in the social and political life of London, Paris, Berlin, Vienna and St Petersburg. Like any other profession, diplomacy encouraged a sense of intimacy among its practitioners, something unknown to the ambassadors of the seventeenth and eighteenth centuries and necessarily inhibited by ideological divisions during the second half of the twentieth century. From 1815 to 1870 a bond of community and understanding developed among sovereigns, statesmen and diplomats which survived even the tensions of the Bismarckian era. Most families entering the foreign service of their country came from the aristocracy or the landed gentry. They were at ease with the French language, they shared common sporting or cultural interests, gravitated towards the same spas as they became older and goutier and discovered that they possessed similar social values, although with differing emphasis according to their country of origin. Between such people it was natural there should be cosmopolitan friendships; and sometimes there were marriage links, too. Frequently, of course, there were also personal feuds and petty jealousies, which sometimes influenced policy. In the continental autocracies many successful diplomats were ultimately given direction of foreign affairs: Metternich, Bismarck, Gorchakov, Bulow, Aehrenthal and Berchtold were all ambassadors before preferment to higher posts. In Britain five Foreign Secretaries, of whom three became Prime Minister, had served as an ambassador: George Canning, the Duke of Wellington, Aberdeen, Clarendon and Kimberley. French practice varied: three of Napoleon III's Foreign Ministers had been ambassadors first; but there were some famous instances of former French Foreign Ministers being subsequently appointed to embassies abroad, notably Talleyrand and Waddington to London and Delcassé to St Petersburg. The diplomatic circle of the European capitals remained small, select and influential.

Within this diplomatic system there was sufficient homogeneity for those who understood its esoteric mysteries to win wide respect, and occasionally envy, from outsiders. Diplomats were a caste apart from the bureaucrats who toiled in other departments of state, especially in St Petersburg, Vienna and Berlin where the sovereign interested himself personally in the shaping of foreign policy. By the last quarter of the nineteenth century the Press, especially in London and Paris, was writing in awe of these men who seemed to determine the pattern of foreign affairs, either as executants or as advisers to their chief. Newspapers referred to them as a collective entity, 'The Chancelleries of the Great Powers' or 'The Chancelleries of Europe'. They could, it seems, receive reports which might 'disturb' or 'divide' them. Occasionally they were 'gratified to learn' of some event. Sometimes, ominously, they were said to have 'met the news with firm resolve'.

Technically, no doubt, there are objections to the use of the phrase 'Chancelleries of Europe'. A chancellery was originally the secretariat of a Chancellor and therefore as much concerned with domestic problems in the great continental empires as with foreign policy. Moreover, purists might argue that there was only a single period of four years, from 1867 to 1871, when there were as many as three Chancelleries in Europe at the same time: Bismarck's in Berlin, Gorchakov's in St Petersburg and Beust's in Vienna. Yet, as Harold Nicolson wrote in the late 1930s, 'The phrase "The Chancelleries of Europe" is in practice indistinguishable from the phrase "The Foreign Offices of the Powers"'. Chancellery diplomacy is at least as valid a concept as the 'cabinet diplomacy' which preceded it or the 'open diplomacy' of the twentieth century.

The following pages outline the history of these specialised ministries of foreign affairs during the era of chancellery diplomacy from the moment when Castlereagh first linked Great Britain with the European states system in 1814 to the fall of the old Europe in the winter of 1918–19. This book does not pretend to discover any new and meaningful interconnection of global forces nor does it claim primacy in historical significance for motives of domestic politics or ideological conflict or the clash of trade rivalry. Basically *The Chancelleries of Europe* is about 'chaps and maps'. It is concerned with the men – and very occasionally the women – who determined policy in Foreign Office, embassy, or Chancellery. It looks at their relationship with one another and with the world around them; and it examines the way in which their conduct of diplomacy kept pace with the quickening communications of a fast-changing century and a narrowing world.

1 Innocent Abroad, 1814

At half-past seven in the evening of Monday 27 December 1813, four carriages pulled away from Lord Castlereagh's London home at the corner of King Street, St James's. 'A large concourse of people', as *The Times* reported next day, 'expressed loud demonstrations of joy' as the Foreign Secretary, his wife, her niece and her nephew entered the first carriage. They were followed down the steps of number 18 St James's Square by a junior member of the government, the Hon. Frederic Robinson, who was to serve for five undistinguished months as Prime Minister in the winter of 1827–8 when he was Viscount Goderich. Joseph Planta, at 26 a senior clerk with eleven years' experience of the Foreign Office, travelled in the second carriage as Castlereagh's private secretary. A copyist, four king's messengers and a handful of coachmen and domestic servants completed the party. It was not an impressive delegation to leave London for what now would be reckoned a 'summit conference', but to the onlookers who cheered that evening in St James's Square the departure of even this small cavalcade seemed proof that the long war with Napoleon was at last coming to an end; for why otherwise should a Foreign Secretary set out for the coast and the continent on a bitterly cold night so soon after Christmas?

Not since 1743, when Carteret as Secretary of State for the Northern Department accompanied George II on the Dettingen campaign, had a British minister responsible for foreign affairs left England on a continental mission. And Castlereagh, a sick man for much of the autumn, never anticipated that he might spend the worst of the winter in Europe. Continental diplomacy was by now accustomed to Foreign Ministers superseding ambassadors and formulating policy while travelling abroad: Metternich, for example, spent six months of his first year as Austria's Foreign Minister in residence at Napoleon's court. But Castlereagh's department of state was still small and compact. Tsar Alexander I of Russia had over 250 officials in the Foreign Ministry at St Petersburg while Metternich could count on a large, well-trained staff in Vienna. There was by contrast something endearingly amateur about the composition of Castlereagh's Foreign Office in 1813: two under-secretaries, two senior clerks and some twenty juniors, the best précis-writers recruited straight from Eton and promised a full £25 bonus as recompense for the extra papers they had to prepare now that peace seemed to be breaking out. Castlereagh himself doubted if the department could stand the administrative strain of an absentee Foreign Secretary. Nor was this the only objection. Castlereagh, though a titular viscount, was an Irish peer and not a member of the Lords but Leader of the House of Commons, where he was the sole government spokesman on foreign affairs. When in late November the Cabinet began to consider the dispatch of a minister to a conference with the allies the Prime Minister, Lord Liverpool, was convinced that the one person he could not spare was Castlereagh.

There was, however, urgent need for Britain to be represented at allied headquarters by someone who could speak and act with authority and understanding. In the third week of October the combined armies of Russia, Austria and Prussia inflicted a severe defeat on Napoleon at Leipzig, forcing him to retreat across the Rhine and bringing war to metropolitan France for the first time in twenty years. In the same month Wellington's army cleared the Pyrenees and invaded France from the south-west. Yet these military successes, which seemed to herald final victory, exposed the essential weakness of the coalition against Napoleon. Britain, Russia and Prussia were linked by the treaties of Reichenbach of June 1813 and the Russian and Prussian armies were subsidised by British gold. Metternich, having first sought to end the war by armed mediation, brought Austria into the coalition two months later. Castlereagh believed it essential that Napoleon's enemies should be united in a formal quadruple alliance, but all attempts to bind the coalition closer together foundered on the growing mutual suspicion of Metternich and Tsar Alexander. Metternich had no wish to see the Tsar replace Napoleon as effective master of Europe; and Alexander, for his part, was convinced that the Austrians were holding back the allied advance beyond the Rhine so as to reach a compromise peace with Napoleon. Despite the presence of three British ambassadors at allied headquarters in Frankfurt, there was complete confusion over the war aims of the British government, and in the first week of December it was agreed that Count Pozzo di Borgo, a Corsican exile serving in the Russian diplomatic service, should travel to London, inform Castlereagh of the difficulties in concluding the quadruple alliance and urge him to come to headquarters so as to save the coalition from disintegration. Reluctantly the Cabinet decided on 20 December that Castlereagh would have to make the journey abroad. Next day the Russian, Austrian and Prussian envoys to London were invited to dinner by Lord Liverpool and told the news. No one at the Prime Minister's dinner party that Tuesday can have appreciated its momentous significance. A British statesman was about to step for the first time into the arena of chancellery politics.

Today a Foreign Secretary might make the journey on which Castlereagh set out that Monday after Christmas in a hundred minutes, from city centre to city centre. It took Castlereagh three weeks: for Christmas in 1813 heralded the most severe weather anyone could remember and Castlereagh's expedition possesses an epic quality worthy of the occasion. As the four carriages trundled eastwards that evening they were enveloped in icy yellow fog. Street lamps projecting from shop fronts became mere luminous dots marking a route through the gloom; the outriders were forced to lead the horses at walking pace, finding their way only with the aid of flambeaux. At Whitechapel Castlereagh ordered his servants to sit upon the trunks and boxes for fear of footpads clambering aboard and cutting them off. Already the Prince Regent, who left Carlton House for Hatfield an hour or two earlier, had turned back in Tottenham Court Road after a mile of London's murky streets. But Castlereagh knew he could not so lightly abandon his journey; at Harwich the frigate HMS *Erebus* was waiting to convey his party, their baggage and their good, English-built carriages across the North Sea to Hellevoetsluis; and somewhere west of the Rhine the allied ministers were discussing, with mounting dissension, the ways to end the war with France. At such a time it was vexing for the British plenipotentiary to seek lodging for the night at an inn in Romford, barely 15 miles from St James's Square. But Castlereagh was by nature too patrician to permit the incidence of bad weather to delay his mission. The four carriages were on their way again soon after six next morning. The travellers reached Harwich at midday to find that, though the fog had lifted, there was no wind. On Wednesday morning the carriages were embarked in *Erebus* and Castlereagh's party was joined by the returning Russian envoy, Pozzo di Borgo. That night the frigate put to sea, only to remain becalmed throughout New Year's Eve and New Year's Day in Harwich Roads. *The Times* on Monday 3 January reported that a wind had sprung up in the small hours of Sunday and that the Foreign Secretary would reach The Hague that evening. This was a false assumption. The wind turned to gale force, icy waves made it impossible to keep a footing on deck, and *Erebus* spent three nights wallowing off the Dutch coast as the captain waited for a pilot who knew the Maas estuary. When the frigate at last approached Hellevoetsluis on 5 January Castlereagh and Pozzo were honoured by what they assumed were salutes from a local fort. As round shot began falling unpleasantly close, someone remembered that this region of Holland had been freed from French occupation only a few weeks previously; and the Dutch distrusted foreign warships which sailed unexpectedly up the estuary.[1]

Castlereagh reached The Hague safely on the evening of Thursday 6 January, eleven days after leaving London. Next morning he discovered that headquarters had left Frankfurt and were established in Basle, over 600 miles up the Rhine. By now the cold was so intense that sections of the Rhine were frozen hard, as also was the Thames in London. Lady Castlereagh, he decided, should remain at The Hague with her niece and nephew. On the evening of 9 January he set out for Basle, with Robinson sharing his carriage along roads that were 'worse than a ploughed field frozen'. Staff and servants followed as best they could in coaches or waggons. 'The last 20 English miles took us 10½ hours', he wrote to his wife from Munster on 11 January. Four days later, from Frankfurt, he reported that 'Robinson and I have hardly ever seen any other object than the 4 glasses of the carriage cover'd with frost which no sun could dissolve, so that we were in fact imprisoned in an Ice House for days and nights'. Only once did he agree to Robinson's suggestion that they might snatch a few hours of sleep at an inn. Otherwise the British mission pressed forward indomitably down the frozen roads. Not until 18 January did Castlereagh, an incongruous figure wearing a fur cap with a gold band, jockey boots and red breeches, at last reach Basle. He was met by the British ambassadors to Russia and Austria, General Lord Cathcart and the Earl of Aberdeen, and by his own half-brother, Major-General Sir Charles Stewart, who was envoy extraordinary to Prussia.

These rigorous days in an icy carriage gave Castlereagh an opportunity to reflect on the problems of wartime coalition. Robinson later recalled some of his companion's conversation during the journey, how he had spoken of the need for statesmen to meet and talk freely so as to avoid the friction caused by negotiation at third hand and long range. He hoped, as Robinson cumbersomely wrote, 'many pretensions might be modified, asperities removed, and the causes of irritation anticipated and met'.[2] Yet in fact Castlereagh knew few foreigners and understood continental politics less than he believed. He was a landowner from turbulent Ulster, born in 1769, forty-eight days after the future Duke of Wellington and fifty-eight days before the future Emperor of the French. Much of his early career was spent in Ireland, where he was Chief Secretary during the years of rebellion and Union from 1797 to 1801. The wars isolated England from the continent, except during the brief Peace of Amiens, and when he became Foreign Secretary in March 1812 there were no Russian or Prussian envoys in London while Austria was represented by an elderly diplomat of low rank, poor hearing and poorer eyesight, so cut off from Vienna that he sold embassy plate to keep himself in funds. When first Russia and then Prussia became enemies of France Castlereagh established polite relations with the diplomats they sent to London, but he remained suspicious of all Austrians, not least because Emperor Francis had been Napoleon's father-in-law since 1810 and Metternich, who negotiated the dynastic marriage, was still Austria's Foreign Minister.

Castlereagh had expected he would find the rulers of Russia, Prussia and Austria awaiting him at Basle. In this he was disappointed. Two days earlier Tsar Alexander I, impatient to accompany the advancing army, left Basle for Langres in eastern France, where the Austrian general, Prince Schwarzenberg, had established field headquarters as supreme allied commander. Emperor Francis and King Frederick William III of Prussia followed Alexander into France, the Tsar having with him his principal foreign policy adviser, Count Nesselrode. Lord Cathcart passed on to Castlereagh a private message from Alexander urging him to come to Langres before consulting the Prussians or the Austrians, but this was out of the question. Waiting for Castlereagh and dominating the conference salons at Basle by his prestige and accumulated experience was Clement von Metternich-Winneburg, created a prince by Emperor Francis three months before in gratitude for his 'wise direction' of Austria's foreign affairs over the previous four years.

The two statesmen met on the day after Castlereagh's arrival. To their mutual surprise they found it easy to collaborate. They were together for only four days – Castlereagh left for Langres on the evening of Saturday 22 January and Metternich followed him next morning – but this brief interlude of discussion was decisive in shaping British prejudices over the next ten years. Much remained beyond Castlereagh's comprehension, for he was still politically an innocent abroad. He did not, for example, begin to understand the importance of the Polish Question to Austria and Russia. He recognised, however, that island Britain – thinking of maritime rights, colonies in the Indies, settlements in southern Africa – judged the merits of any states system in Europe by different standards from those held by the continental land empires. Nothing could shake

Castlereagh's conviction that the first task of the allies was victory in the West and security against another war of conquest by the French, but he found such unexpected support from Metternich that he was prepared, in general, to back Austrian ideas over Europe's frontiers. Above all he accepted that the Austrian Empire, technically created only ten years before, was a European necessity, a potential counterweight to Russia and France and the surest guardian of the German and Italian lands. Small wonder Metternich was delighted with Castlereagh's good sense. 'I get on with him as if we had spent all our lives together', he declared in a private letter written after their third day of talks at Basle. 'Castlereagh behaves like an angel', he told Schwarzenberg enthusiastically a few days later.[3]

Castlereagh found Alexander deceptively co-operative when they met at Langres. Both Metternich and Castlereagh were in favour of an exploratory conference with the French Foreign Minister, Caulaincourt, in the hopes that the war would end without a costly campaign in France. Metternich had maintained that the Tsar would not be content until he had 'blown up the Tuileries' to avenge the destruction of Moscow during the French occupation of 1812. But at Langres Alexander let Castlereagh see that he had no objection to peace talks with Caulaincourt, and he was prepared to humour Metternich by agreeing that the final settlement of Europe should be determined at a great congress in the Austrian capital. Castlereagh travelled to Châtillon as an observer of the conference with the French. To his dismay he found the Russian delegate had no intention of allowing the conference to settle anything. Within a few days Castlereagh received an urgent message from Metternich begging him to return to headquarters and assist him in curbing the Tsar's impetuosity. For Alexander was now proposing to march directly on Paris, dictate peace and summon a convention of eminent Frenchmen, an 'Assembly of Notables', who would choose a ruler for France; they might, he indicated, wish for a regency on behalf of Napoleon's 3-year-old son, for a restoration of the Bourbons, or for a new monarchy under the former Marshal Bernadotte, now Crown Prince Charles John of Sweden and for many months a favourite candidate of the Tsar for the French throne. Nothing said by Metternich or by Castlereagh could make the Tsar change his mind. Frederick William III agreed with Alexander, as so often in the years ahead. The Foreign Secretary's fine hopes for a firm and unified quadruple alliance seemed shattered.

The unity of the coalition was saved not by the good sense of the allied leaders but by the genius and folly of Napoleon. A succession of tactically brilliant minor victories by the French in mid-February ruled out any immediate hopes of a triumphant advance on Paris, and at the same time they convinced Napoleon that he could insist on more generous peace terms than the 1792 frontiers proposed by the allies to Caulaincourt. Momentarily even the Tsar and Schwarzenberg succumbed to a wave of defeatism and it was left to Castlereagh to scoff at the alarmists and to find, from the panic, ways of binding the allies together. He was helped by Napoleon's clumsiness in demanding France's 'natural frontiers' and by clear evidence that the French might make counter-attacks but could not sustain a counter-offensive. The Foreign Secretary's calm impressed the Tsar. By the first week in March Castlereagh could inform Lord Liverpool: 'His Imperial Majesty now encourages me to come to him without form. I see him almost every day, and he receives me with great kindness and converses with me freely on all subjects.'[4] Castlereagh's dignified patience was bringing about that 'habitual, confidential free discussion' which he had told Robinson during the journey to Basle was an essential need of diplomacy during the uncertainties of war and peacemaking.

He achieved his first success with the conclusion of the Treaty of Chaumont of 9 March 1814. Russia, Austria, Britain and Prussia bound themselves in a grand alliance which would remain in being not merely until the defeat of Napoleon but for twenty years after the ending of the war so as to provide security against a resurgent France. There was still imprecision over the future pattern of Europe: provision was made for a confederated Germany, an independent Switzerland, an enlarged Netherlands and restitution, so far as possible, of the old order in the Iberian peninsula and Italy; but nothing was said about the future form of government in France or the fate of Poland. Critics might claim that some of the respect accorded to Castlereagh's views by his allies sprang from relief that the British were increasing their subsidy to £5 million for military operations in the year 1814 and were, at the same time, committed to maintaining a large army on the continent themselves. The Foreign Secretary was well pleased with what he called 'my treaty'. 'This, I trust will put an end to any doubts as to the claim we have to an opinion on Continental matters', he remarked in a note to the senior under-secretary at the Foreign Office. And in a message on 14 March to the ambassador at The Hague he used a significant phrase (apparently for the first time) when he commented on the willingness of 'the Great Powers' to safeguard the new kingdom of the Netherlands.[5] In these last weeks of war the allies assumed a status which, to the British, implied corporate responsibility for the peace of Europe.

At the beginning of March the allies recovered the initiative. By the final week of the month Alexander and Frederick William were again eager to advance on Paris. This time the British and Austrians did nothing to hold them back: Napoleon had wrecked all chance of a negotiated settlement. The allied armies entered Paris on 31 March, Alexander assuming the role of benevolent liberator rather than conqueror. Emperor Francis, Metternich, Castlereagh and the Prussian Chancellor, Karl von Hardenberg, remained in Dijon. The Tsar was left to settle the immediate future of French politics with that master of governmental improvisation, Talleyrand, France's Foreign Minister for all except four months of the ten years from 1797 to 1807. He had helped General Bonaparte become First Consul; now he was easing the Emperor Napoleon on his way to Elba.

Stewart thought it injudicious of his half-brother to allow Alexander and Talleyrand to achieve a working partnership. Urgent messages to Dijon begged Castlereagh to hurry to Paris and frustrate these devilish intrigues. But events played into Castlereagh's hands. The British thought the legitimate king of France, Louis XVIII, would provide the country with its surest guarantee against renewed upheaval. So, for the present, did Talleyrand; and it did not take him long to convince the Tsar that no true Frenchman could believe in any government other than a restored Bourbon constitutional monarchy. By 10 April, when Metternich and Castlereagh arrived from Dijon, Paris had 'decided for the white cockade' of the Bourbons, and Napoleon signed his abdication at Fontainebleau. There was one snag: the Tsar, in negotiations with Caulaincourt, permitted Napoleon to retain the title of Emperor and agreed that he might rule as sovereign of Elba. The Austrians thought the island too close to the Italian mainland for political comfort while the British regretted wasting such a promising naval base on Bonaparte. Yet it did not seem so grave a matter as to warrant renewed friction between the allies. The alternative places of exile – Corsica, Sardinia, Corfu – gave wider scope for trouble-making. No one seems seriously to have considered any island outside the Mediterranean.

The war was over; but the business of diplomacy was only just beginning. Talleyrand, effective head of government throughout April, was confirmed as Foreign Minister by Louis XVIII in May. It was essential for the allies to make peace with the new government as soon as possible and decide on the future political map of Italy, where there was unrest in several cities. Chancellor Hardenberg favoured a rapid settlement of all European questions, but none of the other 'great wigs' (as Castlereagh called them) were prepared to follow the Prussian lead. Castlereagh himself hoped for agreement on western European boundaries and on overseas colonies while the statesmen were in Paris; he feared that if the peacemakers looked eastwards Austro-Russian difficulties would again jeopardise the alliance. Metternich was in no hurry to settle anything except the boundaries of France and of Italy; he was already assessing the advantages that would accrue to Austria from summoning a peace congress to Vienna; and he complained in a letter to his deputy that Paris was 'too much under the influence of the wretched Polish French and Frenchified Poles' for satisfactory discussions. Tsar Alexander, too, believed time was on his side. His army was master of Europe from the Vistula to the Moselle; so slow was the administrative response in his sprawling empire that only now in 1814, when everyone else was ready for peace, was Russia fully mobilised for war. He could profitably play power politics for a few months, tentatively put forward his claims to a free hand in Poland while seeing how far he could collaborate with Talleyrand and the restored Bourbons and testing the durability of the Anglo-Austrian partnership. There was, in consequence, a strange atmosphere of busy futility in Paris that spring and summer. The social trappings of diplomacy served as an excuse for delaying the settlement of intractable problems.

Castlereagh found it all very frustrating. He was chided by the Prime Minister for lingering in Paris instead of returning to London to help the government defend its policy in the Commons. Castlereagh argued that it was important for him to remain 'till this new scene takes shape'. He refused to come himself – 'I really work as hard as a man can do in such a town as Paris' – and he could not spare Robinson so long as there were problems of compensation to discuss in preparing a peace treaty with France. Planta and the copyists were kept fully occupied with proposals for the incorporation of Belgium in a unified kingdom of the Netherlands, for colonial cessions and for the abolition of the slave trade. For preliminary discussions of the problems of Germany and Poland Castlereagh relied on his king's principal Hanoverian Minister, Count Munster, who had no obligations to Liverpool's government but was conscious of a personal bond of loyalty to the Prince Regent. In Paris, as in London, the Foreign Secretary depended for assistance on a small staff but tended to conduct all important business personally, working long hours and rarely delegating authority, even to the three ambassadors who had come with him from Basle. He lived, worked and entertained in a wing of the Ministry of Finance in the Rue Neuve des Capucines, close to the French Foreign Ministry and to Talleyrand's home in the Rue St Florentin.

The Foreign Office archives for the year 1814 show that Castlereagh's six months on the continent cost the British taxpayer slightly more than ten and a half thousand pounds. It is an interesting comment on life in Paris that one-seventh of this sum came from the cook's expenses during the six weeks of peacemaking, when Castlereagh's household was spending almost £40 a day on food; for Paris in that spring pursued pleasure with greedy extravagance, as if making up for the privations of the winter.[6] Castlereagh had told Robinson during the journey from Frankfurt that he thought it essential to find a way in which ministers and diplomats could meet and talk informally. Only two years previously Napoleon had sent a new envoy off to Warsaw with the advice, 'Keep a good table and take care of the ladies'. Now almost by accident Castlereagh was to test the worth of the fallen emperor's advice in his own capital.

On 18 April Lady Castlereagh arrived in Paris with her niece, Lady Emma Mount Edgecumbe, after spending five days in a cramped carriage travelling south from The Hague. As the only allied statesman's wife to make the journey to Paris, Emily Castlereagh felt it her duty to act as hostess at formal dinners or light suppers on almost every evening. She was a virtuous, good-natured woman, rather dull and devoid of any dress sense, but eager to help and cosset her husband. The Rue Neuve des Capucines could not offer the brilliant small talk of Mme de Staël's salon out at Clichy – although the indefatigable Germaine de Staël was careful not to neglect Lady Castlereagh's evening gatherings – but at least it enabled 'conquerors and conquered' to come together amicably. Lord Aberdeen, a widower of 30, despised her hospitality: 'Lady Castlereagh's suppers after the play', he wrote, 'might just as well be in St James Square, except that they are attended here by Englishmen of a worse description and scarcely by any women at all.' But Aberdeen, who had once dined at Malmaison as guest of the First Consul, resented Castlereagh's personal intrusion into European politics and his habit of keeping loquacious envoys uninformed. No doubt the Foreign Secretary was too shy and his Emily too wide-eyed at finding herself a Parisian hostess for the Castlereagh suppers to become a natural rendezvous for intriguers, but their political innocence excited curiosity. 'One evening early', Lady Mount Edgecumbe recalled, 'there arrived without invitation the Duchess of Courland' and two of her daughters, Wilhelmine Duchess of Sagan and Dorothea Countess of Périgord, later the Duchess of Dino. The Duchess of Courland had long served as an intermediary between Tsar Alexander and Talleyrand; Wilhelmine of Sagan was Metternich's principal mistress and eleven months previously had shown superb tact in entertaining him and the Tsar independently on successive days at her Sudetenland château; while Dorothea – then a beauty of twenty – was just beginning a quarter of a century at the side of Talleyrand, her estranged husband's uncle and her mother's devoted lover. Between them these three women were to charm out forty years of Europe's secrets. But not, it would seem, from the Foreign Secretary's wife. They were courteously received in the Rue Neuve des Capucines; pleasantries were exchanged, but nothing of moment was said. When they left, their hostess for once permitted herself a comment: 'Emma', she observed to her niece, 'I am afraid we live in very bad company'. Lady Castlereagh's way of 'taking care of the ladies' was not Napoleon's.[7]

From such purely social gatherings her husband absented himself as often as possible. Once pressure of work even forced him to detail his secretary, Planta, to escort Emily, Emma and the Duke of Wellington to the opera, for Talleyrand's objections to the peace terms needed careful study and refutation. The French, at first willing to accept a return to the 1792 frontiers as the basis of a peace treaty, sought to strike bargains as soon as it became clear that time was wearing thin the unity of the Chaumont coalition. Talleyrand hoped to save the islands of St Lucia and Tobago for Louis XVIII and to secure a string of towns in southern Flanders, and he sounded out Metternich in the hope of winning Austrian support, at least over Belgium. But the Austrians had given up all interest in the Netherlands; Metternich was at that moment drafting a definitive memorandum for the Austrian commanding general in Lombardy and Venetia in which he insisted that the natural condition of the Italian peninsula was political fragmentation rather than unity; and he refused to take up the Belgian Question with Castlereagh at a time when he wanted the backing of the principal naval power in the Mediterranean for his Italian policy. The chief Russian negotiator, Nesselrode, was no more inclined to make concessions than Metternich. When Talleyrand sought to procrastinate he found the British Foreign Secretary ready to counter delays with a threat: if peace could not be made in Paris then Talleyrand would have to come to London and conclude a settlement there. In London he would be without his sources of information and his visit would coincide with the victory celebrations of the allied sovereigns. He preferred to settle for the best terms he could obtain in Paris.

The peace treaty was signed in Paris on 30 May 1814. The frontiers of 1792 were restored, together with additional territory around Chambéry and Annecy and the inclusion of the former papal enclave of Avignon. The French surrendered all claims to territory in what are now Belgium, Switzerland, Italy, Germany and Malta; they ceded Tobago, St Lucia and Mauritius to Great Britain; they recognised that Belgium should be united with Holland to form the larger kingdom of the Netherlands which the British had sought for several years; and they undertook to abolish the slave trade at the end of five years. The terms looked generous: no army of occupation for France, no war indemnity, no return of treasures collected by Napoleon for the Louvre; the French received back their commercial posts in India and were allowed once more to send fishing vessels to the Newfoundland banks. The French, and all the governments who had fought in the recent war, were formally invited by a clause in the treaty to the congress which would be held at Vienna in the autumn. France almost enjoyed the new 'Great Power' status assumed, as of right, by the Chaumont allies – almost, but not quite. For supplementary clauses, outside the main treaty, provided for barriers to check French influence over the frontiers which the Revolutionary and Napoleonic armies had found so easy to dominate. It was agreed there should be some form of federation for the German states and Prussia should control most of the Rhineland; Lombardy and Venetia were to pass under Austrian control, which was to be intensified in northern Italy by a military alliance with Sardinia-Piedmont; and (although this was not settled until after the treaty was signed) the Dutch would receive £2 million from the British as compensation for the retention under British rule of Cape Colony, this money being spent on fortifying the new Franco-Dutch frontier through Flanders and Brabant. The key to the settlement was future security, not vengeance.

Castlereagh, his family and his staff left Paris on the evening after the treaty was signed. They crossed from Boulogne to Dover on 3 June, arriving back in Westminster next day. Although Castlereagh was by nature too austere to win easy popularity, he was cheered when he returned to the House of Commons after five months abroad. His mission had won for Britain a good peace and a wider range of influence. Experience had taught him, however, that peacemaking was a long process. Within three days he was followed to London by Alexander, Frederick William, Metternich, Hardenberg, Nesselrode and a romantic cavalcade of military heroes. For three weeks, as the allies officially celebrated victory, there was further talk of Poland and Saxony, the Rhineland, Spain and Italy with little agreed except that the future must wait on the decisions of the congress in Vienna. Yet Castlereagh was not displeased. For while Metternich and the Tsar were still as befogged over peace aims as in the winter, Castlereagh had already secured his principal objective, a settlement with France. Henceforth he could allow free rein to his gifts as a mediator, seeking to curb 'the restlessness of our time'. During those summer weeks of celebration, the streets, parks and palaces of London were illuminated in honour of the sovereigns and their victorious armies. There was a brisk trade among people of fashion in huge allegorical transparencies and Lady Emily would not miss so proud a moment to advertise her husband's virtues. Outside number 18 St James's Square an oversize dove held an olive branch in its mouth. Small wonder if, to some visitors in the square, it seemed the dove smiled with self-satisfaction.[8]

2 The Christian Conqueror, 1814–15

'I hope Fanny has seen the Emperor, and then I may fairly wish them all away', wrote Jane Austen in a letter from her Hampshire village on 23 June 1814. She was commenting on her niece's longing to set eyes on the Tsar during his visit to London, and her crisp impatience captures the changing mood of the public that midsummer. Alexander came as a popular idol, a soldier hero whose leadership shone with the lustre of victory. One widely read pamphlet lauded his virtues in a catalogue of inspired fabrications; another, written 'by a country gentleman', presented him as *The Christian Conqueror*, adding the explanatory antithesis *Or Moscow Burnt and Paris Saved*. At Westminster the Earl of Harrowby, Lord President of the Council in Liverpool's Cabinet, recalled with respect tinged with apprehension the Grand Design for European peace brought to London by Alexander's envoy when he was Pitt's Foreign Secretary, ten years before; and there were many other public figures prepared to welcome the Tsar as a wise, enlightened saviour of the continent. But Alexander was a paragon whose legend wilted under close inspection. Within a few days Earl Grey, leader of the Foxite Whigs, was dismissing him conversationally as 'a vain silly fellow'. The government found him unpredictable, the opposition thought him indiscreet, the Prince Regent complained of his capacity for intrigue. Several of his hosts were irritated by his restlessness; he even disappointed domestic servants by mean tipping. More seriously, he failed in public or in private to develop the paternalistic ideals for guaranteeing European peace with which, as Harrowby and Castlereagh knew, he had from time to time refreshed his spirit. Only in brief talks with two groups of English Quakers did he recall his quest for a European community pledged to maintain peace through a sense of Christian brotherhood.[1]

Alexander's failure to live up to the expectations of legend during his English visit is characteristic of his conduct of government. No other ruler of the age possessed such an imposing air of grandeur and nobility and none was so infused with an ideal of personal mission. None indeed, from 1814 onwards, could place so large an army into the fields of war. But, as Napoleon himself once remarked to Metternich, there was 'always something wanting' in Alexander. Was he a man of peace or of war, an autocrat or a reformer, a narrow Russian nationalist or a thwarted good European? To these questions his life gave no clear answer. At times it is as if he were seeking to reconcile two personalities in conflict within his mind. The murder of his father, Tsar Paul, in March 1801 left his conscience racked with guilt, for he had known of the plot even though he believed Paul would be deposed and not throttled by drunken officers in his own regiment. The longer Alexander reigned the more he was haunted by the sordid candlelit scuffling in the Mikhailovsky Palace which heralded his accession. To this burden of parricide was added the memory of two humiliations: defeat at Austerlitz in 1805 and a petition from his officers urging him to return to St Petersburg in July 1812 rather than serve at the head of his troops as Napoleon marched towards Moscow. During the black weeks of his life he began to turn in contrition to the scriptures, where he found consolation in the Psalms and a soul-shaking quickening of the spirit in the prophecies of Isaiah, Jeremiah and Ezekiel. This grafting of Cromwellian zeal for the Lord of Hosts on to the mysticism of Holy Russia made Alexander the most unpredictable of allies or antagonists. No one could be certain whether at any given moment the Tsar would be serenely wrapt in spiritual introspection, sombrely assessing the value to his empire of a particular settlement, or preparing a new concept of law among the nations which he would present in the name of the sacred rights of humanity. Occasionally, being by nature a sinner rather than a saint, he would forsake public duties and philander on a grand scale. He confounded contemporaries by his inconsistency. 'His heart and his conscience were honest', commented Metternich soon after the Tsar's death, 'but his mind was false'. It was hard to do business with someone whose motive impulse proved so often at variance with its mode of expression. Alexander gained and retained a reputation for duplicity.

There was, too, a further difficulty for anyone who wished to negotiate with the Russians during his reign. 'It is unfortunately the Emperor's habit to be his own minister and to select as the instrument of his immediate purpose the person who may happen to fall in most with his views', Castlereagh told Liverpool. Technically the titles of Chancellor and Foreign Minister were held from September 1809 until August 1814 by Count Nikolai Rumiantsev, who was originally given charge of foreign affairs in 1807 because he could collaborate with the French. But Rumiantsev was partially paralysed by a stroke in May 1812, and the Tsar used the opportunity of his Chancellor's illness to recruit specialist advisers into the Foreign Ministry and to advance younger men who, by training and temperament, would seek to assist him to shape foreign policy rather than dominate it themselves. Only rarely were these agents of the Tsar's will Russians by birth or by parentage. In London in 1814 he was helped by Karl von Nesselrode, the son of a Westphalian landowner and diplomat, by Prince Adam Czartoryski, head of one of the great Polish aristocratic families, and by the flamboyant Pozzo di Borgo, a Corsican enemy of the Bonaparte clan. Later in the year he was to use the Prussian, Heinrich vom Stein, the Alsatian, Jean Anstedt, the Corfiote, John Capodistria, and his former Swiss tutor, Frederic La Harpe. The only native Russian who played a prominent part in the making of peace was Count Andrei Razumovsky, for many years ambassador in Vienna; and Russian traditions were so alien to Razumovsky that he would never write the Russian language, accepting conversion to Catholicism in place of the Orthodox faith and marrying (twice) into the German-Austrian nobility. Razumovsky is remembered not for his achievements as a Russian diplomat but as a generous patron of Beethoven.

Nesselrode, the Tsar's principal assistant on foreign affairs during the last two years of the war, was 34 when he accompanied Alexander to London. He had been born in Lisbon of German parentage and was educated in Berlin, but he entered Russian service as a midshipman in Catherine the Great's navy when he was 16. He became a diplomat soon after Alexander's accession and served in Berlin, The Hague and Paris before becoming Foreign Ministry representative attached to the Tsar's personal staff during the 1812 campaign. He was never subject to the religious exultation which uplifted the Tsar and other eminent persons at the Russian court from time to time: 'My mother was a Protestant, my father a Catholic . . . I was baptised and became an Anglican for the remainder of my days', Nesselrode wrote in a fragment of autobiography. Strong feelings and convictions were foreign to his character. He rarely set himself against his sovereign, although he was opposed to the incorporation of all the Polish lands in the Russian Empire, as the Tsar wished, and he favoured closer collaboration with Austria than Alexander was prepared to accept, at least in 1814–15. 'I am summoned to him when I am needed, but otherwise I do not push myself forward', Nesselrode had written to his wife soon after joining the Tsar's personal staff in June 1812; to this practice he held true throughout his life. He was self-effacing and diligent, a natural ministerial secretary for an autocrat, and his qualities were fittingly rewarded. When Alexander returned on a brief visit to St Petersburg in the late summer of 1814, he accepted Rumiantsev's resignation as minister and officially created Nesselrode 'State Secretary for Foreign Affairs'. From 1816 to 1822 he was joint Foreign Minister, with Capodistria as his erratic colleague. He was then in sole charge of Russian foreign affairs until May 1856, holding the titular dignity of Chancellor from 1844 up to his death in 1862. Thus Nesselrode, the largely forgotten champion of the *status quo*, controlled the Russian Foreign Ministry for over forty years, a longer span than any other statesman, Tsarist or Soviet.[2]

During the London visit Nesselrode aroused less interest than Pozzo di Borgo or Czartoryski. Both men were already well known in England. Pozzo, exiled leader of the anti-Bonapartist Corsicans, was a British diplomatic agent until 1803, serving mainly in Vienna. He transferred to the Russian foreign service between 1805 and 1807 and rallied to the Russian cause again when Napoleon marched on Moscow. The Tsar sent him on a special mission to Sweden in the spring of 1813 as well as to London later in the year. He continued, after the end of the war, to advise Alexander on the problems of France and Italy, not always to the Tsar's liking. Czartoryski was even more familiar with British political life. He had spent a year in London in his early 20s and retained close links with the Whigs, especially Henry Brougham. The Tories, and Castlereagh in particular, respected Czartoryski for his patient work in bringing together the Third Coalition against Napoleon when he was Deputy Foreign Minister in 1804–5. At that time Czartoryski seemed to subordinate his Polish patriotism to a belief that Alexander, with whom he had been on terms of close personal friendship for nearly ten years, was stirred by beneficent ideals of international morality and justice. Much of Alexander's Grand Design of 1804 – a blueprint for a Europe with frontiers based on natural geographical boundaries and associating in one political unit 'homogeneous peoples able to agree among themselves' – was based upon memoranda drawn up by Czartoryski. Subsequently Czartoryski fell from favour, but he recovered much of his lost influence when Napoleon's puppet Grand Duchy of Warsaw was overrun by the Tsar's armies in 1813. Castlereagh met Czartoryski at allied headquarters in Chaumont early in March 1814 and again in Paris before he crossed to London. Some of the ideas put forward ten years previously were still in his mind, notably the establishment of a German confederation and recognition, in a public treaty, that mediation rather than war should be the natural means of settling disputes between the states. By now, however, Czartoryski saw himself above all as spokesman for the Polish cause. He was strongly committed to seeking a unified Polish kingdom under the Tsar's sovereign protection. Neither Castlereagh nor Metternich could welcome so one-sided a solution of the Polish Question. It seemed to them ominous that Tsar Alexander broke his journey from St Petersburg to Vienna for the Congress at the Czartoryski family estate of Pulawy and talked at length to members of the Polish aristocracy.[3]

On Sunday 25 September 1814 Alexander made a ceremonial entry into Vienna, with Frederick William of Prussia riding by his side, as if to emphasise in the Habsburg capital the dynastic friendship between Romanovs and Hohenzollerns. The Congress was expected to open on the following Saturday, and the Tsar assumed that the peacemakers would finish their task within six weeks. Castlereagh, having reached Vienna twelve days earlier, told one of the German diplomats he would be back in London by the end of November. Metternich, who had hoped to settle some questions before Alexander and Frederick William arrived, was less optimistic. He anticipated trouble with the Tsar over Poland.

The first problems, however, were procedural. They were exploited not by Alexander or his large delegation but by the chief French plenipotentiary, Maurice de Talleyrand. There had been no grand assembly to refurbish a war-weary Europe since the Congress of Westphalia in 1648; inexperience led to doubts and confusion over precedence and representation. Metternich, as Austria's Foreign Minister, was president of the Congress; and he had every intention of maintaining the mastery over lesser powers of the four Chaumont allies. Castlereagh, Nesselrode and Hardenberg agreed with him. Decisions of the Big Four would be presented to the other delegations; there was to be no European forum where ministers would haggle over particular territorial dispositions. Talleyrand, however, raised three objections at his first meeting with the Big Four, on the Friday after the Tsar's arrival. Why, he asked, were the Chaumont allies meeting informally to determine the form of the settlement before the Congress opened? Why were they seeking to perpetuate a wartime anti-Napoleonic alliance, excluding Bourbon France from their counsels? And why were they imposing a new order on Europe rather than taking into partnership the lesser rulers of the smaller states? 'The great need of Europe is to banish for all time the belief that rights depend on conquest alone and to revive the sacred principle of legitimacy from which stems order and stability' he declared.[4]

These were powerful arguments. Hardenberg tried to defend the dominance of the Great Powers: 'We cannot possibly have the affairs of all Europe settled by the Princes of Leyen and Liechtenstein', he said, citing petty sovereigns whose armies numbered, respectively, twenty-nine and fifty-seven men at the last count. 'We cannot have them settled by the ministers of Prussia and Russia, either', responded Talleyrand blandly. And a casual reference to the 'allies' led Talleyrand to another barbed reply: 'Let us speak frankly, gentlemen; if there are still allied powers, this is no place for me.' And he added: 'You would miss me.' All this procedural wrangling effectively postponed the opening of the Congress until the beginning of November. Talleyrand succeeded in having France recognised as a Great Power while Spain, Portugal and Sweden, too, were invited to join the co-ordinating body of the Congress, the 'Preliminary Committee of Eight'. But he achieved little for the status of the lesser rulers. Never once that winter did all 221 royal and princely delegations to Vienna meet in plenary session. Talleyrand commented sardonically on the 'Congress that never was', but he was not greatly troubled. As champion of legitimacy for the princes of Leyen and Liechtenstein the former Vice-Grand-Elector of Napoleon's impromptu empire is not wholly convincing.

Metternich was justified in his fear that Alexander would prove obstinate over Poland. Russian troops garrisoned every Polish city; they were also in the towns and villages of Saxony, whose king (Frederick Augustus) had remained loyal to his Napoleonic benefactor unfashion-ably long, and a Russian general was already established in Dresden to act as administrator of the kingdom. It was Alexander's intention to annex all the Grand Duchy of Warsaw, including the segments of the old Polish kingdom ceded to Prussia during the Partitions of 1792 and 1795, and he hoped to secure by negotiation with Metternich the Polish lands in Austrian Galicia. He would then proclaim a new Polish kingdom, technically independent but united to other parts of the Russian Empire through common allegiance to himself as emperor-king. Prussia would receive as compensation both the kingdom of Saxony and the Rhineland, while Metternich would be offered the Tsar's backing if he wished to consolidate Italy as a Habsburg dependency. Nesselrode and Pozzo thought the Tsar's Polish policy unrealistic. But Alexander was adamant: 'I have conquered the Duchy and I have half a million men to keep it', he told Castlereagh. 'I will give Prussia what is due to her, but not a single village to Austria.' Privately Castlereagh admitted that he feared the Tsar was becoming another Bonaparte.[5]

The Polish-Saxon Question dominated the Congress for the remaining weeks of the year and into January. It stymied the German Committee, whose members were seeking to establish a confederation acceptable alike to Austria, Prussia and some three dozen other German-speaking sovereignties. The committees on Tuscany, on Sardinia-Piedmont and Genoa, on Luxembourg and the former Duchy of Bouillon, on Switzer-land, on the gradual abolition of the slave trade, on diplomatic precedence, on the free navigation of international rivers, and on the collection of population statistics, could all meet and make recommendations of lasting value. But there was no possibility of the Congress completing its work so long as the Chaumont allies were divided into a Russo-Prussian bloc and an Anglo-Austrian bloc encouraged by Talleyrand. Attempts were made, especially by Castlereagh, to win Hardenberg's support for an Austrian compromise solution which would have given Prussia a segment of Saxony and most of the former Prussian Polish lands. Hardenberg, however, was under considerable pressure from the Prussian War Minister, Hermann von Boyen, and a group of distinguished generals who drew up plans for a lightning war against Austria in order to secure Saxony and deny Metternich any voice in the reshaping of Germany; and Frederick William himself peremptorily ordered a halt to his Chancellor's talks with Castlereagh. Metternich was less troubled by the Prussian hotheads than by the Tsar's insistence that he had every right to dispose of lands Russia's armies had conquered. A discussion between the two men on 24 October became so heated that the gossips of Vienna maintained they were about to fight a duel. This, of course, was an exaggeration; but, as Talleyrand contentedly reported to his king, Alexander did 'use language which was so violent that it would have seemed extraordinary even if addressed to one of his servants'. Metternich and Alexander subsequently declined to speak directly to each other for over four months. There was so much noisy sabre-rattling at the Congress that until Christmas outside observers spoke of general war being imminent over Poland.

Yet, in the last resort, only the Prussian officer corps was prepared to risk another winter campaign.[6] Since Prussia lacked the money or the resources to put independent armies into the field the war scares of Vienna seem highly artificial. The Tsar continued to puzzle foreign diplomats and his own advisers. Nesselrode and Pozzo di Borgo were totally out of favour by the middle of November, Razumovsky handling Polish affairs and Capodistria dealing with general matters. As late as Sunday 10 December, the Tsar was scarcely on speaking terms with the Emperor Francis, his host in the Hofburg Palace. But within five days Alexander unexpectedly mellowed. On the following Thursday he invited Francis to join him in two long discussions over Poland; and the Austrians were surprised to learn that he was now willing for Frederick Augustus to retain much of Saxony. He also agreed that Cracow, the earliest cultural centre of the Polish nation, should become a free and neutral city. There followed a strange episode, the significance of which has sometimes been exaggerated. On 3 January 1815 the French, British and Austrians concluded a secret defensive alliance, nominally intended to provide for joint action against Russia and Prussia. Talleyrand made much of his diplomatic success when writing to Louis XVIII – 'Sire, the coalition is dissolved for ever, and France is no longer isolated in Europe' – but, in reality, the treaty was a bluff to call a bluff. Within two days Alexander mentioned to Castlereagh that he was surprised to hear reports of a secret treaty between his former allies and the French, but he continued to seek agreement over Poland and Saxony, and this time he took care to curb the Prussians, too. The worst disputes were over. By the third week in February it was accepted that Prussia would take two-fifths of the former Saxon kingdom and would recover Poznania; Austria would retain Galicia and recover Tarnopol; Cracow would become a free city; and the rest of Poland would form Alexander's kingdom, 'Congress Poland', as it was known for the next half-century. On paper, at least, Czartoryski and Polish nationalism had scored a victory.

Alexander appeared content with his success. The Russians raised few objections to the Austrian policy of strengthening Habsburg control of Italy by defensive treaties and dynastic links. Alexander accepted the boundaries of the British-sponsored united Kingdom of the Netherlands, especially as Castlereagh agreed to settle debts incurred by the Dutch to the Russians out of British funds. He was gratified that Finland, which Russia seized from Sweden with Napoleon's blessing, was recognised as a Russian Grand Duchy and he therefore supported the new territorial arrangements in the Baltic, by which Sweden received compensation through union with Norway. Over German affairs the Tsar personally showed some support for Württemberg in resisting Austro-Prussian domination of the proposed federal diet: his favourite sister, the Grand Duchess Catherine, was about to marry the King of Württemberg's heir. Metternich was afraid Alexander's apparent reasonableness was a sign he was about to interest himself once more in the Eastern Question. Gentz, Metternich's confidant and Secretary-General of the Congress, maintained that Russian expansion southwards was ultimately a greater threat to the Austrian Empire than Czartoryski's Polish designs. He argued that Russian infiltration into Wallachia and Moldavia (then Turkish provinces but now the heart of Romania) would give the Tsar a stranglehold on the Danube; and he feared that Russian backing for Balkan nationalism – whether Romanian, Serb, or Greek – would bring close the disintegration of Turkey and thus threaten any multinational empire. 'The end of the Turkish monarchy could be survived by the Austrian for only a short time', Gentz wrote prophetically. Metternich, a Rhinelander in heart and soul, accepted the logic of Gentz's arguments but – at least in 1815 – hoped that the Eastern Question, if ignored, might never be posed. The immediate danger seemed, in Metternich's eyes, to come from the Tsar's abandonment of Nesselrode and Pozzo and his obvious preference for the Corfiote, Capodistria. Here, Metternich sensed, was an adversary of character and integrity.

The Austrians, though not Metternich personally, first encountered Capodistria when he was serving at the Russian embassy in 1810, three years after the French seized the Ionian Islands, which had been a Russian protectorate since 1802. He was a man of moderate liberal views, entrusted by the Tsar with a special mission to Switzerland in 1813–14 because of his allegedly republican opinions and later honoured with citizenship both in Geneva and Lausanne. Throughout the Congress the Viennese police spies kept him under close surveillance. They found nothing to his detriment, apart from a lack of sympathy with the lavish entertainments which were already winning for the Congress a frivolous disrepute it has never entirely lost. 'The same levity has been adopted everywhere by everyone', he was overheard to say early in January 1815. 'The most important business, the affairs of the whole world, are treated

as one would treat amusing diversions – by whim, and by fits and starts.'[7]
He had a clear idea of Alexander's mission, seeing him as protector of the
Orthodox Greeks within the Turkish Empire, around the Black Sea and
in the Aegean and, of course, in the seven Ionian Islands. Yet, though
Capodistria unquestionably stood high in the Tsar's favour, he could not
greatly influence Alexander's immediate policy at Vienna. The Russian
frontier in the south-west remained along the River Pruth, the Congress
confirming Alexander's possession of Bessarabia, and there were no
incursions into the Turkish Balkans. Alexander even acquiesced in the
establishment of a British protectorate over Corfu and the Ionian Islands,
for he realised that neither Britain nor Austria was prepared to see
a Russian fleet, with a Russian naval base, in the southern Adriatic.
Capodistria consoled himself with the conviction that his native island
was better under a comparatively liberal British protectorate than under
Metternich. Meanwhile he sought to bind the Tsar to the enlightened
ideal of brotherhood between the nations and a just government based on
respect for law. At Vienna he was the most visionary of all the peacemakers.

Capodistria unquestionably contributed to the Tsar's change of mood
in December 1814 – not, however, by turning Alexander's attention to the
Balkans but by encouraging him once more to find inspiration in the
scriptures. For Capodistria was a close friend of the Tsar's private
secretary, Alexander Stourdza, and wished to marry his sister, Roxane,
who was at the Congress as lady-in-waiting to the Tsar's consort, the
Empress Elizabeth. By religious faith the Stourdzas, a family of Greek
origin, were both Orthodox and pietistic. Roxane had already held several
talks with the Tsar on spiritual matters before coming to Vienna. These
conversations were resumed, with the encouragement of her brother and
his friends, in the privacy of the Hofburg Palace during December 1814.
They acquired particular significance because Roxane passed on to the
Tsar exhortations from the Latvian-born prophetess Julie von Krüdener,
whose writings Alexander had hitherto ignored. It was gratifying for the
Tsar to learn that this strange evangelical, who was then in Germany,
recognised in him a 'soul upon whom the Lord has conferred a much
greater power than the World perceives'. Her religious enthusiasm was
reflected in an official note, drafted by Capodistria for Alexander on the
last day of the year 1814. It called on the sovereigns of Europe to purify
their maxims of government and guarantee harmony among the peoples
providentially entrusted to them by basing the political order on
unchanging Christian principles common to all mankind. The note
aroused little comment at the time, for it seemed no more than a pious,
and slightly incomprehensible, New Year message. But the New Year
was 1815; and before it had run its course the Tsar's sentiments were to
appear magnified many times over as a solemn pledge in a Holy Alliance.[8]

By early February such steady progress was being made at the Congress
that Castlereagh decided to return to London and explain his policy to the
House of Commons. His responsibilities as first plenipotentiary were
entrusted to Field-Marshal the Duke of Wellington, late victor of
Salamanca and Vitoria and present ambassador in Paris. Wellington, it

was felt, would press forward resolutely and without subterfuge. He had with him a larger staff of Foreign Office clerks than had ever before left the country as well as two of his former generals from the peninsula, Cathcart and Stewart. At times Wellington's patience was severely taxed by inconclusive sessions with his colleagues in overheated rooms but he was able to strike some order into the committee work, taking a particular interest in the (successful) attempts made to condemn the slave trade as an undertaking unworthy of a Christian state. Talleyrand later recalled the duke's gifts as a diplomat, praising his 'watchfulness, prudence and experience of human nature'. These qualities, together with his habit of incisive command, were certainly needed in the second week of March. News reached Vienna on 7 March, taking eight days to come from both Genoa and Florence, that Napoleon had escaped from Elba. Had Wellington been a less resolute plenipotentiary the allied response might well have been embarrassingly delayed, for even the swiftest King's Messengers could not convey questions of policy and fresh instructions between Vienna and London in less than three weeks. As it is, the old allies were united once more in a matter of days, Alexander and Metternich were on speaking terms, 'Napoleon Bonaparte' was proclaimed an outlaw and decisions were taken on raising an army and on paying for yet another war. The Tsar offered to serve as allied commander, even though the main Russian army was in Poland and could not be ready for service on the frontiers of France until midsummer. He was persuaded to remain in Vienna and approved the selection of Wellington to command the vanguard of allied armies in Flanders. Alexander admired the duke more than any other Englishman and, in a grand gesture of farewell on 29 March, he commended him 'to save the World again'. Six days later Wellington reached Brussels. So, too, did coin and bullion for his army, dispatched by Nathan Rothschild in London with the backing of Solomon Rothschild, who was in Vienna for the Congress. It was a significant development in the conduct of world affairs: a family banking house had broken free from the ghetto of state frontiers to finance an improvised army in the field.[9]

There was something remote and academic about the last months of the Vienna Congress. The Tsar proposed that a series of separate treaties should be concluded, each settling the affairs of a particular region, but Castlereagh instructed the Earl of Clancarty (Wellington's successor as plenipotentiary) to insist on a comprehensive document, a treaty embodying all the decisions of the Congress. Metternich agreed with Castlereagh, and a separate committee prepared the text of the treaty, under the masterly direction of Friedrich von Gentz. Gradually the sovereigns left the peacemaking so as to wage the newest war. Nesselrode, Hardenberg, Talleyrand and Metternich stayed on, occasionally enjoying a hand of whist, while specially recruited clerks were copying out enough versions of the treaty to satisfy all the smaller delegations. The plenipotentiaries of Austria, France, Britain, Portugal, Prussia, Russia and Sweden signed the 'Final Act' of the Congress in the state rooms of Metternich's chancellery on 9 June and the representatives of the smaller powers ten days later. By then, however, Europe had lost interest in the Congress. On 18 June Napoleon was defeated at Waterloo by a combined British and Dutch-Belgian army under Wellington and by the Prussians under Marshal Blücher. On this momentous day the 'Christian Conqueror' of the previous year was still at Heidelberg, with the advanced Russian army corps; and Heidelberg was nearly 300 miles from the field of battle. That incorrigible Bonaparte-baiter, Pozzo di Borgo, was the only 'Russian' general at Waterloo. He had attached himself to Wellington's staff as personal commissioner of the Tsar.[10]

The political and military balance, so much in Alexander's favour a year before, was now tilted against Russia. The Austrians were the chief beneficiaries from the Vienna Settlement. They enjoyed primacy in the new German Confederation and mastery over Italy. Istria and the Dalmatian coast became Habsburg appendages while provinces which had been lost during the Napoleonic transmutations were recovered and enlarged. The Austrian Empire, created only in 1804, was given status and responsibility as Europe's shock-absorber, a protective device against France, against Russia and against what Gentz was to call 'the restlessness of the masses and the disorders of our time'. Britain consolidated the settlement of May 1814; Castlereagh, as he told the Commons, was satisfied 'to have established effectual provision for the general security' at the Congress. Frederick William, although not his generals, was pleased with Prussia's acquisitions: a firm footing on the Rhine and in Westphalia, Saxon lands rich in untapped resources, a strengthened position on the Baltic coast and in Poznania, and the opportunity to challenge Austria within the new Confederation. By contrast, Russia seemed to receive scant compensation for the privations of 1812–13: the creation of 'Congress Poland', and recognition that two earlier conquests (Finland and Bessarabia) might remain within the Tsar's empire. Even Alexander's hope of sanctifying the peace treaty with an affirmation of Christian principles had come to nothing; although the plenipotentiaries did at least sign the 'Final Act' at Vienna 'in the name of the Holy and Indivisible Trinity'.

Alexander left Heidelberg for Paris with a small escort of Cossacks a week after Waterloo. It took him fifteen days to complete the journey across the Saarland, Lorraine and Champagne, apparently because of the risk of attack from fanatics still loyal to the fallen emperor. By the evening of 10 July, when Alexander arrived at the Élysée Palace, the Duke of Wellington was in residence, British troops in the Bois de Boulogne, the Prussians out at St-Cloud and Louis XVIII re-restored at the Tuileries. Everyone, from Foreign Ministers to political courtesans, seemed to have adjourned to Paris from Vienna, or come across from London. Even Lady Castlereagh had arrived with her husband on 6 July, her niece's diary describing their new residence, 'a fine Hotel, splendidly furnished and charmingly situated, with a garden opening on the Champs-Élysées'; it had lately been the home of Napoleon's favourite sister, Pauline, and was about to become – and remain – the British embassy. Talks began on the latest settlement with France two days after the Tsar's arrival, not five weeks after the treaty was signed in Vienna, and less than fourteen months after the first Treaty of Paris. It is hardly surprising if, in their surviving letters and diaries, statesmen and diplomats alike seem peace-weary.[11]

The moves on the diplomatic chessboard were familiar, but the value of the pieces had subtly changed. The Prussians were no longer pawns. Victory at Waterloo placed the generals in the ascendant. They demanded a punitive peace, changes in France's frontiers intended to dissuade the French from ever again shifting allegiance to an emperor on horseback. The Dutch and the Bavarians, too, wanted frontier concessions. Metternich and Castlereagh were strongly opposed to a vindictive peace for fear of encouraging a spirit of revenge. Even the pliable Talleyrand was adamant in refusing to part with any more of France's 'sacred soil', and there was little prospect of a settled period of government under Louis XVIII if his reign marked its newest start with a wholesale surrender of land. Alexander, too, opposed Prussia's demands. He was excessively irritated by the behaviour of Blücher and alarmed by the influence of the Prussian War Minister, Boyen. The Prussian show of independence made him assess, with mounting scepticism, the value of the Hohenzollern–Romanov entente. Yet if he could not rely on Prussia as a partner, where could he turn? Nesselrode, as ever, championed Metternich's Austria. Momentarily, Alexander himself seems to have favoured closer contact with wealthy Britain; to Castlereagh's private dismay, he considered making another journey across the Channel in order to make himself agreeable in London. But, quite apart from the personal hostility towards the Tsar at Westminster and Carlton House, there was a latent conflict of interests between Britain and Russia in the Eastern Question and resentment among many Russians of Britain's worldwide naval power and ruthless competitiveness in expanding commerce. The most natural alliance for Russia was one that straddled Europe and kept watch on the greatest number of Britain's trade routes: Pozzo di Borgo and Capodistria, both men from the Mediterranean, therefore pressed Alexander to seek a new understanding with Bourbon France; and during the late summer and autumn of 1815 the Tsar gave them free rein. Capodistria was prepared to dispute every exaggerated Prussian claim while insisting to his allies that they think in terms of a durable peace rather than of vengeance. More than any other diplomat, he saved France from humiliation.

Alexander took no direct part in the negotiations. Exactly a fortnight before Waterloo, while resting on a Sunday night at Heilbronn in Westphalia, the Tsar was unexpectedly visited by Julie von Krüdener, the prophetess whose messages brought him spiritual comfort in those meetings with the Stourdzas six months previously. 'She spoke to me with words of hope and consolation, as though able to read my very soul', the Tsar later told Roxane Stourdza. For three months Alexander remained spiritually dependent on Baroness von Krüdener, who followed him to Heidelberg and to Paris. His mind, as Castlereagh told Liverpool, took on 'a deeply religious tinge'. He showed as little interest in Parisian social life as in the give and take of conference diplomacy that summer. Julie von Krüdener was housed in Marshal Berthier's former home, number 35 Rue du Faubourg Saint-Honoré, now also part of the British embassy. The house had the advantage of a garden gate which gave secret access to the Élysée Palace where Alexander was in residence. Baroness

Julie's journal records many visits from the Tsar. Generally they talked of religion, of churches, faiths and the Bible. Occasionally, however, he mentioned politics and, in particular, the pressure of Prussia and the other German states on defeated France. She enjoyed, as Castlereagh reported, 'a considerable reputation amongst the few highflyers in religion', and her salon was rarely empty in the evenings. Yet, though people knew she was Alexander's pocket prophetess, only once did she appear beside him in a public ceremony. On 11 September, the Feast of St Alexander Nevsky, she was with him as 120,000 Russian soldiers knelt before seven altars in the natural amphitheatre of the Plain of Vertus so as to share with their Tsar the eucharistic liturgy which he offered to his patron and protector. Foreigners watching this great act of worship – sovereigns, generals and ministers – were deeply impressed but also disturbed by its significance, for military might backed with apocalyptic symbolism made an awesome spectacle. But Alexander himself retained a serene humility. That evening he wrote a letter to Baroness Julie: 'This day has been the most beautiful in all my life', he declared. 'My heart was filled with love for my enemies.'[12]

Less than a week after returning to Paris from the Plain of Vertus the Tsar presented his brother sovereigns with his draft proposals for a pledge by peoples and governments that order among the nations should be based upon 'the precepts of Justice, Christian Charity and Peace'. Contemporary statesmen, trying at that moment to prepare a precise and definitive peace treaty with France, regarded Alexander's project with mingled embarrassment, irritation and derision. There was nothing new in seeking a general code of principles, and Castlereagh had been seeking some form of guarantee for Europe's frontiers for over a year, but the Tsar's romantic mysticism was at variance with all the conventions of diplomatic practice. The 'Holy Alliance', as his project was called, became associated in men's minds with the ceremony in the Plain of Vertus and with Julie von Krüdener. Alexander Stourdza insisted that the original draft of the Alliance was in the Tsar's hand which he, as secretary, had duly copied for the use of the other sovereigns and plenipotentiaries. He denied that Baroness Julie had any direct influence, even though he was himself a frequent visitor to number 35 Rue du Faubourg Saint-Honoré and went to see the baroness there, on the Tsar's behalf, the day before the drafts were handed to Emperor Francis and King Frederick William. It is true that the Tsar's theocratic idealism owed more to the Badenese Jung Stilling (whom Alexander met in 1814) and to the Catholic pamphleteer Franz von Baader than to the confused emotions of Julie von Krüdener, but it is probable that the imaginative phrase 'Holy Alliance' was suggested by her and, of course, her presence in Paris intensified Alexander's spiritual introspection. The Tsar's proposals were received with thinly disguised scepticism and Metternich at once began to revise the draft, erasing phrases which suggested contrition. He made, too, one important modification: the Tsar had suggested that there was a universal brotherhood between subjects as well as between rulers; but Metternich's implied contract was between sovereigns and not peoples. The final version of the Holy Alliance was essentially a conservative statement of the need for orderly government and for solidarity among Christian monarchs faced by the twin dangers of war and revolution. To the general surprise of the other diplomats at Paris, the Tsar accepted Metternich's revision. Alexander, Francis and Frederick William signed the Holy Alliance in Paris on 26 September. It was subsequently signed by every Christian monarch in Europe except the Pope and the Prince Regent of Great Britain, for whose abstention Castlereagh found good reason in the mysteries of the British constitution.[13]

Alexander left Paris as soon as the Holy Alliance was concluded. It was a quiet exit from a stage he had ceased to dominate. Nesselrode and Capodistria were left to complete the negotiations while Pozzo di Borgo became Russian ambassador to France, a post he held continuously from 1815 to 1835. Alexander was in Warsaw, determining how far 'Congress Poland' might revive the traditions of the former independent kingdom, when the second Treaty of Paris was at last signed on 20 November and he showed little immediate interest in its terms. France lost the Saar valley to Prussia, two fortresses to the Netherlands and small areas along the frontier to Bavaria, Sardinia-Piedmont and Switzerland. Against the wishes of Capodistria and his master, the French had to accept allied occupation of seventeen fortresses in northern France, Alsace and Lorraine for at least three years and pay a war indemnity of 700 million francs. It was a harsher peace than its predecessor, but it still left many Prussians disappointed with its terms.

The second Treaty of Paris was not the only international accord concluded that day. Before his departure from Paris the Tsar had shown interest in proposals made by Castlereagh for periodic conferences between the allies. Alexander thought that representatives of the Chaumont allies and France should meet at fixed intervals and discuss common problems. Castlereagh had a broader concept of the new demands of international diplomacy. He wished to continue round table diplomacy, for even the frustrations of the past year had not destroyed his belief in the merits of personal contact when governments needed compromise and reconciliation; but he did not believe Restoration France was as yet sufficiently stable to take part in the counsels of the Great Powers. The inter-allied treaty of 20 November 1815 accordingly differed considerably from the arrangement favoured by the Tsar: it was a quadruple and not a quintuple alliance; Austria, Great Britain, Prussia and Russia were pledged to collective action should France challenge the new frontiers, bring back a Bonaparte to the throne, or succumb to revolution; and it was agreed that the sovereigns or ministers of the four Great Powers should meet from time to time to discuss the general problems of Europe, not merely the well-being of the Alliance. This sixth article of the treaty, added almost as an afterthought and never discussed by the Cabinet in London, created the much-misunderstood Congress System of the years from 1818 to 1825. Castlereagh, patient and unobtrusive through nineteen weeks of negotiation, had scored a diplomatic success as remarkable as in the previous summer.

The last word that year lay, however, with the Tsar, who arrived back in St Petersburg on 14 December. So far the Holy Alliance was a secret bond, known only to the sovereigns who signed it and their chief ministers. But, as a gesture of peace and goodwill, the Tsar published the full declaration of the Holy Alliance for the Russian Orthodox Christmas. Throughout his empire the higher clergy read its 'sacred precepts' to their congregations clause by clause.[14] Yet the text they used was not the revised version of Metternich, with its implied contract of government between sovereigns, but the original draft in Alexander's own hand emphasising the Christian bonds which unite subjects as well as rulers. Thus, even when seeking a moral sanction for the authority of the Great Powers, the Tsar's Russia was of Europe, but outside it. This combination of familiarity and divergence continued to confound the Chancelleries throughout the century.

3 Congress Diplomacy, 1816–22

The first reports of the Tsar's pronouncement appeared in the Press in Germany, France and Britain early in February 1816 and aroused widespread comment. A new parliamentary session was about to open at Westminster, giving the House of Commons an opportunity to debate the peace settlement and to express doubts about 'the Emperor of Russia's treaty'. The Whig opposition disliked the support given to the Bourbons and other 'legitimate' dynasties and were opposed to the stationing of a British army in France. Henry Brougham saw in the Tsar's treaty an autocratic conspiracy against political liberty and Sir Samuel Romilly gloomily predicted a future Russian, Prussian and Austrian 'combination against England'. Whig opinion favoured 'insulation', a vague but fashionable concept which implied withdrawal from any European states' system behind the protective shield of the Royal Navy. There was a feeling that Castlereagh had played into the hands of the allied monarchs, who had come together only when faced by an external danger to their system. Conference diplomacy seemed, by its very nature, repressive and illiberal, a criticism which passed into the legends of historical writing for over a century.

Castlereagh defended both the peace settlement and the new style of diplomacy. On 19 February he told the House that the gravity of the threat from Bonaparte in 1814 and 1815 'would have shivered the confederacy to atoms' had not the sovereigns been present and prepared to meet, with the allied ministers and generals, around the conference table. He also commended Alexander's idealism in promoting the Holy Alliance. 'If the Emperor of Russia chooses to found his glory on such a basis', he replied to Brougham, 'posterity will do justice to the noble determination. Having already done so much for mankind by his arms, to what better purpose could he apply this great influence in the councils of the sovereigns of Europe than to secure for it a lasting and beneficial peace?'[1] The Prince Regent could not himself accede to 'the Emperor of Russia's treaty', but his government appreciated the nobility of the Tsar's desire to appear as peacemaker and mediator.

Alexander was much moved by Castlereagh's words. In a personal letter to the Foreign Secretary he suggested that Russia and Britain should take the lead in 'bringing about in common . . . the reduction of armed forces of all kinds' so as to safeguard peace and remove a 'heavy burden' from Europe's peoples. This approach from the Tsar almost coincided in time with the foundation by his British Quaker friends of the Society for the Promotion of Permanent and Universal Peace, and there is no reason to doubt Alexander's sincerity in putting forward a proposal of this kind. The horrors of the battlefield had produced a revulsion against warfare among many young veterans; Lord Aberdeen, for example, was long haunted by his ride beside Metternich across the field of Leipzig in October 1813. But Castlereagh, who was forever steeling his natural sensitivity, was puzzled by Alexander's letter. However much he might publicly praise the Tsar's good intentions, he was at heart uneasy about Russian policy. 'The Emperor of Russia', he wrote to the ambassador in St Petersburg, 'likes an army, as he likes influence in Europe': why, Castlereagh wondered, did Russia's soldiery remain on a war footing even though there had been cuts in the size of the British, Austrian and Prussian contingents on active service? Moreover, by using the phrase 'armed forces of all kinds' the Tsar was presumably hoping to see naval vessels laid up and seamen paid off.[2] Nothing would induce any statesman, Tory or Whig, to accept restraint on Britannia's sovereignty as ruler of the waves. Politely but firmly Castlereagh brushed aside Alexander's proposal.

Neither Castlereagh nor Metternich was sure who determined Russian policy now the Tsar had returned to St Petersburg. Technically the responsibilities of Foreign Minister were shared by Nesselrode and Capodistria. Metternich tended to blame Capodistria for every intrigue reported by his agents throughout Western Europe and the Balkan lands. Although the Tsar had assured his court that the secretary of state would conduct policy 'from an entirely Russian point of view', Metternich was convinced that Capodistria's one objective was the liberation of the Greeks from Turkish rule. 'The Tsar is, in his hands, no more than an instrument which he believes he can put to good use. One would be quite mistaken in believing that a single genuinely Russian thought ever enters his head', Metternich wrote to the ambassador in London in March 1816. 'He is solely a Greek, a revolutionary independent in the broadest sense of the words.' There was some truth in this judgement, for although Capodistria often concealed his philhellenic sympathies, he tried as early as the spring of 1816 to induce Alexander to accept a forward policy in the Balkans; and he was also rash enough to pay a secret visit to Vienna during which, as the Austrian police duly reported to Metternich, he met several prominent Greek exiles. Such undiplomatic behaviour confirmed the worst suspicions of the Austrians and the British, and Castlereagh came to distrust 'the mongrel minister' (as he called Capodistria) almost as much as did Metternich. Alexander, however, knew his man, and kept him in close attendance at court after the mysterious trip to Vienna. Capodistria could argue that support by Russia for Christians persecuted by the Turks would show the European chancelleries 'the justice and generosity of Russian policy' but, though the Tsar 'smiled encouragingly', he would not be tempted. To carry out such a policy, he declared, 'we would need to set the cannons moving, and that I have no wish to do'.[3]

Shared responsibilities in the Foreign Ministry caused confusion. Nesselrode drafted instructions for the new envoy to the Shah of Persia, Capodistria drafted instructions for the new ambassador to the Sultan of Turkey. German affairs were left to Nesselrode, correspondence with Paris – where a standing Conference of Ambassadors sought to settle disputes arising from the peace treaty – was entrusted to Capodistria. But the real uncertainty over Russian policy in the postwar years arose from the suddenness with which the Tsar's empire had emerged as a major European Power and from the difficulties of communication between St Petersburg and the other great capital cities. A problem raised in Paris at the ambassadorial conference on 15 June 1816 was reported by Pozzo di Borgo immediately but, even with the good road conditions of mid-summer, it was not until 21 July that the matter was discussed in St Petersburg, and it then took the return courier until 10 August to travel back to Paris. Dispatches from Dmitri Tatischev, the ambassador in Madrid, were at least another twelve days out of date by the time they arrived in St Petersburg. Exchanges with London took as long as with Paris, and longer when the Baltic was frozen. Even letters from Vienna only rarely reached St Petersburg within a fortnight.

The foreign services of other powers suffered, too, from poor roads and tired horses. Thus the record for an urgent dispatch from the Austrian embassy in London to Vienna was seven days (in August 1822) and it took over seven weeks for Castlereagh to learn the dramatic news of the hanging by the Turks of the Ecumenical Patriarch in Constantinople (April 1821). But these problems of communication mattered more to Russia's diplomats than to the Austrians, British and French because of the backwardness and inefficiency of the administrative machine in their capital. The accumulated frustrations of delay inclined the Tsar's ambassadors either to act with vigorous independence or to take no initiative whatsoever, pleasantly enjoying the social life of the courts to which they were accredited. Two at least of the ambassadors – Tatischev in Madrid and Pozzo di Borgo in Paris – sought to shape policy rather than execute it.[4]

Tatischev's activities filled the British with misgiving. He was said at one time to be seeking the acquisition of Minorca so as to give the Russians a naval base in the western Mediterranean and at another to be acting as marriage broker for a dynastic link between Madrid and St Petersburg. Castlereagh was especially alarmed at Russian interest in Latin America, a politically sensitive region which offered rich opportunities for trade and investment to England's bankers and merchants. Repeated Russian moves to have the future of Spain's American colonies settled by the Conference of Ambassadors in Paris exasperated him, and he insisted that the ambassadors were concerned with Bourbon France, not Bourbon Spain.

Metternich agreed with Castlereagh, but he put the blame on Pozzo rather than on Tatischev. The Austrians particularly resented the Corsican's political ascendancy in Paris, seeing in Pozzo an outstanding champion of Franco-Russian reconciliation. In September 1815 Pozzo had successfully encouraged Louis XVIII to dismiss Talleyrand and replace him as Prime Minister and Foreign Minister by the Duke of Richelieu, great-great-grandson of a brother of the cardinal and statesman. Pozzo hoped – and Metternich feared – that Richelieu was a Russophile. From 1803 to 1814 he had served Tsar Alexander as resident governor in Odessa, virtually creating the modern city and port; and his statue still overlooks the famous Potemkin Steps, built originally in his honour. But neither Pozzo nor Metternich appreciated that, devoted though Richelieu had been to the welfare of Odessa, he was prepared to spend the last years of his life bound in total loyalty to Louis XVIII. Richelieu knew both Pozzo and Capodistria well enough to outwit them. Moreover, he was sufficiently astute to send as France's ambassador in Vienna the Marquis de Caraman, an old friend of Metternich. By November 1816 Caraman had convinced the Austrians that Paris and Vienna could work together as amicably as in the days of Kaunitz. Metternich continued to complain that Pozzo was too tainted with liberal ideas for the good either of his Tsar or of Richelieu, but in fact it was the French themselves who exploited differences between the occupying powers so as to join the Russians in thwarting Anglo-Austrian collaboration.[5]

Castlereagh's response to rivalry and intrigue in Paris was disconcertingly straightforward. In March 1818 he proposed that the first of the meetings of 'renewal', envisaged in Article VI of the Quadruple Alliance of November 1815, should be held as soon as possible and that it should be primarily concerned with the relations of the four allies to France. Alexander welcomed the proposal of a conference although not of its limited terms of reference: he was prepared to support the Prussians in challenging Austrian hegemony in the Diet of the new German Confederation and he hoped, too, to raise the Spanish questions vetoed by the British in the Conference of Ambassadors. The Tsar had, indeed, for several months been pressing for a resumption of the round table diplomacy which he had affected to despise in Paris during the heady gestation of the Holy Alliance. Metternich favoured a congress provided that it met in a safe and agreeable setting and was restricted in composition. Düsseldorf, Mannheim and Basle were rejected in favour of Aachen, which was in those days still universally known as Aix-la-Chapelle; and a proposal from Capodistria to invite delegations from the smaller German states and from Spain was rejected after Metternich and Castlereagh had reminded the Tsar of the difficulties encountered at Vienna through over-attendance and an imprecise agenda.

The Congress of Aix opened on 27 September 1818 and continued for exactly eight weeks. Never before had Europe's leading sovereigns and statesmen assembled for round table discussion of international problems in time of peace rather than during a war or its immediate aftermath. Aix therefore transcended in importance what was formally agreed by the participants in the Congress. As at Vienna, Friedrich Gentz was appointed Secretary-General but his duties were significantly broadened, so that he became virtually a public relations man. When special correspondents wanted news – for Aix was the first political gathering of its kind covered by Europe's Press – they sounded out Gentz. He it was who listened to Robert Owen (who had hoped to outline his co-operative socialist theories at a higher level) and who arranged the agreeably beneficial luncheon party at which Metternich entertained the brothers Carl and Salomon Rothschild. But the main participants were familiar enough figures – all the big names from Vienna, except for Talleyrand and Czartoryski. The principal task of the Congress, agreement on withdrawing the armies of occupation from France and payment of the last quota of the war indemnity, was accomplished within a fortnight.

Richelieu, as Louis XVIII's plenipotentiary, was then formally invited to associate his king with the pledges of the Quadruple Alliance to uphold the peace of Europe. France thus recovered the status of a Great Power, although her new allies secretly reaffirmed their commitment to act should Paris be shaken yet again by revolution.

So far so good; it was when the Congress began to discuss problems of general concern that the statesmen ran into difficulties. Capodistria, who had induced the Spanish envoy to St Petersburg to travel with the Russians to Aix, raised the question of the relationship between Spain and her rebellious South American colonies. He sought a commercial embargo on trade with Latin America. Castlereagh reacted angrily; the Spanish diplomat was induced to take the waters at Spa, even though an unofficial spokesman for the colonists remained at Aix; and Castlereagh went over Capodistria's head to the Tsar in order to put a stop to all talk of sanctions. Discussion of territorial disputes between Bavaria and Baden, of Jewish rights in Germany's cities and of the rendering of naval salutes by warships at sea proceeded amicably enough. But not so Capodistria's suggestion of an international agency – an 'African Institute' – which would have at its disposal warships from the Great Powers in order to search vessels on the high seas suspected of trafficking in slaves. This farsighted plan was rejected by the Prussians, Austrians and British who saw in Capodistria's initiative a means of maintaining a Russian naval force in distant waters. There was similar suspicion of proposals to hunt down the Barbary pirates of Tripoli, Algiers, Tunis and Morocco; better American frigates in the western Mediterranean than a Russian squadron. The most serious problem of all was the memorandum drafted by Capodistria for Alexander and seeking to convert the treaties between the Great Powers into a single 'Alliance Solidaire'. A league of guarantees would thus bind Europe together, safeguarding even the smallest powers against foreign attack and internal subversion. This magnified Holy Alliance was rejected both by Metternich, who thought the league too large and cumbersome for practical politics, and by Castlereagh, who was opposed to comprehensive obligations which upheld existing systems of government in the various states. To the dismay of Capodistria and Pozzo, the Tsar once again gave way. The Congress ended with talk of 'the moral solidarity of the Alliance'. 'Justice, moderation and concord' had prevailed, said the final communiqué. A French diplomat, who remembered Napoleon's wartime congresses at Erfurt and Dresden, was delighted with the show of harmony; the new diplomacy, he said, offered 'the aspect of amicable conversations entirely devoid of the etiquette, precautions and pretensions of former years'. Metternich's eldest daughter was also pleasantly surprised at the equanimity of Aix. 'It struck me as wholly amusing', she wrote to her mother, 'to see Papa one evening arm in arm with the Tsar.'[6]

Yet Aix was an illusory success for congress diplomacy. The principal achievement – recognition that France was politically able to work her passage as a Great Power – had been agreed in advance, and only the details of formal rehabilitation needed to be settled. Castlereagh's assumption that round table discussion could solve outstanding problems was never seriously put to the test. In the last resort the three autocratic monarchies preferred an outward show of unity rather than risk the discord of debate. The most divisive topic, the 'Alliance Solidaire' proposal, was ruled out of court as too full of 'abstractions', but Metternich, at least, learned much from its fate. He saw that Alexander, who had travelled slowly to Aix across the German states, was uneasily aware of the revolutionary ferment among disappointed liberals and he found it was not difficult to shake the Tsar's confidence in Capodistria or make him doubt the wisdom of collaboration with France by suggesting that Bourbon Paris remained, beneath the surface, a seed-plot of Jacobinism. Metternich readily perceived that Castlereagh no longer exercised the freedom of decision which had made him so valuable an ally at Chaumont. Castlereagh had told him that he would need the backing of his Cabinet colleagues for any shift in British policy, and the Prime Minister and the Secretary for War and Colonies had travelled down to Walmer Castle (7 miles from Dover quay) so that Castlereagh could refer matters to them and receive an answer to Aix within five days. Moreover, midway through the Congress Castlereagh showed to Metternich – and to no other foreign delegate – a long memorandum prepared for his Cabinet colleagues. Ostensibly the memorandum listed Castlereagh's reasons for rejecting Russia's 'Alliance Solidaire'; but it also emphasised the absurdity of seeking to determine whether or not political changes within a state were so dangerous that they justified outside intervention, and it pointed out that even the treaty obligations to intervene in France depended upon clear evidence that the general safety of Europe was at stake. Metternich could see that though Britain might help curb Russian expansion or a resurgence of French nationalism, he could not count on support from London to suppress revolution. That in itself was reason enough for him to walk arm in arm with Alexander.[7]

Capodistria, at his master's suggestion, took several months of sick leave after Aix. He built up his physical strength by wintering in Italy and spending the spring in his native Corfu. Metternich was delighted that a statesman whom he regarded as his personal adversary should absent himself from Russia throughout the first eight months of the year 1819. Meticulously the Austrian police accumulated trivial reports implicating Capodistria in alleged conspiracies wherever he stayed for any length of time. But the Tsar was not yet prepared to desert his 'visionary' minister nor to turn his back on every vestige of liberal constitutionalism. Even when August Kotzebue, German dramatist and Russian intelligence agent, was murdered on 23 March by a radical theological student in Mannheim, Alexander was unmoved by Metternich's warnings of impending disaster. Student unrest so alarmed Frederick William III of Prussia that he hastened to Teplitz to confess to Metternich how wrong he had been to flirt with liberalism when under the spell of his trusted friend and partner, the Tsar. Austrians and Prussians together imposed the illiberal Carlsbad Decrees on the German states, an action criticised not only by Tories and Whigs at Westminster but by the autocrat of the Winter Palace in St Petersburg as well. Metternich, however, had his supporters within the Russian diplomatic service. Nesselrode shared his apparent fear of revolution and so, too, did Dmitri Tatischev, an ambassador for whose judgement Tsar Alexander felt increasing (and exaggerated) respect. On New Year's Day 1820 Major Riego led a mutiny in Andalusia which 'pronounced' in favour of the Spanish liberal constitution of 1812. From Madrid Tatischev reported to the Tsar that Spain's national liberal movement would soon spread to Italy and Portugal; and he succeeded in bringing out into the open the fears first planted in Alexander's mind by Metternich. At the end of April 1820 the Tsar instructed Capodistria to propose collective measures by the five Great Powers in order to help King Ferdinand VII of Spain quench the new revolution before its flames engulfed Europe.[8]

Alexander's initiative embarrassed Metternich and angered Castlereagh. The Austrians had no wish to see a Russian army setting out to cross Europe and stamp down rebellion in Spain, and the British held strong views on all military expeditions in the Iberian peninsula, especially ones which seemed dependent on collaboration between Russia and France. The Duke of Wellington, who knew about such matters, bluntly described foreign intervention in Spain as militarily impracticable. Metternich accordingly worked out an ingenious compromise: the Powers would agree with the Tsar that governments should stand firmly together against the evil of revolution; and they would accept Wellington's advice and keep their armies out of Spain. This characteristic ploy – sententious moralising followed by total inaction – was ruined for Metternich by two lieutenants in the Neapolitan army who raised the standard of national liberal revolt at Nola, east of Naples, and sought to emulate Riego's successes in Madrid. However uninterested Metternich might be in Spanish affairs, he could not ignore a direct challenge to the established order in the Italian peninsula, where Austria's political influence was paramount. He proposed that an ambassadorial conference should be held in Vienna in order to determine how to deal with the Neapolitan revolt. Alexander, however, persisted in linking the Spanish and Italian problems, claiming that the Vienna Settlement was under such pressure that only a gathering of allied sovereigns and ministers could shore up the existing states system. He had already arranged to meet Emperor Francis at Troppau (now known as Opava) in Austrian Silesia, and he proposed to invite Frederick William to join them and to ask the British and French to send their leading ministers. Reluctantly Metternich agreed that the meeting at Troppau, planned for the third week in October, should become the second of the peacetime congresses.

There was, however, never any possibility that Castlereagh would go to Troppau. In the first week of May he had drawn up a state paper, following discussions in the Cabinet, which developed the doctrine of non-intervention he had first outlined at Aix. Lord Liverpool's government expected to be overthrown in the course of the year – by the king, for inept handling of his marital problem, rather than by the people – and it therefore seemed to Castlereagh constitutionally improper to permit the European Powers to believe Britain could become involved in the repression of revolutions wherever they occurred. 'We shall be found in our place when actual danger menaces the System of Europe', he wrote in the final paragraph of his long paper, 'but this Country cannot, and will not, act upon abstract and speculative Principles of Precaution. The Alliance which exists had no such purpose in its original foundation. It was never so explained to Parliament; if it had, most assuredly the sanction of Parliament would never have been given to it.'[9] The state paper was not, as a distinguished historian claimed, 'the end of that system of European co-operation which Castlereagh had done so much to promote', for the Foreign Secretary sent his half-brother, Charles Stewart, as an observer to Troppau (and later to Laibach), held conversations with Metternich himself in Hanover eighteen months after writing the state paper, and was preparing to travel to yet another congress at the time of his death. But the state paper certainly argued that European co-operation was effective only if confined to the limits of the practicable. In encouraging conference diplomacy Castlereagh had never given his blessing to an administrative system designed to maintain established power throughout the continent.

The French, too, contented themselves with observers at Troppau even though Richelieu had pressed for a conference as soon as news of the Neapolitan revolt reached Paris. Metternich was surprised and irritated by this switch in policy. It was caused in part by the instability of Richelieu's government, which made it inadvisable for the Prime Minister or the Foreign Minister to absent himself from Paris, but it also reflected exasperation at the behaviour of Pozzo di Borgo, who assumed that the French would automatically follow Russia's lead. There was still a lingering hope in Paris that France, as a respectable constitutional monarchy, might champion a reform movement in the Italian states and so undermine Habsburg primacy in the peninsula, and Britain's independent stand suggested the possibility of Anglo-French collaboration. For the first time in the century French policy was influenced by a permanent Foreign Ministry official, Count Gérard de Rayneval, whom Richelieu held in high respect. In South America Rayneval intrigued against the British with what Castlereagh testily described as 'the dregs of that old diplomacy which so long poisoned the public health of the body politic of Europe', but he was also strongly anti-Austrian and enjoyed seeing Metternich discomfited over the Italian problem. On the initiative of either Richelieu or Rayneval both Caraman and the ambassador at St Petersburg, La Ferronays, kept a watching brief for France at the Congress. Their instructions were, however, confused and they caused Metternich some moments of wry amusement by contradicting each other.

Troppau was thus essentially a congress of the East European autocrats. Metternich used the occasion to emphasise his belief in a grand international conspiracy of revolutionaries. Capodistria, at Alexander's prompting, proposed that the Great Powers should assert a right of intervention if a revolution challenged the Vienna Settlement but should also promise that any new government would respect the 'dual freedoms', national independence and political liberty. This seemed nonsense to Metternich, who recalled a dictum of Castlereagh that 'The more Russia wishes to transport us to the heights, the further we must descend into the plain'. He turned to Nesselrode and proceeded to undermine Capodistria's position. News from Russia of a 'Jacobin' mutiny in a crack Guards regiment helped Metternich. Alexander withdrew his stipulation that the

Powers should respect the 'dual freedoms'. He disowned the memorandum which he had asked Capodistria to prepare only a week before and ordered him to draw up a new document which would show how the principles of the Holy Alliance could be applied to the revolutionary situation in Italy. Capodistria, with great reluctance, presented the notorious Troppau Protocol to the Congress. It proposed that allied representatives should accompany an army of occupation which would restore King Ferdinand I of Naples to his rightful authority; it invited Ferdinand to meet the allied sovereigns in congress at Laibach, now the capital of Slovenia and known as Ljubljana; and, most important, it gave warning that the Great Powers would 'bring back to the bosom of the Alliance' any state which endangered the security of Europe by revolutionary changes in its constitution. The Protocol was roundly denounced in Press and Parliament in Britain. The French declined to consider themselves bound by its proposals, and Castlereagh duly complained that the allies were assuming 'a moral responsibility of administering a general European police'. Metternich was well satisfied with the turn of events although he concealed his glee from the British envoy. All the unpopularity aroused by the Protocol could be heaped on its unfortunate author, Capodistria. 'Pitiable drafting', Metternich remarked, as he prepared to move on to Laibach; 'hardly a phrase which could be regarded as even satisfactory'. But the New Year of 1821 opened with greater harmony between the Russian and Austrian courts than he could ever remember.[10]

As a congress, Laibach was no more than a Mark II version of Troppau. Frederick William III, realising that Metternich was determined to keep control of the diplomatic machine, did not bother to travel south from Silesia but, with admirable sense, went back to Berlin for Christmas and stayed there. It was agreed that Austria should at once restore orderly government in the 'Kingdom of the Two Sicilies', as Ferdinand's realm was officially styled. Capodistria, trying to explain away the Troppau Protocol, vainly sought to enlist British and French support against Metternich, and indeed against Nesselrode and the Tsar. But even if Castlereagh and Richelieu publicly deprecated the Austrian police action, they still hoped to preserve what the British Foreign Secretary called 'the cordiality and harmony of the Alliance'. Stewart, though only an observer, protested against statements which seemed to commit the Quintuple Alliance as a whole but did not challenge Austria's assumption of a right to intervene in southern Italy. There was little Capodistria could do to recover his position. He 'thrashes about like a devil in holy water', wrote Metternich contentedly in a letter back to Vienna.[11]

Alexander was, with difficulty, restrained from accompanying the Austrian forces as they marched on Naples. He continued to be worried by the Spanish revolution and suggested to Metternich that if Austria dealt with the Two Sicilies, France might be invited to send an army across the Pyrenees and free Ferdinand of Spain from rebel restraint. But Metternich had no wish to lose touch with London and suspected Alexander's interest in Spain sprang from a desire to widen the breach between Britain and the three autocratic Powers. He therefore proposed that the affairs of Spain and of Portugal (where parliament met in January 1821 to discuss a liberal constitution) should be left for the next congress which, he suggested, might gather in Florence in September of the following year. Alexander agreed, and the Congress of Laibach was formally dissolved on the last day of February 1821. But Alexander and his ministers, together with Metternich and a Prussian representative, remained in Laibach until the spring so as to await restoration of order in the Two Sicilies. The final communiqué from Laibach – a vigorous condemnation of all revolution – was drawn up by Nesselrode and Metternich and only issued on 12 May. Capodistria, Nesselrode's nominal partner, did not see the declaration until it was ready for publication.

While the Tsar was still at Laibach news was received of rebellion in Piedmont and of anti-Austrian conspiracies in Lombardy. The Austrians were able to meet these latest manifestations of liberal nationalism by rapid movement of troops and by severe repression. There was no need of Russian help, but Alexander wished to be seen associating himself with the Austrians and he duly sent a courier back to St Petersburg with orders for an army of 90,000 men to be concentrated in southern Poland ready to advance westwards 'to save Europe'. Yet even before the courier reached the Russian capital, a new problem was posed in south-eastern Europe potentially of greater danger to the stability of the continent than any conspiracy in Turin or Milan. On 17 March 1821 the Tsar learned that, a fortnight previously, one of his aides-de-camp, General Alexander Ypsilantis, had crossed the frontier from Russian Bessarabia into Turkish Moldavia with a handful of Greek patriots and raised a revolt against the Sultan of Turkey and his vassal governors in the outlying Christian provinces of the Ottoman Empire. Within a month the Greek Orthodox bishop in the northern Peloponnese gave his blessing to the cause of national rebellion against the Turks. The 'Eastern Question' – ignored at Vienna and Aix, Troppau and Laibach – was forcing itself on the agenda of congress diplomacy.[12]

Metternich was determined to keep it off any such agenda as long as possible. He had feared trouble in the Balkans and blamed the Greek insurrection on the intrigues of Capodistria. Yet, as Metternich himself saw, the news that Ypsilantis had launched his raid across the Pruth and into Moldavia fell 'like a bolt from the blue' on Capodistria. It was remarkably ill timed, and for several weeks Metternich hoped the insurrection would peter out as ineffectually as the disturbances in Piedmont. So long as the Tsar remained in the Austrian Empire, he accepted Metternich's view that rebellion in the Balkans was as rebellion in Spain and Italy. Alexander formally dismissed Ypsilantis from Russian service, disowned him and called on him to lay down his arms and repent. The Tsar also assured his Austrian hosts that Russia would never take independent action in south-eastern Europe. But by early June he was back in St Petersburg and there he found the popular mood favoured war against Turkey. The Sultan had humiliated the Orthodox Church on Easter Day by executing the Patriarch Gregory outside his palace in Constantinople and the Turks heaped insults on the Russian ambassador. Greek Orthodox

Christians were slaughtered by Muslim fanatics, and Capodistria saw to it that every Turkish atrocity reported to the Russian Foreign Ministry was brought to the personal attention of the Tsar. The Orthodox Church was always the most formidable pressure group in Tsarist Russia.

The last section of Capodistria's autobiography vividly shows the conflict which racked the Tsar's conscience in 1821–2.[13] Alexander sought support from Emperor Francis of Austria and from Castlereagh in condemning 'the deplorable affairs in Turkey' and for months on end he allowed Capodistria a free hand in drafting the diplomatic exchanges with Metternich. But after Troppau and Laibach the Tsar accepted unquestioningly Metternich's repeated assertion that there was a 'Paris directing committee' of revolutionaries; Russia could not go to war with Turkey, Alexander told Capodistria in August 1821, because that was precisely what the Paris desperadoes wished to happen in order to break the harmony of the Great Powers. Gradually Capodistria began to lose influence. In February 1822 the Corfiote was allowed by Alexander to draft one last programme of action over Balkan affairs: if the Turks refused to negotiate better terms for their Christian subjects with the Russians, Capodistria proposed that the five Great Powers would withdraw their ambassadors or ministers from Constantinople and prepare joint military and naval operations to coerce the Sultan. Yet no sooner had Alexander approved of Capodistria's programme than he began to dilute it, accepting a proposal from Nesselrode that Tatischev should be transferred from Madrid to Vienna in order to ensure closer Austro-Russian collaboration. Once in Vienna, where he arrived on 6 March, Tatischev assumed he need report progress only to Nesselrode. Metternich and Tatischev between then worked out a compromise which gave the Sultan's ministers time and opportunity to improve conditions in the outlying Christian provinces; and the Tsar was invited to Vienna on his way to the forthcoming Congress. Metternich explained that, as the Congress would be concerned principally with the affairs of Italy and Spain, he thought the Eastern Question could best be discussed at a ministerial conference in Vienna before the Congress opened. Capodistria, realising that the combination of Metternich-Nesselrode-Tatischev called the tune to which the Tsar now listened, left the Russian Foreign Ministry. He was granted indefinite leave for reasons of health in August 1822 although he remained technically in the Tsar's service until after the accession of Nicholas I.

Metternich was elated that 'the reign of Capodistria' was over. But the Austrian Chancellor – a title bestowed on Metternich at the end of the Laibach Congress – did not have such total mastery over the Tsar's mind as Capodistria had feared. Alexander remained obsessed with the Spanish problem and throughout the summer of 1822 pressed Metternich to accept the idea of European intervention south of the Pyrenees. It is probable that Nesselrode and Tatischev were offering the Tsar a means of dignified retreat from the forward position over Turkish affairs into which he had been manouevred by Capodistria. They seem, too, to have believed that Metternich would welcome the Tsar's Spanish initiative as proof of his regard for the doctrines of the Troppau Protocol. Metternich, however, regarded Alexander's suggestion of 'a European Army to which each of the Allies would furnish a contingent' in order to extirpate revolutions as 'utter nonsense'; the Tsar was reverting not to Troppau but to the Holy Alliance, a states system shaped for Europe by the autocrats and not their ministers. Metternich turned for support to Castlereagh, begging him to come to the Vienna Conference as well as to the Congress (which, for reasons of security, was now to be held in Verona and not in Florence). 'What force Russian policy has lost in the East, it will attempt to regain by greater activity in the West', he told Castlereagh, claiming that the British and Austrian governments were 'the two cabinets who understand each other best'. Castlereagh informed Metternich on 29 July that he would leave London for Paris, Vienna and Verona in seventeen days' time.[14]

By the time Castlereagh's letter reached Metternich's summer residence the Foreign Secretary was dead. The strain of long hours drafting his own dispatches and memoranda, together with a parliamentary session that continued until the second Thursday in August, exhausted him physically and mentally. He was the butt of liberal attacks in the Commons and in the Press, and he was troubled by blackmailers who, three years previously, fabricated an incident in which he had appeared about to commit a homosexual offence. His doctor, summoned to St James's Square on the day after Parliament adjourned, found him confused and in poor health. That evening Lord and Lady Castlereagh left for North Cray, his villa near Bexley in Kent and now known as Loring Hall. There, on the following Monday morning (12 August 1822), Castlereagh cut his throat, the only British secretary of state known to have killed himself while in office. Vienna learned the news on 21 August, only three weeks before the Vienna ministerial conference was due to begin. Metternich was distressed at the death of a friend 'for whom I had been waiting here as though he were my second self'. His loss, as Metternich wrote in another private letter, 'is one of those catastrophes which sometimes strike empires as well as individuals'. 'Where', he asked, 'is to be found a man who, to the same degree, can combine knowledge of affairs with knowledge of the people who make the greatest impact on events?'[15] Behind the rhetoric of Metternich's stylistic French ran a fear that no other statesman had the patience to ensure that 'pretensions were modified and asperities removed' around the conference table.

The immediate effect of Castlereagh's suicide was to destroy all hope of Anglo-Austrian collaboration. There was an interlude of five weeks during which the Secretary of State for War and Colonies, Earl Bathurst, served as acting Foreign Secretary while Lord Liverpool gradually persuaded his king and his more Tory colleagues to accept George Canning as Castlereagh's successor. The Duke of Wellington was appointed minister plenipotentiary to the Congress of Verona and followed the route that Castlereagh had planned to take, although Wellington travelled a month later. He reached Vienna to find the ministerial conference over and the Tsar about to set off for Verona next morning. Instead of opposing the Russians at Vienna as he had intended while Castlereagh was alive, Metternich had allowed Nesselrode to decide on the immediate future: Italy would head the agenda at Verona, followed by Spain but not the problems of Greece. As Gentz later wrote, 'It was a matter of courtesy not to mention difficulties in Turkey'. Poor Wellington hurried on to Verona, puzzled over his policy. He had set out with instructions which Castlereagh had drafted for his own use and on which Bathurst had hardly made any comments; but he knew that Canning distrusted commitments in Europe and would not permit him to take the initiative. British policy was now intransigently non-interventionist. 'For "Alliance" read "England", and you have the clue to my policy', Canning was to write a little later in a private letter to a friend.[16]

There were more cast changes on the international stage than the disappearance of Capodistria and Castlereagh. Of the French deputation to Verona only la Ferronays was a familiar figure, remembered by many Russians and Austrians for his incompetence at Troppau and Laibach. Richelieu's government had fallen shortly before Christmas in 1821 and the new Prime Minister, the ultra-conservative Villèle, sent as Louis XVIII's chief plenipotentiaries his Foreign Minister, the Vicomte de Montmorency, and his ambassador in London, the distinguished writer the Vicomte de Chateaubriand. Metternich thought that Chateaubriand was a client of Pozzo, who remained Russia's ambassador in Paris. But Chateaubriand was nobody's dupe. He was one of those French patriots who combat a sense of humiliation by feeding on national pride. The French believed Verona would give them the opportunity to recover authority as the strongest power in Western Europe.

Socially Verona was the most impressive international gathering of sovereigns and statesmen since Vienna: a banquet in the late autumn sunshine within the Roman amphitheatre, Rossini conducting two of his operas at gala performances, competition between ambassadors' wives for the most elegant salon, and grand balls graced by the presence of two emperors (Russia and Austria), three kings (Prussia, Piedmont, Two Sicilies) and the rulers of Tuscany, Modena and Parma (whose Duchess had been Empress of the French for four years). Politically, however, Verona was unproductive. Peace was seen to reign in Italy, and the Congress resolved that Austria's army should be withdrawn from Piedmont and cut in size in Naples. A Greek delegation, which had travelled to Ancona at the suggestion of Capodistria, was refused permission to cross the Papal States and, true to the bargain made at the Vienna Conference, nothing was said about the wrongs of Greece. Spain was the main theme. The French bluntly demanded to know what support their allies would give if it became essential to send an army across the Pyrenees to restore order in Madrid. Wellington no less bluntly made it clear that Great Britain would never approve of the invasion of Spain by a French army or by a European force. Alexander offered 150,000 men to support the French, a suggestion which alarmed Metternich until Montmorency and Chateaubriand turned it down because of the delay in mobilising a Russian army and conveying it across the continent. The Austrians disliked all talk of armies crossing frontiers, and Metternich spent three weeks trying to induce his allies to rely on political pressure rather than on a prestigious show of force. By the end of the Congress the Chancellor was able to claim a diplomatic victory of a sort. The French accepted a measure of restraint; they would take action against the Spanish liberal regime in the name of the alliance only if the political situation in Madrid became so serious that it seemed as if military intervention was essential for the good of Europe as a whole. But, though Metternich had checked Villèle and Montmorency, he had failed in his secondary objective of keeping the British active in the councils of Europe. Wellington refused to associate Britain with even a collective note of warning to the Spanish constitutionalists. Canning had chosen 'insulation'.[17]

The Congress dissolved slowly. Wellington left for home on 30 November, Montmorency and Chateaubriand a few days later, Metternich and Alexander not until the third week of December. There were to be no more congresses attended by a select group of Europe's crowned heads. Tsar Alexander proposed in September 1823 that the Great Powers should gather in congress at St Petersburg the following summer in order to discuss the Eastern Question. Nobody welcomed the idea, least of all Metternich, who had ensured that each of the previous congresses had taken place either within the Austrian Empire or at Aix, an old German imperial city redolent of Hohenstaufen and Habsburg hegemony in Europe. Alexander persisted for several months, but without success. The best he could hope for in St Petersburg was an ambassadorial conference. This indeed became the accepted practice for round table diplomacy throughout the remaining years of the century. Napoleon III sought to revive the congress idea and upgraded the official name of the 'Paris Conference' in 1856 to 'Congress of Paris' when it became certain that Austria, Great Britain and Piedmont would be represented by ministers of state rather than by ambassadors and that there would be discussion of general questions as well as of the specific problem of making peace. It was, too, the high level of governmental representation, and the broad scope of questions discussed, that raised the meeting at Berlin in 1878 to the dignity of a congress. On this occasion, however, not a single reigning sovereign was present at the sessions of the Congress, public or private.

There remained something unique about the congress diplomacy of the years from 1815 to 1822. Sovereigns and statesmen believed they were meeting to anticipate problems and to defend a concept of public international law. Technically they failed. They could not separate instinctive fear of liberalism as 'revolution' from the certainty that frontiers defined by treaty should be guaranteed from invasion. More seriously, the congresses developed the practice of avoiding disputes by ignoring the gravest of problems in the hope that they would go away. To some extent this weakness sprang from the exalted character of the meetings. It was easier for envoys and ambassadors to compromise and trim policies than it was for sovereign heads of government to risk the humiliation of a rebuff, as the tensions at Vienna had shown in the closing weeks of 1814. Yet, with all its fraudulent intrigue and frustrations, the congress idea made a lasting contribution to diplomatic practice. The European Powers continued to collaborate, meeting in smaller conferences with agenda confined to specific issues in dispute. Without the original impetus from the summit, there would have been no precedents and no code of procedure for diplomats who pursued peace at less rarefied heights of negotiation.

4 Dutch Bottoms and an Untoward Event, 1823–30

For eight years after the Congress of Verona the power struggle in Europe was dominated by the policies and legacy of one statesman, a British outsider whom his contemporaries abroad never began to understand. George Canning was the great commoner of the old Foreign Office. Alone among nineteenth-century Foreign Secretaries he was neither a peer of the United Kingdom or Ireland nor the son of a peer. His father died in penury on the boy's first birthday, his mother became an actress and George was rescued from social obscurity by his father's brother, the elder Stratford Canning, whose generosity enabled his nephew to be educated at Eton and Christ Church. Both parents were of Irish descent and from an early age George possessed the sharp felicity of phrase with which so many Anglo-Irish playwrights have been endowed. He became a barrister, a vocation so rare at the Foreign Office that no lawyer served as Foreign Secretary between Canning in 1827 and Lord Reading in 1931. Although he never built up a practice at the bar, Canning's style as a speaker echoed the persuasiveness of a good defence counsel; British public opinion was a jury to be wooed by skilful advocacy of a cause. Poor Castlereagh, whose speeches droned confusedly in a maze of subordinate clauses, never held the Commons enthralled and, as Leader of the House, always had the Press against him. Canning spoke intelligibly, metaphors ringing out crisply to the galleries. Sometimes he positively joked. *The Times*, having damned him as a 'hired advocate' even before he succeeded Castlereagh, consistently mistrusted him; but other newspapers responded to the subtle skill with which he made the exigencies of diplomacy appear dramatic. They welcomed his belief in publicity, his willingness to lay before Parliament for printing and publication dispatches relating to recent problems. This policy, which was thoroughly deplored by Wellington, gave an impression to the public that it was being taken into the Foreign Secretary's confidence. Publicity strengthened Canning's position in the Cabinet and left foreign governments in no doubt of what he affirmed was British policy. He did not originate Blue books, but he was the first minister who used them to appeal to public opinion in the country as a whole.

George IV at first detested him. 'Mr Canning's readmission into the Cabinet' entailed 'the greatest personal sacrifice that a sovereign ever made to a subject or, indeed, taking all the circumstances that man ever made to man', the king told Lord Chancellor Eldon. But the Prime Minister, Lord Liverpool, was a contemporary of Canning at Christ Church and knew that royal displeasure sprang from his earlier friendship with the king's estranged wife, Caroline, and he never doubted his Foreign Secretary's qualities. In 1818 he had insisted Canning be kept informed of the negotiations at Aix and Castlereagh certainly accepted

Canning as a valuable adviser in Cabinet from 1816 to 1820. Canning had, indeed, much experience of foreign affairs: three years as under-secretary (1796–9) and over two years as Foreign Secretary (1807–9), when he originated the practice of heading letters 'Foreign Office' rather than 'Downing Street' as his predecessors had done. From the autumn of 1814 until the spring of 1816 he was ambassador in Lisbon, seeing for himself the problems of an embassy abroad. Many of his personal friends were diplomats: Sir Charles Bagot, who served at Washington, St Petersburg and The Hague had known him well for over thirty years; and so, too, had Lord Granville, the ambassador in Paris from 1824 to 1841. George Canning's cousin, the younger Stratford Canning, was at Washington from 1820 to 1824 but, with four years of valuable service at Constantinople behind him, he was already regarded as an expert on Turkey where he was to become – as Lord Stratford de Redcliffe – the most famous of all British ambassadors in the nineteenth century. Although Stratford was sixteen years younger than George, the cousins understood each other well. The Foreign Secretary remained conscious of a particular debt to this branch of his family; he treated 'Stratty' almost as a brother.[1]

Such close knowledge of the diplomatic machine enabled Canning to bring a touch of professionalism to the Foreign Office. Canning completed administrative reforms begun by Castlereagh towards the end of his life: the staff grew from twenty-eight in 1822 to thirty-six in 1827, with closer distinction of grades in the clerical posts; hours of work were set officially as from noon until five, although the staff had often to remain in the evenings and attend at the weekend. Other changes followed. The messenger service to embassies abroad and the consular service were placed under stricter control. Greater responsibility was given to the permanent under-secretary, Joseph Planta, who was a friend at Eton of Stratford Canning and who had become a Privy Councillor, on Castlereagh's recommendation, in 1819. Yet, although Canning increased efficiency and kept his clerks working for long hours, he retained a firm hold on the conduct of diplomacy, not least because – alone of secretaries of state – he took up residence in the Foreign Office himself.[2] Drafting of dispatches was undertaken by Canning and nobody else, and he insisted on recording in memoranda all important conversations with foreign diplomats, even sending his version to the ambassador or minister for verification. Rather strangely, Metternich considered him casual in the conduct of business, basing his judgement on tales recounted by the Austrian ambassador, Paul Esterhazy, and by that mischievous intriguer Dorothea Lieven, wife of the Russian ambassador and Metternich's mistress at Aix. But Canning was strict, meticulous and hard on his own staff and on diplomats abroad who fell short of his standard.

Occasionally, Canning's self-assurance tempted him into light-hearted asides. When William Wynn, his Cabinet colleague responsible for Indian affairs, sent Canning a worried note in October 1826 to ask if Britain had treaty obligations to assist the Shah in Persia's border skirmishes with Russia, he received a reassuring reply likening the small property owners of Persia to the forty-shilling freeholders of the English unreformed electorate. Wynn was told that the Anglo-Persian treaties of 1812 and

1814 were defensive in character and not operative; the Shah had attacked first, because 'The Priests had gotten ahead and his forty Shillingers were incurably warlike'.[3] There was, too, the famous 'rhyming dispatch' of 31 January 1826 which was caused by the failure of the Dutch minister, Anton Falck, to follow the French example and accept a reciprocal lowering of shipping duties.[4] Canning's friend Bagot (transferred from St Petersburg to The Hague in 1824) was 'up by cock-crow' to help decipher a puzzling dispatch which, 'after an hour of most indescribable anxiety', was seen to read:

Sir,
     In matters of commerce the fault of the Dutch
     Is offering too little and asking too much.
     The French are with equal advantage content
     So we'll clap on Dutch bottoms just 20 per cent
     (Chorus of Customs House Officers and Douaniers)
     20 per cent, 20 per cent,
     We'll clap on Dutch bottoms just 20 per cent.
     Vous frapperez Falck avec 20 per cent.
     I have no other commands from His Majesty to convey to
     you today.

By the time Canning thus allowed his pen to run merrily in dactylic tetrameter he had been shaping British policy for three and a half years; he was certain of his authority in Cabinet and in the counsels of Europe. But it had not always been so. Until the summer of 1825 he reckoned George IV a personal enemy who was prepared to work with Metternich to discredit him and provoke his resignation. His ultra-Tory colleagues long deplored his 'speechifying' and wondered why Lord Liverpool persisted in retaining a Foreign Secretary with such Whiggish sympathy for constitutionalism in Spain and Portugal. They found it hard to understand the purpose of his actions. He had declared that he had no time for 'the predominating areopagitical spirit' of the European conservatives; but was not the alternative a rapid descent into Jacobin international anarchy? It was all very puzzling for Tories who remembered how the pilot, in weathering the storm, had urged the merits of a public law to bind the Powers of Europe in future peace. Yet Canning still saw himself as a Pittite and, in his own mind, possessed a perfectly consistent policy. By refusing to participate in general congresses, he sought the opportunity to intervene with independent objectives, solely in issues of importance for 'England'. The strength and the weakness of thus seeking to recover Britain's freedom of action was well tested by the problem posed, and left unresolved, at Verona – Spain.

     At the end of January 1823 the Spanish parliament (Cortes) rejected a demand from the French, Austrian, Russian and Prussian governments that the constitution should be modified and King Ferdinand restored to absolute sovereignty. Riots in Madrid were followed by the king's enforced removal to Seville and the establishment of a regency. France thereupon claimed the right to intervene and, in the first week of April, the Duke of Angoulême – nephew of Louis XVI and Louis XVIII – led a royalist army across the Bidassoa. The French thus returned to the peninsula from which Wellington had expelled them barely ten years before. It was not, however, a campaign of distinction. 'The hundred thousand sons of St Louis', as a Spanish novelist ironically dubbed the invaders later in the century, met little resistance, except around the stronghold of the Trocadero at Cadiz, the city where the liberal constitution was first promulgated in March 1812. By the end of September 1823 Ferdinand VII enjoyed the trappings of absolute power once more, thanks to French arms. Villèle and Chateaubriand had even rejected proposals from Metternich that the Great Powers – apart from wayward England – should meet and settle the Spanish Question once and for all. This, Europe was told, was a matter for the Bourbons, His Most Christian Majesty in Paris and His Catholic Majesty in Madrid. Legitimism carried odd echoes of old conflicts into the nineteenth century.

Canning could do nothing to influence events in Spain.[5] Lord Fitzroy Somerset – once Wellington's aide-de-camp and later, as Lord Raglan, a scapegoat for inefficiency in the Crimea – was sent to Madrid on a diplomatic mission ahead of the invaders. It was hoped his good sense might moderate Spanish liberal intransigence, but in vain. Once the 'sons of St Louis' were through the Pyrenees, the British confined their efforts to limiting the extent of French military action. In this purpose Canning was remarkably successful. He secured assurances from Villèle that France would withdraw from Spain once anarchy was rooted out and would also respect the territorial integrity of Portugal. Defence of Portugal's independence, whether against alleged French activities in Spain or against successive reactionary governments in Madrid, became a cardinal principle of British foreign policy. Canning ordered a naval squadron to the Tagus and sent a force of 4,000 men to Lisbon in January 1827 in order to protect the legal constitutional government against clericalist reactionaries. The troops were soon withdrawn, but the warships remained at Lisbon, or off the mouth of the Tagus, for another forty years, the most active British presence in the affairs of Western Europe.

The White Ensign over the Tagus moorings was a visible assertion of naval mastery of the Atlantic sea lanes. The strength of the Royal Navy ruled out intervention by other European Powers in Latin America. During the Napoleonic Wars, French subjugation of metropolitan Spain allowed the British to penetrate deeply into the traditionally restricted market of the Spanish and Portuguese colonial empires. Hence, in the postwar years, British support for the independence of the colonies sprang not from admiration of Simon Bolivar or San Martin but from a desire to safeguard an outlet for Britain's manufactured goods and secure a region where it would be profitable for British investors to sink their capital. Canning, MP for Liverpool since 1812, could feel the pulse of Britain's commercial class. 'South America is ours', he wrote in a private note; but he intended the phrase to be no more, and no less, than a statement of commercial fact.[6] Early in October 1823 he held a series of meetings with Prince Jules de Polignac, French ambassador in London, which were summarised in a formal memorandum. This 'Polignac Note' acknowledged

Britain's paramount trading interests in South America, confirmed that France would not interfere in the disputes between Spain and her former colonies and accepted Canning's refusal to take part in any conference to decide the future of Latin America. Significantly the record of the Polignac conversations shows Canning's professed amazement that the European states should consider such a congress 'without calling to their Counsels a Power so eminently interested as the United States of America'. Briefly Canning worked for Anglo-American collaboration over South American problems, but the secretary of state (John Quincy Adams) was suspicious. He did not intend America to serve as 'cockboat in the wake of a British man-of-war'. The principal consequence of Canning's overture was the famous message, drafted by Adams and sent by President Monroe, emphatically informing Congress that the American continent was no place for European colonisation. Adams, who had served as envoy in Russia during the most momentous years of Alexander I's reign, knew Europe too well to allow any administration in Washington to become ensnared in chancellery diplomacy. Britain and the United States had a common interest in preserving the independence of the former colonies in Latin America, but the two Powers were natural competitors for markets rather than potential allies against a threat of intervention which remained largely illusory.[7]

Nevertheless, American policy was indirectly to assist Canning. Not least among his difficulties was handling the more aristocratic members of Lord Liverpool's Cabinet. Gradually he convinced them that British traders needed diplomatic protection so that their enterprises could mature under peaceful and, it was hoped, stable government; and in July 1824 he gained Cabinet approval for commercial attachés to be sent to the new South American republics. But, as he himself said, it was a 'hard fight' to win consent from his colleagues to extend full diplomatic recognition to Mexico, Colombia and Buenos Aires. Ultimately, in the closing weeks of 1824, he swayed the Cabinet by the argument that only formal recognition would enable Britain to frustrate the formation of a Trans-Atlantic League, a project for Pan-American primacy allegedly held by the United States government. Even so, recognition of the three republics shocked the king. He declined to announce in person the government's decision at the opening of Parliament on 7 February 1825, backing up a familiar excuse of persistent gout with the dramatic novelty of lost false teeth. In his absence the speech was read, with obvious distaste, by Lord Chancellor Eldon. Subsequently the ambassadors of France, Russia, Austria and Prussia waited on Canning separately to complain of the patronage he was according rebellious republicanism. He was not impressed by their remonstrances. As he was to tell the Commons at the close of the following session, his backing for British traders in Latin America offset French gains in their occupation of Spain. 'I resolved that if France had Spain, it should not be Spain "with the Indies"', he said in the most quoted of his speeches; 'I called the New World into existence to redress the balance of the Old.' Angoulême and the sons of St Louis returned to Paris with little reward for their campaign other than the battle honour of the Trocadero; but the British merchant companies who had invaded South America were still banking the benefits of Canning's statecraft a century later.[8]

In April 1825, a few weeks after the shock recognition of the three republics, there was a possibility of a meeting between Canning and Metternich. The two men had never encountered each other: Canning was at Lisbon when Metternich came to London in 1814; and although the young Metternich had listened in the Commons gallery to several debates in 1794, nobody had the foresight to introduce him to the newly elected Member for Newtown, sitting on the government benches below. But towards the end of the winter of 1824–5 Metternich's wife, Eleonore, became gravely ill in Paris. He was at her bedside when she died and he remained in France for over a month. Despite his personal sorrow he showed much of his old aptitude for political intrigue, dining with Villèle, with Talleyrand, with Pozzo di Borgo. He was informed that if he came to England George IV would welcome him at Windsor, or even Brighton. But Canning was hostile. His friend Granville, ambassador in Paris, was told that Canning's 'sources of intelligence' led him to believe he was liable 'to be driven from office by the Holy Alliance'. He thought it in Metternich's best interests to come no nearer to England than Paris. 'I wonder whether he is aware that the private communication of foreign Ministers with the King of England is wholly at variance with the spirit, and practice too, of the British Constitution', he added. Granville ensured the warning reached the Chancellor.[9]

Metternich took the hint. So did the 'Cottage Clique', the group of diplomats and court favourites around George IV at Windsor. Canning's veiled threat of embarrassing constitutional revelations in Parliament should he be forced from office by any intrigue at the Royal Lodge silenced 'the continental gossipings'. Gradually George IV allowed himself to succumb to Canning's blandishments. It was pleasant to receive an impression that policies carried out in the king's name were popular with his subjects; and he conceded that 'the damnedest fellow in the world' wrote more entertaining reports of parliamentary business than had his predecessor, Castlereagh. To his amusement Canning found he was now made welcome at the Royal Lodge. Other members of the Cottage Clique hastened to make themselves agreeable. Countess Lieven had spent the best part of three years in convincing Metternich that Canning was a transient phenomenon whose personal following was 'a mere drop in the ocean'. Suddenly she discovered that the Foreign Secretary's wit and originality of mind revealed qualities of hidden statesmanship. Social assessments of this kind, trivial in themselves, mattered in an age when the hearsay of the salons provided hints of policy changes to astute ambassadors, or their wives. Dorothea Lieven was a highly perceptive political animal who, as she once told Metternich, 'quite liked prime ministers'. Her most intimate friends did not always remember that, despite her willingness to give unsolicited advice to the Austrian Chancellor or the leader of the English Whigs or the Duke of Wellington, she was wife of a Russian ambassador and sister of General Benckendorff, the Tsar's chief of police. In a more constrained society than George IV's London some would have thought her a security risk.[10]

Although the Lievens, husband and wife, deplored Canning's Latin American policy, they recognised that what happened in Buenos Aires or Bogotá was of little concern to Russia. The Greek revolt against the Turks was another matter, an act of defiance by Orthodox Christians. At first the War of Independence, which spread from the Peloponnese to the Aegean islands in April 1821, favoured the Greeks. But by 1823 a conflict between rival Greek leaders provided the Sultan with an opportunity to recover lost territory if only he could find a good commander. He called on his most efficient – and most ambitious – vassal, Mehemet Ali, ruler of Egypt, and in February 1825 Mehemet Ali's son, Ibrahim, landed at Modon in the southern Peloponnese with a powerful army, trained by French officers. Ibrahim's arrival transformed the military situation and it began to seem as if such of the Sultan's Christian subjects as survived massacre would be forced back under Ottoman rule. No sovereign of Holy Russia could risk so great a humiliation for the Orthodox faith. Gradually Alexander had come to see that the Greek revolution was not, as Metternich maintained, a peculiarly Aegean manifestation of Jacobinism. Attempts to solve the Greek problem through an ambassadorial conference in St Petersburg were frustrated by persistent temporising on Austria's part, and by the spring of 1825 Alexander was doubting the value of Metternich's friendship. The Greeks, too, were changing their attitude to the Great Powers: they had counted, in vain, on Russian support, relying too much on Capodistria, who was now in exile at Geneva; and, despairing of aid from St Petersburg, they turned to Britain. In July 1825 the provisional government, hard pressed by Ibrahim's forces, formally sought British protection. But Canning was no interventionist. He had recognised the Greeks as belligerents as early as March 1823. To extend them protection was a different matter, for he would not contemplate military action against the Sultan, with whom the British retained treaty obligations. Everything still depended on Russia, the one Power capable of exerting military and naval pressure at Constantinople, and whatever the Greeks themselves might feel, there was little prospect of Anglo-Russian collaboration. Indeed at the end of December 1824 Alexander, piqued by Canning's indifference to the St Petersburg Conference, instructed Lieven in London to give up all attempts to reach agreement with the British over the Eastern Question.

In the second week of July 1825 the Lievens arrived back in St Petersburg on leave. The ambassador had not been home for four years, the ambassadress for thirteen. Their visit coincided with a major change in the Tsar's attitude to his Austrian ally. Reports reached him of patronising remarks made by Metternich during his long stay in Paris; personal rancour thus began to harden his conviction that Russia gained little from partnership with Austria. In mid-August Nesselrode was instructed to inform all his envoys abroad that henceforth Russia would 'follow her own views exclusively and be governed solely by her own interests'. Dorothea Lieven accelerated this 'diplomatic revolution' although she exaggerated and overdramatised her activities. There is, however, no doubt that she spoke favourably of Canning to the Tsar and that, a few hours before the Lievens were due to set out for London on 31 August,

Nesselrode visited her and asked her to let Canning know privately that Alexander was prepared to break with his conservative allies and would look sympathetically at any British initiative over the problems of Greece. It is not clear when this 'living dispatch', as Nesselrode is supposed to have called her, imparted her 'great secret' to Canning. Almost certainly he had some idea that policy was changing in St Petersburg before the middle of October, when he prepared instructions for two newly appointed ambassadors, Lord Strangford (to Russia) and Stratford Canning (to Turkey). The instructions given to both envoys are so vague that it suggests the Foreign Secretary may have anticipated that the diplomatic situation would change before they reached their destination and he was therefore seeking to keep business in his own hands, managed through diplomats in London. But he was as suspicious as ever of hypothetical commitments; the British government had no wish to give any pledge 'that would fetter . . . its decisions upon future contingencies', he said on 14 October.[11]

When Strangford asked for advice on how to deal with Alexander he was told by Canning, 'Just keep him in good humour – that's all'. This, however, he had no chance of doing, for he never met Alexander. The Tsar had left St Petersburg on 13 September intending to winter on the Sea of Azov or in the Crimea. There he contracted a fever and died at Taganrog on 1 December 'from a disease of the liver'. Nothing illustrates more clearly the pedestrian pace of Great Power diplomacy in the 1820s than the slowness with which reports of Alexander's death travelled across the continent. The first major city to hear of it was Warsaw, where a courier arrived direct from Taganrog on 7 December. The Foreign Ministry in St Petersburg did not learn the news until shortly after midday on 9 December. Metternich heard in Vienna about midnight on 13 December, Canning in London on the morning of 18 December, the new British ambassador to Turkey not until 9 January 1826 when HMS *Revenge*, the 74-gun three-decker conveying him unhurriedly to Constantinople, reached the island of Hydra. No one doubted that Alexander's death, which was followed by the abortive Decembrist revolt and the accession of his brother as Nicholas I, marked the end of an era. Both in Vienna and London it was assumed that Alexander had been planning war against Turkey when the snow melted in the Balkan passes. Now there seemed a prospect of a peaceful settlement of the Greek crisis. George Canning told his cousin that he expected narrowly Russian nationalist policies from Nicholas in place of the 'cosmopolitan creed' of the dead Tsar; it would, he thought, be simpler 'to talk Greek' with Nicholas and Nesselrode. All the same, he gave 'Stratty' some practical advice: 'Exaggerate if you can the danger from Russia.' It was not, perhaps, the wisest injunction for a man of Stratford's temperament.[12]

The Foreign Secretary induced George IV to send Wellington as his personal representative at Tsar Alexander's funeral. Canning entrusted the duke with a more important task, one which he felt Strangford too muddle-headed to accomplish. The duke was to join Nesselrode and Lieven (now raised to the dignity of a prince) in working out terms for an autonomous Greek state, which would remain within the Sultan's empire. He was to avoid incurring any lasting guarantee for Great Britain, but was to respond positively to the messages conveyed to Canning by the Lievens. Above all, he was to reach a settlement which would prevent Ibrahim from depopulating the reconquered Peloponnese and establishing there new Muslim communities. The duke and the Russians duly signed a protocol at St Petersburg on 4 April 1826 which provided for mediation between the Turks and the Greeks with the intention of creating a future Greek vassal state. Wellington did not, however, see the implications of every article in the protocol, including one which might be interpreted as giving Russia an excuse for war with the Turks in order to impose a settlement. Canning was far from pleased with the duke and their relations became strained. As Princess Lieven later recalled, Canning 'was not quite sure whether to congratulate himself on a success or to complain of a snare'.[13]

The Austrians, Prussians and French were also 'not quite sure' of the protocol's significance. Outwardly Britain and Russia were once again partners but their union was no love match. Metternich regarded the St Petersburg protocol as a diplomatic defeat for Austria. He was not surprised by any intrigue of that 'malevolent meteor' Canning, but he was thrown from his habitual complacency by the apparent apostasy of Nesselrode and, he suspected, of the Lievens too. Only three months previously he had remarked, in a private letter, on Austria's good fortune in having at the Russian Foreign Ministry so sound a friend as Nesselrode 'who is today a child at my feet'. Now the child had given him a sharp kick on the shin, and others were to follow. Sultan Mahmud II, though in no hurry to accept mediation in Greece, recognised the need to secure his frontiers on the Danube and in the Caucasus from a Russian invasion; and throughout the summer and autumn of 1826 Russian and Turkish diplomats held talks in the small town of Akkerman (now Ovidiopol), near Odessa. The resultant Convention of Akkerman (7 October 1826) conceded considerable rights of intervention to Russia in the internal affairs of the Danubian Principalities (Wallachia and Moldavia) as well as securing safeguards for the autonomy of Serbia and the recognition of Russian rights in the Caucasus and guarantees of Russian free navigation in the Ottoman Empire. All these matters were of major importance to the Austrians, because they strengthened Russia's hold on the lower Danube; but Metternich was barely consulted. He was suffering – and continued for another seven years to suffer – from his ingenuity in having kept Turkish affairs for so long off the agenda of Europe as a 'matter of courtesy'.

In Berlin, and in the Prussian legation at Constantinople, the diplomats still dutifully followed Austria's lead when there was any lead to follow. But in Paris opinion was divided. Charles X, who had succeeded his brother Louis XVIII in September 1824, at first retained the clericalist Villèle as his prime minister with Baron Damas (who had served in the Russian army in 1812) in charge of foreign affairs. Both ministers were uneasy at the apparent change in Russian policy. They were inclined to respond favourably to approaches from Metternich for Franco-Austrian collaboration in the summer of 1826, although there was, at the time, no real purpose behind such an alignment. Charles X himself was a philhellene and ready to look for any means of restoring French influence in the Levant. At the end of September the king received Canning, who was in Paris ostensibly on a private visit to Granville. The two men talked of the problems in both the Iberian and Balkan peninsulas. 'I can turn about even quicker than you', the king remarked significantly, and by the beginning of December Damas had begun talks with Pozzo di Borgo and Granville which were intended to associate France with the Anglo-Russian accord. The negotiations were slow and difficult: the French wanted something more precise than the St Petersburg protocol; and Nesselrode, prompted by Tsar Nicholas, threatened independent action against Turkey. Canning showed great political courage by accepting the idea that Russia might send a squadron into the Mediterranean for joint service alongside the navies of France and Britain. Warships of the three Powers had never before collaborated as allies, nor were they to do so again until 1915; and Canning was revolutionising British strategic assumptions. He carried a reluctant Cabinet with him and on 6 July 1827 a treaty was signed at the Foreign Office which committed Britain, France and Russia to recognise an autonomous Greece and to induce the Turks and Greeks to accept an armistice by concentrating a combined fleet in Greek waters. It was hoped the naval presence would in itself be effective. No one wished the Greek problem settled by the guns of allied warships.[14]

Canning succeeded to the premiership before the treaty was signed and he entrusted the Foreign Office to his friend Lord Dudley. All decisions, Canning assumed, would be taken by the Prime Minister while Dudley attended to routine business. A strong and cohesive government, firmly led and clear in purpose, might have found in the Treaty of London a useful instrument of statecraft. Canning's armed diplomacy was intended to be supplemented by delicate negotiation; a secret emissary was sent off to Mehemet Ali as soon as the treaty was signed in the hope that the Pasha of Egypt could restrain his son Ibrahim even if the Sultan defied the attempt of the Powers to impose an armistice. But the Treaty of London remained Canning's one achievement as Prime Minister. He had taken office on 12 April, already racked with pain from the illness which killed him so suddenly a hundred days later. There was now no one in London capable of operating the checks and balances of Canning's experiment in brinkmanship. The terms of the treaty reached Constantinople on 8 August, the very day of Canning's death; should the Turks reject allied demands for a truce it was left to Stratford and the senior naval commander to make sense of what seemed to them ambiguous instructions.

The death of Canning was seen as 'an event of the greatest significance' by his European rival, Metternich, and as a tragedy by both moderate Whigs and moderate Tories in London. George IV, unwilling to trust government either to the Whigs or the ultra-Tories, settled for 'Goody' Goderich and mediocrity. The new Prime Minister, once Castlereagh's companion on that icy journey to allied headquarters, retained Dudley as Foreign Secretary. This was a grave error. Canning had intended him as a mere tenant and Dudley had never expected to remain long at the Foreign Office. 'In three months I cannot do *much* harm', Dudley had written to Lord Aberdeen.[15] Fate proved him wrong. On 20 October 1827

Vice-Admiral Sir Edward Codrington, one of the most distinguished of Nelson's admirals, led twenty-four British, French and Russian ships into Navarino Bay, where eighty-nine Turkish and Egyptian vessels were at anchor. Technically Codrington's squadron entered the bay in order to persuade Ibrahim to embark his troops and return to Alexandria and the admiral had given orders that no allied ship was to fire the first shot. The Turks regarded the allied presence as a provocation and took the initiative. In a four-hour battle Ibrahim's fleet, which was essential for the supply of his army, was annihilated. News of Navarino reached Dudley in London on 11 November. A resolute Foreign Secretary would have led the three allied Powers to a solution of the Greek Question by the spring, if not sooner.

Metternich was appalled by reports of Navarino. He feared the allied fleet would use its guns to impose peace on Sultan Mahmud in Constantinople as a preliminary to partition of the Ottoman Empire. He need not have worried. There was no follow-up to Navarino by the French or the British. The governments in Paris and London were lamentably weak: the Villèle ministry genuflected its way into a crisis at home in November, while Goderich could not keep discipline in a factious Cabinet; and both Prime Ministers fell in the first week of January 1828. Dudley, rather surprisingly, survived until 30 May. In thirteen months at the Foreign Office his sole success – rare enough to endear him to his staff – was to clear the papers and dispatches in the fourth week of December so that the 'work shop' might be closed and a holiday taken on Christmas Day. Over Greek affairs his under-secretary complained to Granville that Dudley lacked self-confidence and would decide nothing for himself. For five months the Duke of Wellington, as Prime Minister, in succession to Goderich, tried to shape foreign policy by bullying his reluctant colleagues into 'having everything my own way'.[16]

The duke's way was certainly not Canning's. It was Wellington who wrote into the king's speech for the opening of Parliament at the end of January the famous description of Navarino as 'an untoward event'. The phrase was unpopular with the Commons and prompted the opposition to move a resolution which congratulated Admiral Codrington on his victory. But more was at issue in the debate than resentment at an implied slight on the Royal Navy. Wellington was sounding a retreat from Canning's exposed position in Europe, and his critics feared some new accommodation with Metternich and the old order. In this they were wrong. In April he withdrew the troops sent by Canning to Portugal and ordered the naval squadron out of the Tagus as a sign that Britain would no longer meddle in the affairs of the continent. He recognised that Britain retained obligations to defend Corfu but he thoroughly distrusted the popular enthusiasm for Greece. 'All I wish is to get out of the Greek affair without loss of honour and without inconvenient risk to the safety of the Ionian Islands', he remarked to Lord Aberdeen, Dudley's successor as Foreign Secretary. Aberdeen, who as a youthful dilettante archaeologist had excavated the Pnyx at Athens, retained enough sympathy for the Greek cause to check Wellington's drift into total isolation, but he could not allay the Duke's prejudices. The fact that Capodistria assumed office in January 1828 as elected president of a future Greece hardly reassured Wellington. For, although the new president arrived at Nauplion aboard a British warship, no one who remembered him from earlier days could believe he had cut his links with St Petersburg. The duke agreed that the diplomats might meet around tables in Poros and in London to give the new state a frontier and a constitution, but he remained highly suspicious of what was happening in the Peloponnese. 'There never was such a humbug as the Greek affair altogether', he grumbled. 'However, thank God it has never cost us a shilling, and never shall.'[17]

Predictably the chief beneficiaries from Wellington's withdrawal symptoms were the two Powers he most distrusted, France and Russia. Reluctantly, and after several changes of mind, he authorised Aberdeen to back a proposal from Paris for a French force to land in the Peloponnese to supervise the evacuation of Ibrahim's army and thus facilitate the transfer of authority to Capodistria: France remained an influential patron of political life, and commercial activity, in Nauplion and Athens long after the soldiers had completed their turn of police duty. The most decisive action came, however, from the Russians who, exasperated by Sultan Mahmud's prevarication, declared war on Turkey at the end of April 1828. Tsar Nicholas hoped for a rapid victory. 'The Emperor', Nesselrode wrote to Prince Lieven, 'knows well enough that the attitude of the other Powers depends on the speed of our successes.'[18] But Nicholas was doubly wrong: the lightning war failed to flash, and yet Europe did nothing. By the following summer, when the Russians broke through the Balkan mountains, the Powers were concerned only that Turkey should not be partitioned. Nicholas, having won the obligatory Romanov victory against the Sultan, was prepared to be generous. The Peace of Adrianople (14 September 1829) gave Russia gains in the Caucasus and further rights in the Danubian Principalities but the core of Ottoman lands remained intact. Only the Sultan's peripheral rule – in Serbia, southern Greece and Circassia – was constrained and even there Turkish garrisons remained in Belgrade, on the Acropolis and in Erzerum.

Metternich, who for many months had feared a general war, sighed with relief that the peace terms were no worse. That October marked the twentieth anniversary of his appointment as Foreign Minister and he used the occasion to survey the European scene. The crisis in the East was ended, he told Emperor Francis, and it had led to the disruption of Canning's unholy league of Russia, Britain and France. Vienna, he believed, would emerge once more as the centre of European order, for any disaffected Power which sought 'the triumph of the conservative system' would 'sooner or later range itself alongside Austria'. There was a great deal of muddled wishful thinking in Metternich's report and Francis seems to have given it only perfunctory attention when his Chancellor left it with him.[19] The crisis was by no means over; the three signatories of the Treaty of London were to spend three more years of conference diplomacy settling the affairs of Greece. But Metternich was right to see the Peace of Adrianople as a pointer to change in Russian policy. A committee set up by the Tsar to consider Russia's future relations with Turkey reported to Nicholas on 16 September 1829. It claimed that the advantages of preserving Turkey for as long as possible outweighed the attraction of partitioning the empire. To break up Turkey would be to invite Britain, France and Austria to secure footholds in the Balkans or the Levant; it would, as Nesselrode said, 'plunge one into a labyrinth of difficulty and complications each more inextricable than the other'.[20] The Tsar was impressed by these arguments. He instructed Nesselrode to champion the *status quo* in Turkey; only if the Ottoman Empire was about to collapse should Russia be ready 'to ensure that the exit from the Black Sea is not seized by any other Power'. There was henceforth to be no crusade for Orthodoxy and certainly not for the liberties of the Balkan peoples. The sole criterion for action was Russian self-interest – who was to hold the Bosphorus?

Russia thus became once more an upholder of the established order, and the aberrations of Alexander's day were finally over. In France, too, there seemed a new assertion of old principles when, in August 1829, Charles X summoned Prince Jules de Polignac home from the London embassy to serve as Prime Minister and Foreign Minister in a government of 'Church and Throne'. Polignac believed he was honoured with divine revelation. If so, there can be little doubt he got his lines crossed. A proposal forwarded to Nesselrode soon after he took office was more sublime than any holy fantasy of Alexander I; Polignac suggested major territorial changes which included sending the King of the Netherlands to Constantinople where he would rule as a Christian dependant of the Tsar while a French army absorbed Belgium and carried the lily flag of the Bourbons to the Rhine frontier. The Russians, however, wanted the Vienna Settlement, from Warsaw across to Brussels, to remain stable and undisturbed. They wasted little time on the Polignac Plan.[21] Still in search of a prestigious triumph, the French turned to North Africa where the ruler of Algiers had slapped the French consul with his fan in a moment of Barbary anger; and at midsummer 1830 Polignac mounted a crusade against Islam and piracy which enabled the power of France to bridge the western Mediterranean for another century and a quarter. This design, though exciting the Lords of Admiralty in London, was of scant concern to Nesselrode or to Metternich.

Increasingly, these two statesmen, who had known each other for nearly thirty years, were beginning to find a new identity of view on Europe's affairs. They had not met since the autumn of 1823 and when the Austrian Chancellor heard that Nesselrode planned to take the waters at Carlsbad in the last week of July 1830 he arranged to travel to the Bohemian spa with Gentz, who had also known the Russian minister since the turn of the century. The three men came together on Tuesday 27 July. Metternich found Nesselrode 'shy', attentive and ready to co-operate with Austria and Prussia once more in keeping Europe safe and secure. They parted amicably and agreed to meet again before Nesselrode returned to St Petersburg. It was a wise arrangement; for on that same Tuesday another veteran associate of theirs looked out from his window in the Rue St Florentin, heard shouting from a crowd milling over from the Place de la Concorde towards the Tuileries, and remarked that Paris was about to erupt in arms once more. By the end of the week tricolour flags flew from Notre Dame and the Hôtel de Ville, and Talleyrand was preparing to leave the Rue St Florentin to serve a new and bourgeois king. Revolution had returned to Paris.[22]

5 Contest for Leadership, 1830–41

News of the July Revolution reached Metternich speedily. Thanks to the efficiency of the courier service established by the Rothschild brothers, he learned of the fall of the Bourbons on the evening of 4 August, less than sixty hours after Charles X's abdication. He was shocked and alarmed; his doctor maintains that he collapsed at his desk moaning, 'My whole life's work is destroyed'. It seemed to him that, in manipulating the electoral system and muzzling the Press, Polignac and his master had brought the mob once more to the barricades. The chief beneficiary of Polignac's folly was, indeed, not a Jacobin but the wealthiest grand seigneur in France, Louis-Philippe Duke of Orleans, and he was a familiar enough figure in political life, someone with whom the Austrian Chancellor had dined, as a matter of course, during his last visit to Paris. It was, however, hard to believe that the 'King of the French' had come to stay. Metternich's old bogey of a European revolution manipulated by a Parisian directing committee seemed more of a reality in the autumn of 1830 than at any moment since the Chancellor first conjured it up a dozen years before. 'When Paris sneezes, Europe catches cold', he observed with lugubrious fatalism.

On 6 August he met Nesselrode again at Carlsbad. The Chancellor reminded his Russian colleague of the treaty obligations which bound the governments of the Chaumont allies to consult each other if Paris succumbed to revolution, and he suggested calling a conference to review the situation. But Nesselrode wanted a practical statement, a guideline intended as much for the Tsar in St Petersburg as for other chancelleries. Metternich jotted down on a piece of rough paper – the *chiffon de Carlsbad* – a joint declaration of policy common to the 'three Northern courts' (Austria, Russia, Prussia): no intervention in Paris provided the new French government did not seek to extend its authority beyond the frontiers of the kingdom or encourage revolution abroad. The Austrians and the Prussians thereupon followed Wellington's example and recognised Louis-Philippe's government, but Tsar Nicholas was unaccommodating. Although he had met and personally liked the new ruler of France, he condemned the Orleanist usurpation as an affront to the dynastic principle, and he was angry with Nesselrode for concluding the *chiffon* without instructions from St Petersburg. Russian recognition of the King of the French was accorded only grudgingly in January 1831. The Tsar never hid his disapproval of Louis-Philippe and his ministers, an antipathy which ruled out all prospect of Franco-Russian collaboration.[1]

Europe needed more than a Carlsbad *chiffon* to check the revolutionary virus that year. The generation which had reached political maturity in the aftermath of the Napoleonic Wars found the downfall of the Bourbons a stimulus to liberal and national revolt. In Brussels the Belgians sought administrative separation within the Great Netherlands kingdom and there were disturbances as early as 25 August. It was the response of their Dutch masters that turned a rebellion against an alien Protestant system of government into Belgium's patriotic war of secession. There was trouble too in the German Confederation where the people of Hanover, Brunswick, Hesse-Cassel and Saxony demanded – and eventually obtained – constitutional government. In northern Spain the veteran liberal general, Francisco y Mina, endeavoured to stir up civil war with French backing; and early in February 1831 Metternich's hold on the Italian peninsula was shaken by revolts in Parma, Modena and the Papal States, which he believed were inspired by French constitutionalists. At the same time Metternich's old rival, President Capodistria, was complaining that his attempts to obtain stable government and secure frontiers for Greece were threatened by conspiracies originating in Paris; and when Capodistria was assassinated outside St Spyridon's Church in Nauplion on 9 October 1831 one of his murderers did indeed vainly seek asylum in the home of the French resident-general. Yet the most dramatic challenge of all to the Vienna Settlement came in Congress Poland. There, on 29 November 1830 the Fourth Infantry Regiment of the Polish army mutinied in Warsaw. Within two months an army revolt had become a national uprising against the Russian puppet kingdom of Poland. The Tsar King was formally deposed on 25 January 1831 and a provisional government set up with another of Tsar Alexander's former foreign ministers, Adam Czartoryski, as President of the Polish National Council.[2] Czartoryski failed to obtain foreign recognition and although the Poles resisted the Russians for nine months, a new repressive administration was established under a military viceroy in 1832. But the valiant Polish exiles won wide sympathy in France, Britain, Switzerland and the United States. The Warsaw uprising put the Polish Question firmly back on the agenda of Europe, where it was to remain unresolved for another ninety years.

Even Great Britain seemed to Metternich infected with the germs of French constitutionalism in 1830. On 15 November the Duke of Wellington, finding himself rejected by a Parliament which sought electoral reform, resigned as Prime Minister. King William IV sent for Earl Grey, who formed a coalition of Whigs, Canningites and Radicals, thus giving the British their first non-Tory government in twenty-three years. Grey entrusted the Foreign Office to Viscount Palmerston, an Irish peer who reckoned himself a Canningite. Although his Cabinet experience was limited to thirteen months of office, he had sat in the Commons since 1807 and served as Secretary-at-War under five Prime Ministers between 1809 and 1828. At times, to the dismay of his clerks, Palmerston conducted Foreign Office business with a military crack of the whip. 'I think that an Office ought to be like a Regiment', he once minuted on an administrative note to the Chief Clerk. But, unlike other long-serving members of the War Office, he had come to know his Europe. Much of his boyhood was spent abroad; he had visited Paris after Waterloo and on several later occasions, meeting leading political figures there; and, as a follower of Canning, he had tried to master the details of European politics. The famous obituary in the *Daily Telegraph* which described

Palmerston as 'the most English minister that ever governed England' (19 October 1865) gives a misleading impression; there were not many John Bulls who could speak French, Italian and Spanish fluently and no other English statesman of modern times who took the trouble to learn Portuguese. As the Austrian diplomat Wessenberg wrote to Metternich eight weeks after the formation of Grey's government, Palmerston set out to make himself 'in a year's time . . . the best informed minister in Europe'.[3]

He had indeed no alternative if he was to make any success of his tenure of the Foreign Office. By 1830 each of the European Great Powers was perfecting its diplomatic machine so as to deal with problems caused by the projection of old rivalries into new areas of dispute. Diplomacy was becoming more and more complex, and the sheer volume of business transacted in a Foreign Ministry was mounting rapidly as improved communications began to speed exchanges between the major European capitals. The effects of the revolutionary movement of 1830 and the concurrent crisis in the Eastern Question increased the political dispatches handled in the Foreign Office by a third during Palmerston's first two years as Foreign Secretary; and in June 1840 Palmerston himself told the ambassador in Paris that dispatches had doubled in number since he took office and trebled since the Congress of Vienna.[4] Yet, as he remarked in a Commons attack on his successor, he read every document that passed through the department so long as he was responsible for foreign affairs. He bullied his two under-secretaries and his clerks relentlessly, insisting on the rapid and orderly circulation of papers, on prompt answers to queries and on clear penmanship; but every important dispatch was written by himself, and he never sought or received expert advice from his permanent officials.

Other governments faced similar problems but were, at least on paper, more highly organised than the ramshackle establishment in Downing Street. In May 1832 Palmerston's friend and future brother-in-law, Sir Frederick Lamb, wrote to him from the Vienna embassy of his wonder at the assistance which Metternich received from the 'able men' in his Chancellery. 'I wish you could reside here for a week to see the admirable and finished machine which this Foreign Office has been brought to be', wrote Lamb. 'Our country is too poor to afford such a one.'[5] Habsburg foreign policy had been conducted for nearly seventy years from the same baroque palace, number 2 Ballhausplatz, and the long tenure of Metternich gave continuity to a system which had expanded naturally with the changing pattern of work. By 1830 the heads of the ten departments of the Chancellery were old and experienced colleagues. Friedrich von Gentz, who though born in Breslau had been in Austrian service since July 1802, continued to provide Metternich with valuable memoranda until the eve of his death in June 1832. Joseph von Hudelist, who had managed the ministry in Metternich's absence at the end of the Napoleonic Wars, died in December 1818, but he had trained the administrative section of the ministry to function smoothly and efficiently, and it was his organisation that Lamb so admired fourteen years later. Baron Johann von Wessenberg, a former ambassador in Berlin and London who was just six months younger than Metternich, was used year after year as a troubleshooter until the Chancellor's carping criticisms of his alleged liberal sympathies forced him into premature retirement in 1832. Ludwig von Lebzeltern, who had been a special envoy to the Tsar in 1813 and assisted Metternich at Aix, Troppau and Verona, returned from St Petersburg to the Ball-hausplatz in 1826 to help the Chancellor as an under-secretary, but served as resident minister in troubled Naples from 1830 to 1843. Had Lamb inspected closely the machine which so impressed him, he might have found some of the cogs a little rusty, for the defect of Metternich's staff was that, like their Chancellor, they tended to look upon the years of Napoleonic upheaval as the climax of their public careers. Only in 1840, when Karl von Ficquelmont became chief of the War Section in the ministry, did a younger generation begin to influence the Chancellor's decisions. Even so, the ethos of the Ballhausplatz changed little; diplomats trained by Metternich echoed his words and allowed their minds to convolve with his process of thought.

In the eighteenth century the French Foreign Ministry, rather than the Austrian Chancellery, had aroused envy in diplomats from other lands; it appeared efficient, and the number of its specialised departments suggested an awe-inspiring accumulation of detailed knowledge. The Revolution brought momentary chaos, partly through the ravages of the guillotine but also because the principal branches of the ministry had to follow the court from Versailles to a succession of improvised offices in Paris. Orderly reforms were initiated by Talleyrand in April 1800 and completed six years later by one of his closest associates, Count Alexander d'Hauterive, a lapsed member of a monastic teaching order who continued to instruct young diplomats in their craft until his death in July 1830. Yet, despite a continuity in style, the Foreign Ministry in Paris suffered from two disadvantages compared with Metternich's Chancellery: it had no established home or repository of archives, for the imposing building proposed for the Left Bank of the Seine by Napoleon I in 1806 had to wait for completion until the reign of Napoleon III; and – a more serious problem – there was no politician between Talleyrand and Guizot who enjoyed a lengthy period of office at the Foreign Ministry. During the thirty-nine years when Metternich was in charge of the Imperial Chancellery in Vienna, there were three Foreign Ministers in St Petersburg, eight in both Berlin and London, but no less than twenty-one in Paris, seven of whom were in office on two or more occasions. Of these twenty-one Frenchmen, Guizot served as minister for over seven years (October 1840 to February 1848) while no other incumbent held the post for more than forty-five months. The effect of such rapid changes of minister was to increase the responsibility of the senior permanent officials for both the formulation and the detailed execution of policy. The most influential of these civil servants was Émile Desages, who was appointed director of the Political Department in the ministry in 1830 and who became a year later a Councillor of State, at the age of 38. Desages, whose father had also been a high official and a colleague of Hauterive, gained his earliest experience of diplomacy in Warsaw in 1811–12 and he was First Secretary at the embassy in Constantinople from 1824 to 1829.

Knowledge of Polish and Turkish affairs was an asset during the crisis years from 1830 to 1841 and Desages was treated with great respect by a succession of ministers. Experience made him suspicious of all Englishmen, though of none so much as Palmerston, and during the Guizot era his realistic assessment of British intentions soberly countered his minister's historicist Anglophilism. Desages remains an undervalued character in the tragi-comedy of the first entente cordiale.[6]

As director of the Political Department Desages could take advantage of the speediest communications in pre-railway Europe. The French had first used the semaphore telegraph system of Claude Chappe as early as August 1793 and it had assisted Napoleon in his final campaigns. Under Louis XVIII the chain of semaphore towers was extended to Calais, Toulon and Bayonne, largely for military purposes. But in 1829 it began to be used to convey general foreign intelligence: a courier brought news of the election of Cardinal Castiglione as Pope Pius VIII in four days from Rome to Toulon and it was then telegraphed by semaphore to Paris in four hours. Louis-Philippe authorised a rapid extension of the semaphore telegraph while, at the same time, encouraging night and day stage coaches and reducing the time of the courier express diligences between Lyons and Paris from ninety-six hours to seventy-five hours. Railway construction in the years from 1839 to 1848 completely revolutionised the courier service within France and it was soon followed by the almost instantaneous electric telegraph, but even by the autumn of 1831 the speed of communications had improved so rapidly that news of Capodistria's murder in the Peloponnese reached Paris in twelve days, compared with the seventeen taken for the first reports of Navarino to come through, four years previously. The military advantages of this faster news service impressed both the Russians and the Prussians. Tsar Nicholas had not learned of the Warsaw mutiny on 29 November 1830 until 7 December, and one of the immediate consequences of the abortive Polish revolt was the construction of a chain of 226 semaphore towers, from St Petersburg through Pskov and Vilna to Warsaw. The chief tower still stands on the Nevsky Prospekt in Leningrad, although without its wooden signalling arms. This major enterprise was not completed until 1838. Five years earlier the Prussians were able to link Berlin with the Rhineland. Soon afterwards the semaphore system was extended eastwards so that by the end of the decade the Foreign Ministry in Berlin could, by using both signals and couriers, obtain answers from St Petersburg within fifty hours. The Berlin telegraph headquarters was in the Dorotheenstrasse, close to the War Ministry and the Foreign Ministry; Berliners maintained that the semaphore arms above the building were a political barometer, motionless in times of peace but waving when the news was bad.[7]

Throughout most of the half-century which followed Waterloo the Berlin Foreign Ministry was a Cinderella in the Prussian bureaucracy, petted now and again by the king but kept firmly subordinate by the officer corps and the General Staff. It was only in 1819 that Frederick William III purchased the former Russian embassy at number 76 Wilhelmstrasse as an official residence for the Foreign Minister and the home of his newly organised Political Department. A few months previously the king had invited Count Christian Bernstorff, the Danish ambassador, to resign and enter Prussian service, with responsibility for foreign affairs under the ageing Chancellor, Prince Hardenberg; and Bernstorff was offered number 76, 'the most beautiful house in Berlin', to compensate for the loss of his home in Copenhagen. Bernstorff, a tidy-minded administrator, was content to follow Metternich dutifully in Great Power politics while helping to build up a Prussian-dominated customs union (Zollverein) in northern Germany. He fought a long rearguard action against the army chiefs, notably Frederick the Great's surviving nephew, Prince Augustus, who in 1824 wanted officers attached to every important Prussian embassy or legation. Bernstorff maintained that military appointments of this kind would sow mistrust; he wondered if the king appreciated the importance of not harming 'in even the slightest way the confidence and integrity which up until now have happily preserved the ties of alliance and friendship' between Prussia and her partners. But Bernstorff was forced to give way after the July Revolution in France when the first peacetime military attaché, a General Staff captain, was posted to the Paris legation with the official title of 'military expert' *(Militärsachverstandiger)* and a watching brief on the preparedness of the French army for a campaign in Europe. Bernstorff was succeeded in 1832 by a dull Berliner who despised the Prussian squirearchy, Friedrich von Ancillon. He it was who turned down the application of the 20-year-old Otto von Bismarck to serve Prussia abroad because, on interview, the young man seemed to the minister to have 'no vocation for European diplomacy'. Metternich had already decided that Ancillon possessed 'an eminently unsound intelligence', and nothing in the minister's five years of office caused him to revise his judgement.[8]

The year 1829 saw the completion in St Petersburg of the main section of the General Staff Building, with its great 600-yard crescent façade facing the Winter Palace. In one wing of the vast building Nicholas I accommodated his Foreign Ministry and in another the Ministry of Finance, an arrangement which survived until the fall of the dynasty in 1917. There was something symbolic in such a juxtaposition, for under Nicholas I all other departments of government were subordinated to the needs of the army. Nicholas, having been too young to participate in the campaigns of his brother, took pride in emphasising his own professionalism as a soldier. It was said that he conducted much of his diplomatic business on horseback during military parades or manoeuvres and that it was essential for any ambassador accredited to the Tsar to be a good horseman. Nesselrode, always more of a secretary than a director of policy, remained as incumbent of the Foreign Ministry throughout the reign of Nicholas and the six senior officials who dealt with Western European affairs were all of German origin, but for the most part the foreign service was purged of the non-Russians to whom Alexander had extended his patronage. Like his father-in-law, Frederick William III of Prussia, Nicholas preferred the company of soldiers, even though he gave more consistent support to Nesselrode than his brother had done. The Tsar sought, by elevating the importance of his Private Chancery, to create a nucleus of executants at court, independent of his ministers; and his trusted friend General Alexander Benckendorff (Princess Dorothea Lieven's brother) was said to possess more power than Nesselrode or any of his colleagues. The general – an absent-minded philanderer with a roving eye for actresses – was primarily concerned with relieving the Tsar's constant fear of revolution and his influence on foreign policy was therefore tangential. When Benckendorff died in 1844 he was succeeded as security chief (head of the Third Section of the Chancery) by one of the Tsar's favourite generals, Prince Alexei Orlov, who was both an astute social charmer and a ruthless disciplinarian. Orlov was sent as the Tsar's personal envoy on missions abroad from 1830 onwards, occasionally conducting a form of dynastic diplomacy at variance with Nesselrode's immediate policy. He was unquestionably the most skilful Russian-born diplomat in the first half of the nineteenth century.[9]

'I have learned more in the ten weeks that I have spent with you than in the thirty years I spent as an observer of or a participant in the affairs of the world', Orlov told Metternich when he left Vienna in October 1830 at the end of his first special mission. The Austrian Chancellor was delighted by such flattery. He saw it as further recognition of his eminence. But Orlov's remarks may well have misled him, for the Russian was not inclined to remain a dutiful pupil of a master craftsman. What Orlov learned above all in Vienna that autumn was the limitation imposed on Austrian policy by resources which were overstretched in policing Italy and Germany while also seeking to give cohesion to the multinational Habsburg monarchy itself. Metternich was as eager as the Tsar to maintain the *status quo*. There was, however, a difference in method: Nicholas was prepared to use his army to prop up the old order, even in Belgium if he could have found a way to get his troops to the Netherlands; but Metternich knew Austria could not afford a prolonged campaign of repression, let alone a full-scale preventive war; and the Archduke Charles, the most respected of Habsburg field commanders, warned him not to count on the efficiency of the Austrian military machine. Metternich might speak fiercely and portentously; but to solve Europe's problems he looked no farther than the conference table.[10]

Nor, indeed, did Palmerston. He had inherited from Wellington and Aberdeen two conferences, both meeting in London; and within a few days of taking office he was presiding over the long-protracted discussions over Greece and also seeking a speedy solution of the Belgian problem. Palmerston found the new French ambassador, the vastly experienced Talleyrand, readily co-operative over Greece: both Britain and France favoured the establishment of an independent Greek kingdom south of a frontier from the Gulf of Arta to the Gulf of Volo, but the Russians insisted that the Sultan's consent should be obtained by amicable negotiation, a procedure which allowed the Turks to procrastinate – the characteristic resort of Turkish diplomacy throughout the century. Not until the summer of 1832 were the frontiers and dynastic character of Greece finally determined: the Arta–Volo line; and the reign of Prince Otto, second son of the philhellene king of Bavaria, Ludwig I. The Belgian problem should have been settled within three or four months.

Talleyrand and Palmerston collaborated at first, and by the end of December 1830 the British, French, Austrian, Prussian and Russian representatives had agreed that Belgium should form an independent state and that none of the Great Powers would claim Belgian territory. To have persuaded the three Eastern autocracies to accept such drastic revision of the Vienna Treaty was a remarkable achievement on Palmerston's part.[11] It may well have owed less to his skill as a chairman than to Metternich's conviction that Britain and France would inevitably fall out sooner or later over so sensitive an area as Belgium and his belief that the conservative Powers stood to gain from such a quarrel. But Palmerston scored a further success in February 1831; on urgent prompting from his ambassador in London, Louis-Philippe declined the Belgian Congress's offer of the throne to his second son. It was King William I of the Netherlands who, resenting the oracular rulings of the London Conference, postponed a settlement by refusing to recognise the election of Leopold of Saxe-Coburg as King of the Belgians in June 1831. A Dutch invasion of Belgium in August was answered by the Conference with intervention from a French army and a British naval squadron. There were moments in the following eighteen months when Vienna and St Petersburg thought war imminent between the British and the French, who were reluctant to retire behind their own frontier once the Dutch had evacuated Belgian soil. But Palmerston convinced Talleyrand that he was not prepared to compromise over a region of such strategic importance to Britain, and Talleyrand for his part persuaded the French Foreign Ministry that Palmerston was in earnest. Even Louis-Philippe's hope that France might receive Luxemburg, a Grand Duchy of little apparent concern to the British, was firmly squashed by Palmerston who feared armed intervention from Prussia. The Belgian crisis was virtually over by the spring of 1833 when King William accepted the Conference's decisions in principle, but it was not until April 1839 that the Belgians received the formal guarantee of the Treaty of London: Britain, France, Prussia, Austria and Russia acknowledged Belgium as 'an independent and perpetually neutral state'; and the German-speaking core of Luxemburg remained under Dutch sovereignty.[12]

Metternich, who had spent some of his youth at Brussels, resented Palmerston's success in championing Belgium's independence. He cared little whether Catholic Belgium was or was not subject to Protestant Holland; but he was disturbed by the apparent ease with which Palmerston was making London the centre of an alternative diplomatic system. He attempted in vain to have the last stage of the conference on Belgium moved to Aix-la-Chapelle (Aachen) in the closing weeks of the year 1832, but he was supported only by the Prussians. Nicholas, who sent Orlov on a diplomatic reconnaissance of Western Europe in the winter of 1831–2, had soon lost patience with William of the Netherlands. Palmerston kept up a constant stream of protests to Vienna over Austrian repression within the German Confederation and other matters which seemed to Metternich beyond the range of British concern; and the French were almost at war with the Austrians in central Italy, where there had been a series of revolts in the Papal States. A French naval squadron took over the city and port of Ancona in January 1832 as a protest at the occupation of Bologna by Austrian troops and neither city was restored to papal sovereignty until 1838. Metternich might scoff at the French initiative as 'a mere bagatelle', but it was nevertheless a dramatic re-assertion of France's traditional interest in the Italian peninsula, and it effectively ruled out Austro–French collaboration elsewhere in Europe. Metternich exploited the Ancona incident to stir up British suspicion of the French navy, but Palmerston did not worry too much about a French squadron flanking Austria's vital Adriatic seaway.[13]

By the spring of 1832 Palmerston, though in private mistrustful of the French, was prepared to commend the 'cordial understanding' between the two liberal Powers to the House of Commons as a means of main-taining the peace of Europe. For the next two years the entente cordiale remained an effective force in Western Europe, although as Desages was quick to point out in Paris the British assumed the French would follow their lead and there was never any pretence of equal partnership in London.[14] In Portugal the French gave diplomatic support to Palmerston's attempt to safeguard liberal constitutionalism by backing the efforts of the young queen, Maria II, to recover the throne seized by the clericalist conservative pretender, Dom Miguel. This ideological conflict was extended to Spain in the autumn of 1833 when, on the death of King Ferdinand VII, the accession of his 3-year-old daughter Isabella II was challenged as unconstitutional by her uncle, Don Carlos. The Spanish Regent, the Queen Mother Maria Cristina, appealed to Palmerston for help and both Don Carlos and Dom Miguel were ousted by joint naval and military operations in the spring of 1834. The Miguelite cause col-lapsed, but the Carlist rebellion in Spain continued until 1839. The French were disinclined to remain in tutelage to Palmerston over Spanish affairs, even if they conceded Britain's prior historic right of interest in the fate of Portugal. There was mounting friction within the entente, with the French backing the party of Spanish grandees *(Moderados)* while the British tried to gain a favourable commercial treaty from the party of democrats *(Progresista)*. Later still there was a serious divergence over marriage plans for Queen Isabella. Ultimately it was not Belgium, as Metternich had anticipated, but Spain (and Syria) that destroyed what Palmerston called 'the new confederacy of liberal and improving Powers'.

Palmerston and Metternich both exaggerated this division of Europe into ideological camps, an oversimplification which some later writers have taken at face value. Neither statesman was sure of his partners – even Prussian foreign policy under Ancillon occasionally irritated the Austrian Chancellor by a splutter of independence. There was a closer affinity between the main protagonists than either would admit to himself. Both wanted peace in Europe, political stability and the orderly conduct of international relations, ideally through conferences over which they themselves presided. Their rivalry was a contest for leadership rather than a conflict of principles. The greatest difference between them as prac-titioners of statecraft lay in their range of vision. Metternich's world was one essentially familiar to him; it was watered by the Rhine, the Seine and the upper Danube. Palmerston had been a Junior Lord of the Admiralty in

1807 when the post-Trafalgar navy was gobbling up distant islands as spoils of victory, and he was accustomed to the images of sea power and commerce. Metternich once remarked, 'Asia begins at the Landstrasse', the highway eastwards from Vienna, a route he neglected or ignored. Palmerston, by contrast, behaved as if he thought the Portsmouth Road was a gateway to the Orient, and was glad of it. Metternich always deplored the posing of the Eastern Question; there was nothing in it to gain for Austria, only a fear that partition of one multinational empire would be followed by the disintegration of another. Palmerston may not have welcomed the problems of the Eastern Question, but he was determined to benefit from them to bolster Britain's political and commercial interests at Constantinople and throughout the Levant. Eventually Turkey was to give him the most striking diplomatic triumph of his career.

Yet, curiously enough, his first encounter with the Eastern Question ended in rebuff.[15] In the summer of 1832 Mehemet Ali of Egypt, resenting Sultan Mahmud II's inadequate rewards for Egyptian services against the Greeks, encouraged his son Ibrahim to seize the fortress of Acre as a preliminary to securing control of Syria and Lebanon. When the Turks belatedly sent an army against Ibrahim, it was routed at Konya (27 December 1832) and within five weeks the Egyptians had advanced into Anatolia and captured Kutayha, a mere 150 miles from the Bosphorus. There seemed nothing to prevent Ibrahim from marching on Constantinople when the spring came unless Mahmud could win the backing of the Great Powers. Even before Konya a succession of emissaries to London had implored Palmerston to help Britain's 'ancient ally' in the East to meet the Egyptian incursion. Palmerston behaved correctly but indecisively: the Royal Navy was fully committed off the Tagus and the Scheldt, and his Cabinet colleagues were alarmed at the expense which would be incurred if additional vessels were commissioned for the Aegean; and it seemed to the Foreign Secretary that the Great Powers should jointly send a remonstrance to Mehemet Ali, requiring him 'forthwith to retire to Egypt and rest contented with that fertile country'. Both Metternich and Tsar Nicholas had let Palmerston know they would be glad if a British naval squadron entered the Dardanelles, but meanwhile the Russians had independently offered the Sultan both ships and soldiers. At the beginning of February 1833 Mahmud, desperate for aid, asked the Russians for an army of 30,000 men to be sent through the Balkans in order to defend Constantinople. By the end of April the Turkish capital was virtually under Russian occupation while three squadrons of the Tsar's warships were moored in the Bosphorus and off the Golden Horn. Heavy diplomatic pressure from the British and the French induced Mehemet Ali to make peace, the Turks allowing him to add to his dominions Syria, Lebanon and Adana (although all his lands remained tributary states within the Ottoman Empire). But the dramatic outcome of the crisis was the privileged position which Russia was seen to enjoy at Constantinople. And for this change of fortune much blame rested with a dilatory and cheeseparing Cabinet in London.

Tsar Nicholas immediately sought to capitalise his advantage. Orlov was sent to Constantinople with instructions to secure a lasting agreement with the Turks. He behaved with consummate tact, abasing himself in the presence of Sultan Mahmud, distributing thousands of medals to the Turkish soldiery as tokens of the Tsar's respect for their courage in not running away, and arranging for Russian troops and warships to leave as soon as Ibrahim's army had withdrawn from Anatolia. On 8 July 1833 Orlov had his reward signed: the Treaty of Unkiar Skelessi was a pact of mutual assistance valid for eight years, but it contained a secret clause by which the Russians waived the obligation for Turkish aid in repelling an attack provided the Sultan closed the Straits between the Mediterranean and the Black Sea to foreign vessels of war. Orlov was elated, and so was Nicholas. The Tsar believed – until corrected five years later by Nesselrode – that Russia now had a right to move warships through the Bosphorus and Dardanelles, which would remain closed to other navies. While Nesselrode assured the British, French and Austrians that Turkey assumed no fresh commitments under international law, Orlov was telling the Tsar that Unkiar Skelessi perpetuated a Russian protectorate at Constantinople. 'In a year or two at the most we shall be summoned back', Orlov declared, 'but we shall have the great advantage of coming back, thanks to our antecedents, without arousing suspicion and of coming back in such a way as never to leave again, if need be.'[16]

The news of Unkiar Skelessi surprised Metternich, who had thought himself in the Tsar's confidence, and disturbed Palmerston and the Duke of Broglie, the French Foreign Minister. It was suspected the treaty had secret clauses binding Turkey even closer to Russian policy. The British and French were far from reassured by a flurry of diplomatic activity in central Europe that autumn. Emperor Francis and Metternich met Frederick William III at Teplitz in August for the first time in six years and Tsar Nicholas travelled to Bohemia three weeks later and spent ten days at Münchengrätz (Mnichovo Hradiste) as a guest of the Austrians. This informal conference gave Metternich the opportunity not only to meet the Tsar for the first time but to hold long discussions with Nesselrode and Benckendorff on the problems of Turkey, Poland and the German Confederation. The Münchengrätz Convention (18 September 1833) had, like most such treaties, public and secret clauses: Europe was told that Russia and Austria pledged themselves to uphold the existing structure of the Ottoman Empire, but the unpublished articles of the agreement provided for joint action if Turkey appeared close to disintegration. A convention concluded on the following day guaranteed the existing settlement of the Polish lands and promised mutual aid to quell any fresh rebellion. Finally a joint declaration, agreed after consultation with Ancillon and published in Berlin a month later, reaffirmed the willingness of the Russian, Austrian and Prussian governments to help sovereigns who were threatened by internal upheaval. Collectively these three conventions are called the Münchengrätz agreements.[17]

There was nothing in them to alarm the British or the French. Palmerston was, however, inordinately suspicious of any gathering of 'the northern courts' while Broglie – or, more probably, Desages – interpreted the Berlin Declaration as a warning to the French, whom

Metternich considered were stirring up trouble in the Rhineland and in Italy. At the end of the year the octogenarian Talleyrand, still the most stylish ambassador in London, cajoled Broglie into authorising him to seek a defensive alliance between Britain and France as a response to the Münchengrätz agreements. Palmerston was unenthusiastic. 'We do not much fancy treaties which are formed in contemplation of indefinite and indistinctly foreseen cases', he explained; and, to Talleyrand's sorrow, nothing more was heard of the proposal. A few months later, however, Palmerston began to negotiate a formal Quadruple Alliance which would link Britain, France, Spain and Portugal: but he committed the diplomatic solecism of inviting French adherence after concluding his talks with the envoys of Portugal and Spain. 'Old Talley', as blandly precise as ever, had the satisfaction of securing from Palmerston the rightful status for France in an alliance which he seems to have convinced Paris was his creation. Rather oddly, Palmerston, too, boasted of it as 'a capital hit and all my own doing'. Technically this Quadruple Alliance of April 1834 was a pledge to uphold constitutionalism in the Iberian peninsula but, as the Foreign Secretary wrote in a private letter to his brother, 'It will serve as a powerful counterpoise to the Holy Alliance of the east'; and he added characteristically, 'I should like to see Metternich's face when he reads our treaty'.[18]

The Austrian Chancellor did, indeed, affect disgust at finding Palmerston patronising 'revolution incarnate in its most dangerous form'. He was delighted when, a few months later, the Tories formed a new government under Sir Robert Peel with the Duke of Wellington as Foreign Secretary. Yet it was merely an interlude, from November 1834 to April 1835, and the Duke left no mark on the Foreign Office, apart from gaining a reputation for 'short and full and clear' minutes[19] He did not like the polarisation of Europe into 'liberal' and 'autocratic' camps, nor did he trust the French diplomats in Madrid, but he was given no chance to initiate a policy of his own. Melbourne and the Whigs were back in office by the spring, although there was some doubt whether Palmerston would return to the government since he had lost his seat in South Hampshire at the general election in January. Both the Austrian and Prussian ambassadors let the Prime Minister know that they thought it would be possible for their governments to have friendlier relations with a different Foreign Secretary, an approach which annoyed both Melbourne and Metternich, who was appalled at such rash interference by one of his envoys in the affairs of a parliamentary democracy. Palmerston duly became Foreign Secretary again on 26 April, although he had no seat in the Commons until returned unopposed at a by-election in Tiverton two months later.

During his second tenure of the Foreign Office Palmerston seemed at first more responsive to shifts in public opinion; its vagaries had, after all, cost him a parliamentary seat and more than half the annual salary of the secretary of state in electoral expenses. Russophobia was rife, at court (where William IV, entertaining Pozzo di Borgo to dinner at Windsor, could not bring himself to toast the Tsar's health), in the Commons (where there was a radical lobby sympathetic to the Poles) and among journalists and pamphleteers.[20] Palmerston had already clashed personally with Tsar Nicholas I, who in 1833 refused to accept Stratford Canning as ambassador at St Petersburg. A long dispute culminated in the recall of the Lievens after more than twenty years at the London embassy, a humiliating loss of status for Princess Dorothea, who blamed Palmerston for the whole episode and never forgave him. Her lamentations helped create a legend that Palmerston had expelled the Lievens and, on his return to the Foreign Office in 1835, he was slightly surprised to find himself lauded by the Radicals for having got rid of the arch-intriguer. For two years Palmerston remained the darling of the Radicals, who approved of his general policy of bolstering Turkey so that the Sultan could resist pressure either from the Tsar or from Mehemet Ali. But Palmerston's vision of international politics went farther afield. It was only with reluctance that he accepted Melbourne's advice not to give support to the Circassians in their long guerrilla campaign against Russian settlement of the Caucasus; but the Cabinet accepted his pleas for action to safeguard the northern frontiers of India. 'Afghanistan must be ours or Russia's', Palmerston said; and an Anglo-Indian army made ready to march for the first time on Kandahar and Kabul. A British presence in Afghanistan, he reasoned, would undermine the ascendancy of the Tsar's agents in neighbouring Persia and thereby strengthen the position of the Sultan in Constantinople and 'place the Dardanelles more securely out of the grasp of Russia'.[21] There were moments when it seemed as if Palmerston's world picture compressed the vastness of Asia into the orderly shires of the English Midlands, but unerringly his eye focused on the Straits as the central problem. In January 1834 he gave the British ambassador, Lord Ponsonby, authority to summon the Royal Navy to the Straits if he thought its presence would deter the Russians from seizing Constantinople and the British regularly used sea power as an instrument of policy in the eastern Mediterranean for the following twenty years. Palmerston was as anxious over the growing strength of the Russian Black Sea fleet as he was over Russian infiltration into Afghanistan, but he wanted if possible to avoid a further crisis in the Near East.

Midsummer in 1839 brought new panic to Constantinople. A Turkish incursion into Syria led to disaster in the battle of Nezib, where the Turkish commander foolishly ignored advice from Prussia's military observer, a Captain Helmuth von Moltke. Within a few days and before the tidings of defeat were made public in Constantinople, Sultan Mahmud drank himself to death and the Turkish fleet sailed for Alexandria, preferring service under Mehemet Ali to the possibility of a Russian commander-in-chief. To lose army, Sultan and fleet so carelessly gave a novel twist even to Turkey's history. Yet despite this colourful scenario, Europe's Chancelleries remained calm and acted responsibly. Nesselrode urged the Tsar not to intervene with soldiers and warships, if only because the state of Russia's finances ruled out expensive unilateral action. Already Palmerston had instructed Ponsonby to let the Grand Vizier know the Turks could not count on any assistance in a campaign started by themselves. The way was clear for Metternich to take the initiative and show that the diplomatic system which he had tried to preserve over so many years could assume collective responsibility and stamp out the embers of war.[22]

Metternich proposed that a conference should gather in Vienna to discuss the Eastern Question in general and the current crisis in particular. Approval came speedily from France and Prussia and grudgingly from Palmerston. The Chancellor believed he could count on his Russian ally and drafted a note which was presented by the ambassadors of the five Great Powers to the Sublime Porte (the Turkish government) on 27 July. Though not the most precise of documents, the note showed, clearly enough, that the Powers would arbitrate in the Turco-Egyptian War. Back in Vienna, Metternich prepared for a conference over which he had every intention of presiding. His wife complained that he was at his desk working for fifteen hours without a break. Even Palmerston wrote to Lamb that if Metternich pulled off a settlement of the Eastern Question he would have done more for European peace than any man since Waterloo. 'And why should not Austria have the merit of settling it?' he added magnanimously.[23]

Yet Metternich consistently overrated his influence with the Tsar. Soon after meeting the Chancellor at Münchengrätz, Nicholas had told his wife, 'Every time I come near to him, I pray God to preserve me from the Devil'. The Tsar was even more suspicious of diplomatic finesse than Alexander had been. Closer acquaintance mellowed his judgement, but he remained convinced that Metternich was seeking to ensnare Russian policy. On 7 August Ficquelmont – then Austrian ambassador at St Petersburg – arrived in the Ballhausplatz and informed Metternich that the Tsar would not accept Vienna as a centre for discussion of the Eastern Question; he was, moreover, indignant with the Austrians for associating the Münchengrätz allies with Britain and France before hearing the views of Russia. For three days the Chancellor tried to save his conference in talks with the Tsar's envoys in Vienna, but they were now uneasily conscious of their lack of authority to act independently, and the pressure of events ruled out constant reference back to St Petersburg. A telegraph wire or speedy railway expresses might have enabled Metternich to win over the Russians, but the electric telegraph was still an experimental novelty in St Petersburg and work had only begun that year on a railway to link Vienna with Warsaw. As it was, the strain proved too much for Metternich. His nervous system gave way. By 14 August he was so ill that Ficquelmont had to take over the conduct of foreign affairs, a responsibility he continued to exercise until the end of October while the Chancellor recovered his strength, resting on his estate in the Rhineland. These ten black weeks in the autumn of 1839 marked the beginning of the end for Metternich's primacy on the continent.[24]

Yet, bitter though it may have been, he had the satisfaction of having halted the fighting in the Levant even if he could not resolve the political crisis. By the collective note of 27 July both the Turks and the Egyptians could see that 'Europe' assumed a right to impose a settlement. The difficulty was that by now the French, who had provided Mehemet Ali with military instructors for over twenty years, were falling out of step with the other Great Powers. Mehemet Ali was effective ruler of Egypt, Palestine, Syria, the Sudan and all the Arabian peninsula. Although he was 70, his heir was his son, the redoubtable Ibrahim (who, in fact, died in 1848, nine months before his father); and the French maintained that the Levant would prosper more securely under the dynasty of Mehemet Ali than under other viceroys appointed by the new and young Sultan, Abdul Mejid. Both the British and the Russians suspected that the French wished to convert Mehemet Ali's dominions into a commercial satrapy, exploited by the banking families who flourished under Louis-Philippe's bourgeois monarchy. Palmerston was hostile to Mehemet Ali on two counts, strategic and economic: his authority threatened the shortest route to India; and his monopoly of trading concessions over such a vast area of the Levant deprived the British of advantages accruing from an Anglo-Turkish commercial treaty, concluded in August 1838. All in all, Mehemet Ali appeared a more tiresome adversary than the Russians.[25]

At this point, in mid-September 1839, the Tsar sent to London one of Nesselrode's key advisers. Baron Philip Brunnow was authorised to propose an Anglo-Russian agreement, providing for joint pressure on Mehemet Ali and Ibrahim in return for international recognition of the principle that the Straits should be closed to foreign warships in time of peace.[26] Palmerston liked these proposals, which implied non-renewal of the Unkiar Skelessi treaty; but he could not carry the Cabinet with him. In December Brunnow returned to London on a second mission; the Tsar was willing for an arrangement by which, if the Sultan asked for aid, the Royal Navy might enter the Dardanelles and the Black Sea fleet enter the Bosphorus. Palmerston still faced difficulties with his colleagues, some of whom feared an Anglo-Russian accord would lead to an irreparable breach with the French. But French policy was in itself devious, especially after Adolphe Thiers became Prime Minister in March 1840. There were rumours that France was seeking an independent settlement of the Turco-Egyptian crisis; and the French Press became stridently Egyptophile, rejoicing in the happy coincidence that the birth of Mehemet Ali at Kavalla fell under the same zodiacal sign of the same year as the birth of Bonaparte at Ajaccio.

On 15 July 1840 Palmerston had his way, and yet another Treaty of London was signed. Austria, Britain, Prussia and Russia undertook to observe the peacetime closure of the Straits to foreign warships and to compel Mehemet Ali to submit to the Sultan's authority within a prescribed time limit or face action from the Powers and the loss of his dominions. Thiers responded by threatening war in the Mediterranean and a crusade in Europe against the whole Vienna Settlement. Palmerston refused to take the war scare seriously, nor for that matter did Metternich; but some of the Cabinet made public the divisions within the government and the Foreign Secretary's Radical allies of 1835–6 began to denounce him for having 'sold out' to the Russians. The worst aspect of French bellicosity was the encouragement which it gave to Mehemet Ali to defy the Powers. In September and again in October a British naval force bombarded the coast of the Lebanon, with an Austrian squadron in support. There was a fierce battle in the hills to the north of Beirut in which British and Austrian marines supported Turkish infantry and Christian Lebanese rebels against the Egyptians. Ibrahim was forced to retreat, a naval bombardment of

Acre emphasising how exposed were his communications to flank assaults from the sea. Louis-Philippe refused to allow the French naval squadron to intervene. At the end of October he replaced Thiers with Marshal Soult as Prime Minister, while the astute Francois Guizot became Foreign Minister and the real head of the government. A month later Mehemet Ali gave up the struggle: an armistice in Alexandria left him with the promise of hereditary possession of Egypt but destroyed the Arab empire he had sought to build in the East.[27]

Palmerston's triumph was almost complete: London had become the pivot of diplomatic consultation over the fate of Turkey. Yet Metternich continued to put himself forward as a natural disinterested arbiter with suggestions to preserve peace. A congress, perhaps, in Wiesbaden? A permanent ambassadorial conference at Vienna which would tender long distance advice to the young Sultan Abdul Mejid? Such proposals echoed emptily around the chancelleries. Ironically Metternich's sole diplomatic success in the early months of 1841 consummated Palmerston's achievement. For it was the Austrian Chancellor who persuaded Guizot that France could not remain isolated from the European Concert. The Straits Convention, signed in London almost exactly a year after the four-power treaty, reaffirmed the principle of keeping the Dardanelles and Bosphorus closed to warships; and this time the French added their signatures to the agreement.[28] The privileged position which Orlov won for the Tsar had been wrested from his grasp without a major war to free Turkey; and France, too, was once more in tune with the European Concert. The long crisis had shown that the new diplomatic system, with its emphasis on collective responsibility for peace, possessed enough flexibility to stand the strain of rival ambitions, whether personal or national. Yet the real challenge to the international order was still to come. For twenty-five years no Great Power had sought to impose drastic revision on the map of Europe. It remained to be seen whether this sense of restraint sprang from an undefined code of public law or from the selfish fear that policies of military adventure would uncork the jinn of revolution among vanquished and victors alike.

6 Ministers of Peace, 1841–48

Less than two months after signing the Straits Convention, Palmerston was out of office. The change was welcomed in Europe, where the increasing belligerence of British policy caused concern in St Petersburg and Vienna despite the improved relations of those governments with London. Sir Robert Peel succeeded Lord Melbourne and formed a moderate Conservative ministry which brought the Earl of Aberdeen back to the Foreign Office. He was a familiar figure to Europe's statesmen. Metternich, who had dubbed him 'that dear simpleton of diplomacy' in 1813, continued to patronise him abominably. 'A good fellow but his range is extraordinarily limited', he commented in a letter to London; and he had already warned his ambassador against Aberdeen's habit of expressing his thoughts verbally with different intent from the considered opinions which he would give in writing. Nesselrode had always rated Aberdeen more highly, and in Paris Guizot was pleased at the appointment of a Foreign Secretary whom he knew and respected. There was, too, a personal link between Aberdeen and Guizot. When Princess Lieven had left London, Aberdeen assured her, 'Whether in office, or out of office, you may depend on my being a regular and frequent correspondent'. In September 1835, having left her husband, she settled in Paris and by 1841 was identifying herself intimately with the statecraft of Louis-Philippe's chief minister. This remarkable woman, Metternich's mistress at the age of 32, became Guizot's mistress at 51 and shared his political fortunes for the remainder of her life while maintaining her purely platonic friendship with Lord Aberdeen.[1]

Everyone recognised in the virtuous Scottish Earl a man of peace and good intent. He wished to keep on amicable terms with Russia and Austria, improve the strained relations with France and ease the recurrent tension with America over the Maine and Oregon boundaries with Canada. His work was hampered by unresolved conflicts from the Palmerston era, notably in Afghanistan and China, and by the rapid spread of old rivalries to new areas in the Pacific, in North Africa and even in Texas. He suffered from an inability to make a speech in or out of Parliament which was either memorable or inspiring and, like other members of Peel's government, he was overshadowed in Cabinet by the massive authority of Wellington, an elder statesman without departmental responsibilities. Nor were Aberdeen's relations with the lower house always happy. He complained, privately, that the Commons, unlike the Lords, was swayed by gusts of nationalistic pride and did not trouble over the niceties of diplomacy. He even told the Earl of Clarendon – like himself an ex-ambassador – that Peel's handling of foreign affairs in the Commons led the Prime Minister into verbal indiscretions which someone 'in the trade' would have avoided.[2] There was a patrician aloofness in Aberdeen's approach to politics coldly reminiscent of poor Castlereagh.

Yet he possessed one considerable advantage over his immediate predecessor at the Foreign Office: friendship with the royal family. Over the past sixty years British sovereigns had intervened less and less in foreign affairs and in 1837 Palmerston assumed that the accession of 'a totally inexperienced Girl of 18 just out of a Strict Guardianship' would free ministers from any concern with the sovereign's role in shaping policy. He was prepared to explain problems to the young queen patiently and at times light-heartedly; and when in November 1838 she came across such puzzling placenames as Herat, Kabul and Kandahar he arranged for a map of Asia to be sent at once to Windsor Castle. But Palmerston had a clear sense of priorities. 'The less you send the Queen this week . . . the better, as her time will be much occupied by Ascot', he told the permanent under-secretary in June 1838.[3] He saw no reason why Victoria's marriage to her conscientious cousin from Coburg should change the relationship of Crown and Foreign Office. Aberdeen, on the other hand, immediately recognised Prince Albert's deep concern for European politics and took his conversation and long memoranda to heart. The prince, for his part, valued the earl as a tactful, calm and earnest public servant; and Albert's approbation guaranteed for Aberdeen the lasting confidence of the queen. The two men between them ensured that, by 1855, Victoria had a respected voice in the courts of Europe, an influence intensified by family ties and mature experience during her long years of matriarchal widowhood.

The European autocracies, though not displeased to see the voters smile on Peel's conservatism, deplored one consequence of the British electoral system; changes of government from Whig to Tory or from Tory to Whig involved ambassadors, too, in a game of general post. Peel and Aberdeen continued the practice of exercising political patronage within the foreign service. Aberdeen's brother, Sir Robert Gordon, held the embassy at Vienna as had Castlereagh's half-brother some years earlier. Lord Stuart de Rothesay was given St Petersburg in 1841 largely to gratify his former crony, the Duke of Wellington, while the Duke's brother, Lord Cowley, went to Paris, an embassy he had sought for thirty years. Peel soon regretted both appointments, and induced Aberdeen to recall the 'utterly unfit' Stuart de Rothesay in 1843. Cowley, a septuagenarian whose spoken thoughts often lost themselves in benign confusion, remained ambassador until the duke retired from party politics in 1846, even though Queen Victoria was so alarmed by his inadequacies that she had written anxiously to Aberdeen about Cowley as early as October 1843. But probably the most exasperating aspirant for preferment in 1841 was Stratford Canning, who had sat as a Tory backbencher since resigning from the diplomatic service in 1829 and hoped for government office. Peel thought little of his skill in debate, Aberdeen found him a trying colleague; and he was therefore offered the embassy at Constantinople 'on the ground of political disappointment', as Peel explained privately to one of his more powerful party managers.[4] Stratford duly arrived back in the Bosphorus in January 1842 and was accorded a privileged status by Sultan Abdul Mejid; all ambassadors to the Porte were given the courtesy title of 'Elchi Bey'; Stratford was 'the Great Elchi', almost a pro-consul.

Successive governments in London preferred him to pass his middle years of life in splendour at the ambassadorial palace in Pera or the summer embassy by the shore at Therapia than as an authoritative Russophobe among the nuisances of Westminster.

At first Aberdeen was more concerned with the Paris embassy than with Constantinople, Vienna, or St Petersburg. To bring trust and confidence back into Anglo-French relations was a formidable undertaking. Guizot, with his French Protestant sympathy for the English Establishment, might favour an entente, but for many public figures on either side of the Channel there seemed something unnatural in such an association. Aberdeen and Guizot could, however, count on full support from the two royal families. The long personal isolation of the British monarchy from continental affairs came to an end in September 1843 with a five-day visit by Queen Victoria and Prince Albert to King Louis-Philippe and Queen Marie Amélie at the Château d'Eu in Normandy. No crowned sovereign of England had paid a courtesy visit to a French king since the famous meeting of Henry VIII and Francis I at the Field of Cloth of Gold in 1520. Eu, rather than Paris, was chosen partly because it was only 2 miles inland and there was a good anchorage for the new royal yacht at Le Tréport, but also so as to emphasise the private character of the visit. Nevertheless Victoria and Albert were accompanied by the Foreign Secretary and Guizot was in attendance on Louis-Philippe. Dynastic marriages, which had played so decisive a role in the diplomacy of earlier periods, still mattered greatly in the nineteenth century; and in 1843 Queen Isabella II of Spain celebrated her thirteenth birthday and was declared of age by the Cortes. There was mounting speculation over her 'choice' of a husband, and the matter was gravely discussed at the Château d'Eu.

It is from Guizot's letters to Dorothea Lieven that we receive the clearest impression of the royal visit to upper Normandy.[5] He described Victoria's simple delight at all she saw, and he recorded Aberdeen's first words to him – 'I beg you to look upon this visit as clear evidence of our policy, not only over the Spanish question but over all matters.' Aberdeen, for his part, was impressed by 'the very great earnestness' with which Louis-Philippe talked to him of Europe's affairs. Little was, in fact, settled at the Château d'Eu. Guizot, however, convinced himself that he had won British recognition of French diplomatic primacy in Madrid; he was prepared to count the Eu talks as a victory which wiped out the humiliations of France's misadventures in the Mehemet Ali crisis. On 27 December 1843 Louis-Philippe opened the Chamber with a speech which contained the first friendly reference to Great Britain in seven years of royal orations; and Queen Victoria's speech from the throne five weeks later reciprocated. As she told her uncle, Leopold of the Belgians, the speech included a generous reference to France 'for the first time since 1834'. Tsar Nicholas and Metternich began to fear a new ideological division between the Eastern and Western Great Powers of Europe.

There followed, however, two unhappy years in which Anglo-French relations stumbled clumsily through a series of misunderstandings. Admiral Dupetit-Thouars had proclaimed a French protectorate over

Tahiti in 1842 and his action caused lingering resentment in Great Britain, where Polynesia had been treated as a region of Protestant missionary endeavour for several decades. Tension mounted in the summer of 1844 when Dupetit-Thouars arrested George Pritchard, who was both Britain's consul in Tahiti and a respected missionary. Although Pritchard was soon released, the incident fed Francophobia in the London Press and there were hotheaded speeches in Paris as well as in London. Such displays of popular prejudice exasperated Aberdeen. 'It would be deplorable if you and I, two Ministers of Peace, should be condemned to quarrel about a set of naked savages at the other end of the world', he wrote privately to Guizot.[6] Hostility to 'England' was strongest in the French navy and French naval writings were examined critically and suspiciously in London. The Francophobes accordingly received a further fillip when the French navy bombarded Tangier after the Arab nationalist leader Abd-el-Kader carried armed rebellion against colonialism from his native Algeria into Morocco. It was difficult for the 'two Ministers of Peace' to persevere when there was so little genuine cordiality behind the entente.

The royal exchange of visits continued, nevertheless. As soon as the Pritchard affair was settled, Louis-Philippe came to Windsor, where he was created a Knight of the Garter. In September 1845 *Victoria and Albert* again carried her royal and princely eponyms to Le Tréport, with Lord Aberdeen once more in attendance.[7] On this occasion the marriage of Queen Isabella was discussed in greater detail. The dynastic ambitions of the Orleanist monarchy wanted a marriage link with Madrid but Aberdeen was as insistent as earlier British statesmen that there could be no union of the French and Spanish thrones. The Foreign Secretary was convinced that in these second Eu talks Guizot committed France to an arrangement by which Isabella would marry her first cousin, Don Francisco de Asis, and that once a child was born to them her sister, the Infanta Luisa Fernanda, would be able to marry Louis-Philippe's son, the Duke of Montpensier. Even though several Cabinet colleagues deplored his willingness to appease the French, Aberdeen hoped that time would vindicate these efforts at preventive diplomacy. He had, however, not allowed for two imponderables: the changing political moods of Madrid; and the uncertainty which Palmerston's return to the Foreign Office would arouse in Paris. The fabric of the Aberdeen–Guizot entente was mere gossamer.

Tsar Nicholas regarded the Eu and Windsor meetings as evidence of a new diplomatic phenomenon, a display of monarchical solidarity in *Western* Europe. For it was in *central* Europe that the practice of conducting dynastic diplomacy through meetings of sovereigns had been revived, after many centuries: Joseph II of Austria exchanged visits with Frederick II of Prussia and travelled to St Petersburg, Kiev and the Crimea at the invitation of Catherine the Great. This initiative was developed further by both Napoleon I and Alexander I, although still primarily intended as a show of legitimate majesty within central Europe. Tsar Nicholas, like his brother, believed that rulers should be seen to stand together. His first response to the growing friendship of the French and British monarchs was therefore to emphasise the links between the Eastern autocrats. He visited his brother-in-law, Frederick William IV (who had come to the Prussian throne in June 1840), and he then proposed to Metternich that the rulers of Austria, Prussia and Russia should meet in Germany in the summer of 1844 to discuss the possible partition of Turkey should the Sultan's empire finally collapse. Metternich, however, was unco-operative, not least because in Austria, too, there had been a change of sovereign. The Emperor was no longer Francis I but his kindly and feeble-minded son, Ferdinand, who could never pull his weight in any monarchical troika. Nicholas, rebuffed at Vienna, then decided to renew contacts with the British monarchy and turn for diplomatic support to London.[8]

This change of approach was neither so sudden nor so unexpected as it seemed to the contemporary Press in England. Shortly before Christmas in 1839 the Tsar had suggested to the British ambassador that the two Powers might reach a 'clear understanding'. He explained that he did not so much want a formal treaty as 'a gentlemen's agreement' for collaboration between Britain, Russia and her Münchengrätz allies in countering any threat from France. Palmerston rejected the proposal: verbal undertakings, he explained, were only binding to the ministers who made them; and the parliamentary conventions of England precluded the acceptance of obligations 'with reference to cases which have not actually arisen'.[9] The Tsar, however, persisted in his efforts at wooing the British; he realised sooner than Palmerston or Aberdeen that the two peripheral states possessed a capacity for conflict outside Europe which made the problem of their mutual relationship different from the familiar rivalry of the inner continental Great Powers and ultimately more menacing. Baron Brunnow's success on his diplomatic mission to London in 1839 induced the Tsar to appoint him as ambassador. Brunnow remained at the London embassy for thirty-four years, longer than any other ambassador in modern times. He became something of a favourite with Queen Victoria, perhaps because he had accompanied Orlov to Britain to offer Nicholas's congratulations to the young queen on her accession in the summer of 1837. But Brunnow, one of the least flamboyant of diplomats, was always a faithful executant and not inclined to shape policy himself, as Tatischev or Pozzo di Borgo had tried to do. He was useful to Nicholas in offsetting the suspicion of the Tsar's intentions among the British governing classes, but Russia needed an envoy of stronger personality if there was to be concerted action to forestall another crisis in the East. And who better to come to London than Nicholas himself? Had he not been told by successive British ambassadors that their queen would welcome a visit?

The Tsar appears to have decided to journey to England on his own initiative and at the last minute. Brunnow travelled down to Woolwich on 31 May 1844 anticipating the arrival of Prince Orlov in one of the new Dutch steamers running a packet-boat service between the Scheldt and the Thames; he found Orlov accompanied by his imperial master in person. The Tsar was at first accommodated in the Russian embassy, for the queen and Prince Albert were entertaining Frederick Augustus II of Saxony, nephew of the king who was so nearly deprived of his sovereignty by the Russians at the Congress of Vienna. *The Times* records a surprise encounter in The Mall when the Tsar of Russia's carriage and escort met the King of Saxony's carriage and escort travelling in the opposite direction and 'the two rulers recognized each other'. Subsequently they were both accommodated at Windsor Castle, the Queen excitedly describing in a letter to her uncle Leopold how she had entertained 'the dear good King of Saxony' and 'this greatest of all earthly potentates' to breakfast at Adelaide Cottage in Frogmore. Tsar and King accompanied their royal hosts to Ascot on Thursday 6 June, and Nicholas was accorded a 'most brilliant' reception by the racegoers. 'A great event and a great compliment his visit certainly is', Victoria told her uncle. But no surfeit of royal superlatives could hide the fact that Ascot Week was a poor time to talk high politics. Peel and Aberdeen did indeed meet the Tsar, Orlov and Brunnow on the Tuesday and Wednesday of that week at Windsor. They agreed on the need to maintain the Turkish Empire as long as possible and to enter on discussions if the fall of the empire seemed imminent. The Tsar said that he did not want to see any one foreign Power dominant on the straits, not even Russia, and that he did not believe in the possibility of a new Byzantine empire. The British ministers, too, made plain what they did not want in the Levant: a powerful and hostile government in Egypt which might endanger 'the commercial road' from Alexandria to Suez, the shortest route to India and the Orient. Yet, though both governments talked vaguely of their fears for the future, nothing positive was said. As Aberdeen assured Guizot a few days later, 'the Emperor did not propose a plan nor let me see any project which could be applied to the various eventualities which anyone can envisage'. The Tsar and Orlov sailed for home on 9 June after what a later age would have described as 'successful exploratory talks', nothing more and nothing less.[10]

Aberdeen should, however, have realised by the end of the year that the Russians attached greater significance to the Windsor conversations than he did himself. Three months after the Tsar's departure, Nesselrode (who was by now titular State Chancellor as well as Foreign Minister) came to England, ostensibly on a visit to Brighton. On 19 September 1844 he left with Aberdeen a memorandum which embodied the Russian version of the verbal agreement made in June. Nesselrode's summary showed the Russian and British leaders as men of peace who were willing to exercise self-restraint in maintaining the balance of power in the East through concerted diplomatic action by the European states. Aberdeen confirmed formal acceptance of the Nesselrode memorandum as something 'to be kept in view during all our negotiations connected with the Levant' on 21 January 1845. It was, in his eyes, a working agreement binding solely on the Peel government and on the Tsar and his ministers. Had Nicholas recalled Palmerston's objections to his proposal of December 1839 he, too, might have been content to regard these verbal exchanges as a mere step towards some future understanding. Wrongly he believed he had wrung from Aberdeen a lasting British commitment. In this illusion he was sustained by Nesselrode and by Brunnow. It was a misunderstanding that led Russian diplomacy into serious error eight years later.

Tsar Nicholas, as Metternich complained, was unpredictable. More and more he resembled his brother Alexander. There was indeed no searching for spiritual satisfaction as in Alexander's later years, but there was a similar reliance on personal relationships, a similar pride of family and a similar restless desire to speed to distant places, as if the racing wheels of a post-chaise could bring him understanding of Europe. At times Nicholas wished the Romanov and Habsburg dynasties could become as closely linked as the Romanovs and the Hohenzollerns; and for some years he had sought marriage between his daughter Olga and Archduke Stephen, son of the Palatine of Hungary and first cousin of the ruling emperor, Ferdinand. Metternich distrusted the proposal, suspecting Russia of favouring the eventual establishment of an independent Hungary, with Stephen as king, Olga as queen and the full weight of Nicholas's army to sustain them. The abortive marriage project bedevilled Austro-Russian relations in the years 1843–5 at the very moment when Metternich's spy system was reporting that Polish exiles planned a new insurrection. Nicholas left St Petersburg suddenly in October 1845, met Stephen in Prague, travelled the length of Italy and across to Sicily, and returned to Rome, where he became the first reigning Tsar received in audience by a Pope. Eventually on 30 December he arrived in Vienna, with as little warning as at Woolwich eighteen months before. He told Metternich that the Münchengrätz allies needed to strengthen the bonds between them and that it was essential to maintain the Ottoman Empire for the general peace of Europe, a sentiment with which Metternich concurred. The Tsar indicated he was also prepared to see Austria as heir to the Turkish Empire in Europe should the Sultan's government disintegrate. But his three days in the Austrian capital were not a success. Nicholas was angered by the Chancellor's dilatory approach to politics; he found him unaccommodating over the marriage project and unwilling to define spheres of influence in case the Turkish lands came up for partition. The Tsar thought the new generation of Habsburgs spineless, stupidly insistent that Olga should renounce Orthodoxy and embrace Catholicism before marrying the future Palatine. It seemed a personal rebuff: in the following July Olga married her first cousin, Charles of Württemberg, whom she dominated as crown princess and queen for nearly half a century; and no bride was ever found for Stephen. Nicholas nursed his resentment at Metternich's behaviour for several years and the two men did not meet again until 1852. Austria, Nicholas told his wife early in 1846, was 'sick, very sick' – the anthropomorphic metaphor came naturally to the Tsar when his will was thwarted in an empire other than his own.[11]

After Nicholas's stormy visit to Vienna the only common cause still binding the Münchengrätz allies together was the need to suppress Polish nationalism. Social unrest in Galicia, caused for the most part by agrarian distress, led to anarchy around Tarnow and Lemberg in February 1846, with numerous landowners murdered by their peasants. In neighbouring Cracow – constituted a free city by the Treaty of Vienna – Polish patriots seized public buildings and proclaimed an independent republic. Luwik Mieroslawski, an agent sent by the exiled Polish Democratic Society from Paris to co-ordinate a general insurrection in the three regions of partitioned Poland, was arrested by the Prussians soon after he had left

Cracow for Poznania, and the Polish rebellion went off at half-cock. The ten-day Republic of Cracow succumbed to an Austrian army attacking from the south and a Russian army moving in from the north; by the end of the first week in March the Polish lands seemed once more pacified. But Metternich was eager to destroy the revolutionary nest in Cracow, not least because he feared that if the free city was allowed to survive, the Tsar would annex Cracow to the Congress Kingdom of Poland and Russian troops garrison a region of considerable strategic importance to Austria. On 6 November 1846 Cracow was absorbed in the Austrian Empire.[12] As the cynics pointed out, by now even Metternich was tearing up the Treaty of Vienna.

The timing of Austria's annexation of Cracow was determined by events in Western Europe. Aberdeen had recognised the need for Austrian troops to restore order in March 1846 but he made it clear to Metternich that he hoped there would be no change in the city's status. So long as there was a conservative government in London, the Austrian Chancellor took care not to infringe international law by a unilateral breach of the Vienna Treaty. But all was changed in the third quarter of the year. Peel resigned on 29 June 1846; Lord John Russell, who succeeded him as Prime Minister, brought Palmerston back to the Foreign Office. If the news of his return did not exactly please Metternich, it spread despondency in Paris, alarming not only latent Anglophobes like Desages but the complaisant Guizot, too. No other Foreign Minister of France habitually placed such stress on personal understanding as Guizot, and he regarded Aberdeen's departure as a sad blow to France's interests. 'The new and distinctive characteristic common to the attitude of Aberdeen and myself was the abolition of the spirit of national rivalry and personal vanity between us', Guizot explained to Princess Lieven. 'Palmerston will bring it all back again', he added mournfully.[13]

Guizot's letters that summer show two obsessions dominating his mind: the urgency of achieving a diplomatic triumph in Madrid, and the conviction that Palmerston regarded the revived entente cordiale as harmful to Britain's interests. The Spanish marriage problem pushed aside all other considerations in Guizot's policy. He suspected that Palmerston wished to back a Coburg candidate for Queen Isabella's hand and the Duke of Seville for her sister, the Infanta Luisa; and with the first signs that the British were undermining Orleanist family influence in Spain, Guizot abandoned the Eu agreements. On 1 September 1846 he told the British ambassador that Isabella would marry her cousin, Don Francisco, and the Infanta would marry Montpensier in a double ceremony at Madrid. It was, Guizot insisted, a 'family affair'.[14] There followed a month of angry denunciation and diplomatic protests, but Palmerston achieved nothing. The double marriage took place in Madrid on 10 October, with the British ambassador absenting himself from every ceremony. The entente was in shreds; the only beneficiaries from the absurd marriage imbroglio were the Münchengrätz allies. It is significant that in the week preceding the annexation of Cracow, Metternich received rival approaches for support over the Spanish Question from Palmerston and from Guizot. The problem of the new Duchess of Montpensier's right of succession to the Spanish throne plagued Europe's chancelleries for another eighteen months, until the fall of her father-in-law's monarchy in Paris made the whole issue as antiquated as the Treaty of Utrecht.

Palmerston and Guizot made separate protests to the Münchengrätz allies over the suppression of Cracow. Nesselrode wryly observed that the tone of Palmerston's note was restrained, a contrast to his speech at the Lord Mayor's banquet which delighted the Polish exiles. Guizot's indignation, too, was muted, although, given the publicity electorally desirable so long as the French Chamber found time each year for a parliamentary motion deploring the subjection of Poland. As Palmerston explained to the septuagenarian exiled patriot, Adam Czartoryski, Western liberals all sympathised with the Poles but could do nothing to help them.[15] The truth was that Palmerston, despairing of backing from Metternich, still hoped for support from Russia and Prussia against French diplomacy in Spain and in Portugal, where renewed civil war had brought British frigates once more to the Douro and Tagus estuaries. Guizot, for his part, turned in the first instance to Metternich, although he was forced to conceal his approaches to Austria from other members of the French government, who remained as suspicious of Vienna as of London. Oddly enough, Guizot was the only leading French politician whom Metternich had never met, but the Chancellor welcomed Guizot's secret emissary to his home in the Rennweg. He convinced himself that Louis-Philippe's Foreign Minister was dedicated to maintaining the conservative order in the face of revolutionary upheaval. This was, in fact, an oversimplification. Guizot thought of himself not as a conservative pillar of order but as a wise and cautious reformer. He was confident, moreover, that he could lead Metternich rather than follow him as a pupil.

From the autumn of 1846 until his final flight into exile eighteen months later the Austrian Chancellor did not once leave Vienna to seek rest or recuperation on his estates in Bohemia and the Rhineland. He toiled away at his papers for weeks on end, even though he no longer signed every document and could rely on Ficquelmont to assist him with the day-to-day business of the Chancellery. Sometimes he tried to update the tactical forays of his earlier statecraft: thus when exasperated with Palmerston in 1847 he resorted to the ploy used unsuccessfully against Canning in 1824–5 and approached, first, the Duke of Wellington and, then, the court at Windsor in the hope that they together might unseat the Foreign Secretary; but Palmerston was not even jolted in the saddle, for the duke was now in retirement and Prince Albert was certainly not George IV. Metternich's letters to Guizot show the Chancellor's difficulty in coming to terms with the present.[16] He warmly approved of steam power, railways and speedier communications but when he looked at the strategic map of Europe he tended to ignore the intrusion of such innovations; and he would add to his labours by recalling, at great length, the comments which Napoleon had made to him forty years before on the problems of the continent. It was as if he wished to convince himself, rather than the recipient of his letters, that little had changed with the passage of two generations in central Europe or the Italian peninsula.

Yet Italy was by now something more than the 'geographical expression' of Metternich's famous apophthegm. The people of the peninsula were already looking for a liberator who would give them unity and independence when Cardinal Mastai-Ferretti was elected Pope in the summer of 1846, and there were many believers who convinced themselves that Pius IX (as the reforming cardinal was styled) would be the 'liberal Pope' who would invoke God's blessing on the cause of Italy. Disorders in Ferrara, a city in the Papal States with a citadel of strategic importance, led the Austrian commander to institute a military occupation in July 1847, a move undertaken with Metternich's warm approval. But, to the Chancellor's amazement, the Ferrara crisis produced more response from Europe than the annexation of Cracow. The King of Piedmont protested, the Pope protested, Palmerston protested – and British naval vessels ostentatiously showed the flag in the Adriatic and Ligurian seas. Palmerston even sent the Prime Minister's father-in-law, the Earl of Minto, on a special mission to Turin in order to assure King Charles Albert of Piedmont of British support for liberal constitutionalism throughout the peninsula. Minto, a Cabinet minister without departmental responsibilities and a friend of Palmerston for almost half a century, showed no political inhibitions as he travelled from Turin to Florence, Rome and Naples. He happily elicited cheers for 'independent Italy' whenever a curious crowd gathered around the 'English lord' in a six-month tour of revolutionary trouble-spots. With so eminent a public figure showing such indiscretion, it is small wonder that at Christmas Metternich complained to his ambassador in London that 'We see the English Cabinet everywhere allied to the parties which desire revolution'. [17] How different was the behaviour of that good honest bourgeois, François Guizot: no encouragement of the Piedmontese; no naval swashbuckling at Ancona or any other port; and an assurance that if Pius IX's apparent liberalism provoked revolution in the Italian states then Metternich could count on French assistance in restoring order. Only with the coming of the new year in 1848 did Metternich sense a danger that Guizot might extend French patronage to the Italian reform movement so as to outbid Palmerston and Minto. After the Spanish marriages, the rift between Britain and France ran so deep that their Foreign Ministers seemed more intent on upstaging each other than in following a coherent policy for Europe as a whole.

The policies of Palmerston and Guizot also clashed in Switzerland. [18] Twelve of the nineteen Swiss cantons supported the demands of the liberal and radical parties for a stronger central government. They maintained that nineteen separate tariffs and nineteen variations in civil and commercial codes of law hampered the economic growth of the country; they also claimed that, in the predominantly Catholic areas of the Confederation, the Church sought to preserve archaic institutions and social customs. In December 1845 the seven Catholic cantons (mostly around Lake Lucerne) formed a Separatist League *(Sonderbund)* to defend cantonal rights against federal authority and to champion the old order against radicalism. Metternich was afraid that, with 'radicalism in control', the Swiss would export revolution to their neighbours and when, in January

1847, the central government in Berne denounced the *Sonderbund* as illegal the Austrians withdrew their envoy in protest, an action dutifully followed by their Prussian and Russian allies. Guizot, too, distrusted Swiss radicalism and proposed an international conference to consider the Swiss problem. His initiative was warmly backed by Metternich, but Palmerston maintained that the Great Powers could not deliberate on a domestic issue in Swiss politics. While the Powers were still considering the legality of Guizot's proposed conference, Swiss federal troops began a civil war against the *Sonderbund*, claiming that the seven cantons were threatening to secede from the Confederation. It was a brief campaign (4–30 November 1847), fought mainly around the principal city of the *Sonderbund*, Lucerne, and there were no more than 128 casualties on the two sides. But Europe's liberals saw the Swiss Civil War as an issue of 'progressives' versus 'reactionaries' and took heart at this easy victory over 'detested despotism'.

Guizot tried desperately to save something from the wreck of his Swiss policy. In late October he had seemed about to manage the Concert of Europe and he could argue that only Palmerston's obstinate hesitancy denied him such eminence. He even suspected that the British encouraged the Federal army to attack the secessionists and resolve the crisis by armed force while the projected conference was still under discussion. A week after the fall of Lucerne Guizot pressed yet again for a conference on Switzerland, proposing that it would meet in Neuchâtel (a Swiss town in which the King of Prussia enjoyed hereditary rights) where it would seek the restoration of liberty of action within the *Sonderbund* cantons and their evacuation by Federal forces. Palmerston thought further discussions on Switzerland superfluous: the civil war was over, and the Great Powers had no reason now for intervention. Guizot's plans were defeated, however, not by the British but by a revolt of his own ministers who maintained that there would be demonstrations of liberal sentiment in Paris should France be seen in league with the despoilers of Cracow and Ferrara.[19] It was, they warned him, enough to bring down the government. Five days before Christmas Metternich was told by the French ambassador that Guizot had abandoned the idea of a conference. A collective note was presented to the Swiss Diet by the envoys of France, Austria, Prussia and Russia which demanded that cantonal rights should be respected. But the Swiss radical leader, Ulrich Ochsenbein, was not impressed for he could see that time was on his side; had the Powers been confident of their cause they would have backed a collective note with military movements on the frontier. Switzerland successfully defied the Big Four. Privately Nesselrode agreed with Ochsenbein: Guizot's collective note seemed to him so ineffectual that he dismissed it as 'a declaration scented with rose water'.[20]

'It would not surprise me if Guizot was to go out at last', Palmerston commented on 9 January 1848. Others, too, thought the days of the French government numbered. It survived a scathing attack in the Chamber of Deputies at the end of the month, the opposition accusing Guizot of aligning the nation with reactionary Austria, as his colleagues had anticipated. One deputy, Alexis de Tocqueville, warned the government against social complacency, speaking of the 'disorder deep in the people's hearts' and ending his speech with a minatory 'The storm is brewing'. The deputies received the prophecy with 'sardonic laughter'. They were tired of the Minister of Peace, but it seemed absurd to suggest that the Orleanist monarchy itself was in danger. The harvest of 1847 was good, after two bad years; and the hungry unemployed were not sacking bakers' shops in the Paris faubourgs as they had done twelve months before. It is true that the electorate, composed entirely of men with some property, was uneasily aware that seven years of Guizot's foreign policy no longer 'enriched' France. Credit was short and there were hints of financial scandals. Gradually the Deputies began to shift allegiance from Guizot to Thiers, showing thereby an interesting preference for the historian of the Consulate over the historian of the Long Parliament. Such gestures do not, however, signal revolution. 'Society is calm on the surface', Alexis de Tocqueville admitted in his speech of 27 January. 'There is no visible sign of revolt.'[21]

Within a month Guizot and Princess Lieven were in a train for Calais, escaping to England before workless navvies tore up the track they had so recently laid south of Creil. Within five weeks King Louis-Philippe and Queen Marie Amélie were seeking refuge at a Newhaven hotel under the overworked alias of Mr and Mrs Smith. Within a year Count de Tocqueville was at the Foreign Ministry, and a nephew of the First Consul had become Prince-President Louis-Napoleon. The pace of events was to leave Europe in disarray, with only the Tsar and Palmerston standing out as familiar landmarks. But for the moment, as January 1848 gave way to a strangely mild February, the ambassadors in Paris could report how M. Guizot had triumphed in the Chamber, and how public attention was moving from foreign affairs to franchise reform. It seemed a harmless diversion.

7 Europe in Disarray, 1848–51

Metternich, unlike the French Deputies, had long anticipated political disaster. He was not, however, unduly disturbed by the reports he received during the early winter of 1847–8. On 2 January he amused himself by drawing up a political horoscope for the year 1848: he predicted that radical forces would emerge and confound society; the danger-spots were not in France or Switzerland and certainly not in the Habsburg Empire, but in Italy, and especially in Rome. This seemed a reasonable prediction. An insurrection in Palermo in the second week of January was followed by the grant of a constitution in Naples and by liberal demands in Tuscany. February began with street riots in Milan, troop movements in Piedmont and news that Pius IX had authorised a government for the Papal States which was to include, for the first time, laymen. It was not until the last weekend of the month that the horoscope was knocked awry. Ominous rumours reached Vienna from Paris: it was said that Guizot had banned a demonstration in favour of extending the franchise, and a 'reform banquet'; that students and radicals had taken to the streets in protest; and that, after shots were fired, the barricades had gone up. There were reports, too, of a disturbing display of red flags; and Princess Metternich was heard to remark, 'If Guizot goes, we are all of us lost'.[1]

In fact, by that weekend Guizot had already gone. A combination of political resentment and economic distress led Louis-Philippe to dismiss his minister on the afternoon of 23 February, only to find that he had himself to set out for exile in England on the following morning. So chaotic was the situation in Paris that, despite improved communications, Metternich heard of Louis-Philippe's abdication only in the early evening of Tuesday 29 February, and the alarming news that a Republic had been proclaimed in Paris did not reach him until Wednesday morning. At the same time he received a false report that the French had concentrated 50,000 men in Savoy and were about to launch a revolutionary war of national liberation in Italy. Hurriedly the Austrian Chancellor sent a dispatch to Turin, offering Charles Albert a defensive alliance. 'We are returning to the most unhappy days of the First French Republic', Metternich wrote, 'and for the moment our common safety should be our only concern.'[2]

The analogy with 1792 was in everybody's mind. The Prussian army on the Rhine was placed on the alert on 4 March, King Leopold arranged for some valuable possessions to be shipped from Brussels to London, the King of the Netherlands offered Belgium aid to keep her 'neutrality and independence', while in Vienna there was a run on the banks, with investors eager to exchange paper money for the security of silver. The most extraordinary reaction was in St Petersburg, where Tsar Nicholas silenced a ball at the Winter Palace with the dramatic order, 'Gentlemen, saddle your horses! France is a republic.' More soberly, he discussed with Chancellor Nesselrode and Prince Orlov the dispatch of an army of 30,000 men to help the Prussians on the Rhine but he was persuaded that so great an unheaval would finally shatter peace on the continent. He contented himself, on 11 March, with putting all Russia's armies at the ready for war.[3]

Nicholas, Frederick William IV of Prussia and Metternich appealed to the British for joint action against France should the new republicans rip apart the Vienna Settlement. Palmerston, however, did not share the general apprehension. His initial suspicion of the republican movement was allayed by reports from Lord Normanby, who had succeeded Cowley as ambassador. Normanby possessed some feeling for the cultural life of France; he knew the republican Minister of Foreign Affairs, Alphonse de Lamartine, and respected him as an outstanding Romantic poet and as an historian of the Girondins. Lamartine told Normanby as early as 28 February of his hopes for 'a lasting and sincere alliance between two great nations who ought always to be friends'. Palmerston was pleased at Lamartine's initiative. He praised his moderation and instructed Britain's envoys in Vienna, St Petersburg and Berlin to oppose all attempts by 'the three Northern Courts' to take up arms against republican France. Privately he doubted if Normanby's friend could restrain his countrymen from a revolutionary crusade – 'Large republics seem to be essentially and inherently aggressive', he warned the ambassador – but he did not believe there was any immediate threat of war, and he ended his message to Normanby with a final flourish of optimism. 'For the present, *vive* Lamartine', Palmerston wrote.[4]

He needed his imperturbable jauntiness that February. The Paris revolution coincided with the climax of a Radical campaign against Palmerston at Westminster. David Urquhart, a diplomat dismissed by Palmerston from his post as First Secretary at Constantinople in 1837 for seeking to provoke an Anglo-Russian conflict, was returned to the Commons at a by-election in 1847. He immediately began to mobilise Radical and Chartist support for the impeachment of Palmerston as a Russian agent, allegedly in the pay of the Lievens as far back as 1827, when he was Secretary at War. This ridiculous campaign culminated in a motion of impeachment against the Foreign Secretary in February 1848, the principal charges being made by an Irish barrister, Thomas Anstey, who spoke in all for some six hours to rapidly emptying Houses on 8 February and again on 22 February, the Tuesday on which the first barricades went up in Paris. Palmerston replied to Urquhart and Anstey in one of his most famous speeches on the following Wednesday (1 March), a few MPs showing sufficient interest in the lunatic accusations to come to the House. After patiently answering each of the twelve counts against him in a defence which filled fifty-five columns of Hansard, Palmerston used the opportunity to develop his general principles of foreign policy. His peroration was clearly related to the mounting crisis in Europe and the call of the autocracies for a new anti-revolutionary coalition. 'I hold that the real policy of England – apart from questions which involve her own particular interests, political or commercial – is to be the champion of justice and right', he declared. 'It is a narrow policy to suppose that this country or that is to be marked out as the eternal ally or the perpetual enemy of England. We have no eternal allies, and we have no perpetual enemies. Our interests are eternal and perpetual, and those interests it is our duty to follow.' He ended by invoking the tradition of George Canning and asserting that 'with every British minister the interests of England ought to be the shibboleth of his policy'.[5] Urquhart, Anstey and their Radical friends were routed; and the first and last attempt to move the impeachment of a Foreign Secretary was soon forgotten in the rush of dramatic news from the continent.

Four days after Palmerston's speech Lamartine published a manifesto in *Le Moniteur Universel* defining the foreign policy of a French republic. 'To return after half a century to the principles of 1792 or the desire of the Empire for conquest would be to step backwards rather than to progress. Our revolution is a step forward . . . toward peace and fraternity', he said.[6] The Republic had no wish to make war, for a nation at war suffers loss of liberty and France had no desire 'for a Caesar or a Napoleon'. He denounced the treaties of 1815 but recognised them as an existing fact in international relations, and he pledged French support for the people of Switzerland and 'the independent states of Italy'. Palmerston was well satisfied by the manifesto, although uneasy over the reference to Italy, and he wished the Great Powers to assure Lamartine that no aggression would be committed against France provided the republican government did not itself resort to aggression. Metternich was more suspicious of French intentions, for the references to Switzerland and Italy seemed a deliberate challenge, but he, too, gave Lamartine an undertaking that Austria would not intervene in France so long as the Republic abstained from violating existing treaties. The Prussians and the Russians, as well as the Austrians, were surprised that the manifesto held out no promise of support to the Polish cause, despite the sympathy shown for the Poles in Paris ever since the last years of the Empire. The omission of Poland from the manifesto was interpreted in St Petersburg, Berlin and Vienna as a hopeful sign that this newest revolutionary government in Paris might prove less disruptive to the European states system than had its predecessor in 1830. But as a precaution, Frederick William IV sent to Vienna General von Radowitz, his most trusted military adviser, with an offer of Prussian military support to Austria in return for allowing Prussia greater control of the German Confederation. General and Chancellor held preliminary talks in the second week of March and agreed to meet again after the weekend; and Metternich's secretary made an appointment for Radowitz to return to the Ballhausplatz on Monday 13 March.[7]

What the two men decided that morning mattered little, for by nine in the evening Metternich had fallen from power. He was toppled not by shock waves from Lamartine's revolution but by a movement indigenous to the Habsburg lands. Over the previous four months the Hungarian Diet, meeting in the city now known as Bratislava, had formulated demands for reform which, under the inspired leadership of Lajos Kossuth, culminated in proposals for a virtually autonomous Hungary with a responsible government elected on a broad franchise. News of

Kossuth's programme provoked a double response in Vienna: a provincial assembly, the Estates of Lower Austria, sought civil rights and some form of parliamentary government, while students at the university demonstrated in favour of abolishing censorship and greater freedom in education and worship. The two protests came together on 13 March. They seemed so menacing that Archduke Ludwig, uncle to the emperor and effective spokesman for the dynasty, induced Metternich to resign both as Chancellor and Foreign Minister in order to save the capital from serious rioting.

The Chancellor's fall was welcomed in Vienna as a prelude to domestic reform. Farther afield it was interpreted as an event of greater significance, the end of a supranational repressive system. Liberal unrest, already stimulated in northern Italy, Germany and central Europe by the example of Paris, was given a specifically nationalistic character as radical leaders repudiated Habsburg primacy in Hungary, Milan, Venice, Prague and Frankfurt. It was this second revolutionary impulse that produced such uncertainty in Berlin, where news of Metternich's fall was received on the morning of Thursday 16 March. King Frederick William IV, torn between fear of liberalism and a muddle-headed romantic German patriotism, rejected the advice of his generals and promised a parliamentary constitution for Prussia and Hohenzollern support for the German national cause. He was even prepared to order the Prussian army to protect German soil from Russia as much as from France, but as a gesture of revolutionary goodwill Prussia's largest minority, the Poles around Posen, were promised some form of national recognition. There was even, momentarily, a possibility that exiled Poles would launch a war of liberation from Posen (Poznan) against the Russian-occupied Congress Kingdom, but so dangerous a policy held no appeal for Frederick William. As early as 10 April Prussian regular troops reported that they were under attack from Polish 'insurgents' near Posen. Thereafter German national sentiment remained as hostile to Polish liberties as Tsar Nicholas himself.

Nesselrode and Orlov ensured that the Tsar behaved with shrewd restraint throughout the crisis months of 1848. Russia was directly concerned with two neighbouring regions, Poland and the Danubian Principalities of Moldavia and Wallachia – the outlying Romanian provinces of the Turkish Empire. Nicholas knew he could rely on Marshal Paskievič, his viceroy in Warsaw, to keep a vigilant eye on the Poles, whether within or beyond the Russian frontier. But he was so alarmed by the activities of Romanian patriots in Bucharest that he ordered the Russian army to take both Moldavia and Wallachia under its protection, a military move which he claimed was in accordance with Russia's rights under the Treaty of Kutchuk Kainardji of 1774. The Russian invasion caused scarcely a ripple in international relations. Only Great Britain among the Powers chiefly interested in the Eastern Question was in a position to protest, and Palmerston thought the Tsar's action justifiable.[8] Like Nicholas, he had no desire to see the revolutions spreading to the Turkish Empire and posing new problems at Constantinople. The southward movement of the Tsar's forces meant that by midsummer in 1848 the Russian army was spread around the arc of the Carpathians and able to cross the passes into Transylvania and the heart of Hungary should the Habsburgs need effective proof of conservative solidarity. But the time to intervene in Austria's affairs had not yet come.

Palmerston adjusted himself serenely to the new European scene. He entertained Guizot and Dorothea Lieven to dinner at Carlton Gardens and called courteously on the exiled Metternich at his hotel in Hanover Square. Old animosities were not perhaps entirely forgotten; for when the House of Lords debated foreign affairs, Guizot could be seen in the visitors' gallery listening impassively to Aberdeen attacking an imprudent attempt by Palmerston to interfere in Spain's internal affairs. Some of the exiles – notably Louis-Philippe – held Palmerston responsible for their downfall and sought to convince the queen and Prince Albert that the Foreign Secretary was recklessly directing revolution in one European state after another. Yet, in reality, Palmerston consistently opposed any threat to the international order whether from revolution or reaction. He instructed Lord Ponsonby, the ambassador in Vienna, to use 'all proper means in your power' to ensure maintenance of 'the Austrian Empire as united and as strong as possible'.[9] And, again like the Tsar, he was determined to check and localise any military conflict arising from revolutionary unrest.

The greatest danger lay in northern Italy, as Palmerston had long ago foreseen. Charles Albert of Piedmont could not resist the appeal of his subjects to answer the call of Italian patriots in Milan and Venice and seek the incorporation of Lombardy-Venetia in his kingdom. The Piedmontese declared war on Austria eleven days after Metternich's fall and inflicted a defeat on the demoralised Austrian army at Goito on 8 April. The British offered to mediate, for Palmerston hoped it would be possible not only to stop the fighting but to induce the Austrians to surrender Lombardy-Venetia to Piedmont and then assume the status of a protective power over the whole of northern Italy. By this means Palmerston hoped the peninsula would be safeguarded, once more, from the contagion of French ideas and, indeed, from French territorial aggrandisement.

The policy came near to success.[10] Metternich's coeval Baron von Wessenberg, fetched from 16 years of retirement to become Austria's Foreign Minister in early May, immediately sent a peace envoy for talks with Palmerston in London. The Austrians were willing to cede Lombardy to Charles Albert while retaining Venetia within the Habsburg Empire, although with a measure of autonomy. As Palmerston found that the French, too, were offering to mediate – with a plan for two buffer republics in Lombardy-Venetia – he was eager for an early settlement. But the Foreign Secretary ran into two unexpected obstacles: his Prime Minister, Russell, was always more firmly committed to the Italian cause than he was himself and therefore regarded the Austrian concessions as minimal; and the Milanese revolutionaries wanted to detach from Austria not merely Lombardy-Venetia but the Italian areas of the southern Tyrol as well. The envoy returned to Vienna for fresh instructions; some attempt was made to formulate joint Anglo-French proposals for mediation; but the Austrians suddenly regained the military initiative, and with

Field-Marshal Radetzky's victory at Custozza on 25 July Lombardy returned to Austrian rule while Charles Albert accepted an armistice on 9 August. Proposals to use the British and French as joint peacemakers continued to be made in Vienna for another two months, but with the coming of winter, real authority in Austria passed to Prince Felix Schwarzenberg and his brother-in-law, Prince Alfred Windischgraetz, iron-nerved aristocrats with little inclination for a negotiated settlement. Windischgraetz had ended Czech hopes of national freedom and dispersed a Slav congress of radicals by ordering the bombardment of Prague and the occupation of the city hill by hill and street by street soon after Whitsun; and in October he dealt no less drastically with a radical rising in Vienna itself. He was not the man to temporise, and he gave the backing of his army to Schwarzenberg's policies, including the intrigue by which Emperor Ferdinand abdicated on 2 December in favour of his 18-year-old nephew, Francis Joseph.

In northern Europe, too, revolutionary nationalism led to a localised war, fought in a region of historic concern for both peripheral Powers, Russia and Britain. Schleswig and Holstein, the so-called 'Elbe Duchies', were confirmed under the suzerainty of the Danish king by the Treaty of Vienna although Holstein was admitted to the German Confederation, an acknowledgement that the population of this southern Duchy was almost entirely German in speech and background. Commercially the Duchies looked naturally to Berlin rather than Copenhagen, especially during the years of Prussia's economic growth under the protective umbrella of the Zollverein. Assertions from within the Duchies that they acknowledged the Salic law of succession whereas the Danish Crown might pass down through a female line aggravated feeling in Copenhagen, where the childless and dissolute Frederick VII came to the throne in January 1848. Danish national and radical sentiment wanted an end to such archaic feudal concepts of succession and the incorporation, once and for all, of Schleswig-Holstein in a unitary Danish kingdom. This uncompromising attitude encouraged assemblies of the duchies at Altona and Kiel to secede during the heady liberal days of March 1848 and appeal for protection to Prussia and to the all-German Frankfurt Assembly. King Frederick William IV, pleased at that moment to place his regiments in the service of the German national cause, sent an army into Holstein in the second week of April. By the end of the month the Danes were ousted from the Duchies and the war was carried across the border into Jutland. Prussia thus acquired not only a commanding position in the Baltic but an opportunity to garrison for the first time the littoral of the North Sea. It was with some confidence that the Danes appealed to Britain and Russia to uphold the integrity of their kingdom. They were convinced that neither Power wished to see Kiel, the Elbe estuary and much of the Jutland peninsula in the hands of a potential rival. This was still true of the British; but the Russians were no longer so concerned with locking their Baltic doorway as in earlier years.

A council of ministers discussed the Danish Question in St Petersburg during the first week of May.[11] It was decided that the Duchies had lost much of their strategic importance for Russia now that the empire's main trade artery ran southwards through the Bosphorus and Dardanelles; but it was agreed that Nicholas should protest to Frederick William at the use of Prussia's army against a brother sovereign in a revolutionary 'national' cause. At the same time Nesselrode proposed a common-sense solution: Holstein would be recognised as a German state, Schleswig would be partitioned along a clearly defined national boundary. Yet, having delivered this oracular judgement, Nesselrode left Palmerston to determine the line of partition; and this proved impossible. The Danes were no more inclined to accept Nesselrode's plan than the Italians to accept a compromise in Lombardy. For, though the Danish army might have difficulty in checking German incursions, the Danish navy was strong enough to ruin Prussia's maritime trade if the crisis dragged on. It was a ridiculous situation: neither Britain nor Russia would impose a settlement by force of arms; and neither the Danes nor the Prussians had the will or skill to gain a decisive military victory. At last, on 26 August, Frederick William IV authorised the signing of an armistice at Malmö. Yet even this action was taken, not because the British, the Russians and the Swedes came forward as mediators, but because Frederick William had a nagging fear that the Tsar might, perhaps, be right in accusing him of selling his good monarchical soul to an evil German national movement. The king had lost the Pan-German enthusiasm which excited him in the second half of March. When, in September, radical demonstrators sought to make the Frankfurt 'Parliament of the German People' denounce the King of Prussia's apostasy and resume a patriotic war against Denmark, they were dispersed by Prussian and Austrian troops. The counter-revolutionaries were firmly in the saddle.[12]

Next month an international conference opened in London, with Palmerston resuming his search for a compromise over the Elbe duchies. The dispute dragged on for nearly two years, and the Prussians and Danes fought each other again in the spring and summer of 1849. Eventually Palmerston hacked out an agreement: Schleswig and Holstein remained inseparably united, but their link with Denmark was solely through the person of the Danish king, who would also be Grand Duke of Schleswig-Holstein. The Treaty of London of May 1852 confirmed this arrangement: the five European Great Powers recognised as heir to all the Danish king's territories Prince Christian of Glucksburg, whose mother was a first cousin of the reigning sovereign, Frederick VII. The Duke of Augustenburg, claimant to the Elbe Duchies under Salic law, saw his rights passed over. It was an improvised settlement, testimony to Palmerston's persistence rather than to any deep understanding of the problems of the Duchies. There was some hope that the Powers' willingness to respect treaties drafted by concerted agreement after long negotiation might give Schleswig-Holstein a few decades of peace. No one, however, could predict that national feelings would retain such fervour once revolutionary passion died away.

Despite the fine talk of unity against revolution, the Tsar remained as yet a distant spectator of events; Russian diplomacy did little in Denmark and less in Italy. But the third military conflict of 1848–9 involved the Russians deeply in central Europe's affairs. During the early days of the revolution within the Habsburg Empire the Magyars, under Kossuth, secured a series of reforms which gave Hungary an administration of her own. These concessions, however, frightened the subject nationalities living within the historic boundaries of the old Hungarian kingdom, minorities who traditionally resented Magyar exploitation. Foremost among these subject peoples were the Croats, who in 1848 had a new and militant governor *(Ban)*, General Baron Josip Jellačić. When, in the autumn of 1848, Kossuth's radicalism began to threaten the existing social order, the Austrians encouraged Jellačić to lead his Croatian regiments northwards and invade the Hungarian heartland. This incursion was repulsed by the brilliant 30-year-old commander of the Hungarian militia, General Gorgei. The successes of the militia inflated the national patriotism of the Magyars even higher and, for a time, they threatened Vienna itself. What was at first a struggle for political rights became an assertion of national independence in April 1849 when the Hungarian parliament, meeting in Debrecen, declared that the House of Habsburg had forfeited the throne and authorised Kossuth to serve as provisional head of state.[13]

Tsar Nicholas had not originally intended to intervene in Hungary. But Kossuth's eloquence and Gorgei's victories attracted to Buda and Debrecen revolutionary leaders who had earlier waited on conspiracy in Paris and Geneva. Among these exiles were two Polish veterans, Generals Bem and Dembinsky, who had fought against the Tsar's army in 1830–1. Nicholas regarded their arrival as extremely ominous. He feared that Hungary would become the revolutionary springboard of Eastern Europe. 'The symptoms of a general plot against everything sacred, and especially against Russia, are clearly visible in the Hungarian rebellion', he wrote to his Polish viceroy, Marshal Paskievič, on 7 May 1849. And he added: 'At the head of the rebellion, and acting as the principal instruments of it, are our eternal foes, the Poles.'[14] Nicholas therefore readily responded to a request from Francis Joseph for Russian assistance. Two Russian armies, from the north and the east, advanced into Hungary, with Paskievič himself in command. The British chargé d'affaires at St Petersburg thought it unfortunate Austria could not restore order without Russian aid, and he told Nesselrode so. Nesselrode, with forty years of diplomacy behind him, blandly agreed that it was indeed a matter of regret. No other protest was made. However much Palmerston might sympathise with the liberal cause, he still believed in the merits of a tranquil and orderly continent. 'The maintenance of the Austrian empire', he told the Commons on 21 July, should be 'an object of solicitude to every English statesman . . . Austria stands in the centre of Europe, a barrier against encroachment on the one side, and against invasion on the other. The political independence and liberties of Europe are bound up, in my opinion, with the maintenance of Austria as a great European Power.'[15] If the Tsar, thinking primarily of Poland, also wished Austria restored as a Great Power, so be it.

Russian intervention completed the defeat of the Hungarians. They were faced by Windischgraetz and Jellačić in the west, by Serb irregulars in the Danubian plain, by German and Romanian groups in Transylvania, and by the full weight of two Russian armies. Four thousand Hungarians and 800 Poles escaped across the frontier and, with Kossuth and the Polish generals, found refuge in Turkey. Gorgei's army was trapped in south-eastern Hungary, hopelessly outnumbered. It capitulated to the Russians, on honourable terms, at Vilagos on 13 August 1849. Only the isolated Danubian fortress of Komarom continued to defy the counter-revolutionaries, not surrendering to the Austrians for another seven weeks.

'Hungary lies at the feet of Your Majesty', Paskievič reported to the Tsar after Vilagos. Militarily he was right; but how could Nicholas benefit from his soldiers' victory? Certainly not by territorial gains from his Habsburg ally. The only tangible reward for Russia's one military incursion into central Europe between 1813 and 1944 was a collection of fifty-eight Hungarian flags surrendered at Vilagos and housed in St Petersburg beside insignia from more exacting campaigns. Yet Nicholas gained almost all he wanted. Gorgei's capitulation ended the cycle of revolutions within central Europe. The Poles gave no more trouble in the lifetime of Nicholas or Viceroy Paskievič. Austria could restore the Germany of the Vienna Settlement: no doubt the old Confederation had its weaknesses but the Russians saw it as a harmless safety-valve for those nationalist sentiments which had erupted so aggressively on Metternich's fall. Russia's prestige after Vilagos seemed to Nicholas as high as in 1815. It was convenient that Francis Joseph should begin his reign under a debt of political gratitude. The Tsar was prepared to treat his brother autocrats in Austria and Prussia graciously: he would receive them or their ministers in Warsaw, separately; and he was pleased to come to Vienna in state, to be thanked for his services; but there would be no Münchengrätz and no revived Holy Alliance. The gendarme of Europe was never a visionary. With one exception – the coming disintegration of Turkey – he calculated his policy pragmatically from day to day, not in terms of some hypothetical balance of future forces.[16]

Yet Nicholas, despite this rapid ascendancy over Europe's affairs, was far from being master of the continent. He suffered a tiresome rebuff in September and October 1849 when the Turks, encouraged by Stratford Canning, Palmerston and a British naval squadron off the Dardanelles, declined to surrender four Polish generals to Russia or Kossuth and his supporters to Austria. Not even the peremptory withdrawal of the Russian and Austrian ambassadors from Constantinople could induce the Sultan to change his mind. Nor indeed was there complete accord between the Tsar and his Austrian partner. He deplored the summary execution of thirteen Hungarian generals at Arad, not least because the Austrian commander, the notorious General Haynau, ordered the officers who had surrendered to the Russians to be hanged while those who had surrendered to the Austrians had the privilege of being shot. Of more lasting significance was the Tsar's mistrust of Prince Schwarzenberg, who had become head of the Austrian government and Foreign Minister eleven days before Francis Joseph's accession. Schwarzenberg was arrogant and contemptuous of his fellow aristocrats for allowing the Habsburg Empire to be rocked by revolution, but in Nicholas's eyes his own past was suspect, since he had befriended one of the Decembrist conspirators when he was in St Petersburg in 1825. Nicholas credited Schwarzenberg with a greater capacity for intrigue than he, in fact, possessed – 'Palmerston in a white uniform' was the Tsar's damning comment on the prince after they met in Warsaw – but there were moments when his suspicion of the Austrian minister was fully justified. 'Austria will astonish the world by the extent of her ingratitude', Schwarzenberg is reported to have said after Vilagos. He had assumed that the Russians would force Gorgei to surrender to Austrian commanders rather than claim the final victory over the revolution for themselves.[17]

The real test of Austro-Russian friendship came over the German Question. Schwarzenberg did not want to restore the old German Confederation, as Nicholas and Nesselrode assumed. He wished to replace it by what was, in effect, a 'Great Austrian' Confederation, to include all the lands of the Habsburgs, German and non-German. The Prussians, too, were reluctant to put the clock back to the Metternich era; Radowitz had discussed proposals to change the form of the Confederation with the Austrian Chancellor during his visit to Vienna in March 1848. By the spring of 1849, when Radowitz became chief minister of Prussia, he was favouring the idea of an enlarged confederation organised in two loosely integrated units: the Habsburg Empire, and a 'small' Germany, dominated from Berlin. Schwarzenberg was resolutely opposed to the Radowitz solution, and he encouraged the mistrust of Prussian intentions shown by the other German kingdoms, Bavaria, Hanover, Saxony and Württemberg. In March 1850 Radowitz set up an embryonic confederation, the Erfurt Union, only to find the four kingdoms coming together in a rival league, sponsored by Schwarzenberg. Tsar Nicholas, as the King of Prussia's brother-in-law, was in a quandary. He was uneasy at Schwarzenberg's ambitions for a central European state, but he thought Frederick William IV weak and vacillating and suspected that Radowitz would chance war rather than accept Austrian primacy in Germany again. A conflict in Germany ran counter to Russia's interests, not least because it would disturb the balance of power in partitioned Poland if Prussia or Austria emerged as a clear victor. Nicholas therefore gave qualified support to Schwarzenberg and the opponents of the Erfurt Union.

Tension continued between Prussia and Austria throughout the summer and autumn of 1850. A Russian assessment of the military strength of their two former allies rated Prussia higher than Austria, and the Tsar was worried that if war broke out, the Austrians might find themselves in difficulties and Francis Joseph would again appeal to him for help. He wished to avoid the embarrassment of having to choose between Berlin and Vienna. These fears were groundless. Frederick William's lack of confidence played into Austria's hands. In November 1850 the king dismissed Radowitz and sent a new chief minister, Otto von Manteuffel, to meet Schwarzenberg at Olmütz (Olomouc) in Moravia; the German affair should be settled once and for all, felt the king. Significantly the Russian ambassador to Austria accompanied Schwarzenberg to Olmütz and encouraged the two German Powers to sink their differences. By the 'Olmütz Punctation' of 29 November 1850 Prussia agreed to dissolve the Erfurt Union and participate once more in the work of the German Confederation.

There was, however, one matter unresolved: should the Confederation be enlarged? A conference of the German princes gathered at Dresden in January 1851 to discuss the question. Not one of them wished to see Schwarzenberg's Greater Austria astride the land mass from the Baltic to the Adriatic. Nesselrode, too, made it clear in March that Russia disliked the plan. By the spring it seemed that Schwarzenberg faced diplomatic isolation; and this at a time when he was worried over the future of Austria's possessions in Italy, where French influence was by now stronger than during the Metternich era. Ironically Manteuffel, whom Schwarzenberg despised at Olmütz, came to Austria's rescue; he offered a secret three-year military alliance by which Prussia would guarantee the whole of the Habsburg lands provided that the territorial and constitutional settlement of 1815 was retained within Germany. On 16 May 1851 Schwarzenberg, with an eye on Italy, accepted Manteuffel's terms. Austria and Prussia were once more partners. The new Prussian envoy to the Diet of the Confederation deplored its resurrection; but as yet no one attached much weight to the complaints of Herr von Bismarck.[18]

Overshadowing the German crisis was uncertainty concerning the role of France in Europe's affairs. The Second Republic had puzzled foreign observers since its inception. Lamartine's radicalism had been challenged by the socialist experiments of Louis Blanc until the brutal street fighting of the 'June Days' culminated in the appointment of General Cavaignac as dictator by a cowed National Assembly. But Cavaignac, though pitiless in his treatment of the Parisian socialists, permitted the preparation of a basically democratic constitution and allowed his name to go forward as a candidate for election to the presidency. By the autumn of 1848, however, it was clear that the favourite contender was Prince Louis Napoleon, the little known and long-exiled nephew of the great Emperor. His campaign caused concern outside France, and especially in Russia. An envoy sent to St Petersburg in an attempt to secure diplomatic recognition for the Republic from the Tsar noted the alarm of the Russians at news of a Bonapartist candidature. 'They fear Louis-Napoleon Bonaparte, they dread his election, they feel that this will bring war', the envoy reported to Paris, in the second week of November.[19] But the French voters thought that the prince could both protect a just social order and restore the nation's prestige in Europe. The presidential elections of 10–11 December 1848 gave Louis Napoleon some 75 per cent of the votes, 4 million more than General Cavaignac, and over 300 times as many votes as the former radical idol, Lamartine. The prince was inaugurated President, for a four-year term, on 20 December. Not a single Bonapartist was included in the government. The Prince-President appointed a former Orleanist diplomat, Édouard Drouyn de Lhuys, to head the ministry of foreign affairs. His appointment was interpreted by the Russians as a sign that French foreign policy would be traditionalist rather than revolutionary in character.

Louis Napoleon and Drouyn inherited from the Cavaignac administration a French commitment in the Italian peninsula. Disillusionment with the allegedly liberal Pope culminated in revolution at Rome in November 1848, forcing Pius IX to flee to Gaeta in Neapolitan territory. When he asked for assistance from Catholic Europe to suppress the revolution in Rome, General Cavaignac announced that French warships would sail to Civitavecchia and an expeditionary force would be concentrated at Marseilles and Toulon to safeguard the temporal authority of His Holiness. The force was ready to sail at the time of the presidential election and on 23 December, at the first Cabinet presided over by the Prince-President, Drouyn proposed that France should forestall Austria and dispatch the expedition to Civitavecchia immediately. His Cabinet colleagues agreed with him; for this was, after all, a familiar device of French policy – Ancona had been under French naval administration from 1832 to 1838. But the Prince-President refused to authorise intervention. He similarly declined to intervene militarily in March 1849 when the Piedmontese, having rashly reopened their war with the Austrians, were decisively defeated by Field-Marshal Radetzky at Novara. The most Louis Napoleon would do was to collaborate with Palmerston in putting diplomatic pressure on the Austrians to save Victor Emmanuel II, the new king of Sardinia-Piedmont, from beginning his reign under punitive peace terms. But Austria's success in the north of Italy inevitably made urgent some decision over the Papal States; and in the last week of April 1849 a French naval squadron escorted 9,000 troops from Toulon to Civitavecchia. Even so, Mazzini (principal triumvir in the new Roman Republic) hoped that General Oudinot and his French expeditionary force had come to protect Rome from Austrian, Spanish and Neapolitan 'reactionaries' who were competing for the honour of restoring Pius IX to his holy city. Oudinot insisted on entering Rome. His march was resisted by the volunteer redshirts of Giuseppe Garibaldi who routed the invaders in a sharp battle on the western hills of Rome and forced the survivors to retreat to the coast. Thus, within five months of becoming President, Louis Napoleon had allowed the confusion and hesitancy of his policies to bring the French their first military defeat since Waterloo.[20]

The repulse of Oudinot condemned Louis Napoleon to support papal authority. A truce arranged by the French diplomat Ferdinand de Lesseps was brushed aside by the Prince-President, and as soon as reinforcements reached Civitavecchia, Oudinot was ordered to destroy the Roman Republic. 'We have to finish this wretched Roman affair by cannon shot', Louis Napoleon wrote to an old Bonapartist friend; 'I deplore it; but what can I do?'[21] By the end of June Rome was controlled by French troops. Apart from an interlude of eleven months in 1866–7, they were to remain in Rome as defenders of the Pope until needed to defend France herself in the late summer of 1870. Louis Napoleon's blundering policy may have ensured that throughout the 1850s the influence of France was greater in the peninsula than the influence of Austria, a reversal of roles from the Metternich era. But Louis Napoleon, not for the last time, became the captive of his own ingenuity. His uncle, at the start of the century, made certain he was master of the Pope and master of the Italian peninsula at the same time. The nephew, an opportunist crusader rather than a conqueror, spent years propping up the papacy, as an almost good Catholic, while claiming he was 'doing something for Italy', as an almost good Bonapartist. There lay the difference between Napoleon the Great and Napoleon the Less.

By the summer of 1849 the Prince-President was freeing himself from dependence on Orleanist veterans in government. Drouyn became ambassador in London and was succeeded at the Foreign Ministry by Alexis de Tocqueville, but the initiative in foreign affairs was increasingly taken by special Bonapartist emissaries. Louis Napoleon's former companion in exile, Count Persigny, was sent to Berlin to discuss a possible frontier rectification in the Rhineland in return for an offer of French support over the German Question. Other envoys were sent to St Petersburg and to Vienna. Such cloak-and-dagger diplomacy, invariably rebuffed, tended to discredit its author, although it remained his trick of trade as President and as emperor. Conventional attempts to find an ally were hardly more successful, not always through any fault of Louis Napoleon. He valued especially the friendship of England during the years when he was unsure of the continental autocracies and there were a few months in the winter of 1849–50 when he spoke of Britain and France as 'the Liberal Powers'. Against Tocqueville's advice he insisted on sending French warships to support Admiral Parker's squadron as it lay off the Dardanelles in October 1849; he wished Europe to see that France would back Britain in encouraging the Sultan to protect the refugees from the fighting in Hungary. Unfortunately, Palmerston had a further objective in mind for Admiral Parker's squadron, which was to lead within six months to yet another war scare in Anglo-French relations.[22]

At Easter 1847 an anti-Semitic mob in Athens wrecked the home of David Pacifico, a money-lender who was a leading member of the Jewish community in the city. Don Pacifico, a former Portuguese consul in Athens, was of Spanish descent but, as both he and his father were born in Gibraltar, he enjoyed British citizenship. The Greek government, at that time dominated by a pro-French faction, rejected his claims for compensation, beginning a legal wrangle which dragged on interminably throughout the year of revolutions. Relations between Palmerston and the Greeks were already bad: there was a dispute over the sovereignty of some small islands off the Peloponnese which the British insisted fell within their Ionian Protectorate; and Palmerston was incensed by the action of King Otto of Greece who sequestered the Athens villa of the Scottish historian George Finlay because he wished the land enclosed within the park of his new royal palace. Exasperation with the Greeks over all these matters induced Palmerston to order Admiral Parker to sail from the Dardanelles to Phaleron Bay and enforce the pecuniary claims against the Greek government of Don Pacifico, George Finlay and other British citizens with cause for complaint. The British squadron remained off Athens for several months, seizing Greek vessels and effectively blockading Piraeus.

France and Russia – who, with Britain, were the recognised Protecting Powers of the Greek kingdom – deplored this naval bullying. Louis Napoleon used Drouyn as a mediator throughout the early months of 1850, only to find Palmerston set hard against compromise or concession; there was a suspicion in Europe that London wished to oust King Otto and find for the Greeks a sovereign more susceptible to British blandishment. At the height of the crisis, in May 1850, the French ordered Drouyn to return to Paris in protest at Palmerston's high-handed policy. It was said the French ambassador had been cheated and insulted. There was a press campaign which maintained that the right answer to Palmerston's conduct was war. Louis Napoleon had no intention of allowing the hotheads to stampede him into disaster. Characteristically he let Russell (the Prime Minister) know privately that he had not been present at the Cabinet meeting which resolved to recall the ambassador. He still hoped eventually to bring about an Anglo-French alliance.[23]

Never has so dubious an incident aroused such anger nor involved the deployment of so many warships. In the end, Pacifico received about a sixth of the £35,500 compensation he had claimed for loss of furniture, valuables and documents while Finlay was awarded a token sum. But the Don Pacifico affair transcended in importance the petty claims of particular individuals. There was a strong feeling among British Conservatives that the Foreign Secretary had behaved injudiciously; and the government was defeated in the Lords on a motion censuring Palmerston's policy towards Greece. Lord John Russell refused to resign, to dismiss Palmerston, or to appeal to the country. He did, however, encourage a radical MP to table a motion congratulating Her Majesty's Government on a foreign policy 'calculated to maintain the honour and dignity of this country'. The consequent 'Don Pacifico debate' of 24–8 June 1850 became the gala performance of Victorian parliamentary oratory. Palmerston defended himself in a famous speech lasting four and a half hours, through the brief darkness of a midsummer night. He reviewed every aspect of his policies on the continent, but the speech is best remembered for his assertion that a British subject had as good a right as an ancient Roman citizen to expect privileged treatment, that 'in whatever land he may be . . . the watchful eye and the strong arm of England will protect him against injustice and wrong'.[24] Peel, Gladstone, Cobden and Disraeli all spoke against Palmerston, Gladstone insisting that it was a Foreign Secretary's duty 'to exalt in honour among mankind that great code of principles which is termed the law of nations'.

Palmerston's patriotic peroration, received with resounding cheers, virtually decided the debate before the other speeches had been delivered: the Commons endorsed his policy by 310 votes to 264. There were rumours, to which Disraeli later gave credence, that 'Lord Aberdeen had planned the attack on Palmerston under the inspiration of Madame Lieven and Guizot'. Even the Radicals who tried to impeach Palmerston two years before now rejoiced that he had frustrated the knavish tricks of envious foreigners; a dinner in his honour at the Reform Club greeted him with 'Rule, Britannia!' Only at Buckingham Palace was there a sour note: Lord John Russell told the queen that her Foreign Secretary's speech was 'one of the most masterly ever delivered' and that it 'appealed from time to time to great principles of justice and freedom', but Victoria thought the whole affair 'a most disagreeable business'. 'The House of Commons is becoming very unmanageable and troublesome', she complained to King Leopold in Brussels.[25]

Yet once the Britannia euphoria evaporated, it became clear the Palmerstonians were celebrating an empty triumph. Their champion had won a political battle comparable to Custozza and Novara – victories which gave Radetzky a patriotic Strauss march but which denied Austria lasting gains since the vanquished enjoyed powerful protection from other states. Palmerston had shored up his position within Russell's Cabinet, provided he continued to please the backbench Radicals; but were he to slip from popular favour by treating too indulgently one of the foreign bogeys, then he would find against him the Crown and every experienced minister from both political parties. He remained Foreign Secretary, largely on sufferance and perhaps without realising his precarious position. When in December 1851 it was found he had privately congratulated the French on Louis Napoleon's coup d'état, he offended government policy, his queen and public opinion, and he was turned out of the Foreign Office for good.

The real victor from the Don Pacifico affair was Louis Napoleon himself. A high tone of respect for the public law of Europe, an insistence on Great Power mediation, a show of injured dignity when forced to recall Drouyn from London – all these attributes won the Prince-President support from Russia, Austria, Prussia, and indeed from Holland, Spain and Portugal, too. In the previous October he had touted for an English alliance; in May he stood up to Palmerston, and thereby enhanced his status in Europe. When, denied the constitutional amendment which would have allowed him a second term of office, he was forced to retain power by a coup d'état, he received not only the ill-conceived message from Palmerston but the congratulations of the Tsar and the chief ministers of Austria and Prussia as well. Any ruler who could dam 'the red fool-fury of the Seine' and help repair a politically devastated system on the continent could be certain of support from his European neighbours. But that did not mean they would welcome the proclamation of a Second Empire, a term which filled the imagination with fears of war and conquest. There was nothing wrong with Louis Napoleon as head of state, provided he forgot to be a Bonaparte.

8 The Primacy of France, 1852–56

The abrupt removal of Palmerston from the Foreign Office in December 1851 left Europe without a dominant statesman for the first time in forty years, and it was by no means clear who would step on to the vacant pedestal. Palmerston's immediate successors were of small account: the young and amiable Earl Granville was swept into opposition within a couple of months when Russell's government was defeated in the Commons on a Militia Bill; and the new Conservative Foreign Secretary, Viscount Malmesbury, was little known outside England – except, curiously enough, to Louis Napoleon, who had been his personal friend for over twenty years. The Prince-President of France aroused more interest abroad than any other political figure but, as yet, he was too concerned with domestic affairs to give Europe a clear lead.

Unquestionably the statesman with the widest experience that winter was State Chancellor Nesselrode, in St Petersburg. He remained, however, as self-effacing as ever, ready to tender advice in skilfully penned memoranda but not seeking to determine policy himself. Tsar Nicholas was content with the equilibrium of the restored European order. He was prepared to back expansive projects in the Caucasus or in the eastern regions of his empire, where there were outposts along the Pacific, but he stood on the defensive in Russia's western borderlands. The Tsar could count on support from Frederick William IV in Berlin and his chief minister, Otto von Manteuffel, a military bureaucrat with few pretensions to statecraft. Nicholas also believed that the Austrians would collaborate with the Russians in any major European crisis, and he continued to put an exaggerated emphasis on the gratitude allegedly owed to Russia by Francis Joseph for her intervention in Hungary in 1849. This was a curious miscalculation, for the Tsar had already been surprised on several occasions by Schwarzenberg's independent initiative and, in particular, by Austrian support for Louis Napoleon's pro-papal policy in central Italy.

Prince Felix Schwarzenberg was young by the standards of the Habsburg monarchy, a mere lad of 51 at the time of Palmerston's dismissal. There seemed no reason why he should not shape Austrian policy for the rest of the decade and even longer. It was hoped in Vienna he would win for Francis Joseph a Napoleonic ascendancy over central Europe, creating a Greater Austrian 'Empire of seventy millions' by diplomatic negotiation and economic enterprise rather than by war. Schwarzenberg's Vienna had some claims to be a natural capital for the European Concert. By 1852 improved communications linked Vienna to the other great cities of the continent: by rail northwards to Prague and Berlin (whence lines already radiated to Brussels, Antwerp, Calais and Paris), eastwards to Warsaw and Budapest, and southwards to Laibach (although the first trans-Alpine route, through the Semmering Pass, was not formally opened until 1854); and by electric telegraph, not only to Berlin and Paris but indirectly with London, too, after the inauguration in November 1851 of a cable under the Channel. Schwarzenberg and his colleagues were fully alive to the significance of Vienna's key position in the centre of the continent. They showed greater interest than their predecessors in the lower Danube as a trade route and in dominating the Balkan lands as far east as Constantinople. The prospects for Austrian primacy in Europe were better in the winter of 1851–2 than at any moment since the Seven Years' War, and Schwarzenberg appeared the likeliest new leader of the European system.[1]

Unfortunately the gift of longevity, enjoyed by the Metternich, Radetzky and Wessenberg families, was denied the Schwarzenbergs. The great Field-Marshal Prince Karl Schwarzenberg, victor at Dresden and Leipzig, had died suddenly at 49; and now, on 5 April 1852, his nephew Prince Felix was felled by an apoplectic stroke as he buckled himself into a tight-fitting hussar uniform for the Easter court ball. Emperor Francis Joseph mourned the statesman who had arrested his monarchy's decline. At 21, however, he was determined to rule, not merely to reign; and he looked for a dutiful secretary of state, an Austrian Nesselrode, rather than a masterful leader of men. He believed he would find just such a Foreign Minister in the career diplomat Count Ferdinand Buol-Schauenstein.

Schwarzenberg appears to have thought highly of Buol, although his record was unimpressive: as envoy to Turin in 1847–8 he had failed to prevent Charles Albert from embracing the Italian liberal-national cause; as ambassador in St Petersburg from 1848 until 1850 he succeeded in offending Tsar Nicholas by his 'civilian bearing' during the interminable military reviews at Tsarskoe Selo. Buol had few illusions about his capacity for office. He had no intention of shaping Habsburg foreign policy without advice from the elder statesman who had befriended his father and appointed him to the diplomatic service in the first place. On the very day he became Foreign Minister he rode out to the Metternich villa on the Rennweg and sounded the opinions of the fallen Chancellor. By the end of that week Metternich was commenting at length on dispatches from the Austrian ambassador in London. Soon he was casting his eye over anything of interest from Paris, Dresden, or Berlin. Buol had enough confidence to handle St Petersburg himself – perhaps because the Tsar's ambassador in Vienna, Baron Meyendorff, was his own brother-in-law – but Metternich's influence was considerable throughout the remaining months of the year. He had no wish to take the centre of the diplomatic stage again; he did not even visit Buol in the Ballhausplatz until the following February; but foreign envoys recognised the familiar touch of Europe's eldest statesman and responded appropriately. At midsummer 1852 Otto von Bismarck, sent from Frankfurt to serve for a month in Vienna during the illness of Prussia's ambassador, took a carriage to the Rennweg villa at the first opportunity. When Tsar Nicholas paid a state visit to Francis Joseph later that year he called privately on Metternich within twenty-four hours of reaching Vienna and returned for further political discussions a few days later.[2]

Metternich's re-emergence made certain the brake was applied to policies begun by Schwarzenberg. He could still analyse problems but he was too out of touch to offer constructive ideas. Sometimes he seemed tediously preoccupied with comparatively trivial matters, such as whether the new Emperor of the French ought really to be styled 'Napoleon V', and his long homilies assumed that Austria could perpetuate the old Concert of Europe by postponing the search for answers to the German Question, the Italian Question, or the Eastern Question. Yet the experience of many decades made him alive to new dangers as soon as they began to trouble the diplomats. Earlier than any other public figure in Europe Metternich perceived the risk of war implicit in the rival claims of the Russian-backed Orthodox clergy and the French-backed Catholic clergy to protect the Palestinian Holy Places of the Turkish Empire. Gloomily he warned Buol that, as an instrument for disrupting peace, religious fanaticism was 'as old as the world itself'.[3] Buol, however, was unimpressed; Tsar Nicholas might be in earnest, for it was clear to every emissary to St Petersburg that the official trinity of Autocracy, Orthodoxy and Nationalism was one and indivisible; but it was hard to believe that Napoleon III's sense of mission rested on an alliance of Second Empire and Catholic Church.

There was nothing unusual in tension over the Holy Places. Louis XVIII's government had revived a Bourbon claim to speak out for Catholic rights in Jerusalem, Nazareth and Bethlehem in 1819, but had dropped the matter as soon as the next elections showed the countryside supporting the king's ministers. In 1842 Guizot claimed a French right to be consulted over maintenance of the fabric of the Church of the Holy Sepulchre, as if he wished to show that his Protestant upbringing did not preclude action on a traditional Roman Catholic issue. It is not surprising that ten years later the Austrians – and, for that matter, the British – assumed that once Louis Napoleon won popular support for his new imperial title from the clergy-dominated French provinces he, too, would lose interest in a sectarian contest for control of distant shrines. Only Tsar Nicholas affected to believe that Napoleon was deliberately, and insultingly, picking a quarrel with Russia. To Nicholas, long uneasy over the condition of the Turkish Empire, it seemed that each gesture of appeasement made by the Sultan provoked Napoleon into more extravagant demands, either for his church or for his empire. This sensitivity of Nicholas to the new imperial Bonapartism broadened the chronic wrangling of rival monks and churchmen into a new and critical phase of the Eastern Question. Ultimately the conflict of prestige in Constantinople led to the Crimean War.

In the spring and summer of 1852 France twice displayed naval might in order to secure concessions from the Turkish authorities: the three-decker ninety-gun warship *Charlemagne* was allowed up the Dardanelles and into the Bosphorus conveying the French ambassador back in state, and under steam power; and a squadron trained its guns on the city of Tripoli to force the Turkish pasha to return two French deserters to whom he had given sanctuary. These incidents exasperated the British as well as the Russians. Significantly, in a survey of the year's events drawn up at Christmas 1852, the British chargé d'affaires in Constantinople gave pride of place to the impression made on the Sultan's ministers by the arrival, six months previously, of the *Charlemagne* 'conveying successfully her mass of artillery and men against the most rapid currents . . . by the sole power of the screw'.[4] The point was not lost on the Tsar. He suggested to Nesselrode that, in face of the French menace, Britain and Russia should come closer together, as in 1840, and on this occasion he wished to draw up plans for the eventual partition of the Ottoman Empire. Nesselrode was uneasy. After quizzing the British ambassador on his government's attitude to the problems of Turkey he wrote a powerful memorandum in which he urged the Tsar not to put forward 'proposals for partition or plans for an uncertain future'. An approach to London, Nesselrode argued, would be 'both dangerous and utterly useless', possibly swaying the British into lasting hostility.[5]

The State Chancellor could hardly have spoken out more strongly. Like that other great survivor, Metternich, he had seen the warning signals. But Nicholas was convinced events were moving in his favour. He was delighted to learn that Lord Derby's Tory government had fallen in the last days of 1852, giving way to a Whig-Peelite coalition under the Earl of Aberdeen, with Lord John Russell as Foreign Secretary and an almost chastened Palmerston grappling with gout and the Home Office. Nicholas respected the Peelites and valued Aberdeen's judgement and good sense. On 9 January 1853 the Tsar's widowed sister-in-law, Grand Duchess Elena Pavlovna, celebrated her birthday with a dinner party in the Mikhailovsky Palace. Among her guests was the British ambassador, Sir Hamilton Seymour, and it was here, in this white-columned masterpiece, that Tsar Nicholas exchanged parting pleasantries with Seymour and made his famous comment likening Turkey to 'a sick man on our hands'. Almost casually he pointed out that it would be as well to make 'all the necessary arrangements' before the invalid 'slipped away from us'. The Tsar was genially benevolent and promised Seymour an early private audience.[6]

It is one of history's minor ironies that, within a matter of hours, the Russian court itself could say, 'We have a sick man on our hands'. For a week the Tsar was seriously ill, 'sweating violently' in what his wife described as an 'exhausting . . . salutary crisis' which anticipated in many details the fatal attack of influenza he was to sustain two years later. Only on 21 January was he strong enough to receive Seymour and so begin the series of conversations over the Eastern Question which were to continue intermittently for a couple of months and provide muddled Russophobes, during and after the Crimean War, with 'proof' of Tsarist cynicism and perfidy. In reality, Nicholas was careful to pay lip-service to Nesselrode's warning: he never presented Seymour with a clear-cut partition plan, alluding hypothetically to distant problems rather than focusing attention on immediate issues. Once again, as in 1839, the Tsar scorned any formal agreement. 'A general understanding . . . between gentlemen is sufficient', he told Seymour in the third week of February.[7]

Had the conversations taken place in a diplomatic void, with no other sign of Russian interest or activity in Turkey, they might have achieved Nicholas's purpose and dissipated the suspicion which prevented

Anglo-Russian collaboration. The Tsar believed that, despite his illness, he was taking great pains to reassure the British; they now knew he did not wish to destroy the Ottoman Empire by some precipitate act, that he would not revive the Byzantine Empire or create a Greater Greece and that, should Turkey disintegrate, he was prepared to allow Britain to take Egypt and Crete. But the British were far from convinced of his goodwill. During Nicholas's illness the Austrians prevented a Turkish invasion of Montenegro by the simple expedient of sending a special emissary to Constantinople with a ten-day ultimatum; and in February – at the very time Nicholas was striving for his 'gentleman's agreement' – the Russians resolved to follow the precedents of France and Austria by subjecting the Sultan and his ministers to a show of force. On 28 February a special envoy from the Tsar arrived in Constantinople, not the skilful veteran Prince Orlov (as both Nesselrode and Seymour had wished), but the arrogant Turcophobe soldier, Prince Alexander Menshikov. Even the warship which brought him to the Bosphorus was named *Gromovnik* (*Thunderer*).

Menshikov's instructions were drafted by Nesselrode: he was to secure the dismissal of Mehemet Fuad, the Foreign Minister who had given 'the Latins' rights at the Holy Places, and then conclude a convention with the Turks reasserting Orthodox privileges in Palestine and restricting the concessions accorded to the Roman Catholics to the Church of the Nativity. Finally he was to obtain formal acknowledgment from the Turks of Russia's right to protect the Sultan's Orthodox subjects throughout his empire, clergy and laity alike. Menshikov engineered the fall of Fuad by insulting him, the minister resigning in pique – as he was meant to do. The Russians even secured a compromise with the French and the Turks over the Palestinian Holy Places, a settlement which owed much to the mediation of Stratford Canning (now Lord Stratford de Redcliffe), who arrived back in Constantinople on 5 May 1853, after an absence of ten months. But the final demand, with its apparent right of protective intervention throughout the Sultan's domains, was too much for Turkish opinion to accept. For a fortnight Menshikov allowed the Turks, and the diplomatic corps in Constantinople, to see his fanatical loathing for every aspect of the Sultan's government – he had been castrated by Turkish round shot in the campaign of 1828–9 and his prejudice was traumatic in origin. At last, on 21 May he left for Sebastopol, frustrated and threatening vengeance on the Turks and on the British ambassador. Stratford, he alleged, had 'bewitched' the Sultan's ministers by his 'frantic activity'.[8]

'Our unhappy quarrel with the Turks has had such a deplorable issue – thanks to the infamies of Stratford Canning – that war is imminent', wrote Tsar Nicholas to his sister, Anna, a few days later.[9] But Nicholas was wrong on two counts: Stratford did not put direct pressure on the Sultan's Grand Council to reject Menshikov's proposals even though the new Turkish Foreign Minister, Reschid, mischievously sought to convince the Russians that he was to blame for the failure of negotiations; and there was still a good prospect of keeping the peace. For Menshikov's bombast alerted the Great Powers to the danger of general war, which no government at that time desired. Buol, prompted by Metternich, strained hard to win acceptance in London, Paris and St Petersburg as a neutral mediator, although Anglo-Austrian relations were at low level because of British resentment over Austrian measures against the property of political refugees, particularly the wealthy Lombards who had defied Radetzky in 1848–9. Nesselrode successfully restrained the Tsar from declaring war on Turkey as soon as Menshikov arrived home, and he was supported by Orlov and Paskievic, who feared an insurrection in Poland should the Russian army be bogged down in a Balkan campaign. British policy was indecisive, largely because Lord Clarendon (who, in a Cabinet reshuffle, succeeded Russell as Foreign Secretary at the end of February 1853) was acutely conscious of anti-Russian public feeling, while Aberdeen favoured collaboration between the Great Powers and 'their firm but friendly representations at St Petersburg'. To satisfy public opinion the Mediterranean fleet was ordered to sail from Malta on 2 June to an anchorage in Besika Bay on the Turkish Asiatic coast, 10 miles south of Kumkale and the entrance to the Dardanelles. The warships reached Besika Bay on 13 June; they were joined a day later by a French squadron from Toulon which had been moored in Greek waters off Salamis for the past nine weeks as a token of Napoleon III's continued interest in the power struggle at Constantinople.[10]

Alexander Kinglake, who began his eight-volume history of the Crimean War while the sun of the Second Empire was at its zenith, claimed that Napoleon III deliberately provoked a conflict between the Powers in order to gain new triumphs for France and avenge his uncle's humiliation by the armies of the Fourth Coalition in 1813–14. This theory distorts Napoleon III's objectives. The Second Empire certainly responded to the will of liberal patriots, who respected the revived imperial army and navy as guarantors of orderly society at home and protectors of France's influence abroad; but this dual role required victories of prestige, political successes which benefited French trade, rather than the glory and misery of fresh battle honours. Napoleon and Drouyn, who was Foreign Minister for the first three years of the Empire, wanted France to cut a decisive figure in Europe's affairs, preferably in partnership with Great Britain, who had no continental ambitions; but they were concerned not so much with avenging the great Napoleon's defeat as with revising the peace treaty that followed it. Ideally the Second Empire sought to change the map of Europe by agreement round a conference table, with Paris rather than London or Vienna accepted as the centre of Europe's diplomacy. What Napoleon provoked in 1853 was not a war but a crisis, which called for solution. Throughout the six months which followed the Menshikov fiasco Napoleon's diplomatic strategy sought to preserve peace, sometimes to the exasperation of his ministers.

Early in July the Russians crossed the River Pruth and occupied the Danubian Principalities of Moldavia and Wallachia. They had done so before, as a precautionary measure to curb incipient Romanian nationalism in July 1848 and had remained south of the Pruth for two and a half years. But this time they intended the occupation to put pressure on the Turks; Nesselrode made it clear that Russian troops would hold the

Principalities until the Sultan accepted all Menshikov's demands. The Russian action infuriated Buol, for it left the lower Danube waterway under control of the Tsar's troops. Hurriedly Buol convened a conference of Austrian, British, French and Prussian diplomats who, within a fortnight, produced a compromise intended to settle the Russo–Turkish dispute. This 'Vienna Note' was accepted by the Russians but rejected by the Sultan's Grand Council. Turkish resistance was in part stiffened by the attitude of Stratford de Redcliffe, who found it hard to conceal his belief that the compromise unduly favoured Russia. But the Sultan's ministers were also influenced by a general elation which followed the arrival of Egyptian soldiers and warships to strengthen the defences of the Bosphorus.

Turkey's obstinacy gave Russia a moral advantage. This was, however, soon dissipated by publication in a Prussian newspaper of a confidential letter from Nesselrode which indicated that the Russians had convinced themselves the Vienna Note would give them the protectorate over the Sultan's Christian subjects which they had sought since the spring. The British and the French responded to this allegedly 'violent interpretation' of the Vienna Note by authorising their naval commanders to leave Besika Bay, where vessels could easily drag their anchors in a westerly gale, and pass through the Dardanelles, in defiance of the Straits Convention. Stratford de Redcliffe still hoped for a diplomatic solution to the crisis and did not summon the fleet until 20 October, more than a fortnight after receiving permission from London to bring the warships into the Straits. Nothing, however, could quell the fanatical anti-Russian fury in the streets of Constantinople or hold back the Sultan's commanders in the field. At dawn on 23 October 1853 Turkish troops were silently ferried across the Danube and attacked Russian outposts facing Tutrakan, the nearest point on the great river to Bucharest.[11]

Russians and Turks had fought each other in four long campaigns over the previous ninety years; and only once – at Navarino – had other Great Powers participated in the contest. Now, in the autumn of 1853, both Nicholas I and Napoleon III sought to prevent the war from spreading. The Tsar travelled to Olmütz, Warsaw and Potsdam for talks with Francis Joseph, Frederick William IV and their ministers. While he was at Olmütz, he encouraged Buol to publish a revised version of the Vienna Note, although in his further conversations he tried to tempt his old Münchengrätz partners into a formal military alliance, as a means of deterring France and Britain from intervening in the Black Sea.[12] Napoleon was ready to accept Buol's Olmütz compromise and join the British in compelling the Sultan to fall into line with the peacemakers but, for the sake of French prestige, he would not make the first gesture of appeasement. In his struggle to raise the diplomatic status of France he placed great emphasis on collaboration with Great Britain. Having posed the Eastern Question in its newest form by championing the 'Latins' in Palestine in the first place, he was now content to follow Aberdeen's lead in seeking a peaceful solution to the crisis.

Aberdeen, however, could give no lead, either to his colleagues or his extemporised French ally. Alone among the great names around the

Cabinet table – Russell, Palmerston, Clarendon, Granville, Gladstone – he had seen for himself the carnage of a European battlefield, and he hated war from the depths of his soul. Moreover the crisis of 1853–4 offended Aberdeen's sense of enlightened achievement; he believed the aristocratic diplomats of his generation had created a Concert of Europe, an entity which could rationalise disputes into settlement by negotiation or deter potential aggressors by the united opposition of the Powers; there had to be a way of restraining Russia short of war. Palmerston, Russell and Clarendon did not share his hesitancies, nor did public opinion, which was for the first time showing the aggressive self-consciousness that was to build the most extensive of empires over the following ninety years. It was a basic Whig assumption that the autocrats who had repressed Poles and Magyars could not be trusted. 'The proposition from Olmütz is intended only to deceive', Russell bluntly told Clarendon. 'If Nicholas, or Nesselrode or Buol were to act honestly all might be settled in half an hour.'[13] And Clarendon agreed that Buol, in particular, was a weak character, overshadowed by the personality of his brother-in-law, the Russian ambassador in Vienna. This prejudice against Buol was groundless, as the British ambassadors in Vienna and St Petersburg emphasised on several occasions, but it persisted in London until Russell met Buol in person in March 1853 and told Clarendon, somewhat naïvely, that he was 'much impressed' by the Austrian's sincerity. By then it was too late to use Buol's unique position as a means to preserve the old Concert of Europe.[14]

Once the Turks had crossed the Danube at Tutrakan, there were three courses of action available for Aberdeen personally: to see that Britain gave military and naval backing to the Sultan, in the hope that a resolute commitment would induce the Tsar to drop Russia's demand for a protectorate and come to the conference table; to disavow support of the Turks for having precipitated the war; or to resign as Prime Minister, leaving the conduct of policy to Palmerston and the Whig hawks. But Aberdeen, largely for domestic reasons, was determined to sustain the fragile Whig-Peelite coalition. Weakly, he did nothing and waited on events. On 30 November six Russian warships destroyed a Turkish flotilla in the harbour of Sinope. News of the Russian victory, magnified by the Press, made Sinope appear as a decisive engagement which tilted the naval balance in Russia's favour. Peace, *The Times* declared on Tuesday 13 December, was 'no longer compatible with the honour and dignity of the country'; on Friday Palmerston's supporters found that their *Morning Post* condemned Sinope as 'a violent outrage' to which the only true English answer was 'immediate war'. Aberdeen refused to allow the newspapers to stampede him. But Napoleon's ministers, too, were exerting pressure on their reluctant emperor and, over the weekend, the British government gained the impression that France might act alone if Aberdeen continued to prevaricate. This seems to have been a groundless fear and, as if to emphasise Napoleon's desire for peace, the Empress Eugénie invited the Russian ambassador to be her opening partner at the New Year's Day ball of 1854. Yet only three days later the Anglo-French fleet sailed through the Bosphorus and into the Black Sea with orders to safeguard the Turkish shores from a Russian attack. Negotiations to keep the peace of Europe continued for another ten weeks, with Napoleon III vainly seeking to persuade the Russians to evacuate the Danubian Principalities as a first stage towards a settlement. This final initiative was, perhaps, primarily a gesture of propaganda, an attempt to have Paris rather than Vienna accepted as the natural diplomatic centre of the continent. It was certainly too late to check the drift into war. Britain, France and Turkey concluded a formal alliance against Russia on 12 March 1854. France declared war on Russia on 27 March, Great Britain a day later.[15]

No other war gestated for so long. Yet it was by no means clear why at that moment the Forty Years' Peace came to an end. Queen Victoria assured Aberdeen the war had been 'brought about' by 'the selfishness and ambition of *one* man and his servants', the sovereign and ministers of the Russian Empire, a belief shared by many of her subjects. Within a few months responsibility for the war was being laid on the shoulders of Stratford de Redcliffe, who was held to have encouraged the Turks to reject all overtures for peace from the Great Powers. This myth, together with the later Victorian conviction that the diabolical Napoleon III was to blame, has been demolished by modern historical writers.[16] There is no doubt that the French stimulated the renewed Russian interest in the Ottoman Empire by championing the Latin cause in the Holy Places dispute, that French commercial interests in the Levant benefited from Napoleon's collaboration with the Sultan, and that the Emperor was pleased by any crisis which challenged the states system based on the Treaty of Vienna. But no one person and no one country was responsible for allowing the Powers to drift into war. The notion of a general crusade of liberal Europe against Russian tyranny had long appealed to Radicals in the West, and it is significant that Walewski – French ambassador in London from 1851 to 1855 and a natural son of the great Napoleon – first entered high politics as a spokesman for the Poles, trying as early as 1832 to win over the British Prime Minister to the anti-Tsarist cause. The Crimean War was never directly concerned with liberating the nationalities along Russia's borders, nor did it become popular with England's Radicals. For, as Cobden complained, the main issue was that 'mischievous delusion', the balance of power. The British, the French and ultimately the Austrians convinced themselves that the accepted restraints of the new international order applied as much to the Near East as to the nearer West; the Russians, on the other hand, assumed that the affairs of Turkey were extra-European, akin to the rivalries of central Asia rather than to the unquestionably European problems of Lombardy-Venetia or the Danish Duchies. Among contemporaries Napoleon III came nearest to 'explaining' the war. 'Sovereignty over Constantinople means sovereignty over the Mediterranean', he told his Senate and Legislative Chamber as the expeditionary force began to muster. 'Why are we going to Constantinople? We are going there with England in order to defend the cause of the Sultan and equally to protect the rights of the Christians; we are going there to uphold the freedom of the seas and to safeguard our rightful influence in the Mediterranean.'[17]

The first allied troops landed at Varna in June, prepared to hold the line of the Balkan mountains against a Russian assault on Constantinople. But the Balkans soon ceased to be a war zone. Throughout the first seven months of the year, diplomatic negotiations had continued intermittently in Vienna, the gifted Prince Orlov adding his experience to the efforts of Meyendorff and Gorchakov (who succeeded Meyendorff as ambassador in July). The Russians hoped to secure the armed neutrality, and sympathetic backing, of the two other conservative monarchies, Prussia and Austria, but they were disappointed. Francis Joseph, influenced by Metternich's advice, insisted that Buol should safeguard the lower Danube basin and stay out of the war until Austria's intervention could become decisive – an updated version of Metternich's policy in 1813. In April 1854 Austria concluded a treaty of mutual defence with Prussia, fear of isolation drawing the German rivals together now that they had repudiated the Münchengrätz link with Russia. In July Buol concentrated on securing a statement of war aims from the British and the French (who assumed that his activity would be followed by Austrian participation in the war) and on securing from the Russians and the Turks the creation of a neutral buffer in the Danubian Principalities (which would be occupied by Austria pending a final peace settlement). On 6 August Buol seemed to have gained a diplomatic triumph: the allies defined their war aims in the 'Four Points'; and Gorchakov informed Buol that Russia had evacuated Moldavia and Wallachia and that Austrians troops might move in. From August 1854 to March 1857 the Austrian army stood guard along 1,400 miles of the Danube, from Passau to the marshy delta. There seemed to Austria no advantage in entering the war when it was possible to make such gains by keeping out of it. Point One and Point Two of the allied programme – a European guarantee of the Principalities and free navigation of the Danube – were now entirely dependent on Austria's will. Point Three (revision of the Straits Convention 'in the interests of the European Balance of Power') and Point Four (a collective guarantee of the status of the Christians in Turkey) could be discussed at greater length by the belligerents and the two neutral allies, Austria and Prussia; and where better for a conference than Vienna?[18]

Buol was therefore the first beneficiary from the Crimean War. He was also largely responsible for ensuring that the Crimea was, indeed, the theatre of war. For, deprived of a Danube front against Russia in Wallachia, the British and French slowly, reluctantly and incompetently committed themselves to a seaborne military expedition against the main base of Russia's Black Sea fleet; and from September 1854 the fortress of Sebastopol was besieged for 349 days before young veterans of the Imperial Guard hoisted the French tricolour from the smoking ruins of the Korabdelnaya Admiralty buildings to end a folly which cost besiegers and besieged the lives of almost a quarter of a million men. British public opinion, frustrated by the elusiveness of victory, turned against Lord Aberdeen and forced him from office at the end of January 1855. The unfortunate earl was blamed not for the catastrophe of being at war, for which his weak leadership was seriously at fault, but for the shortcomings of the army and navy, the responsibility of a system rather than of any single government. Aberdeen was succeeded as Prime Minister by Palmerston, who was popularly supposed to have disapproved of every measure of the outgoing administration, of which he had been a member since its inception. Legend commended him as a pugilistic, though septuagenarian, war leader.

He began, however, with a step towards peace. Lord John Russell set out for Vienna on 26 February, briefed by Palmerston and Clarendon, who remained Foreign Secretary. Russell was the first Cabinet minister entrusted with the authority of a plenipotentiary at a conference abroad since Wellington went to Verona in 1822 and when he reached Vienna six days later, after talks in Paris, the prospects for peace looked good. The Austrians were eager to end the war, not least because Piedmont-Sardinia had joined the allies in January 1855 in a bid to secure Anglo-French goodwill for the next round in the long contest with the Habsburgs for supremacy in Italy. Buol was able to tell Russell that Russia, too, seemed now to desire peace. Nicholas I had died on 2 March and the new Tsar, his son Alexander II, had indicated that he would accept honourable terms based on the Four Points rather than allow the war to drag on. Not until several days later did Francis Joseph receive a stern letter from Alexander blaming the man whom his father had thought 'a faithful friend and ally' for having come 'closer to our enemies' and threatened a 'fratricidal conflict' between the armies of Russia and Austria.[19]

Yet, despite this ominous note, the Vienna Conference opened under Buol's presidency on 15 March. Three weeks later, on 6 April, the French Foreign Minister, Drouyn de Lhuys, travelled to Austria convinced that the talks in Vienna would bring peace back to Europe. The outstanding personality at the conference was not Buol, Russell, or Drouyn but the Russian plenipotentiary, Alexander Gorchakov, who as a young diplomat attended the Congresses of Laibach and Verona only to rusticate for fourteen years as envoy in Stuttgart and Frankfurt before coming to Austria as ambassador. Gorchakov poured scorn on the initial allied attempt to secure the neutralisation of the Black Sea. He argued that this had not been one of the original issues in dispute and that it could only be conceded by a defeated Power, which Russia was not – Gorchakov's cousin was commander-in-chief in the Crimea at the time. On the other hand Gorchakov showed some flexibility, and Buol believed he was prepared to compromise over the future size of the Black Sea fleet and to join Britain, Austria, France and Prussia in a guarantee of Turkey's independence. These proposals were embodied in a plan drawn up by Buol on 15 April and accepted, with modifications, by Drouyn and Russell during discussions held in the following week. But Napoleon III, Walewski, Palmerston and Clarendon were opposed to the Buol Plan, or indeed to any compromise Gorchakov might offer. Public opinion, they believed, demanded the spoils of a victory and not merely a negotiated settlement. 'Were we to adopt Buol's plan', Clarendon wrote to the ambassador in Vienna privately, 'none of us would feel safe from attack in the streets, and serve us right.'[20] The British and French governments took the unprecedented step of rejecting their plenipotentiaries' work. Drouyn promptly resigned as Foreign Minister. Russell stayed on in the Cabinet as Colonial Secretary until early July when, finding his position an embarrassment, he too left office. The war, so near an end in April, still had six months to go before the guns fell silent.

The failure of the conference had the incidental effect of confirming the primacy of France among the European states. If the home governments could disavow such distinguished envoys as Drouyn and Russell, there was no hope of settling the conflict at Vienna or any neutral capital. Napoleon III, though persuaded to give up the foolish idea of going to the Crimea as supreme commander, reached the peak of his personal influence on events. He was fêted in Windsor and London during April. In August he had the satisfaction, denied all the Valois and Bourbon kings of France, of welcoming a reigning sovereign of England on a state visit to Paris. As at Eu in 1843 and 1845, the Foreign Secretary accompanied Victoria and Albert to France.[21] Clarendon discussed questions of peace and war with Napoleon and Walewski, who had succeeded Drouyn at the Foreign Ministry. The French – like the Russians – were angry with Austria; they believed Buol had committed Austria to war against Russia if his conference failed to bring peace, and, so far from going to war, the Austrians actually stood down reservists at midsummer. While the British were planning for another twelve months of war and reviving old projects for expeditions to the Baltic in collaboration with Sweden, Napoleon was looking forward to the peace conference and the happier task of redrawing the map of Europe, erasing here and there the frontier lines of 1815. Something should be done for Poland, the French told the British, and Piedmont would need rewarding for the expeditionary force which that spring had brought 'the flag of Italy' to the trenches outside Sebastopol. Above all, peace should be made in Paris where, on the Quai d'Orsay, an impressive Foreign Ministry was at last nearing completion.

When Sebastopol fell in September, the French behaved as though the war was as good as ended; the last battles, and in particular the storming of the Malakoff fort, were a triumph of French arms. The British, repulsed in these final attempts to break into the city, were prepared to mount further amphibious operations in the Black Sea. Alexander II, too, was willing to continue the war and spent six weeks that autumn in Nicolaev supervising the construction of a base to replace Sebastopol. But back in St Petersburg, Nesselrode was already telling the Austrian ambassador that Russia would listen with interest to any peace proposals offered to her. In November Walewski secretly contacted the Saxon envoy in Paris (who was Nesselrode's son-in-law) and proposed a settlement based on neutralisation of the Black Sea and territorial concessions in Bessarabia and the Caucasus. At the same time – with another characteristic twist of family diplomacy – Napoleon III's half-brother, Count Charles de Morny (who was also Talleyrand's grandson), secretly contacted Gorchakov in Vienna. Even so, it was only under an Austrian threat of an immediate declaration of war and a warning that Prussia might enter the conflict that Alexander II agreed to make peace.[22] On 1 February hostilities formally ceased with the signing of a preliminary convention in Vienna, but Palmerston still growled belligerently, and the British subsequently imposed a relatively short time-limit on the armistice.

Napoleon III had his way. A conference opened in Paris on 25 February

1856, soon being elevated to a 'Congress' and turning its attention to Europe in general once the peace treaty was signed on 30 March (a day before the armistice was due to expire). Procedure owed something to the Vienna precedents of 1815. The host country's Foreign Minister again presided, Walewski showing – at least in his dealings with Britain – some of the dexterity of Metternich at his prime. France, too, supplied the Secretary-General, Vincente Benedetti, a conscientious diplomat recently at Constantinople who bustled agitatedly through the unfamiliar new salons with black brows furrowed, as though determined to leave some mark on history. He was to have his moment of fame, at Ems in 1870. The emperor remained in the background, present only on gala occasions.

The foreign delegates were familiar figures. At 75 Nesselrode was too decrepit to cross Europe and was preparing to hand over the Russian Foreign Ministry in April to Gorchakov (whom he personally detested). Prince Orlov, now entering his 70s, headed the Russian delegation; among the military orders on his green and gold uniform, he defiantly wore miniatures set in diamonds of the three Tsars whom he had served as soldier and diplomat. The second Russian envoy was Brunnow, from the London embassy, but Orlov depended personally on Peter Shuvalov, a young cavalry officer hotfoot from the Crimea, whom Orlov was grooming for high office in the state. Buol was Francis Joseph's plenipotentiary, while Clarendon tried to be a latterday Castlereagh, no easy task with Palmerston rather than Lord Liverpool as Prime Minister. At first British indignation over Prussia's refusal to enter the war denied Frederick William representation, but (on Buol's insistence) Manteuffel and the Prussian minister to Paris were admitted to the fourth week of the Congress when the Straits Convention, of which Prussia was a signatory, came up for discussion. The westernised Mehemet Fuad, Menshikov's old adversary, was a recipient of decisions rather than an active spokesman for Turkey. Buol would have liked the delegates from Sardinia-Piedmont similarly cut down to size; it was, he maintained to Clarendon, essential not to 'erect Sardinia into a first-class Power, which could disturb the settled order of things in Europe'. Clarendon, however, vigorously supported the Piedmontese, whom public opinion in Britain greatly favoured. Their principal delegate at the Congress was Count Cavour, Prime Minister and Foreign Minister since 1862, a man of deceptive appearance, the underlying fanaticism in his political beliefs showing itself at the conference table only when his ill-fitting rimless spectacles slipped down his nose and gave his myopic vision a fiercely concentrated stare. For Cavour everything was subordinated to the need to unify Italy under the House of Savoy. Within a few days of reaching Paris he even (as he said) 'enrolled in the diplomatic service' a beautiful 18-year-old cousin 'to flirt with the Emperor and seduce him' in the belief that this might offset the influence of the pro-papal Walewski on Napoleon. Her cousin's agreement accorded well with the Countess of Castiglione's skills and desires; but there is no evidence that it furthered the cause of a united Italy.[23]

There were fewer of these extraneous political allurements in Paris than at the earlier congresses. Napoleon wanted a speedy settlement, not least because Morny and his friends on the Paris Bourse thought a peaceful Russia would prove a rich field for investment. The British approach was cruder. Palmerston and Clarendon had hoped the peace treaty would deprive Russia of all capacity for aggression. They were disappointed; Russia was placed under restraint, not destroyed. Theoretically the Black Sea became as neutralised as any Swisss lake – not a warship on its waters, not a fort, an arsenal, or a naval dockyard around its shores. Southern Bessarabia was ceded to Moldavia, thus denying Russia riparian contact with the navigable Danube – a waterway safeguarded by the creation of two international commissions, to clear the channels of the delta and determine rules of navigation and police control along its course. The British were satisfied that a check had been administered to Russia's thrust into Asia by the return to Turkey of the key Caucasian fortress of Kars, which the Russians had stormed in 1829 and again in 1855. Clarendon was also gratified by a diplomatic success in the Baltic: the Russian-held Aaland Islands, a strategic archipelago at the entrance to the Gulf of Bothnia, were neutralised.

Yet Palmerston remained uneasy over Russia's future intentions. He realised the Treaty of Paris imposed superficial humiliations, and these he thought would invite retaliation, possibly in seven years, perhaps in ten. In the third week of the Congress the Prime Minister wrote to Clarendon voicing his suspicions; Russia, he thought, had made peace in order that the new Tsar could develop his empire's vast resources, 'preparing at leisure the means of making war by and by'.[24] Palmerston welcomed a proposal from Buol that Britain and France should join Austria in guaranteeing the independence and integrity of the Ottoman Empire, the three Powers declaring that any attack on Turkey would be seen as an immediate cause of war. The French agreed to the guarantee with considerable misgivings and the Triple Treaty was concluded in the third week of April only when Walewski won acceptance for the principle that it should not be aimed specifically against Russia. The Foreign Minister's concern heightened Anglo-Austrian fears that the Congress would be followed by a 'Tilsit reconciliation' between the old enemies.

The Congress of Paris confirmed the primacy of France. It did not, however, leave a neo-Bonapartist imprint on the map of Europe. Napoleon was still hoping for a drastic reshaping of the continent as late as the spring of 1855, when Walewski took over from Drouyn. But the Congress was an essentially conservative gathering, the delegates for the most part striving to bring harmony back to the European Concert. In February, before the Congress opened, Napoleon received Buol and briefly mentioned to him the Polish problem. It was a topic of concern to Palmerston, too; he had even suggested, twelve months earlier, that the time had come for reviving 'a substantive Kingdom of Poland'. Polish exiles waited expectantly in Paris. But, in April, Orlov asked that the Polish Question should not be raised at the conference table as it would hinder his sovereign's efforts to improve conditions in the old 'Congress Kingdom', and the British and French accepted his request – although more probably to discourage the Partitioning Powers from coming together again than to spare Alexander II political embarrassment. The

Romanian émigrés, making much capital of their nation's Latin origin, fared better than the Poles. Wallachia and Moldavia, nominally restored to Turkish suzerainty, were permitted 'independent national administrations', assemblies which successfully brought a Romanian state into being over the following six years. The Principalities continued to enjoy Napoleon's patronage until the fall of the Second Empire.[25]

Most surprisingly of all, the Congress left the political system of Italy unchanged: Austrian troops still kept order in Tuscany and the Romagna while the Habsburg double-headed eagle flew from the battlements of Milan and over the Palazzo Ducale in Venice. Cavour had hoped at least to secure the cession of Parma; but the Crimean expedition gained no territory for Sardinia-Piedmont. However, for one day in the nine weeks of the Congress the Powers discussed the Italian Question. On Tuesday 8 April Cavour had the satisfaction of hearing the British Foreign Secretary indict papal misgovernment, the Austrian protective occupation of the Romagna and the injustice of Ferdinand II's repressive rule in Sicily and the south. Clarendon's speech – strangely intemperate for a minister proud of his diplomatic finesse – served notice to Europe: the focus of public attention in Britain, more concerned now with foreign affairs than in Victoria's early years, was moving away from Constantinople to Rome and Naples. Over Italy the British upper classes held strong views, the product of a classical curriculum, a traditional prejudice against popes and a taste for the poems of Shelley, Clough and the Brownings. After that Tuesday's memorable sitting, Cavour believed he could win the armed support of Britain for a war of liberation in Italy, a mistake compounded from wishful thinking and Clarendon's genially polite table talk. But Cavour was justified in telling parliament in Turin that the Congress had laid 'the cause of Italy before the bar of public opinion'.[26] Napoleon III, who had supported Italian nationalism in his conspiratorial youth, readily perceived the significance of that Tuesday's sitting and the publicity given to Clarendon's speech in the British, French and liberal Italian Press. He sensed that in the peninsula France could achieve a diplomatic masterstroke which would consolidate her leadership of Europe. But victory in the Crimea left the fundamental contradictions of Bonapartism as starkly exposed as ever. Catholicism, which had served Napoleon well in the Levant, was a hindrance in Latium where a French garrison still protected Pius IX from his compatriots. How was he to make his policy coherent? The dilemma plagued Napoleon III as he fumbled between the advice of Walewski, of Morny and of the Empress Eugénie. It was a dilemma he never resolved.

9 Subverting the System, 1857–61

It has long been recognised that the Crimean War and the peace congress which followed it form the great divide in nineteenth-century diplomatic history. Before 1854 the statesmen of the continent pursued, not always successfully, an ideal of peace through collective responsibility; after 1856, for at least fifteen years, they were ready again to choose war as an instrument of policy, reverting to the practices of pre-Congress Europe as though there had never been any concept of public law between the nations. During those fifteen years there were four separate conflicts on European soil, each of which involved at least two Great Powers. Moreover, this belligerency was not confined to Europe: the British sent military expeditions against Persia and China; and French armies, too, were in action in south-east Asia and in Mexico. It is true that the longest and bloodiest wars of the period – the five-year struggle of Paraguay against Brazil, Argentina and Uruguay and the 'irrepressible conflict' which racked the American Union – were not caused by the machinations of Europe's statesmen. At least in Europe the new breed of 'realist' political leaders were determined on localised wars of brief duration, for no government was prepared to see the economy disrupted or the social order imperilled by long campaigns; and there was as great a need for competent statecraft within the Chancelleries to check the spread of the fighting as there was for effective planning in the War Ministries. But if the work of diplomats and their chiefs proliferated, the prevailing mood in the Chancelleries differed from earlier decades. It seemed now to mock the conscious striving for a Concert of the Great Powers which had, at times, uplifted the labours of Aberdeen, Nesselrode, Metternich and even the younger Palmerston.

John Morley, completing his famous biography of Palmerston's Chancellor of the Exchequer soon after the turn of the century, could find nothing of merit in either the war aims or the peace settlement of 1856: 'The vindication of the standing European order proved so ineffectual that the Crimean War was only the sanguinary prelude to a vast subversion of the whole system of European States,' he wrote. Yet, at the time, Gladstone was himself more optimistic. In Paris Lord Clarendon had received a delegation from the British Peace Society and, to please them, secured the insertion in the Peace Treaty of Protocol 23, which 'expressed the desire that States . . . before appealing to arms, should have recourse . . . to the good offices of a friendly Power'. This innovation impressed Gladstone. 'The principal nations of Europe have given an emphatic utterance to sentiments which contain at least a qualified disapproval of the results of war', he declared. But Clarendon's initiative fell some way short of the pacifists' proposals. They had asked for 'some system of international arbitration'; the protocol merely voiced a pious plea for mediation. Not once in any later crisis of the century did a Great Power pause, on the brink of war, and seek the 'good offices' of a mediatory neighbour as Clarendon had hoped, although the neutrals themselves came forward as peacemakers on several occasions after the fighting had begun.[1]

Common sense urged an era of peace after the tale of muddle in high places which was the fruit of victory in the Crimea. Economic forces seemed to militate against war in Europe. Less than eight years after the fall of Sebastopol two-fifths of the shares in tne principal Russian railway company were held by British investors and most of the remainder by the French, whose emperor had given his special patronage to the Crédit Mobilier, the financial house controlling the whole enterprise. There were close commercial links, rather than industrial rivalry, between British firms and the cities of northern Germany and the Rhineland. The Habsburg Empire was as dependent as the Russian Empire on foreign capital, mostly French and British, while Prussia and France concluded a commercial treaty in 1862, only eight weeks before Bismarck became head of government. One traditionally radical group in British politics, the survivors of the Anti-Corn Law League, believed it was possible to create a new relationship between the nations based on the need for open commerce. Bright and Cobden, spurned for their anti-war agitation during the Sebastopol campaign, could count on a wide following in northern England and the Midlands three years after it was over. When Bright told the people of Birmingham that an active foreign policy, with 'its regard for "the liberties of Europe" and its excessive love for "the balance of power"', was 'neither more nor less than a gigantic system of outdoor relief for the aristocracy of Great Britain', his words were received with sympathetic laughter and applause. Technically, Bright's scorn was already outdated by events, for in 1856 Clarendon made entry into the foreign service subject to competitive examination in a half-hearted attempt to bring new, and non-blue, blood into the diplomatic system; but the public, as a whole, continued to share Bright's suspicion of foreign affairs and of the socially narrow élite who shaped policy towards other governments. People in London or Newcastle might fête Garibaldi on his visits to England, enterprising salesmen even appropriating his name for a blouse and a biscuit, but only a few eccentrics so admired their hero that they wished to intervene in continental affairs. When Cobden roundly declared 'No foreign politics', there were plenty who welcomed his cryptic veto, whatever it meant; not everyone found the intrusive bluster of Palmerston's premiership congenial. Cobden went so far as to claim that 'Free Trade is God's diplomacy, and there is no other way of uniting people in bonds of peace'.[2] In this conviction, and with Palmerston's backing, he responded to Napoleon III's initiative for an Anglo-French 'Free Trade Treaty' during the winter of 1859–60. The agreement brought material gain and also eased tension between the two former allies over Napoleon's Italian policy. Cobden, it seemed, was proved right. Only after 1865 – the year in which both Cobden and Palmerston died – did the mounting productivity of American, German and Russian markets challenge Britain's economic pre-eminence and question Bright and Cobden's assumption that Free Trade was 'the great panacea'. In their constructive idealism there was certainly no sign of the 'vast subversion' of the states system which Morley was retrospectively to condemn.

Nor, indeed, was there in the diplomacy of defeated Russia during this period. Here the most significant change was the retirement of Nesselrode, after forty years at his desk overlooking the great square before the Winter Palace. On the eve of resignation he drafted a final testament to guide Alexander II into the postwar world: the Tsar should develop his empire's 'moral and material forces' by concentrating on internal affairs rather than following a forward policy beyond its borders. Gorchakov, who formally took over the Foreign Ministry in April 1856, did not agree with all his predecessor's recommendations, in particular his claim that Russia's security was better served by a Vienna–St Petersburg axis than by reconciliation with France, but he too told the Tsar it was essential 'to heal by domestic measures the wounds inflicted by the war'. Like most Russian landowners who had long lived abroad, Gorchakov favoured emancipation of the serfs and reforms which would modernise the administrative system, the army and the judiciary. He was himself prepared to bring a new look to the Foreign Ministry, while waiting patiently to realise his ambition of encouraging the victors in the Crimea to fall out amongst themselves and thus secure revision of the Treaty of Paris. Some five months after taking office he thought it necessary to explain the passivity of his policies abroad in a circular dispatch sent to every embassy and legation. Characteristically, since he had nothing constructive to propose, Gorchakov elegantly turned an epigram. 'Russia, they say, is sulking', he wrote; 'Russia does not sulk; Russia communes with herself.'[3]

This image of autocracy plunged in meditation gave Alexander II the interlude he desired. He established committees which eventually freed his empire from the inhumanity and inefficiency of serfdom, set up regional self-government and looked to filling the emptiness of Russia's plains by railway enterprise and commerce. By comparison, Gorchakov's reorganisation of his own department was a modest venture. Entrance to the ministry and to the diplomatic service was, from 1860 onwards, made dependent on passing a written examination, although good connections and impeccable French eased the process. At the same time, the day-to-day running of the Chancellery was entrusted to three senior civil servants, nominated by the minister, and destined to exercise considerable influence over the wording of dispatches and instruction for some fifteen to twenty years. The Asiatic Department of the ministry – specialists who thought they knew every minaret from Sarajevo to Kabul and every pass across the imperial frontiers from the Caucasus to Sinkiang – defied the attempts of Gorchakov and his 'Europeans' to control its work and personnel. Significantly, the Asiatic Department remained staffed overwhelmingly by Russians, headed successively by the explorer Igor Kovalevsky, General Ignatyev and Petr Stremoukhov: the Chancellery, on the other hand, was dominated by Vladimir Westmann (a Baltic German), Alexander Jomini (a Swiss general's son) and Andrei

Hamburger (whose family were apparently Frankfurters by origin). Despite Gorchakov's insistence that now, at last, a minister of good Russian stock determined foreign affairs, his closest collaborators were as alien to the Orthodox Slav tradition as the advisers of Alexander I during the Vienna Congress. This 'European' and 'Russian' division within the ministry assumed some importance in the late 1860s and 1870s, not least because of the Press campaigns of the nationalist Moscow publicist, Mikhail Katkov, a proto-Hearst or proto-Northcliffe in Russian journalism; but in his earliest years as minister, Gorchakov found a more serious challenge to his authority came from other members of the Tsar's family. Alexander II's brother, Grand Duke Constantine, commanding admiral of the Russian navy, at times tried to pursue a foreign policy totally independent of the ministry. This trait of the Grand Duke was so marked that the British ambassador (who, as Lord Kimberley, was later to become Foreign Secretary) thought Constantine's behaviour worth a long dispatch to London. The widowed empress, Alexandra Feodorovna, sister of the King of Prussia, supported Constantine's waywardness until her death in November 1860.[4]

Prussia, like Russia, embarked on a 'new era' in the aftermath of the Crimean War, although its consequences were less apparent to outside observers than the 'great reforms' in St Petersburg. Frederick William IV was incapacitated by a stroke in October 1857, the responsibilities of government passing to his 60-year-old brother, William, Prince of Prussia. During the war the prince had vainly urged the king and his chief minister, Manteuffel, to seek agreements with Palmerston and Napoleon III and so help impose peace on Russia. In so far as he had any clear ideas on foreign policy, the prince favoured a British alliance and when, in the autumn of 1858, he became Regent, he purged the government of the ultra-conservatives who had backed Manteuffel since the Olmütz Punctation eight years before. Otto von Bismarck, still Prussian envoy to the Diet of the German Confederation in Frankfurt, hoped for ministerial advancement. He presented the prince with an unsolicited 92-page memorandum urging him to seek support from German nationalist sentiment by pitting the Prussian state against the multinational Austrian Empire. The new Regent, however, wanted no adventurous escapades. He did, indeed, promote Bismarck, but not to government office. He was sent to St Petersburg as minister-plenipotentiary, 'placed in cold storage on the Neva', as Bismarck himself complained. The Foreign Ministry went to Alexander von Schleinitz, who had held the post briefly in 1848 and 1849–50, a competent quill-pusher, personal friend of the Regent and admirer of English ways and institutions.[5]

Schleinitz's political outlook was not unlike that of Gorchakov – nor, for that matter, of Buol-Schauenstein, whom Francis Joseph persisted in retaining at the Ballhausplatz. Each of these three ministers saw himself as an enlightened conservative, too astute to commit the follies of a predecessor, too staid to compromise with the radical nationalism which realist politicians were seeking to tame. Theoretically there was no reason why Schleinitz or Buol or Gorchakov should not create a 'liberalised' Holy Alliance of the Eastern autocracies, with a programme of peace, investment and reform to tempt bankers abroad. But rival vanities and old resentments precluded the collaboration of Gorchakov and Buol, while Schleinitz was too colourless to set the pace of events. Moreover, during the period that Russia was communing with herself, Gorchakov unhesitatingly accepted the primacy of Napoleon III in Europe's affairs. Tsar and emperor, Gorchakov and Walewski met at Stuttgart in September 1857 to emphasise to the German states the reality of a Franco-Russian entente. If Napoleon sought the diplomatic isolation of Austria, then Gorchakov was prepared to act as if there had never been a Münchengrätz or a Holy Alliance.

By the time of the Stuttgart meeting the 'vast subversion' of the European system had begun, with Napoleon III as prime conspirator. After the Congress of Paris, the emperor decided that the only way to bring coherence to his Italian policy was to gain for France the mastery of the peninsula which Austria had secured by the Treaty of Vienna. But whereas Metternich believed in political fragmentation, Napoleon accepted the need for some form of unity. He was convinced that, with French patronage bestowed equally on the patriots and the papacy, it would be possible to create a liberal-conservative (as opposed to radical-national) Italian state. Such an achievement would win prestige for the Second Empire and new outlets for its businessmen, now suffering in a postwar depression. He hoped, too, there was some possibility of redrawing the south-eastern frontier of France, imposed on a defeated nation by the 1814–15 settlements; revision of the Vienna map of Europe would be a good fillip to Bonapartist sentiment. Throughout 1857 Napoleon accordingly concentrated on isolating Austria, while maintaining friendly relations with his former ally, Victor Emmanuel II of Piedmont-Sardinia. At Stuttgart Walewski acted as intermediary between the Piedmontese and the Russians over proposals for establishing a Russian naval coaling station at Villefranche which – like neighbouring Nice – was then a Piedmontese port.[6] But on 14 January 1858 this incipient Franco-Russian-Piedmontese partnership was abruptly disturbed by one of the most notorious terrorist attacks of the century – the attempted assassination of Napoleon and his empress as they drove to the Paris Opera. The plotters were Mazzinian radicals angered by the continued presence of a French garrison in Rome, and their leader was Count Felice Orsini, a dedicated revolutionary and author of a book which had sold widely in Piedmont. Eight onlookers died from the blast of Orsini's bombs and over 150 people were injured. Inevitably, after so grave an outrage there was a rift between the governments in Paris and Turin. Walewski, a good Catholic often made uneasy by his emperor's policy, peremptorily ordered the Piedmontese authorities to suppress the Mazzinian movement within its borders. Not unnaturally, the Austrian ambassador, Baron von Hübner, laid stress on the menace of radical nationalism when he conveyed his sovereign's sympathy to the imperial family at the Tuileries.

In later years Hübner hinted that the Orsini plot induced Napoleon to take up the Italian cause for fear of a second, and successful, assassination bid. This tale was accepted by some of Napoleon's critics in London, including Disraeli, but it has never stood up to close examination.[7] For several months before the assassination attempt Napoleon was planning to destroy Austria's hold on the peninsula, as the Russians had seen clearly enough at Stuttgart. Hübner sent warnings to Vienna and so, too, did Metternich's son, Richard, who had been serving under Hübner in the Paris embassy. Curiously enough, the most immediate effect of Orsini's plot fell not on French policies at all but on life at Westminster, for when Palmerston discovered that Orsini's bombs were made in England the Prime Minister proposed to seek a strengthening of the laws protecting political asylum from abuse. In this he misjudged public opinion. The 'Conspiracy to Murder' Bill was unpopular with Tories and Radicals alike; and Palmerston, of all people, found himself accused of giving way to foreign pressure. So strong was feeling in London that he was defeated in the Commons on 19 February, and the Conservatives came back to office after five years in opposition. It was therefore not the experienced team of Palmerston and Clarendon that met the latest twists of the Italian Question over the following sixteen months but Derby and Malmesbury once again. Cavour looked on the departure of Clarendon as a misfortune, pro-Italian sentiment being traditionally regarded as a Liberal attribute in English party politics. This assumption oversimplified the fickle enthusiasms of the moment; but Derby and Malmesbury were certainly opposed to plans for dismembering the Habsburg Empire.[8]

Orsini's plot may not have frightened Napoleon into partnership with Cavour, but it increased his natural deviousness. Walewski, as Foreign Minister, continued to regard every Italian politician inside and outside Piedmont with the gravest suspicion. Napoleon, acting independently of the Quai d'Orsay, sent his personal friend and physician, Dr Conneau, to Turin to reassure Victor Emmanuel and Cavour within eight weeks of the assassination attempt; and it was subsequently arranged that the emperor would meet Cavour secretly in the spa town of Plombières, where Napoleon was in the habit of taking the waters for some weeks each summer. They met for four hours in the Grand Hotel, Plombières, on 20 July 1858 and in the evening went for a carriage drive alone through the wooded hills of the Vosges. There was no 'Pact of Plombières', merely a verbal agreement which was later committed to paper by Cavour. But what was settled in these talks was momentous, enough indeed to arraign host and guest before an international war crimes tribunal had the meeting occurred in 1938 rather than in 1858. Napoleon and Cavour completed plans to launch a war of aggression against the Austrian Empire. Provided Cavour could provoke the war, France would aid Piedmont in the subsequent campaign. The peace settlement would establish a kingdom of Upper Italy under Victor Emmanuel, while the rest of the peninsula was to form three political units (the Two Sicilies, the Papal States and a central Italian kingdom) which, together with Upper Italy, would be linked in a federation presided over by the Pope. France was promised Nice and Savoy after the war and, before it began, there would be a dynastic marriage, the emperor's 36-year-old cousin, Prince Napoleon, taking as his bride Victor Emmanuel's elder daughter, Princess Clothilde, aged 15. All in all, Plombières was a cynical bargain.

An absurd incident well illustrates the confusion of the times. While Napoleon was closeted with Cavour at the Grand Hotel on 20 July, he received a message from Walewski warning him that intelligence reports indicated that the Piedmontese Prime Minister had secretly entered France and was involved in some political intrigue.[9] Walewski seems first to have learnt of the meeting two days later from the newspapers, a journalist having recognised Cavour at Plombières. He did not resign the Foreign Ministry, presumably hoping he might yet check the irresponsible drift to war. But Napoleon continued to make Walewski's position difficult by persistent use of private emissaries. Thus, in September 1858, he sent the princely bridegroom-to-be to Warsaw as a personal envoy to the Tsar. Alexander II was not flattered, especially as Prince Napoleon was known as a champion of the Polish exiles in Paris; and when the Prince began to sound out Gorchakov over Russian diplomatic aid to France should war come to northern Italy, it was made clear he was a greenhorn in such matters, unsuited for so important a mission. Even so, Napoleon III sent another confidential agent to St Petersburg before allowing Walewski and the professionals to take up negotiations for a Franco-Russian entente soon after the turn of the year. Eventually, on 3 March 1859, a secret treaty pledged Russia to observe benevolent neutrality in a Franco-Austrian war, while the two Powers would seek treaty revision in each other's interests at any subsequent peace congress – an undertaking which Alexander II convinced himself would shake off the restraints imposed in the 1856 settlement. The French were disappointed – they had hoped for a Russian naval presence in the Ligurian Sea as a gesture of anti-Austrian solidarity – but Napoleon was relieved of the fear that the Eastern autocracies would once again come together against him.[10]

At the New Year reception of ambassadors on 1 January 1859 Napoleon III went up to the Austrian ambassador and said, 'I regret that our relations with your government are not as good as in the past; but I beg you to tell the Emperor that my personal feelings towards him remain unchanged'. These words did not seem particularly menacing to Hübner, for everyone could see that Franco-Austrian relations were poor, and an optimist might have drawn comfort from the tone of regret. But Napoleon III was at times a victim of his uncle's style of business; Thiers's best-selling volumes on the consulate and empire had made the public familiar with the occasion in March 1803 when the First Consul greeted the British ambassador in front of other envoys with a hectoring 'So you are bent on war?' nine weeks before the Peace of Amiens ended; and there was a similar scene at the imperial birthday reception of 1808 when Napoleon I asked Austria's representative (Metternich) 'Well, and is Austria arming much?', the opening gambit in a war of nerves which culminated in the Wagram campaign and a French occupation of Vienna. It is hardly surprising that reports of the emperor's remarks led, in 1859 as in 1808, to a disastrous slump in share prices on the Paris Bourse. Avid readers of *The Consulate and Empire*, including Cavour and Malmesbury, assumed that Napoleon III meant war – and so, indeed, did Thiers himself and that arch-survivor in Vienna, whom Francis Joseph still consulted in times of crisis. Only Buol, irritated by old Metternich's messages about Italy (for he had, after all, served in Turin himself), insisted that France and Piedmont were bluffing. This belief matched in folly his sanguine assumption of loyal support from Prussia and the other German states.[11]

Both Britain and Russia tried to keep the peace. Malmesbury collaborated closely with Schleinitz in Berlin in January and February, months which were marked by a rare wave of Prussophilism as Londoners celebrated the birth of Queen Victoria's first grandchild, the future Kaiser William II. Lord Cowley, the British ambassador in Paris, was sent on a mission to Vienna in the hope that he could persuade Buol to accept a Russian proposal for a congress to settle the future of Italy.[12] By late March it seemed the diplomats rather than the generals would resolve the crisis after all. Napoleon drew back from the brink of a war which most of his ministers considered pointless. When Cavour hurried to Paris to remind Napoleon of the Plombières agreement he was received by Walewski, and rebuffed. Buol, however, refused to consider the possibility of a congress until the Piedmontese demobilised their overswollen army, and he made it clear he would not sit at any conference table with Cavour. Buol wanted a diplomatic victory and, sensing that the Franco-Piedmontese combination was breaking apart, he resolved to give Cavour the final push: on 22 April the Piedmontese Prime Minister received an ultimatum from the Austrians requiring him to withdraw the army from the Lombard frontier and agree to general disarmament within five days. Cavour, confident Napoleon would stand by his public pledge to defend Piedmont 'against every aggressive act on the part of Austria', rejected the ultimatum. The Austrians crossed the River Ticino and engaged the Piedmontese forces on 27 April. Six days later, true to the style of his uncle, Napoleon III issued a rousing proclamation of war against the Austrian invaders.

The news from Paris seems, unaccountably, to have surprised Vienna. Buol, who had thought he was ousting Cavour, was himself dismissed from office; and, on the advice of the dying Metternich, Francis Joseph brought the shrewd and experienced Count Rechberg to the Ballhausplatz. It was too late to stave off disaster. The Austrians were defeated in the two extremely bloody battles of Magenta and Solferino, encounters which left Napoleon III aghast at the spectacle of carnage. The French, however, could not exploit their victories. Behind the Lombard plain stood the famous Austrian 'Quadrilateral', the fortresses of Peschiera, Verona, Mantua and Legnano, a defensive network capable of checking an advance into Venetia for several months and so turning a short campaign into a war of attrition which Napoleon could not risk. The discovery that he needed siege artillery, a fear that he might be faced by four Sebastopols, weakened Napoleon's military resolve. Reports that Prussia was mobilising six army corps beyond the Rhine inclined him further to make peace for, though Schleinitz might merely be hoping for concessions within the German Confederation from a grateful Austria, it was always possible the Prussians would cross the frontier and march on Paris while the main French army was engaged south of the Alps. The Prussian threat decided the outcome of the campaign. Napoleon and Francis Joseph ended a costly war with a personal meeting at Villafranca, where preliminary peace terms were agreed on 12 July. Cavour was not consulted.[13]

This brief war of 1859 was unique for, in a sense, each sovereign who mobilised his army was a loser. Francis Joseph surrendered the Lombard plain to Napoleon who handed it over to Piedmont. Napoleon had hoped for Nice and Savoy, but despite the long list of battle casualties he dared not claim his reward after seeking a premature armistice. Victor Emmanuel went to war looking for a kingdom 'from the Alps to the Adriatic' and for primacy in a reorganised Italy but had to content himself with Lombardy, less the fortresses of Peschiera and Mantua. Prince Regent William of Prussia, counting on Austrian gratitude, found himself treated with contempt by Francis Joseph for alleged opportunism; and Tsar Alexander II, who had thought sabre-rattling along the Galician frontier would win Gorchakov a chance to dispute the 1856 settlement at a European congress, came gradually to realise the truism that a localised war needs only a localised peace to end it. It could even be argued that the country gaining most from the war was, quite fortuitously, Great Britain. Malmesbury had worked hard to prevent war in the first place, and his efforts at mediation improved British standing in Berlin, Vienna and St Petersburg; but he had no illusions about his one-time friend, now Emperor of the French, and even less about his Piedmontese partners. 'That Europe should be deluged with blood for the personal ambitions of an Italian attorney and a tambour-major, like Cavour and his master, is intolerable', he told Lord Cowley.[14] However, halfway in time between the battles of Magenta and Solferino, Lord Derby's government was defeated over a reform bill; Palmerston came back as Prime Minister and Lord John Russell took over the Foreign Office from Malmesbury. Three warm supporters of the Italian cause – Palmerston, Russell and Gladstone, the Chancellor of the Exchequer – now dominated a Liberal Cabinet. They distrusted Napoleon III even more than Malmesbury had and they were able to capitalise on the improved prestige of Britain's leading diplomats to encourage acceptance by the European Chancelleries of their principle of non-intervention in Italy's own affairs. The British attitude in the critical summer months of 1859 ensured that when eventually a unified kingdom of Italy was created it was free from French patronage or papal supervision and willing to look for support to the European Power best able to stimulate its industries and give naval protection to a long vulnerable coastline. 'I am very Austrian north of the Alps, but very anti-Austrian south of the Alps', remarked Palmerston in private conversation. It was a sound enough formula for most of his Cabinet.[15]

The immediate test for the doctrine of non-intervention came in central Italy. As soon as war began on the Ticino, popular risings in Parma, Modena and Tuscany swept their rulers into exile, and when the Austrians withdrew their troops from Bologna, papal Romagna joined the three duchies in seeking union with Piedmont. However, the Villafranca Peace threatened to impose a return of the old regimes. Cavour, disgusted at the premature ending of the war, resigned office although not before he had advised the liberal leaders in Florence and Bologna to speak out in favour of the Piedmontese connection. Palmerston and Russell saw no reason why the people of the central duchies should be forced to take back their unpopular rulers, and for five months the British campaigned in favour of Cavour's return as Prime Minister in Turin so as to complete the union of upper Italy.[16] On 20 January 1860 he was back in office. He proposed that the male inhabitants of the Romagna and the central duchies should decide by plebiscite for or against union with Piedmont. Russell supported the proposal, but it posed a new problem for Napoleon. In theory he always favoured plebiscites, and a vote by universal male suffrage provided the Second Empire with its basic claim to sovereignty in France itself. Napoleon, however, was still seeking some specifically Bonapartist success, an erasing of the frontiers imposed on France in 1814–15. He therefore countered Cavour's proposal with a demand of his own, echoing the bargains struck at Plombières: France would approve a plebiscite in central Italy provided that the people of Savoy and Nice were given the right to decide whether they wished to become French citizens. A treaty signed in Turin on 24 March 1860 settled the bargain, the duchies and the Romagna having already voted for union with Piedmont twelve days earlier. Nice and Savoy chose French rule in plebiscites held on 18 and 22 April. There is no doubt most people in both districts favoured integration under Napoleon III; but the manner in which the emperor secured his modification of the 1815 settlement incensed the other Great Powers, especially Britain, and clouded his good relations with Russia.

Walewski resigned as Foreign Minister in the first days of the year 1860. He was succeeded by Édouard de Thouvenel, a career diplomat lately ambassador at Constantinople. At 40, some nine years younger than Walewski, Thouvenel was the first Foreign Minister of any Great Power to come from the post-Napoleonic War generation. Thouvenel retained a certain zest in his leisure hours – a Piedmontese diplomat once regaled Cavour with an entertaining account of the minister's performance, partly in drag, at one of Eugénie's Fontainebleau charades – but professionally he was self-effacing.[17] His genuine sympathy for the Italian national cause helped moderate French policy in the dramatic crises with which Garibaldi confounded the other European Chancelleries during the spring and summer of 1860. A conservative, like Drouyn de Lhuys, or a practising Catholic, like Walewski, would have supported the empress in urging Napoleon to reinforce his garrison in Rome, curb the Piedmontese and defy liberal sentiment on the continent and in Britain. Thouvenel wished not so much to make policy as to accommodate his assumptions to Napoleon's needs. He was so faithfully eager to echo his master that he deserved a consistent sovereign who would speak with only one voice on the problem of the moment; but clarity of purpose seems never to have been a characteristic of the Bonapartes.

It was, however, the most devastating of Garibaldi's virtues. Most of Europe assumed in the spring of 1860 that there would be months, or more probably years, of diplomatic negotiation before the map of Italy was further revised. But Garibaldi, incensed at the plebiscite in Nice which had made him 'a foreigner in the town of my birth', was eager to exploit the patriotic enthusiasm which followed the union of central Italy with the northern kingdom. On 5 May Garibaldi and his expedition of redshirt volunteers sailed from Genoa for an unknown destination. The Thousand landed at Marsala in Sicily six days later and kept the Italian Question on the boil for the next nine months, determining by arms the task haltingly begun by the diplomats. Garibaldi put himself at the head of a rising of Sicilians against their Bourbon king in Naples, the 24-year-old Francis II, a weedy and devout son of the hated 'King Bomba', who had died twelve months before. The redshirts defeated a Neapolitan army at Calatafimi, entered Palermo on 27 May and made Garibaldi master of the island by the fourth week in July. A failing autonomist rising was thus converted by Garibaldi into a national movement of unity. Europe was faced by a new Italian revolution, for it was clear Garibaldi would soon cross the Straits of Messina and set the peninsula aflame. The tone of his speeches in Palermo left no doubt that his principal objective was Rome, where his redshirts had gained legendary fame in their struggle against Oudinot in 1849. Here was a threat which no Great Power could ignore, except perhaps Britain, whose Foreign Secretary had declared: 'Let the Italians govern their own affairs – that is my motto'.[18]

Other Foreign Ministers could not share Russell's sublime confidence in self-determination. Russia, Austria and Prussia protested at the ease with which Garibaldi had fitted out his expedition on Piedmontese soil and evaded the inconstant vigilance of the Piedmontese navy as he sailed south to Sicily. Cavour was not unduly worried by this spectral gesture from the Holy Alliance Powers; he knew there was little possibility that Rechberg or Gorchakov would conjure up a new Laibach Congress, for both the Austrian and Russian empires were occupied in that summer of 1860 with problems of internal reform. Prince Regent William of Prussia, on the other hand, was extremely active: he met Napoleon III at Baden-Baden in late June, Francis Joseph at Teplitz in late July and Queen Victoria (with Russell in attendance) at Coblenz early in October. Yet each of these meetings was frustrating for the Prussians; William found the Emperor of the French unreliable, Francis Joseph obstinately disinclined to allow him greater influence in German affairs, and the British opposed to any revision of the 1852 Treaty of London on the status of Schleswig-Holstein, a gesture which would have gratified German nationalists within his kingdom. Moreover, Anglo-Prussian relations were soured throughout the winter of 1860–1 by a trivial incident at Bonn railway station in September when an arrogant British tourist, Captain Macdonald, fell foul of an equally arrogant Prussian railway official and exchanged the comforts of a first-class compartment for the privations of a prison cell. The Macdonald affair, which dragged on for over a year, stimulated that impulsive Don Pacifico style of patriotism which always marred Palmerston's better judgement; and on this occasion he was supported by scathing attacks on Prussia in *The Times*. It is curious, with hindsight, to peruse the London Press and Hansard during the consummation of Italian unity and find long columns devoted to an episode which has fallen out of all the history books.[19] Prince Regent William and the naturally Anglophile Schleinitz were driven back to dependence on Russia.

Such diversions indirectly assisted Cavour. He had already been pleasantly surprised at a mild reaction from Thouvenel to Garibaldi's incursion into Sicily, although his minister in Paris shrewdly reminded him that 'France is not paid to serve as gendarme for the Bourbons'. His chief concern was to prevent the uprising becoming a Mazzinian insurrection, and he was prepared to exaggerate the threat of unbridled radical republicanism so as to win support abroad for his own brand of liberal-monarchist nationalism. But, while Thouvenel was cool-headed and reasonable, Napoleon was coy and evasive. As Garibaldi was advancing on Naples, so Napoleon and Eugénie left Paris for a state entry into Savoy and Nice. At Chambéry, on 28 August, two envoys from Turin caught up with the imperial progress and there followed a meeting which accorded well with the traditions of subversive diplomacy exemplified two years before at Plombières. Cavour's emissaries told Napoleon he wished to send the Piedmontese army southwards through papal territory in order to halt Garibaldi's revolutionary force before it marched on Rome. Napoleon gave the plan apparent approval, provided Cavour acted swiftly; he indicated he would summon a congress to settle the reordering of the peninsula. 'The diplomats will make a great fuss', he told the envoys, 'but will let you get away with it.'[20]

The Piedmontese crossed the frontier of the Papal States on 11 September and were confronted by an international army commanded by the French Orleanist general Louis de Lamoricière, which gave battle to the invaders at Castelfidardo a week later. Nothing could check the Piedmontese troops, who thrust southwards towards Garibaldi's position on the River Volturno, although carefully respecting papal sovereignty over the 'Patrimony of St Peter', the region around Rome. On the day of Castelfidardo the Emperor of the French was completely cut off from the authorities in Paris and without news of events in Europe for nearly sixty hours. He landed at Algiers on a state visit in the morning of 17 September, having told the Quai d'Orsay that the new underwater cable from Toulon would keep him informed of developments. But the cable was found to be inoperative a few hours before Napoleon stepped ashore – which was not surprising as two vessels were still laying it. The so-called 'snapping of the cable' left the emperor as isolated as his uncle in the closing stages of the Russian campaign.[21] As in 1812, it was up to the Foreign Minister to handle the general European crisis.

Thouvenel did his job well. The diplomats were able to have their 'great fuss' in the emperor's absence, while Thouvenel treated both French clericals and the Piedmontese minister with dignified restraint. He also prepared memoranda to convince the Russians that his imperial master was not hand in glove with revolution. When Napoleon arrived back in Paris, nearly a week after Lamoricière's defeat, the political storm had blown itself out. Napoleon cut diplomatic links with Turin in a show of indignation, insisting privately that Cavour had misunderstood his advice at Chambéry. At the same time Thouvenel sent off his proposals to St Petersburg: no support for Piedmont in a new war against Austria for Venetia; a pledge of stability in south-eastern Europe; and a tentative offer of backing for any Russian initiative to recover Bessarabia. Alexander II and Gorchakov were pleased. The French proposals, even more than his unconvincing rupture with Turin, perched Napoleon back alongside the angels. To gratify Rechberg and Schleinitz, Alexander had agreed that the three Eastern autocrats should meet at Warsaw in the final days of October to discuss the Italian Revolution. Now Gorchakov considered inviting Thouvenel to Warsaw as an observer; but on reflection he contented himself with reading to the Tsar's guests an edited version of Thouvenel's comments on the future of Italy.[22]

This last weekend of October 1860 proved a decisive moment in Italy's history. On Friday 26 October Garibaldi met King Victor Emmanuel II at Teano, north of the Volturno, and greeted him in the customary theatricality of the Risorgimento with a resounding 'Hail to the King of Italy'. Next day, in London, Lord John Russell completed a historic dispatch to the British minister in Turin giving enthusiastic support to events in the peninsula. He compared Victor Emmanuel's southward march to the liberating mission of William of Orange in 1688, that most hallowed episode in Whig mythology. Russell could see no reason to censure Piedmont as Austria, France, Prussia and Russia proposed. 'Her Majesty's Government', he concluded, 'will turn their eyes rather to the gratifying prospect of a people building up the edifice of their liberties, and consolidating the work of their independence, amid the sympathies and good wishes of Europe.'[23] His dispatch, as Cavour realised when it was read to him, constituted the first clear acknowledgement from a Great Power that a new nation state was in being. Victor Emmanuel II was formally proclaimed King of Italy on 17 March 1861, although Rome and Venetia remained outside his realm. Cavour's revolution from above was almost complete, the triumph of a national cause instigated by the least radical social class in the least Italian state of the peninsula.

In Warsaw, on that same Saturday of October on which Russell penned his spirited endorsement of Piedmont's policy, Austria failed to rally support from Russia and Prussia against the Italian Revolution. Alexander II showed more interest in Thouvenel's proposals than in the fate of the peninsula, while Prince Regent William fell in dutifully behind the Tsar as had his father in 1815. This first meeting of the Eastern monarchs in seven years accomplished nothing. When, on Saturday evening, Alexander heard of the grave illness of his mother, he apologised to his guests and hurried back to Tsarskoe Selo. Francis Joseph returned to Vienna conscious of a diplomatic defeat to set alongside the lost battles in Lombardy of the previous summer. Bitterness disinclined him to seek partnership with his fellow autocrats after the Warsaw rebuff. Not until the autumn of 1872 did the three monarchs come together again; and then they met in newly imperial Berlin rather than in Poland's old capital. It was not everyone who, in that winter of 1860–1, could perceive the significance of Cavour's achievement, but shrewd observers were already calculating where the new Italy would stand in the European states system. From his legation beside the Neva, Prussia's envoy – who was less than five years Cavour's junior in age – sent his considered verdict to Schleinitz in Berlin: 'Although I may be wrong', Bismarck wrote, 'I feel convinced that the establishment of a strong Italian state in the south between France and Austria is to Prussia's advantage.'[24] This was hardly Napoleon's intention when he began to cultivate Cavour after the Congress of Paris.

10 Prussia Triumphant, 1862-70

On 18 October 1861 a ceremony of great significance took place in the Schlosskirche at Königsberg, the old city of the Teutonic Knights. The former Prince Regent William, who had acceded on the second day of the year, was acknowledged as sovereign amid the red velvet and gold canopies of the chapel in which the first Hohenzollern king was anointed with consecrated oil 160 years before. Prussian coronations were rare events, most Hohenzollerns finding thrifty comfort in Frederick the Great's dictum that 'a crown is merely a hat that lets the rain in'. William, however, revived the rite of coronation so as to stress his ideal of kingship. Solemnly he placed the crown on his head before the altar, took up sceptre and sword of state and, turning to the assembled notables in the congregation, proclaimed, 'I receive this crown from God's hand and from no other'. This faith in Divine Right, reiterated in a speech at the castle after the service, scorned the compromises of constitutional liberalism which permitted the sovereigns of France, Belgium and Italy to rule by 'grace of God and the will of the People'. William was serving notice that the enlightened conservatism of Prussia's 'new era' was over. As a professional soldier through and through, his greatest desire was to possess a large, well-disciplined and well-trained regular army; and he had no intention of allowing a parliament to limit the length of military service or the size of his army budget.

Lord Clarendon had travelled the thousand miles to Königsberg as his queen's personal representative. The Prussian kingdom seemed less stable to him than France or the new Italy, now mourning Cavour who had collapsed from physical exhaustion that summer. 'The King, a man of perfect honour, has no idea of the Duties of a Constitutional Sovereign', Clarendon reported from Berlin. He added: 'Besides His Majesty is unfortunate in not possessing a single statesman in his Kingdom.'[1] Among the Prussian politicians so lightly dismissed by Clarendon was Otto von Bismarck, who was present at the coronation. When Queen Victoria met Bismarck briefly at Versailles in 1856 he had impressed her, though hardly favourably; but five years later his prospects for advancement to high office looked poor, and it is not surprising that Clarendon failed to perceive in him the parliamentary skills and world outlook he had admired in Cavour. Bismarck had indeed been recommended to King William in the preceding summer by General von Roon, the Minister of War, but his policies seemed too wild for an old-fashioned soldier monarch of natural caution to accept. Bismarck's objective was to defy Austria and secure Prussian domination over all Germany outside the Habsburg Empire; and he urged the king to take over the moral leadership of the national cause, saving it from liberal demagogues. William, however, wanted nothing so drastic. All he sought was a politician who could induce the lower house of Prussia's parliament (the *Landtag*) to accept his plans for expanding the army. When Schleinitz's health gave way later that summer the king chose as his successor not Bismarck but Albrecht von Bernstorff, Prussia's minister in London, who formally became Foreign Minister a week before the coronation.

From Königsberg Bismarck travelled back to St Petersburg. There Gorchakov, more perceptive than Clarendon, was already cultivating Bismarck as Prussian Foreign Minister of the future. No doubt Gorchakov's patronage sprang partly from the coincidence that the two men had known each other for more than ten years; the Russian liked to gratify his vanity by claiming Bismarck had been his 'pupil' when they were both envoys to the Frankfurt Diet. But he could also see, by perusing dispatches from Berlin, that despite wrangling between king and *Landtag* over revenue for the larger army, Bernstorff was embarking on an ambitious foreign policy which challenged Austrian primacy within the German Confederation. Rightly Gorchakov assumed that Francis Joseph and Rechberg would respond by seeking to isolate Prussia diplomatically. If an external crisis coincided with the constitutional conflict in Berlin, the Prussians would need a minister more dextrous and experienced than Bernstorff and better versed in chancellery politics than any general to whom William might be tempted to entrust a military coup. Bismarck possessed every attribute except, as yet, the confidence of his king.

The eleven months which followed William's coronation were as decisive as any in nineteenth-century Prussia. It was still possible that the King might change course and accept both parliamentary control of the army budget and Austria's continued mastery of the German states. Prussia's liberals feared a military putsch instigated by General Edwin von Manteuffel, the ambitious cousin of the former chief minister. At best they hoped King William would abdicate in favour of the Crown Prince rather than compromise the principles he had proclaimed at Königsberg. The triumph of either 'constitutional government' or the generals would have left Bismarck's name in the margin of history, remembered in passing as a failed diplomat with a penchant for the grand gesture. But Roon, who had long distrusted General von Manteuffel and his cronies, continued to urge the king to send for Bismarck as tension grew between the *Landtag* deputies and the Crown. Bismarck spent the remaining winter months in St Petersburg, served for a mere eight weeks as ambassador in Paris, visited London briefly and took a long holiday at Biarritz. Back in Paris he received a famous telegram from Roon: the constitutional crisis was wearing down the will of the king, who contemplated abdication, and Roon urged Bismarck to return to Berlin as speedily as possible. He was received by William at Babelsberg on 22 September 1862 with some suspicion, but he assured the king that he could form a government and carry through a modernisation of the army with revenues which he would raise, if necessary, independent of parliamentary consent. A vigorous and successful foreign policy would, he argued, soon silence liberal nationalist critics. At once the king appointed him acting Minister President ('prime minister') and Foreign Minister. A week later, speaking to some two dozen members of a budget committee, Bismarck remarked – almost as an aside – that the 'great questions of the day' would be settled 'by iron and blood'. Only when the newspapers gave emphasis to this passage of his speech later in the week did Europe begin to talk, anxiously, of the Junker 'Cavour-ism' of Prussia's new chief minister.[2]

During these months of constitutional crisis in Berlin the Foreign Ministries elsewhere had been concerned primarily with matters other than the affairs of Germany. The American Civil War posed direct problems, particularly those caused by the Northern blockade and by Southern commerce raiders, and more general questions, notably whether the Union would survive or whether, as Gladstone believed, the Confederate leaders had 'made a nation'. By 1862 Russell, though thinking that Gladstone had gone 'beyond the latitude which all speakers must be allowed', raised with Palmerston the possibility of recognising the Confederacy and seeking an end to the Civil War. Palmerston favoured recognition and joint mediation 'at one and the same time by England, France and some other Powers'. News that Lee's thrust north of the Potomac was checked at Antietam gave Palmerston second thoughts. When, early in November 1862, Napoleon III proposed that Britain and Russia should join France in seeking a six-month armistice, the Cabinet rejected the idea of mediation – as also did Gorchakov. Napoleon III had wider interests in the Americas than any other European ruler of his day. The Bonapartist Catholic faction, headed by the Empress Eugénie and Walewski, encouraged him to intervene in Mexico against the anticlerical radical president, Benito Juarez, a mid-nineteenth-century Fidel Castro. Originally in 1861 Spain and Britain had sent forces to support France's attempt to make Juarez pay the debts of his European bondholders. But by the spring of 1862 Napoleon's Mexican project went further than Palmerston and Russell or the Spaniard, General Prim, thought practicable. Napoleon was prepared to send a large army to Mexico to establish a new monarchy there, and as early as March 1862 was discussing with the Austrian ambassador in Paris the possibility of creating Francis Joseph's brother, Archduke Maximilian, Emperor of Mexico. Although Maximilian did not accept the imperial crown until April 1864, the French presence in Mexico weakened the effectiveness of Napoleon's influence on the European continent throughout the first five years that Bismarck was Prussia's chief minister. Napoleon III's Mexican misadventure was the earliest instance of a Great Power heavily committing itself to a totally artificial stake in a faraway land. Like later ill-considered gambles, involvement in Mexico ended in humiliating withdrawal and demoralisation in an army raised to meet a different kind of challenge.[3]

There were problems, too, for the European Foreign Ministers in Asia and the Balkans.[4] Palmerston and his Cabinet colleagues spent much of the early 1860s trying to enforce strict observance by China merchants in London and the Far East of the treaty limitations on trade accepted in negotiations with the Chinese authorities at Tientsin in 1858. If it was hard to convince British merchants that China could not become a second India, it was even harder to reassure the Russians. Count Muravyov-Amursky, Alexander II's proconsul in eastern Siberia, had founded Vladivostok in 1860 to celebrate Russia's 'dominance of the East', and he could not believe that his British rivals did not harbour similar ambitious designs around Peking, Shanghai and Canton. Muravyov-Amursky was supported by the young General Nikolai Ignatyev, who in 1861 became head of the Asiatic Department of the Foreign Ministry at the age of 29 after two profitable diplomatic missions to Peking. Already Ignatyev had been brilliantly successful in sowing discord between the Chinese, the British and the French, who were at that time consolidating their newest colonial empire, in Cochin-China. In later years Ignatyev became the most famous of all Russia's ambassadors in Constantinople, and as soon as he took over the Asiatic Department he was able to exploit Anglo-French differences of approach to the Eastern Question, making certain that the Crimean alliance was finally dead and buried. To suspicion of Napoleon III's championship of Romanian nationalism in Bucharest was added British resentment at French activities in the Lebanon and Egypt. A Greek insurrection in October 1862, which ended the reign of the colourless and childless King Otto, also reopened old conflicts between the diplomats of the three Protecting Powers (Britain, France and Russia) when a search began for a new ruler. The Franco-Russian entente came forward with a nephew of the Tsar, much to the annoyance of Palmerston and Russell, and a Greek assembly caused dynastic embarrassment by promoting the candidature of Queen Victoria's second son. Eventually in July 1863 an Anglo-Russian compromise led to the accession of George I, younger son of the King of Denmark and brother of the new Princess Alexandra of Wales. King George eventually married Grand Duke Constantine's daughter, Olga. Austria, and to a lesser extent Prussia, were displeased by the dynastic change in Athens, partly because the deposed king was a Bavarian by origin, even more from hostility to King George's Danish family, the House of Schleswig-Holstein-Sonderburg-Glücksburg. National sentiment over the Danish duchies, so intense in 1848–9, still ran high within the German Confederation.

Italy, too, formed a constant leitmotiv in the international politics of these years. Cavour's early death left the problems of Venetia and Rome unresolved. Garibaldi began collecting men and arms for an advance into Venetia, probably in the spring of 1862, but the Italian Prime Minister, Urbano Rattazzi, had no wish to see Austria provoked into a war for which he was not ready militarily or diplomatically; his police effectively scotched the conspiracy. Both Napoleon III and Eugénie urged Metternich's son Richard – by now ambassador in Paris – to recommend to Rechberg that Austria should cede Venetia to Italy, advice the ambassador firmly declined to pass on. Thouvenel still believed that French troops should be withdrawn from Rome and the Pope left to settle his fate with the Italian government, but Eugénie and Walewski held that millions of French Catholics would see the abandonment of the Holy Father as an act of spiritual treachery. In the summer of 1862 the indefatigable Garibaldi travelled to Sicily, denounced Napoleon III in a speech and openly recruited supporters under the slogan 'Rome or Death!' Once more he crossed the Straits and began to march through Calabria but, in the last days of August 1862, his force was surrounded by Victor Emmanuel's troops in the foothills of the Aspromonte north of Reggio;

Garibaldi was wounded in the foot, and the venture ended in bathos. This apparent threat to the Pope's sovereignty hardened the mood of the Bonapartist Catholics in Paris, who vetoed Thouvenel's attempt to negotiate a settlement of the Roman Question. Thouvenel left office, to be succeeded in October by Drouyn de Lhuys, recalled to the Foreign Ministry after seven years, much of which he had spent denouncing, confidentially, his emperor's 'radical' anti-Austrian prejudices. There seemed at the time no reason why Thouvenel, who was only 44, should not make a similar comeback when Napoleon's shifting principles of policy drifted free from their conservative captors. By then, however, in the autumn of 1866, Thouvenel was dead and Napoleon was left to improvise expedient designs with ministers who knew little of the European states system.[5]

But in the autumn of 1862 Napoleon still enjoyed prestige as arbiter of the continent. A month after becoming Prussia's chief minister, Bismarck visited Paris, met Drouyn and had a long private conversation with the emperor at St-Cloud. He found Napoleon affecting a pose of masterful strength through sphinx-like reticence, listening as his guest spoke of Prussia's need to oust Austria from north Germany's affairs but declining to commit France in support of either rival Power. Drouyn was unhelpful, favouring Austria whereas Thouvenel had encouraged Prussia. Shortly after their meeting Drouyn let Bismarck know that in any German conflict, France would make certain of her own security, a frank warning that Napoleon's disinterestedness was based on a realistic opportunism. But so too was Bismarck's policy: less than eleven weeks after taking office he told Francis Joseph's ambassador in Berlin – Count Aloys Karolyi, a Hungarian landed magnate – that the time had come 'for Austria to shift her centre of gravity from Germany to Hungary'; and he gave Francis Joseph a choice of abandoning Germany and gaining Prussian support for forward policies in Italy and the Balkans or of seeking to preserve the old system in Germany and forcing Prussia into partnership with France in any future war, for example one caused by the Venetian Question. The veiled threat was ignored. Small wonder if Rechberg, who had long known Bismarck personally, reckoned him a dangerous head of government 'with no real political sense'. By the end of the year 1862 Rechberg, Drouyn and Palmerston had all decided, independently of each other, that the Bismarck ministry was a passing phenomenon. In the third week of January even the Prussian Prime Minister's private banker could write: 'The resignation of Bismarck seems close at hand.'[6]

So, indeed, it appeared for much of the new year. In January and February 1863 the attention of Europe was concentrated on Polish affairs, where rebellion in Warsaw revived the radical crusading zeal of 1830 and 1848 in liberals and old-style Bonapartists on both sides of the English Channel. The Russians, however, never lost control of Warsaw or any large town; it was an insurrection and never a civil war. France, Britain and even Austria petitioned the Tsar to keep the liberties granted to Congress Poland in 1815, but Bismarck's Prussia stood apart from the European bloc. Hurriedly Bismarck sent to St Petersburg General Alvensleben, a personal emissary of King William, with instructions to conclude a military convention providing for joint Russo-Prussian collaboration against Polish dissidents. The Russians duly signed the convention, though they could see no need for it; and the chief effect of Bismarck's initiative was to bring down on his head the abuse of Europe's professional enlightened opinion. *The Times*, for example, was indignant at Prussia's behaviour. 'Whatever may be our hostility to the bear, there is no doubt of our feeling towards the jackal', an editorial declared on 21 February.[7] A joint diplomatic protest at Prussia's proposed intervention from Britain, France and Austria alarmed King William, who was unaccustomed to finding himself in discreditable isolation. King and minister rode out the storm, for Bismarck was still essential to William in his battle against Prussia's parliamentarians. But the Polish affair brought no benefit to Prussia. It did not even win Russian gratitude, for neither Gorchakov nor the Tsar welcomed interference from Berlin in what they thought was a task for Russia's soldiery and police. They feared that Prussian military support would breath new fire into the old Crimean coalition. 'Aid for a war against France and England: no thanks', minuted the Tsar on a report from Berlin. Whatever Bismarck may have written later in his memoirs, the Alvensleben Convention was at the time extremely unpopular with Alexander and his ministers. It prompted sardonic remarks in St Petersburg on that army reservist lieutenant in the Wilhelmstrasse who was hoping to emulate Frederick the Great. 'Our dear Bismarck is a terrible blunderer', Alexander commented on 22 February. When, six days later, Gorchakov informed Russia's envoy in Berlin that 'I am in such despair over the humiliation of our dear friend Bismarck', crocodile tears must have stained the paper on which he was writing.[8]

The final twist of irony belonged, however, to Bismarck. Later in the year continued remonstration from London and Paris over Russia's treatment of the Poles began to alarm Alexander II. Early in June he wrote personally to his royal uncle in Berlin and asked for Prussian co-operation in case 'France and England' should go to war with Russia for the sake of Polish autonomy. King William referred the matter to Bismarck, who thought the contingency too remote and hypothetical to take seriously; and William's answer evaded the question entirely. By midsummer Bismarck had lost interest in Poland and was seeking a diplomatic success within Germany itself. When, early in August, he induced William not to attend the Austrian-sponsored 'Congress of German Princes' at Frankfurt, he wrecked Austria's plan to reform the Confederation, for the other rulers would not commit themselves to drastic changes in the absence of the King of Prussia. Yet this first political triumph of Bismarck was a negative achievement, the imposition of his will on an obdurate sovereign so as to frustrate others. He remained without a positive victory which would raise Prussia's status in Europe and mute the protests of liberal nationalists, indignant at the way in which he had passed a military budget without the consent of parliament.[9]

All in all, however, the year 1863 brought more success to Bismarck than to Napoleon III. The Polish insurrection was a major setback for France. Traditionally the Polish cause was championed by both Bonapartists and French Catholics, and popular indignation in Paris effectively put an end to the Franco-Russian entente. At the same time, Anglo-French relations, strained since the acquisition of Savoy and Nice, were little better than in the final days of the Guizot era. Desperately both the emperor and his empress searched for a substitute policy. In the last week of February Richard Metternich informed Rechberg of an extraordinary three-hour conversation with Eugénie in which she had outlined proposals for a new map of Europe: a reconstructed Polish kingdom, under an Austrian or Saxon ruler; a Prussian-dominated Germany, with Silesia ceded to Austria and the Rhineland to France; a divided Italy, in which Victor Emmanuel II took Venetia but allowed the central duchies and the south to form separate states within an Italian confederation. Nor was revision confined to Germany and Italy: the Ottoman Empire would be dissolved, Austria acquiring the south Slav lands, with Constantinople going to the Greeks and Asiatic Turkey to the Russians. France would surrender nothing, and there was no suggestion that the carvers might toss a morsel to the British. Perhaps the conversation should have been regarded as a variant on those party games in which Eugénie delighted at Compiègne and Fontainebleau. Rechberg, however, took Metternich's report at its face value, especially when a few days later the emperor himself spoke oracularly of new partnerships in Europe. Such fantasies were to be discouraged, whether they originated with Eugénie or her husband; and the ambassador was told he should emphasise Austria's 'total repugnance' towards proposals of this kind, particularly any concerned with the German Question.[10] Even Tsar Nicholas I had never put forward partition plans so comprehensive or so dangerously imprecise.

A general suspicion that Napoleon III favoured such grandiose schemes devalued his most constructive diplomatic proposal as soon as it was made. On 4 November 1863 he invited the sovereigns of Europe or their plenipotentiaries to a congress in order to settle the outstanding problems of the continent, which Drouyn later listed as Poland, Venetia and Rome, the Danubian Principalities, and Schleswig-Holstein. Not since Verona in 1822 had there been a peacetime congress of this character, and it could be argued that in the intervening years a more complex diplomatic system and speedier communications rendered such a gathering superfluous. Alexander II, angry that other rulers might discuss the problems of his Polish kingdom, wanted Gorchakov to send a peremptory refusal but the Russian Foreign Minister was prepared to temporise, shrewdly waiting to see the reaction of Palmerston and Russell. Rechberg, gloomily anticipating that such a congress would lead to general war, was also inclined to wait on London's response; and so, for that matter, was Bismarck too. The British Cabinet discussed the proposed congress on 19 November and unanimously advised the queen to decline Napoleon's invitation since, as Palmerston said, 'such a meeting could only tend to bring out in bolder relief all those differences of opinion and conflicts of interest which are at present kept in the background'. Unfortunately the British refusal was published in the official *London Gazette* before the ambassador in Paris had an opportunity to present it privately, an accidental rebuff which incensed Napoleon III. The other foreign ministers insisted that 'a congress without England' would be worthless, although

Bismarck encouraged his king to please Napoleon by accepting the idea of a congress in principle – whatever that meant.[11] The British decision marked the end of the Anglo-French alliance forged at the coming of war in March 1854. Thus, within a few months, Napoleon had lost his remaining links both with Russia and with Britain. As the year ended, he began to look not unfavourably on Prussia. It is an interesting comment on Bismarck's mounting prestige that when, on Christmas Eve, the Prussian Prime Minister light-heartedly told Napoleon's personal envoy, General Fleury, that 'he would sooner cede our Rhenish province' than allow other countries to discuss the affairs of Prussian Poland, Fleury thought the casual mention of the Rhine was worth a telegram sent directly to his emperor. The hint – if such it may be called – was duly noted at the Tuileries.[12]

By now Bismarck had taken the measure of his antagonists, at home and abroad. He had, in fact, embarked on what fourteen years later he called 'the diplomatic campaign of which I am most proud'.[13] Pan-German sentiment in the Elbe Duchies of Schleswig-Holstein and Lauenburg remained strong even after the Treaty of London had confirmed the dynastic link between Denmark and the Duchies in 1852. It was not, however, a cause which interested Bismarck until Danish nationalists tried to impose a unitary constitution which swept away local franchises. The death of King Frederick VII of Denmark and the disputed succession of Prince Christian as his successor in November 1863 brought new life to the Schleswig-Holstein Question throughout Germany, the liberals supporting the claim of Frederick of Augustenburg as Duke of an independent Schleswig-Holstein-Lauenburg. The Austrians would never back Frederick since his cause depended on a claim of national self-determination, a principle totally alien to the Habsburgs; and Bismarck was prepared to collaborate with Austria, partly to discredit the liberals but even more because he hoped Prussia would herself eventually annex the Duchies. He therefore proposed, and Rechberg accepted, an agreement by which Austria and Prussia would seek to uphold the 1852 treaty and at the same time settle the future of the Duchies jointly should the dispute lead to war. On 14 January 1864 – three days before the Austro-Prussian alliance was signed – Bismarck remarked to Karolyi that some people in Berlin favoured the incorporation of the Duchies in Prussia but that he rejected any such idea; and he also mentioned, with studied irrelevance, Austria's need of secure frontiers in northern Italy. If, as seems likely, these remarks were intended to suggest that Prussia should have a free hand in the Duchies in return for supporting Austria south of the Alps, the offer made no appeal to Vienna. But Francis Joseph was prepared to authorise the use of Austrian troops beyond the Elbe rather than allow the dispute with Denmark to excite the Frankfurt brand of German nationalism.

Hanoverian and Saxon troops, acting in the name of the German Confederation, crossed into Holstein in the last days of the old year. A month later the Prussians moved in, and on 1 February 1864 entered Schleswig alongside Austrian troops. By mid-April the two armies had taken every fortified position on the mainland of Denmark, and Bismarck had given up all pretence of fighting on behalf of 'Germany'. The pretenders in 1864 were Palmerston and Russell, both threatening intervention by the Royal Navy to uphold Denmark's integrity, both knowing that their queen, their Cabinet colleagues and their compatriots in general would never accept a need to fight for Denmark. To save face Palmerston convened a conference in London which he hoped would revise the 1852 treaty and induce Austria and Prussia to pull their troops out of Denmark. But nobody except the British seems to have wished the London Conference to succeed: Denmark refused all concessions; the Austro-Prussian allies resumed their advance; and a new government in Copenhagen, uninterested in British attempts to mediate, negotiated directly with the representatives of Bismarck and Rechberg. The Duchies were handed over to Austro-Prussian military administration, pending a general settlement. In its broadest terms the whole affair of Schleswig-Holstein was a defeat, not simply for Palmerstonian bluff but for the diplomatic system which had developed in the era of Metternich and Nesselrode. In 1864, as in earlier centuries, war was the final arbiter, not ambassadors around a conference table nor sovereigns in some congress conjured from Napoleon III's fantasies.

In the last days of August Francis Joseph and William, Bismarck and Rechberg met in the Habsburg summer palace of Schönbrunn to discuss a final settlement of the Duchies.[14] Bismarck's solution was simple: let Prussia manage Schleswig-Holstein, and in return he would support Austria's interests elsewhere in Europe, perhaps even assisting Francis Joseph to recover Lombardy. Rechberg distrusted Bismarck's imprecision but he was inclined to work with him as a conservative realist. Francis Joseph wanted compensation if he was to forgo his share of the Duchies; he had in mind the retrocession of a small region annexed by Frederick the Great more than 120 years before. But King William cut short these discussions. He had no sympathy with all this talk of bartering provinces, and he made it clear that he did not even feel he had a right to claim Schleswig-Holstein – a rebuff to Bismarck from his own sovereign. The Schönbrunn conversations settled nothing, except perhaps the fate of Rechberg, for Francis Joseph had no wish to retain a Foreign Minister who seemed to handle Prussia softly.

At the end of October 1864 Rechberg was duly replaced by Count Alexander von Mensdorff-Pouilly, a first cousin of Queen Victoria, their mothers being sisters. Mensdorff, ambassador at St Petersburg when the Crimean War began, remained in the Ballhausplatz for almost exactly two years. 'There is not in this world a more honest, straightforward or chivalrous man', wrote the American historian and diplomat John Motley. Austrian policy over German affairs was, however, determined not by the amiable Mensdorff but by a senior counsellor in the Foreign Ministry, Ludwig von Biegeleben, a Darmstadter who believed passionately in Austria's mission to dominate central Europe from the Baltic to the Adriatic. Biegeleben – like Gentz before him in Vienna and Desages, Holstein and Eyre Crowe in other capitals – was an adviser with unusually strong opinions, a dogmatist skilled in expounding his convictions on paper but unwilling to become a public figure. More than anyone else

Biegeleben was responsible for turning Francis Joseph against Rechberg. He took charge of the Austrian Foreign Ministry's correspondence on the German Question until he retired in the summer of 1872, at the age of 60.[15]

Biegeleben encouraged Mensdorff to seek support from the other German states in the Federal Diet and even to tolerate an agitation in favour of Augustenburg's claims in the Duchies rather than make concessions to Prussia. The Austrian reaction suited Bismarck admirably. By February 1865 he could cite so many instances of Austrian intransigence that he won over King William and the more conservative generals to a policy which would place the Duchies totally under Prussian control. By the end of May the king and his Crown Council were prepared for 'a war of brothers' against Austria rather than risk a second humiliation. of Olmütz by giving way to pressure from Vienna. Bismarck was not, in fact, ready for such a war; he needed to be certain of the attitude of the other Great Powers. But he knew that Francis Joseph's empire was near to bankruptcy and politically as divided as ever between the claims of rival nationalities. Austria could no more hope for victory in a short campaign in 1865 than in 1859; and Francis Joseph, largely of his own accord, stepped back from the brink of war. On 14 August a compromise settlement was reached at Gastein: Prussia would administer Schleswig, Austria would administer Holstein and Francis Joseph would sell his share of rights in the small duchy of Lauenburg to William who would then incorporate the region in his kingdom. The Austrians also gave Prussia military and naval concessions in Holstein, including the right to convert Kiel into a naval base and to construct a strategic canal from the Baltic to the North Sea. 'Just fancy finding an Austrian diplomat willing to sign a thing like that', Bismarck said to a colleague as he looked over the draft of the treaty.[16]

The Convention of Gastein is sometimes represented as a trap, to be sprung on Austria when Prussia wished to fight the next round. This is an oversimplification which ignores the material gains acquired by Prussia, the kingdom's first territorial expansion for half a century, and assumes that Bismarck regarded an Austro-Prussian war as inevitable. This he did not. In November he proposed that Austria should hand over Holstein, Francis Joseph selling his rights there as in Lauenburg, and he still hoped Austria would belatedly follow his advice and shift her centre of gravity to Hungary. If there was a change of heart in Vienna, he was ready to promote a rapid reconciliation. Every proposal was brushed aside by the Austrians, who were determined to keep their outpost on the Elbe and their last provinces in Italy. Relentlessly, in the face of Austrian obduracy, Bismarck began to manipulate the Magyar exiles, Czechs, Italians and every other enemy of the Habsburgs, seeking to commit them to action in case of war but avoiding the assumption of any obligations himself. Austrian intelligence reports indicated that a Prussian general had been seen in conversation at cafés in Belgrade one week and in Bucharest the next; there were rumours of attempts to incite Czechs, South Slavs and Romanians within the Habsburg Empire into rebellion; and Garibaldi was said to be fitting out an expeditionary force of Magyars and Croats (an improbable combination) which he would land on the coast of Austrian-held Dalmatia. Yet, in reality, Bismarck was less successful in his efforts at encirclement than he had hoped although there was a good prospect his agents could raise a 'Magyar Legion' of liberators commanded by General Klapka. The one certain enemy of Austria remained Italy, the kingdom which Francis Joseph still declined officially to recognise. It was when, in the second week of March 1866, Karolyi reported the arrival of an Italian military mission in Berlin that Mensdorff and Biegeleben became seriously alarmed.[17]

Bismarck rightly anticipated no risk of intervention in German affairs from either of the fringe Great Powers, Russia or Britain. Tsar Alexander made muted protests at the cavalier way in which Bismarck treated the Danish monarchy, a dynasty with whom the Romanovs were forging marriage links. Gorchakov emphasised yet again the preoccupation of his country with internal affairs. The British, too, had problems of their own. Palmerston, who had become more sympathetic towards Prussia in the closing months of his life, died on 18 October 1865. He was succeeded as Prime Minister by Russell, while Clarendon returned to the Foreign Office. But the principal interest of both Whigs and Tories over the following two years was franchise reform. Although willing to mediate in order to stave off a general war, neither Russell nor Clarendon believed that Britain could take a lead in shaping Europe's future at a time when political feeling was running so high in the country at large and the life expectancy of any government at Westminster was necessarily brief. Britain thus retreated into exaggerated insularity as the Bismarckian revolution on the continent reached its climax. Indeed on 3 July 1866, the day of Königgrätz-Sadowa, the largest and bloodiest battle in Europe in the ninety-nine years which separate Waterloo and Tannenberg, there was technically no government in office at Westminster, Russell having resigned a week previously and Derby and Disraeli still trying to create an endurable Conservative ministry. Eventually Derby took the premiership, his son (Lord Edward Stanley) became Foreign Secretary and Disraeli Chancellor of the Exchequer. Never before or since have two such important posts in a British government been held by father and son. Foreign observers thought the Cabinet narrowly based and Stanley a lightweight compared with his predecessors. The Prime Minister did nothing to dispel this belief by his first speech in the Lords after assuming office. 'It is the duty of the Government of this country', he declared, 'to endeavour not to interfere needlessly or vexatiously with the internal affairs of any foreign country, nor to volunteer to them unasked advice with regard to the conduct of their affairs.'[18] Derby and Stanley, not uninfluenced by Britain's comparative military and naval weakness, firmly turned their backs on the spacious pugnacity of the Palmerston era.

Of far greater concern to Bismarck was the attitude of France. He was anxious, if possible, to secure the benevolent neutrality of Napoleon III in any Austro-Prussian war. When he met Gorchakov briefly in Berlin in November 1864 he maintained that he 'only had to say the word' and France and Prussia would reach an understanding 'within twenty-four hours'.[19] This boast was prompted by conversations which Bismarck had held with Napoleon and Drouyn at St-Cloud and Paris in the previous month. Later reports from the ambassador in Paris led him to moderate his optimism. Drouyn and the Empress still favoured reconciliation with Austria, Eugénie maintaining close links with the Austrian ambassador, Prince Richard von Metternich, and his wife, the much fêted Princess Pauline. Bismarck was angered by Drouyn's condemnation of the Gastein settlement as a cynical bargain which rested on no foundation other than force and, during his autumn holiday, he sought a chance to talk privately to Napoleon, away from Drouyn and the officials of the Quai d'Orsay. The two men accordingly met at Biarritz on 4 October 1865, coming together again for luncheon a week later. Early in November they talked once more at St-Cloud, although on that occasion Napoleon seemed to his guest less speculative and more restrained than at his seaside villa in the Basses-Pyrénées.

Bismarck himself was largely responsible for the myth that Biarritz served as Germany's Plombières. There is no real parallel between the two encounters. Cavour in 1858 had struck a bargain; Bismarck seven years later was prepared to give Napoleon nothing, except the attention offered by a shrewd listener. He was reassured to hear from the emperor that there was no prospect of a Franco-Austrian alliance and he took the opportunity to let Napoleon know that the Gastein Convention contained 'no secret concessions to Austria', that 'we had given Austria no guarantee about Venetia'. Napoleon was well satisfied by the talks. He was confident that Bismarck recognised France's desire for compensation should there be extensive recasting of Europe's frontier lines on the map. Bismarck was surprised at Napoleon's continued preoccupation with Italy, and in particular with the fate of Venetia. In fact, Napoleon – independently of Drouyn – was seeking to interest the Italians in the acquisition of Venice so as to distract them from Rome, where he had committed himself to the eventual withdrawal of the French garrison. Only in the following spring, when Bismarck induced William to sound out Napoleon on the possibility of 'a closer and more special entente between our two governments', did the emperor turn his attention to France's eastern frontier and tentatively angle for concessions in the Rhineland.[20]

Throughout the first four months of 1866 Bismarck sought to provoke Austria, particularly by encouraging unrest within Holstein. He wanted to put Francis Joseph in the wrong, partly in the hope that this would lessen support for Austria from the smaller German states and partly to prevent William's God-fearing royal conscience from dutifully accepting Habsburg leadership again, as in the Schönbrunn conversations. Yet Bismarck was prepared to accept any plan which would give Prussia dominance over north Germany without a campaign against Austria. General Ludwig von Gablenz, the Austrian military governor of Holstein, had a brother, Anton, who was in Prussian service; and in April 1866 Bismarck supported the attempts of the two brothers to settle the mounting tension between Austria and Prussia. But the 'Gablenz Mission' had little chance of success in Vienna. It required Francis Joseph to acknowledge Prussian military primacy north of the River Main at a time when he could see the Habsburg hold on northern Italy finally slipping from his hands. Most outside observers thought Austria would defeat Prussia in war, especially if Prussia's forces were also deployed against the troops of Saxony, Hanover and Bavaria. Every French officer 'from the Minister of War to the most junior subaltern' was convinced Austria would be victorious, Richard Metternich wrote to Mensdorff from Paris. The long-postponed conflict broke out in the small hours of 16 June 1866.[21]

Neither for the first nor for the last time in his reign, Francis Joseph was manoeuvred into a declaration of war for which his empire was ill prepared militarily or financially. The Austrians did indeed have little difficulty in defeating the Italians, with whom Bismarck had concluded a secret military pact on 8 April operative only if fighting broke out between Austria and Prussia within three months. The other German states offered little resistance to the Prussians. But the decisive battle was fought on 3 July in Bohemia, near Sadowa and 7 miles from the fortress of Königgrätz (now appearing on maps of Czechoslovakia as Hradec Kralove). Like Waterloo the battle was a 'near run thing', settled by the arrival of the Second Prussian Army, commanded by the Crown Prince, when the Austrians were already weakened by five hours of 'heavy pounding'. Technically the war continued for another three weeks, but as soon as news of Austria's defeat reached Paris Napoleon III announced that he would mediate, and in the second half of the campaign there was more activity around the council table at Prussian headquarters than on the battlefields. It was only with great difficulty that Bismarck induced the king to abandon his ambition of entering Vienna and dictating peace from the capital of the enemy he had been so reluctant to fight. The preliminaries of a settlement between Prussia and Austria were signed at Nikolsburg on 26 July, with the final peace treaty concluded in Prague four weeks later. The German Confederation was dissolved, Austria losing her status as a Germanic Power. Prussia annexed Schleswig-Holstein, Hanover, Frankfurt and a large part of Hesse. Francis Joseph handed over Venetia to Napoleon III, who transferred it to Italy. Thus the most dramatic and extensive revision of the Vienna Settlement of 1815 had been accomplished by a war of seven weeks, not by the conference diplomacy on which sovereigns and statesmen had based their hopes for half a century.[22]

'It is France that has been defeated at Sadowa', observed Napoleon's Minister of War, Marshal Randon. More precisely, it was the two thwarted revisionist Powers, France and Russia, that had been defeated at Nikolsburg. Gorchakov reacted sharply. He called for a European congress to consider so drastic a change in the map of Europe. There was something wrong in 'a great European negotiation being conducted under the mediation of a single Power', the Russian ambassador complained to the Foreign Secretary in London, and he added that the Tsar 'would take amiss the extinction of the small German States, several of whose Princes were connected by ties of kindred with the Imperial family of Russia'.[23] Napoleon, too, favoured a congress. But Bismarck was not interested. Gorchakov and Alexander II were left in no doubt that Russia must either accept the new ordering of Germany or jeopardise the 'old and faithful' partnership between the Hohenzollerns and the Romanovs. By mid-August Gorchakov was saying that he was satisfied to leave German affairs as they stood. Had he been sole master of France's foreign policy, Napoleon also would have accepted the settlement. There is no reason to suspect he was already preparing for another devious round of diplomacy, in which he would play off the four south German states (Baden, Bavaria, Hesse-Darmstadt and Württemberg) against the Prussian-dominated North German Confederation which Bismarck was creating north of the Main. Drouyn, however, shared Randon's view of Sadowa. If the battle had tilted the balance of power in Prussia's favour, he wanted France to receive compensation in order to offset Bismarck's gains. Drouyn therefore ordered Benedetti, the French ambassador in Berlin, to seek some territorial acquisition. On 5 August Benedetti accordingly proposed a secret agreement by which, as Bismarck wrote, 'Prussia gives France the frontier of 1814 . . . as compensation for our annexations' while Bavaria and Hesse-Darmstadt would be required to hand over to France all their lands on the left bank of the Rhine, receiving an indemnity which Prussia would pay. These demands were curtly rejected by Bismarck. They were, he felt, an insult to national pride and to German public opinion.[24] So angry were the Prussians that Napoleon considered it expedient to jettison Drouyn, who left office at the end of the second week in August. As it was the height of the French holidays, Napoleon decided to entrust the Quai d'Orsay temporarily to one of his staunchest supporters, Eugène Rouher, whom his critics derided as the 'vice-emperor'.

Rouher was a prototype of the ministers who were to scramble for office under the Third Republic. He was a small-town lawyer from the Auvergne, an astute businessman, excellent at handling peasant voters. At heart he was as much a bargain hunter as the discarded aristocrat, Drouyn. If, Rouher argued, Bismarck could not spare a pair of Rhenish fortresses or a cast-off frontier here or there, perhaps he might fancy an alliance in exchange for allowing Napoleon a free hand to grab Belgium or Luxemburg. The bargain was broached by the indefatigable Benedetti, and Bismarck showed interest. He preferred, however, his own brand of conspiratorial diplomacy; and the French obligingly gave him in writing a draft treaty by which Prussia would recognise French claims to Belgium and Luxemburg in return for French approval of a federal union between northern Germany and the four southern states. At this point, in the middle of September 1866, Bismarck became ill, Benedetti protected his own health by seeking the spa waters of Carlsbad, and Rouher left the Quai d'Orsay, finding more congenial work in presiding over the Council of State, a post which gave him patronage over the civil service and over suppliants for the Legion of Honour. Rouher's foray into chancellery politics achieved nothing, but it left the draft of a treaty, filed away in the Wilhelmstrasse for future reference.[25]

Bismarck watched the growing isolation of France with satisfaction. In the four years following Sadowa French foreign policy was a succession of bad guesses, false initiatives and setbacks as Napoleon, racked by poor health, sought to assert his lost hegemony. The emperor claimed, in a speech of February 1867, that by insisting on mediation in the previous July he had halted Prussia's armies at the gates of Vienna without moving a single French regiment; but the boast seemed to echo hollowly round the

Palais Bourbon. It seemed as if Napoleon could do nothing right. From Mexico the news was always bad, and his hopes of unravelling his Italian policy were dashed in November 1867 by the need to send yet another French expedition to defend the Pope and defeat the latest Garibaldian incursion, at Mentana. The most serious of the European crises came in the spring of 1867, when negotiations by which France sought to purchase the Grand Duchy of Luxemburg from the King of the Netherlands were leaked to the Press in London and Berlin.[26] Napoleon had believed he could count on Prussian backing for the deal but so intense was the feeling engendered by the crisis that Bismarck had to warn Benedetti that it would be difficult to avoid a war if Luxemburg passed into French hands. In the first week of May 1867 the British convened a conference in London to discuss the Luxemburg problem. The Grand Duchy was accorded neutral status and remained part of the dominions of the sovereign of the Netherlands until 1890 when, on the accession of Queen Wilhelmina, it gained independence under the senior branch of the House of Nassau. Never again did France seek to secure Luxemburg, nor indeed were any further attempts made to gain German consent for the revision of France's frontiers.

Only one Great Power took France's side in the Luxemburg crisis, and that was Austria. Francis Joseph remained unreconciled to the loss of Habsburg leadership in Germany. At the end of October 1866 he dismissed Mensdorff from the Foreign Ministry and gave the post to Count Ferdinand von Beust, formerly in charge of foreign affairs in Saxony, where he had gained the reputation of being a determined opponent of Bismarck. Originally Francis Joseph intended Beust to organise an anti-Prussian league, comprising Austria, the four south German states and any other government made uneasy by Bismarck's policies. Beust was not, however, to contemplate another military campaign: Austria, Francis Joseph told him in his formal instructions, would have 'to renounce all idea of war for a long time'.[27] Although Beust improved Austro-French relations, there were two main obstacles to fulfilling the programme for which he was appointed: secret treaties bound the lesser German states to Bismarck's new North German Confederation; and the Habsburg Empire itself was convulsed in the winter of 1866–7 by the political negotiations with the moderate Hungarian liberals which produced the Compromise *(Ausgleich)* of 1867 and transformed Francis Joseph's empire into the Dual Monarchy of Austria-Hungary. Beust travelled to Budapest within a few weeks of taking office and was largely responsible for the final agreement with the Magyar leader, Ferenc Deak, and his closest associate, Gyula Andrassy, who became Hungary's first Prime Minister. This intervention by Beust in purely Habsburg affairs was followed, within the Austrian lands of the Monarchy, by a series of administrative reforms which he had recommended. It was clear by the summer of 1867 that Francis Joseph hoped Beust would be his new strong man at the helm. Already in February he had taken office as Minister President, with responsibilities transcending the duties assigned to a Foreign Minister.

At Beust's personal request he was given the title of Chancellor. In

Vienna this rank had been enjoyed previously only by Metternich and by Kaunitz in the eighteenth century. Francis Joseph calculated that the new dignity would assure the ex-Saxon minister of status and prestige within the empire and abroad. Significantly, Gorchakov had been created Chancellor on 25 June 1867 to mark his golden jubilee in Russia's foreign service, and it was the title now borne by Bismarck as head of government in the North German Confederation. Beust's critics – mostly German-Austrian Catholics suspicious of his foreign liberal Protestantism – maintained that the appropriation of a rank which placed him on an equal footing with Bismarck was the sole overtly anti-Prussian action of his chancellorship. This was slightly unfair, as he was known to be conducting long negotiations with the French, but it is clear that when he moved from Dresden to Vienna Beust became first and foremost a champion of 'European values' allegedly menaced by Slavdom. In conversation with Francis Joseph he would talk of Europe's need for 'a united front binding Germans and Hungarians against Pan-Slavism'.[28] He was disinclined to make concessions to the Czechs at home or to underestimate the activities of Russian agents in the Balkans and the threat from Russia's army on the borders of Galicia. Beust therefore looked rather down the Danube than to the Main and the Rhine. He would willingly join France in war with the new Germany once he was convinced the French were on the verge of victory, but he had no intention of being for a second time on the loser's side against Bismarck. Napoleon III, failing to perceive the full subtlety of Beust's opportunism, mistook assurances of goodwill for a sign that Austrian and French armies would one day march together. Such a concept was indeed conjured up conversationally by Francis Joseph when the two emperors met at Salzburg in August 1867; but before leaving Vienna for Salzburg, Francis Joseph received from Beust a memorandum which might almost have been a carbon copy of the instructions the emperor had given his new minister the previous autumn. 'Austria has an absolute need of peace for a long time', Beust wrote.[29] In fact, though it seemed improbable, Austria was to be granted the longest respite from war in Habsburg history, for the peace was not broken for another forty-seven years.

There was never any real prospect of a war to avenge Sadowa. Not even a project for linking France, Italy and Austria in a grand alliance against Prussia and Russia had much chance of success, although it was discussed intermittently in Paris, Florence and Vienna between December 1868 and June 1869. Napoleon employed Rouher again, hoping he might draw up some business deal gratifying to Austria and to Italy, too. But the task was beyond Rouher's ingenuity. Talk of a Brenner Pass frontier, of moving Italy's capital to Rome, of vague commitments in the area known even more vaguely as the 'Near East', left everything unresolved. The nearest Napoleon came to ending France's isolation was when Field-Marshal Archduke Albrecht – a much-esteemed soldier, first cousin to Francis Joseph's father and therefore, with an odd echo of past attachments, a first cousin to the Empress Marie-Louise – came to Paris in April 1870 and discussed strategy with General Leboeuf, Napoleon III's new Minister of War.[30] But when the French came to examine the archduke's war plans they reluctantly decided that Francis Joseph was out to cheat them: the Austrians claimed that they would not be able to march until the French had been engaged for six to eight weeks with the German armies. By then, it was felt in Paris, the fortunes of war would have gone one way or the other. Archduke Albrecht was merely embellishing the 'heads I win, tails you lose' approach of Beust.

In Paris there was no sense of imminent disaster, or even of an inevitable war with Prussia, in that spring of 1870. Franco-Prussian relations had been cordial for the past three years. King William was a guest of Napoleon in Paris in 1867, his first journey there since he marched in behind Alexander I in 1814; and the visit had gone well, with Bismarck promising as the royal train left the French capital that they would come back again. Yet there was nothing quite like a conflict with France, whether in the form of threatening speeches or the confrontation of armies, to fan German patriotic enthusiasm along the length of the Rhine, both inside and outside the borders of Prussia. Few people now believe that Bismarck deliberately provoked the French to war in 1870 by encouraging a Hohenzollern to seek the Spanish throne, left vacant by the flight of the allegedly nymphomaniac Queen Isabella II in 1868. It was impossible for anyone, even Bismarck, to anticipate that French national pride would transform a dying crisis beyond the frontier of the Pyrenees into a live challenge on the Rhine. But there is nevertheless no doubt that Bismarck strongly favoured the Hohenzollern candidature as a source of potential mischief in Europe, a rallying point for Pan-German feeling at a time when he was faced with opposition from North German liberals to his attempts to Prussianise the structure of the new Confederation.[31] Bismarck manufactured a crisis, if he did not provoke a war.

At the end of February 1870 an envoy from the acting Regent of Spain met Prince Charles Anthony of Hohenzollern-Sigmaringen, head of the Roman Catholic branch of the dynasty, and offered the throne of Spain to Prince Charles's eldest son, Leopold. The Hohenzollerns were unenthusiastic and King William positively hostile to the idea; he complained petulantly, but realistically, that Spain was 'a nation which for the last forty years has wantonly proceeded from one revolution to another'. On the other hand Roon, as Minister of War, and Moltke, as Chief of the General Staff, favoured the Spanish proposal: a Hohenzollern in Madrid would, by his presence there, force France to keep an army in the southwest in any future Franco-German crisis, thereby effectively weakening any concentration around the vital garrison cities of Metz, Strasbourg and Châlons. Bismarck backed the two generals and even the Crown Prince, often an opponent of the Chancellor, was impressed by their argument. The king left the decision to the Sigmaringens. On 19 June Prince Leopold at last accepted the offer, which was still a secret. News of the candidature leaked out in Madrid in the last days of the month. By 4 July it was in the French Press. So violent was reaction in Paris that William, who thought it absurd to go to war with France over such a project, sent an emissary to Sigmaringen and induced Leopold to withdraw his candidacy on 12 July. Once again, as at Schönbrunn in August 1864, the king had struck at the heart of Bismarck's policy. Briefly the Chancellor contemplated resignation.

Roon and Moltke let him know that should Napoleon commit some foolish act and precipitate a war every advantage lay with Prussia that July. But when the Chancellor met Gorchakov, who was on a private visit to Germany, on Wednesday 13 July, he assured the Russian that it would be against his religious principles and his instinct of humanity to take any step which would make war certain.[32]

On that same Wednesday the French ambassador met King William on the promenade in the spa town of Ems. On instructions from Paris, Benedetti asked William for a guarantee that he would never consent to a renewal of the Hohenzollern candidature. The king politely but firmly declined to say anything more on the subject. Benedetti, however, had received instructions to secure an assurance, not because the French believed a renewal of the candidature likely but because the government in Paris hoped to emphasise Prussia's humiliation, perhaps forcing Bismarck from office and thus weakening the hold of the North German Confederation over the four southern states. It was Benedetti's attempt to secure a second audience with the king which caused William I to send an irritated telegram to Bismarck from Ems in which he authorised the Chancellor, if he thought it advisable, to make public the whole episode with Benedetti. Publication of the telegram, with slight excisions by Bismarck, made the encounter between king and ambassador appear more dramatic than it had been in reality. The French thought they had suffered a rebuff, the news breaking in Paris on the *Quatorze Juillet*, of all days in the good patriotic Frenchman's year. Napoleon III, a sick man no longer in control of events, allowed himself to be stampeded into a declaration of war on 19 July. Only the veteran statesman Thiers and the politicians of the left called for peace and common sense.[33]

By Europe's reckoning France thus placed herself in the wrong. Bismarck hammered home the point in his propaganda, notably by publishing the draft proposals of four years back, with their hint of 'compensation' in Belgium and Luxemburg. No other Power offered France diplomatic support, let alone military assistance. At Sedan on 1 September the principal field army of the Second Empire was, as Moltke remarked, 'caught in a mousetrap'. Total victory for Prussia was followed by the personal surrender of Napoleon III to King William in Bismarck's presence at the small manor-house of Bellevue, some 2 miles west of Sedan. The fallen emperor left next day for captivity at Wilhelmshohe, near Cassel, while a republic was proclaimed in Paris. The victorious king turned westwards, where the road to France's capital seemed to lie open. Prussia had triumphed, and the south German states were now prepared not merely to enter the North German Confederation but to establish a unified German state under Prussia's leadership.

Four months later, even while Paris was still resisting a grim siege, the king who had crowned himself in East Prussia less than ten years before was proclaimed 'German Emperor' in Louis XIV's Hall of Mirrors at Versailles. But the ceremony brought him little pleasure; on the previous afternoon he had wept at the thought of 'bidding farewell to the old Prussia'.[34] At Königsberg he had proudly received a crown 'from God's hand and no other'. At Versailles he stood before Germany's princes as reluctant high priest in the apotheosis of popular nationalism. Only the fortunate coincidence that this Wednesday, 18 January 1871, was the one hundred and seventieth anniversary of the coronation of Prussia's first king reconciled William to what he scornfully termed Bismarck's 'Emperor charade'.

11 The Three Emperors, 1871–79

When, on 3 September 1870, news reached St Petersburg that Napoleon III and his army had surrendered to the Prussians, Alexander II is reported by the British ambassador to have made the sign of the cross and exclaimed, 'Thank God, Sebastopol is now avenged'.[1] Few statesmen in Europe shared the Tsar's certainty that providential retribution had prevailed mysteriously at Sedan; most, however, recognised that the day-long battle around the grey citadel on the Meuse had changed the political balance of the continent. A unified Germany, stronger in military capacity and industrial potential than any of its neighbours, was replacing the ineffectual confederation of the Metternich era. The fall of the Second Empire threw into jeopardy client dependencies elsewhere in Europe, in south-eastern Asia and in North Africa. It was a time for other governments to adjust their policies so as to benefit from the eclipse of France before a new system was dictated from Berlin.

The immediate beneficiary was Italy. French troops hurriedly withdrew from Rome, and on 20 September Victor Emmanuel's army finally solved the Roman Question by breaching the walls of the papal city and forcing Pius IX to confine himself to the palaces of the Vatican. Before the end of the year Rome had become the effective capital of united Italy, a nation striving to act as a Great Power at the very moment when neighbouring France was relegated to a lower status. No other nation gained so much from the fall of the Second Empire. Ultimately the British benefited in Egypt and the Levant from the disappearance of Bonapartist political and commercial patronage of the Arabs. More immediately the Gladstone government – with Granville back at the Foreign Office after Clarendon's death in July 1870 – looked to the traditional areas of British concern in the Low Countries. Bismarck's revelation of earlier French designs on Belgium so alarmed the British that Granville concentrated his energies on securing new pledges from the signatories of the 1839 Treaty of London to ensure respect for Belgium's neutrality. To some extent the Belgian Question distracted the British from other issues and, at least until the bombardment of Paris, hardened public opinion against France, as Bismarck intended.[2]

News of the first Prussian victories at Wörth and Gravelotte soon dissipated any enthusiasm there may have been in Vienna for renewing the contest with Germany. A ministerial council, under the emperor's presidency, met at Schönbrunn on 22 August to decide on policy. The tentative feelers put out by Archduke Albrecht were ignored; this was no time for gestures of Franco-Austrian friendship. Beust wished to collaborate with Britain and Russia, mediating between the combatants in the hope of safeguarding the integrity of France and so prevent drastic changes in the map of Europe. The most significant comment at the council came from Beust's rival, Gyula Andrassy, the Hungarian Prime Minister. 'Austria's mission remains, as before, to be a bulwark against Russia', Andrassy declared. 'Only so long as she fulfils this mission does her existence remain a necessity for Europe.'[3] Not for many years had Francis Joseph heard so clear a statement of principle at a ministerial council. Although Andrassy's views seemed closer to those of Archduke Albrecht, Francis Joseph was inclined to follow the advice of his empress and entrust the conduct of foreign affairs to her Magyar favourite; but not yet. He could not risk a conflict with Russia. Chancellor Beust was authorised to seek friendly collaboration with Chancellor Gorchakov, Francis Joseph assuming that Saxon ingenuity would somehow explain away the awkward fact that the Austrians had been undertaking military preparations for some months along Russia's Galician frontier. And, in case of failure, a Saxon expatriate was more easily expendable than Count Andrassy.

The Austrian attitude puzzled and irritated the Russians. Beust and Gorchakov had similar objectives: neutral mediation to limit German supremacy on the continent. No one in St Petersburg could understand why Vienna insisted on fortifying Galicia and purchasing horses for a likely winter campaign while giving pledges of neutrality. The possibility that Francis Joseph had to find a safety-valve for Archduke Albrecht's sabre-rattlers well away from the theatre of war does not seem to have occurred to the Russians. Yet St Petersburg, too, suffered from influential pressure groups. There had long been a pro-German 'lobby' at court, headed by the Grand Duchess Elena, last surviving sister-in-law of Alexander I and by birth a Württemberg princess. The Grand Duchess, an indefatigable sexagenarian of great prestige and personality, spent much of August seeking to improve relations between St Petersburg and Berlin, holding several conversations with the Prussian ambassador and the Tsar while making certain that the elusive Gorchakov paid attention to her views by submitting them in writing. For good measure she gained the backing of Katkov's newspapers in Russia and was able to use her German relatives to badger King William at his field headquarters. The Grand Duchess's plan was simple enough: Bismarck would suggest that if the Tsar wished to abrogate the Black Sea clauses of the Treaty of Paris Russia could count on German support, provided that the Tsar in his turn recognised that Germany needed to annex territory from France. Bismarck encouraged his ambassador to support the Grand Duchess's initiative, and Gorchakov took up the proposal four days after news of Sedan reached St Petersburg. 'Should the Prussian Government have decided not to relinquish their conquests of Alsace and Lorraine', the British ambassador reported Gorchakov as saying, 'he fears that the Neutral Powers could only look on with regret.' Henceforth two distinct political issues – Alsace-Lorraine for the new Germany, a re-militarised Black Sea for Russia – were more closely interrelated than the other Foreign Ministries of Europe appreciated at the time.[4]

It was not until the end of October that Alexander II finally resolved to denounce the Black Sea clauses and he embodied his decision in a diplomatic circular sent to embassies abroad early in the following month.

Reaction to the unilateral abrogation of treaty obligations was predictably hostile in London and Vienna. The outcry in the British Press and Parliament even distracted attention from events in France. Gladstone deplored loose talk of waging another war against Russia, but Bismarck affected to take the threat seriously. He induced Gorchakov to withdraw the circular and submit claims for revision of the Treaty of Paris to a conference which opened in London on the day before the great 'Emperor charade' at Versailles. The talks continued intermittently for two months until a convention was signed which restored Russia's sovereign rights in the Black Sea and pledged the Sultan of Turkey to open the Bosphorus and Dardanelles to allied and friendly warships in time of peace. The settlement was well received. Britain was satisfied that treaty revision had come by agreement round the conference table, Russia that it had come at all. Alexander II 'prayed with signs of deep emotion' at the tomb of his father, telling his attendants as he left the cathedral in the fortress of St Peter and St Paul that 'the shade of the Emperor Nicholas would now be appeased'.[5]

Bismarck, too, welcomed the London Conference and its negotiated settlement. He could claim the Tsar's gratitude for his role in securing revision of a hated treaty and he was well satisfied by an exchange of telegrams between the German and Russian rulers emphasising the friendship of their two empires. But his principal concern was to finish off the war with France, secure 'a safe frontier' for Germany and win acceptance by the remaining Great Powers of the new Prussian-imposed system in Europe. Above all, he was eager to end the fighting before the London Conference tried to dictate a settlement on the Rhine as well as on the Black Sea. The minimum programme of annexation acceptable to Prussia and her allies in Germany was agreed between William and Bismarck soon after the victory of Sedan: cession of all Alsace, including Strasbourg, and much of Lorraine, including the fortress of Metz. These terms, first communicated to a French envoy on 19 September 1870, were condemned by foreign governments as liable to perpetuate friction between the two Great Powers of Western Europe. France fought on until the new year, accepting an armistice on 28 January and signing peace preliminaries four weeks later. The formal treaty was concluded at Frankfurt on 10 May 1871: Belfort remained in French hands, but most of Alsace and Lorraine passed under German rule, and a German army of occupation remained in France until the defeated enemy paid the victors an indemnity of 5 milliard francs. The Treaty of Frankfurt was a greater humiliation than the settlements of 1814 and 1815 simply because it was imposed not by four allied powers but by a single newly united empire convinced that France would seek revenge and determined to weaken her militarily and industrially by the annexation of the two disputed provinces.[6]

With the signing of the Treaty of Frankfurt Bismarck became as much a champion of the established international order as Metternich in his prime. Once again, as in the forty years before the Crimean War, there was talk of a European system, with Gladstone even reviving pious hopes of a Concert of Europe. Bismarck, however, was a pragmatist who believed that an orderly and balanced community of nations depended not upon acceptance of a common moral purpose but upon constant adjustment of the relationship between the states by improvised alliances, limited both in time and in purpose. He was prepared to borrow themes from the old chancellery diplomacy, conjuring up a bogey of international socialism where Metternich had spoken of the 'Jacobin peril' and hoping, from time to time, to revive a Holy Alliance, although with more mundane credentials required for membership than in Alexander I's day. But Bismarck was never the slave of ideological purity. He sought and enjoyed greater flexibility than his predecessors had known, and he kept ready an alternative route along any line of policy rather than accept the humiliation of retreat.

Bismarck never possessed the authority of a dictator. He found it essential to tighten ministerial control over his subordinates. This was made clear to the German public in 1872 and 1874. On the first occasion he dismissed from office Hermann von Thile, the 'State Secretary for Foreign Affairs', who had begun to seek opportunities to determine policy; the Chancellor regarded the State Secretary as an administrative official, not a person of political or executive rank. Two years later the famous conflict between Bismarck and Count Harry von Arnim served as a warning to other envoys who might (like Bismarck himself in earlier days) wish to offer their sovereign an alternative foreign policy; for the Chancellor broke the career of Arnim, the Junker aristocrat whom he had appointed ambassador in Paris three years previously, because he lacked 'the discipline, loyalty and obedience which a supreme general in the field has a right to expect from his brigade commanders.'[7] Yet, ironically, the hardest of Bismarck's bureaucratic battles was against these loyal and disciplined generals. Military attachés tended to form a separate foreign service who would give advice from other capitals and courts direct to the Chief of the General Staff or to their war lord, the German emperor. Although Bismarck checked the intrusive influence of the General Staff on several occasions – notably in 1871 and 1887 – he could not establish total mastery over the officer corps, a failure which helped to precipitate his downfall in the reign of a younger and headstrong emperor.[8]

However successful Bismarck's policies might appear to outside observers, he remained unsure of his position in the state. He was particularly on guard against ambitious soldier diplomats. This insecurity contributed to the relatively low level of ambassadorial competence in the Bismarckian era; the Chancellor did not encourage potential rivals. Some ambassadors were merely conscientious pen-pushers, two were distinguished officers who saw themselves as representatives of their emperor abroad and had scant regard for the Chancellor, others were society idols, a few were sycophants, and almost all the senior diplomats were despised by Bismarck and ignored by him so far as possible. The outstanding exception was Count Paul von Hatzfeldt-Wildenburg, 'the best horse in my diplomatic stable', successively envoy at Madrid and Constantinople. After three years as State Secretary in Berlin, Bismarck sent Hatzfeldt to London where he was ambassador from 1885 to 1901. As Bismarck grew older so his suspicion of ambassadors increased. More and more he turned for information to a few trusted cronies, of whom the most versed in public affairs was the banker Gerson Bleichröder, whom Disraeli considered the one person who dared speak the truth to the Chancellor. This was no doubt an exaggerated judgement, but it is clear that, at least from 1878 onwards, Germany's ambassadors and foreign envoys in Berlin treated Bleichröder with the awed respect accorded to a mystery man of influence and perception.[9]

There was too much inspired improvisation about Bismarck's foreign service for it to arouse the envy of other diplomats. Even after the disasters of 1870–1, the quality of France's ambassadors – many of them aristocrats with scant sympathy for the republic they represented – continued to arouse wide respect. The diplomatic tradition of France remained superior to all rivals. There was a regular exchange of postings; diplomats did not spend too long in one capital and they had frequent spells of work in the Quai d'Orsay itself, thus enabling them to acquire a more comprehensive view of world politics. The system worked admirably, although it was sometimes said by officials from other ministries in Paris that overstaffing made the Quai d'Orsay inefficient. During the 1870s the French were fortunate in having only three Foreign Ministers and, at the end of the decade, a first-rate director of political affairs at the ministry, Baron de Courcel, later an equally effective ambassador in Berlin and London. The concise lucidity which Talleyrand and d'Hauterive had tried to instil into the young attachés and secretaries earlier in the century still set the tone of the communications between members of the French diplomatic service; and the printed dispatches of French ambassadors throughout the Third Republic remain models of dispassionate reporting and judicious assessment.[10]

The Austro-Hungarian foreign service in the 1870s and 1880s suffered from the two inherent weaknesses of the Monarchy itself, social exclusiveness and racial division. The snobbishness which made an ambassador of the French Republic, himself a royalist Marquis, recruit his staff solely from the nobility so long as he served in Vienna, found its counterpart in Austria's embassies in other capitals, while a diplomat's strong feelings for (or, more probably, against) Germans or Slavs influenced the reports back to Vienna as well as decisions within the ministry itself. Nevertheless, the Austrians had the good sense to send Karolyi back to Berlin in 1871 as soon as ambassadors were exchanged again after the humiliations of the Seven Weeks' War. No one else knew Bismarck's strength and weakness so well. The ablest of the German-Austrian diplomats, Baron Heinrich von Haymerle, ambassador in Rome from 1877 until he became Foreign Minister in 1879, possessed a remarkably non-Austrian efficiency, but he had difficulty in disciplining his almost pathological hatred of everything Slav.[11]

If there was any collective characteristic among the Tsar's representatives in the Bismarckian era it was a discrepancy in levels of professional competence. Ignatyev, who by 1870 had six years' experience of Constantinople to add to his earlier achievements, stood out as a unique figure, a powerful rival to Chancellor Gorchakov. By contrast, Oubril – ambassador at Berlin from 1862 to 1880 – was a bumbler, much despised by Bismarck but kept at his post through the obstinacy of Gorchakov, whose colleague he had been in earlier years. Novikov (in Vienna 1870–80, Constantinople 1880–82) was an outstanding scholar on the Hussites, a preoccupation which allowed him to remain happily ignorant of weakness and inefficiency within his own embassy. Until 1874 the ambassador in London was still Brunnow, whose first mission had been to congratulate Victoria on her accession; but he was succeeded by a more remarkable personality, the great landowner Peter Shuvalov, who had made his debut at the Paris Congress but later became notorious as head of the Tsar's security service, the 'Third Department'. It is an interesting comment on the partialities of society in London that, despite his ill repute as a police chief, the wealthy Shuvalov was soon accepted as the most polished social charmer accredited to the Court of St James. He was also, though he concealed the fact, the ambassador with the shrewdest intelligence.[12]

The presence of such able envoys as Shuvalov and (later) Hatzfeldt and Courcel emphasises how much foreign governments regarded London as a key post. There were two main reasons for this importance: Britain was an uncommitted Power, rich in banking interests and worldwide trade; and the British persisted, especially after Lord Salisbury became Foreign Secretary in March 1878, in conducting diplomacy so far as possible at home rather than allowing the pace of negotiations to be set abroad. The Foreign Office, which moved into its present neo-Palladian Venetian *palazzo* in 1868, was no longer the 'dingy and shabby . . . picture of disorder, penury and meanness' which the elder Sir Horace Rumbold could remember from the late 1840s.[13] It remained self-contained and small, with its personnel still kept rigidly distinct from the diplomatic service, a separation unknown in most other capitals. Odo Russell, who had the advantage of being Lord John Russell's nephew, served briefly in the Office between diplomatic missions to papal Rome and newly imperial Berlin, but this was exceptional. The earliest senior transfers from the Foreign Office to the diplomatic service took place in 1889 when Julian Pauncefote, permanent under-secretary for the past seven years, became minister in Washington, and in 1894 when his successor at the Foreign Office, Philip Currie, was appointed ambassador to the Sultan.

The strength of the Foreign Office as an efficient institution in the 1870s and 1880s was derived from the achievements of Edmund Hammond, permanent under-secretary from 1854 to 1873. Hammond, who had begun climbing the bureaucratic ladder of the Office as early as 1824, gave continuity to British diplomacy, especially under the less dynamic Foreign Secretaries who separate Palmerston from Salisbury. From Hammond's day onwards, the 'permanent head' supervised the work of the key political departments and much of the administration, too. He expected to deal directly with the Prime Minister and other members of the Cabinet as well as with the Foreign Secretary. The three assistant under-secretaries of state annotated incoming dispatches with relevant references to past papers. Occasionally, if they possessed particular knowledge of a country's problems, they might suggest a line of policy for the Foreign Secretary to follow. At least one senior clerk, Sir Percy

Anderson, came to exert an influence on policy out of all proportion to his nominal ranking in the Foreign Office hierarchy. As effective supervisor of the African Department from 1883 to 1896, Anderson understood the problems of a continent neglected by more senior administrators, his natural Francophobia giving a bias to Foreign Office decisions which was not perceived until some seventy years after his death. Yet, apart from Anderson, the mandarins of the Foreign Office seem to have remained executants rather than formulators of policy until the very end of the century.[14]

Most of Britain's embassies and legations abroad were staffed by talented aristocrats with large private incomes, although there were also some well-informed outsiders, such as Sir Joseph Crowe, the commercial attaché in Berlin. The 'professionals' in the Foreign Office, natural conservatives to a man, tended to regard the luminaries of the diplomatic service as gifted amateurs – elderly Whigs believing in ordered liberty and low taxation, younger Liberal high thinkers, often from Jowett's Balliol, seeking to perfect a Platonic statecraft in which a morally valuable end is attained by a rationally chosen means. Some British ambassadors enjoyed great influence because both the home government and the government of the sovereign to whom they were accredited held them in high regard and trusted them to ease mutual tension. Among such envoys were Lord Lyons (at Paris from 1867 to 1887), Odo Russell (Berlin, 1871–84) and the archaeologist Sir Henry Layard (Constantinople, 1877–80), although both Russell and Layard were criticised from time to time in the Commons and the English Press. Several ambassadors were lightweights; Disraeli, who like Bismarck thought little of his top diplomats, complained that Sir Andrew Buchanan (Vienna, 1871–81) was a 'hopeless mediocrity' and that Lord Augustus Loftus (Berlin, 1861–71, and St Petersburg, 1871–9) was 'a mere Polonius . . . afraid even of Gorchakov's shadow'.[15] Yet these strictures reflect the Prime Minister's mounting irritability rather than any general weakness in the foreign service. The greatest fault among the ambassadors was a tendency to despise all matters concerned with trade. There remained, until after the First World War, a marked gap between the diplomatic service and the consular service, even though one of Salisbury's most respected ambassadors, Sir William White (Constantinople, 1886–91), had spent his early years in the consular branch, concentrating on commercial affairs.[16]

The more cautious British diplomats were inhibited by a threat of partial publicity, a problem long unknown in the foreign service of governments whose ministers remained independent of parliamentary control. Palmerston had made use of Blue books more extensively than his predecessors, and it was reasonable to assume that as Parliament became more representative so the newly enfranchised would be given more and more selections from the archives, since Foreign Secretaries would wish to justify their case or stress particular aspects of policy. This was, in fact, a false assumption. During the last quarter of the nineteenth century Foreign Secretaries considered world affairs too serious a matter for widespread Blue book publicity, and it was the continental Chancelleries who began to select material from their archives for propaganda purposes – the French as early as 1861, the Austrians from 1868, the Germans after 1870. There remained nevertheless in Britain a certain public pride in the openness of 'the English diplomatic tradition'. At Oxford, for example, the Chichele Professor of International Law and Diplomacy, lecturing to undergraduates on 'Diplomacy as a Career', used a claim that 'our diplomatic agents . . . more than others have worked, and are likely to work, in the daylight' as the climax of his concluding remarks. 'Base motives and crooked designs shrink from the daylight', Professor Bernard told his pupils. 'Falsehood and dissimulation spin their webs in dark places.' 'We do not want a stirring or a brilliant diplomacy,' he added. 'Better that it should err, if at all, on the side of inaction.'[17]

Such precepts were well suited to the needs of post-Palmerstonian England, whose interests by the early 1870s were primarily outside Europe. Yet, curiously enough, in one sense Bismarck would have agreed with the professor now that peace had been formally settled by the Treaty of Frankfurt. Bismarck's Germany was a 'satiated Power' and, after 1871, inaction was preferable to change. Provided France remained isolated, other governments might even initiate diplomatic ventures. All Bismarck asked was that Berlin be consulted, so that he could adjust his policy and benefit from any proposals put forward by Germany's neighbours. He would not, of course, risk weakening Prussian Junker control of the Reich by measures which might harm the landed interest, and he was prepared to use alleged threats from other governments as a means of distracting the German people from grievances nearer home, but in general he favoured a stable, conservative and co-operative European system. Not surprisingly, he welcomed the ideas of any statesman who was opposed to policies of territorial expansion. It is significant that the 'League of the Three Emperors' *(Dreikaiserbund)*, an informal grouping that gave Bismarck's diplomacy its most characteristic form throughout the 1870s, was created in the first instance not by the German Chancellor but by Count Andrassy, whom Francis Joseph appointed Foreign Minister in November 1871.

The emperor-king's decision to replace Beust by Andrassy caused surprise in Vienna and in foreign capitals. Andrassy had, after all, been an exiled rebel under sentence of death at the start of the emperor's reign and Beust was widely respected abroad. But Francis Joseph had become alarmed by the extent to which his Saxon-born Chancellor concerned himself with the internal affairs of the Dual Monarchy. With astonishing suddenness the title of Chancellor was dropped from Habsburg constitutional usage, Beust sent off to London as ambassador and Andrassy brought to number 2 Ballhausplatz – where, in exultant moments, he would amaze the staid officials of the ministry by doing handstands on Metternich's old desk. Lord Lytton, First Secretary of the British embassy, described Andrassy as 'a soldier, a sportsman and something of an elegant, with a dash in his temperament of the gypsy chief', much as Disraeli seven years later told Victoria that Andrassy was 'a picturesque-looking person but apparently wanting calm'. These thumbnail sketches, tributes to a superficial Magyar exoticism, missed the one fundamental Hungarian assumption in every aspect of Andrassy's policy – the conviction that Austria-Hungary must never increase its Slav population.[18] Although Archduke Albrecht and the military party around him in Vienna might wish to absorb the two Turkish provinces of Bosnia-Herzegovina, Andrassy contended that such a move would swell the Serb and Croat minority within the Monarchy and he feared it would endanger the racial balance established by the 1867 Compromise.

Soon after Andrassy became Foreign Minister, Lytton reported that he wished to collaborate with Germany, Italy and Britain so as to keep the revisionist Powers, France and Russia, 'on their best behaviour'. Gladstone and his Foreign Secretary, Granville, were cautious; there was widespread hostility in England and Scotland to the supposedly evil machinations of continental diplomacy, and Gladstone fought shy of any European commitment.[19] Andrassy, too, was really still feeling his way towards a policy. Although he remained convinced that Austria should serve as a bulwark against Russian expansion, he was prepared to test the mood in St Petersburg and seek reconciliation with the new Germany at the same time. Thus in July 1872 Archduke Albrecht made a – highly successful – goodwill visit to the Tsar while Andrassy induced a reluctant Francis Joseph to accept an invitation from Berlin for early September. Two and a half weeks before Francis Joseph was due in Prussia, Alexander II informed the German ambassador that he wished to pay a courtesy call on his uncle, the Emperor William, during the Austrian visit. This gathering in Berlin, an unexpected fillip to the ideals of monarchical solidarity, enabled Andrassy to broaden the scope of his policy and work with Russia through a loosely knit League of the Three Emperors rather than seek Bismarck's support in a narrow Austro-German alliance.

The Berlin meeting aroused widespread concern, particularly in Paris and London, where there was the customary newspaper talk of a resurrected Holy Alliance. Bismarck made much of the imperial visits. 'For the first time in history', he boasted to Odo Russell, 'three emperors have sat down to dinner together to discuss peace.' Gorchakov, less inclined to prandial generalisation, thought the meeting of 'enormous significance', although he regretted that there was 'nothing for the diplomatic archives'.[20] Andrassy and Gorchakov found they could work together. Austro-Russian relations were, indeed, better than Austro-German, for Francis Joseph was irritated by a German interest in his empire's railway projects and especially in the future of the port of Trieste. The imperial round of visits continued, nevertheless, over the following eighteen months: William to St Petersburg in April 1873 and to Vienna in the following October; Alexander in state to Vienna in June 1873, with Francis Joseph braving St Petersburg's snow and ice to return the compliment in February 1874. On each occasion the visiting sovereign was accompanied by his Foreign Minister. An Austro-Russian Convention, signed at Schönbrunn during the Tsar's visit, bound the two emperors to consult each other, even when their interests differed, so as to uphold European peace. Emperor William acceded to the Convention when he came to Schönbrunn four months later. This Schönbrunn agreement was the sole protocol linking the Three Emperors' League of the 1870s. Technically it was a triumph for Andrassy. The Habsburg capital was again the hub of Europe's diplomacy, even if the true arbiter between governments was Germany's Chancellor, not the Foreign Minister in Vienna.

Yet there is no doubt that Andrassy was chief beneficiary from the so-called 'War in Sight' crisis which Bismarck engineered in the spring of 1875. The bitterness of the divisive church and state conflict within Germany (the *Kulturkampf*) induced the Chancellor to seek an easy diplomatic success as an escape from his domestic political differences. In early April he encouraged newspapers in Cologne and Berlin to suggest that the rapid rearmament of France was a sign that Paris wanted a war of revenge. The newspaper scare was followed by indiscreet remarks from influential figures at the Prussian court and by mysterious warnings received in Paris from a 'royal prince' sympathetic to France.[21] In early May the French and British Press began to draw alarming parallels with the crisis weeks of 1870. Emperor William, too, was disturbed; he had been so eager for better relations with France that he surprised the new ambassador of the Third Republic by wearing the sash of the Legion of Honour when he welcomed him to Berlin only seven months after the Treaty of Frankfurt;[22] and William now made it clear to Bismarck that he would not allow his Chancellor to provoke new battles with the French. It was easy enough for Bismarck to reassure his sovereign, for he had never contemplated a war. What disturbed the Chancellor was the reaction outside Germany. He had counted on an abject French climb-down, something to boost his prestige in the most Roman Catholic regions of western Prussia. Instead he received a stern warning from the British government and evidence that London and St Petersburg were prepared to work together rather than risk another upheaval in Western Europe. On 10 May the Tsar and Gorchakov arrived in Berlin as spokesmen for 'Europe'. Gorchakov asked for an assurance from Bismarck that he would never go to war with France, a more arrogant request than any demand made by the unfortunate Benedetti at Ems. It says much for Bismarck's self-control that he was willing to give way to Gorchakov and allow the Russian to believe he had saved the peace of Europe. So angry was Bismarck, however, that for the rest of his life he regarded Gorchakov as a personal adversary. By contrast, Austria–Hungary remained silent throughout the crisis, thereby convincing Bismarck he could henceforth count on Andrassy's loyal partnership.[23]

Vienna's silence was not entirely a sign of Andrassy's determination to stand dutifully beside Bismarck. Indeed, in private he made it clear he thought Bismarck was making a tactical blunder. The truth was that throughout April 1875 the Austrians were more concerned with the Adriatic than with any war scare along the Rhine. Against Andrassy's wishes, Francis Joseph set out on a month-long tour of Dalmatia, beginning with a visit to his former possession, Venice, where he was entertained by his old enemy, Victor Emmanuel II, in one of those placatory gestures of wound-healing which mark the misadventures of the House of Habsburg. From Venice, Francis Joseph sailed down the Adriatic to Ragusa (Dubrovnik), where he was greeted by both Orthodox and Catholic Christians who had crossed the frontier from Turkish Herzegovina. At Cattaro (Kotor) Prince Nikita, the 34-year-old ruler of independent

Montenegro, came down from his capital, Cetinje, and pledged his people's support for any Austrian move to end Turkish sovereignty over Bosnia and Herzegovina. Small wonder that within eight weeks of Francis Joseph's tour of southern Dalmatia all of Herzegovina and much of neighbouring Bosnia was in revolt against the Sultan's rule and the Muslim faith.[24]

Contemporaries blamed the troubles on Russian agents. Ever since 1858 foreign observers were obsessed with the activities of a body known as the 'Moscow Slavonic Benevolent Committee' and, from 1870 onwards, by the Panslav enthusiasm of Katkov's newspapers. But in 1875 the flame of revolt was kindled not by the Russians but by the Austrian military party who were anxious to acquire Bosnia-Herzegovina in order to make the long finger of Dalmatia more defensible and safeguard the Monarchy and its commercial interests in south-eastern Europe. Andrassy remained totally opposed to such ideas, but Francis Joseph was sympathetic to them. In Venice he had warned Victor Emmanuel that the Austrian army might soon have to move into Bosnia-Herzegovina, and when Francis Joseph passed through Zagreb after meeting Prince Nikita he told his garrison commander, General Anton von Mollinary, to hold himself ready to seize the two Turkish provinces should they begin to slip from the Sultan's grasp. Yet neither Francis Joseph nor the war party realised that the Dalmatian tour would stimulate risings against Turkish misgovernment, not merely in the western Balkans but in Bulgaria too, where every disturbance of the established order seemed inevitably to benefit Russia.[25]

The Great Eastern Crisis, begun by the Herzegovinan rising in the summer of 1875, dominated European diplomacy for the next three years. The decisive events, as terrible as anything in Greece's war of liberation earlier in the century, came in the spring of 1876 in the high villages of the Rhodope Mountains, around Philippopolis. There, less than 200 miles from the Sultan's capital, Turkish irregular soldiery – generally known as the 'Bashi-Bazouks' – killed over 12,000 Bulgarian men, women and children in six weeks of merciless reprisals. These atrocities, widely reported by the *Daily News* in England and the *New York Times* across the Atlantic, transformed localised revolts into a liberal crusade which was supported by those who had championed the Greeks, the Neapolitans in the prisons of 'Bomba', and the whole romantic adventure of the Italian Risorgimento. At the beginning of September 1876 Gladstone's thunderous pamphlet *The Bulgarian Horrors and the Question of the East* appeared in London, selling 40,000 copies in the first week; and by the end of the month a translation was available in St Petersburg and Moscow, with 10,000 copies put on sale, an unusually large edition for Tsarist Russia.[26] It was impossible for the governments to ignore the popular mood of anger with the Turk, however much they might deplore the reopening of the Eastern Question.

As early as November 1875 Bismarck told Odo Russell that Germany had no direct interest in European Turkey, adding that as he wished to prevent Russia and Austria from quarrelling over 'the Sick Man's Inheritance' he would 'adhere strictly to the part of peacemaker'.[27] He remained convinced that the Balkan peninsula was not worth a war, and for once he chose to stay as long as possible in the wings of the diplomatic stage, hoping Gorchakov and Andrassy would settle the affair through the loose entente of the Three Emperors' League. Andrassy, on the whole, preferred inaction, which had served him well in the 'War in Sight' crisis. He still did not want Francis Joseph to annex Bosnia-Herzegovina and he was especially worried in case Montenegro became what he called 'an Eastern Piedmont', drawing the South Slavs together 'to our own cost and peril'.[28] Fortunately, until the opening months of 1878, Andrassy found it possible to co-operate with Gorchakov and so contain the crisis to the Balkan lands themselves rather than risk a general European war. Ingenious efforts were made to settle the problems of both Bosnia and Bulgaria: the 'Andrassy Note' of December 1875 did not go far enough to satisfy the Christian rebels; the 'Berlin Memorandum' of May 1876 – drafted by Andrassy under Bismarck's patronage and with Gorchakov's grudging support – proposed a truce between the Turks and the insurgents while consular representatives of the Great Powers enforced a series of reforms, but it was rejected by Britain as a step towards the disintegration of the Sultan's empire; and the 'Constantinople Conference', which met in the Sultan's capital from 12 December 1876 to 20 January 1877, proposed reforms which the Turks promptly rejected. 'I much desire that we shall reach a general agreement', Alexander II had publicly announced shortly before the Conference opened. 'If this is not possible . . . then I firmly intend to act independently . . . and may God help us to fulfil our sacred mission.' Already, in the previous August, Andrassy and Gorchakov had reached an oral agreement when they met at Reichstadt for a possible division of the Balkans into Russian and Austrian spheres of influence. Now, after Alexander's warning and the obvious approach of a Russo-Turkish war, further secret agreements – the Budapest Conventions of January 1877 – assured the Austrians of a free hand in Bosnia in return for benevolent neutrality while declaring that 'the establishment of a great compact State, Slav or otherwise, is out of the question'.[29]

When, in April 1877, Sultan Abdul Hamid finally rejected an Anglo-Russian scheme for supervising reform within his empire, Tsar Alexander lost patience and the Russian armies marched southwards 'for the cause of Orthodoxy and Slavdom'. By the middle of July they controlled the main range of the Balkan mountains, but they were held up throughout the late summer, autumn and early winter by Turkish resistance at Plevna. It was not until the last weeks of the year that the Russian liberators entered the heartland of the Bulgars, around Sofia, while the Serbs, Bosnian South Slavs and Montenegrins tied down Turkish forces in the western Balkans. By now the mood of London – though not of other cities in Britain – was strongly anti-Russian and in favour of 'our old ally, Turkey'. The queen advised her Prime Minister, the Earl of Beaconsfield (as Disraeli had become in August 1876), to 'be very firm and decided', for subservience to Russia would make 'England . . . become a second-rate Power'. When in February the British sent a naval squadron through the Dardanelles, the Russians advanced a force of 10,000 men to occupy the town of San Stefano, only 8 miles from Constantinople and looking out on the Sea of Marmora, where the British warships lay at anchor some 10 miles off the coast. Britain and Russia seemed close to war.[30]

The other Great Powers had not, of course, been mere spectators of these events. At the beginning of August 1876 Gorchakov urged Bismarck, as Chancellor of a Great Power 'neutral' over Balkan affairs, to summon a congress which would settle the Eastern Question for all time. Metternich or Napoleon III would have welcomed an opportunity to preside over Europe in such a way. Bismarck declined. Privately he explained that Russia, Austria, or Britain would have returned from such a Congress 'ill-disposed towards us because not one of them would receive from us the support which he expected'; and he added that he thought a confrontation of Gorchakov and Beaconsfield, 'two ministers of equally dangerous vanity', would endanger peace rather than make it more secure.[31] Eighteen months later the diplomatic scene had changed, and for the worse. The European states collectively had the alternative of recognising a Russo-Turkish solution of the Eastern Question irrespective of its effect on the general balance of power or of meeting in congress to patch up a new settlement acceptable to the traditional custodians of the East, the signatories of the Treaty of Paris. Bismarck consoled himself by the thought that Gorchakov was so unwell that he spent most days in a wheel-chair and that Beaconsfield's asthma and bronchitis made it unlikely he would break a twenty-year habit and venture out of Britain. Even so, Bismarck suggested the congress should meet in Paris or in Vienna rather than in Berlin. He insisted that the anglicised French Foreign Minister, William Henry Waddington – an old Rugbeian who had rowed for Cambridge in the Boat Race when Andrassy was fighting for Kossuth and Bismarck campaigning against the Frankfurt liberals – would make an excellent chairman of an international conference, an honour Waddington hastily declined. Andrassy would have welcomed a second Congress of Vienna, but the Russians insisted that they would come to Berlin and to nowhere else. Eventually Bismarck, still leaving the initiative to Andrassy so as to avoid unwanted responsibilities, authorised the Austro-Hungarian Foreign Minister to invite the Powers to a congress in the German capital in the summer.

The invitations to the Congress of Berlin, circulated to Austro-Hungarian embassies and legations at the end of the first week in March, coincided with news of the peace terms imposed by Russia on Turkey at San Stefano.[32] The settlement was the work of Ignatyev and the Panslavs rather than of Gorchakov – and the details were not even referred back by Ignatyev from Russian field headquarters to the Foreign Ministry in St Petersburg. To the indignation of the Austrians the Treaty of San Stefano created a 'Big Bulgaria', an autonomous Slav national state whose existence ran counter to the spirit of the Reichstadt and Budapest agreements. Andrassy was especially angry that almost all the Sanjak of Novibazar – a strategic corridor between Serbia and Montenegro already connected by rail with the Vardar valley and Salonika – should have been awarded to Prince Nikita. Despite Andrassy's Magyar reluctance to associate more Slavs with the Monarchy, he now demanded the right to occupy (though not annex) both the Sanjak and Bosnia-Herzegovina. The British, too, were enraged by San Stefano, not only because it represented a victory for Panslavism in the Balkans, but because Ignatyev's old interests in central Asia had left their mark on the Russo-Turkish boundary in Armenia. Layard from Constantinople sent back to the Foreign Office a 32-page dispatch in which he listed the enormities of the treaty and, in particular, the advance of Russia's frontier so as to control the famous caravan route from Trebizond through Erzerum to Tabriz.[33] It seemed as if the Russians held the Ottoman Empire in a vice, masters of the Balkan passes in the west and the Armenian plateaux in the east.

The hostile reaction of Andrassy and of the Beaconsfield government made Alexander II weigh carefully the chances of success in a major war to safeguard Ignatyev's gains. Gorchakov and Milyutin (the War Minister) persuaded the Tsar that Russia faced certain defeat in a European war, Reutern (the Finance Minister) adding for good measure that Russia faced certain bankruptcy, too. In Vienna Francis Joseph's principal military adviser, General Beck-Rzikowski, rated Austria–Hungary's prospects just as lowly, the appalling condition of the army being exceeded only by the grim state of the Monarchy's finances. Hurriedly both Austria–Hungary and Russia found shelter under the umbrella of the Three Emperors' League. Ignatyev, told by Gorchakov to get himself out of the mess he had himself created, travelled to Vienna in March, convinced that Austria's failure to appreciate his achievements arose from the personal antagonism of ambassador Novikov. But Ignatyev's mission was fruitless. He failed to win over Andrassy and was forced, both in Vienna and in St Petersburg, to encourage intrigues which he vainly hoped would bring a Russophile to the Ballhausplatz in Andrassy's place.[34] It was virtually the end of Ignatyev's diplomatic career; in May he was appointed Minister of the Interior. Shuvalov, the ambassador in London, was called on to rescue Russian policy and he visited Germany in order to make certain of Bismarck's support as well as seeking to ease the tension in Westminster. Bismarck was convinced that Russia would be represented by Shuvalov at the Congress. Here, he felt, was a chief delegate with whom he could do business.

But would there, in fact, be a Congress? At the end of March it seemed unlikely. The differences between Britain and Russia were so great that there was little point in hoping for agreement round the conference table in Berlin. On 2 April Beaconsfield strengthened his government by appointing Lord Salisbury to succeed Derby who had resigned as Foreign Secretary when he thought the Cabinet was set on war. Salisbury, who had represented Britain at the Constantinople Conference, was regarded as more resolutely anti-Russian than Derby, largely because as Secretary of State for India over the past four years he had kept a vigilant eye on Russian intrigues in Afghanistan. In fact, however, Salisbury's experiences in Constantinople convinced him it would be foolish to see in Turkey 'a genuine reliable Power' and Shuvalov found it easier to make progress with the new Foreign Secretary than with his predecessor. In two months of discussion and hurried communication with St Petersburg, Shuvalov recognised that San Stefano would have to be renegotiated. An Anglo-Russian agreement, signed by Salisbury and Shuvalov on 30 May, erased 'Big Bulgaria' from the map and pushed back the Russian frontier in Armenia. Further secret agreements with the Austrians and the Turks pledged Britain to support Francis Joseph's claim to occupy Bosnia-Herzegovina and guaranteed Asiatic Turkey against Russian attack in return for the Sultan's consent to the stationing of British naval and military forces on the island of Cyprus. So much was agreed in advance that on 3 June Beaconsfield announced that he would himself head the British delegation to the Congress, which was due to open in Berlin ten days later. Salisbury and Odo Russell would assist him. Never before had a Prime Minister and a Foreign Secretary left England for a congress or conference abroad.

Beaconsfield's decision finally induced Gorchakov to go to Berlin in person. He would prove he was again in control of Russia's foreign policy after the eclipse of Ignatyev; he would prevent Shuvalov from stealing the show; he would thwart Bismarck. More than half a century ago Gorchakov had attended the Congresses of Laibach and Verona; now, in his eightieth year, he would make Berlin positively his last gala appearance. 'I do not wish to be extinguished like a lamp that is smoking', he declared; 'I want to sink down as though I were a star.'[35] His sense of theatre never failed him. The train from Warsaw arrived in Berlin on the morning of 13 June; five hours later, with no preliminary conversations, Gorchakov made his entrance into the ballroom of the old Radziwill Palace, just as the first session of the Congress was beginning. Bismarck greeted him with frigid courtesy.

Although so many aspects of the new settlement had been worked out in advance, the four weeks of the Berlin Congress showed the latent suspicion behind the attempts of the Powers to decide questions of detail. Bismarck remained as impartial as possible, backing Russian claims in the eastern Balkans and Asia Minor while supporting Austria in Bosnia-Herzegovina and the Sanjak, although he appears at one time to have tried to induce Andrassy to modify his claim of compensation in the western Balkans so as to safeguard the unity of the Three Emperors' League. Gorchakov left every important decision to Shuvalov; the third Russian delegate, Oubril, kept on good terms with almost everybody through the sheer excellence of the cuisine when he dispensed hospitality, but his knowledge of cis-Danubian Europe was scanty. Andrassy, Karolyi and Haymerle formed the strongest trio of representatives. Beaconsfield left day-to-day business to Odo Russell and Salisbury. The Foreign Secretary's vigorous and self-confident individualism irritated Bismarck; he was puzzled by an English aristocrat who, as *The Times* reported, travelled 112 miles from Berlin to Dresden at the weekend so as to worship in an Anglican church and who privately made it clear that his greatest pleasure during his days in Berlin were the discussions he held with the physicist Hermann Helmholtz on problems of electro-magnetism. Bismarck preferred Beaconsfield: 'In a quarter of an hour you knew exactly where you stood with him', he would reminisce in later years.[36]

But at the time, Beaconsfield was more of an enigma than Bismarck chose to remember. There was, for example, the strange episode of the special train. On the morning of 21 June the Russians seemed unwilling to meet British proposals for the presence of Turkish troops in the semi-autonomous Bulgarian province of Eastern Rumelia. The Prime Minister, out walking with his private secretary, told him to see if a train could be made ready to take him back to Calais should there be no progress in the next round of talks with the Russians. That afternoon new instructions from the Tsar allowed Shuvalov to satisfy the British; and no carriages were shunted at Beaconsfield's request. But the special train legend impressed Bismarck and passed into chancellery folklore. It also boosted the prestige of the British delegation who, only a few days earlier, had been embarrassed by publication in the *Globe* newspaper of a secret agreement between Shuvalov and Salisbury which met Russian demands over the port of Batum. This revelation, leaked to Fleet Street by an underpaid copyist at the Foreign Office, made the Prime Minister's Jingoistic critics complain he was too soft with the Russians; and he was not displeased when, early in July, gossip in the London clubs said that 'Dizzy' had ordered his special train in Berlin rather than appease Russia over Bulgaria.[37]

Technically the Congress of Berlin was a success, run so speedily and efficiently that the final treaty was signed a mere thirty days after the opening session. Autonomous Bulgaria was limited to a region between the Danube and the crest of the Balkan range while the area around Philippopolis, where the first massacres took place, acquired a particular status within the Ottoman Empire as a semi-autonomous region, Eastern Rumelia. The Austrians occupied Bosnia-Herzegovina and garrisoned the Sanjak while Russia strengthened her hold on the southern Caucasus and received Bessarabia from the Romanians, who were allowed to detach the Dobrudja from the Ottoman Empire as compensation. Provided that the three principalities of Serbia, Montenegro and Romania gave equal political rights to the people of all religious faiths, they were promised international recognition of their independence. This provision was extended in the case of Romania so as to ensure the protection of foreign traders, too – an attempt to stamp out Romanian anti-Semitism. Andrassy and Gorchakov disliked these concessions, partly because of their significance for the Jewish problems in Russia and Austria-Hungary, but also because they feared that a ready recognition of the principle of nationality would create greater difficulties in the future. This was especially true of Macedonia, whose peoples were handed back to direct Turkish sovereignty after being included in the Big Bulgaria created by the Treaty of San Stefano. The strength, and the weakness, of the Berlin Settlement lay in the fact that it was imposed by the Concert of Europe, almost in harmony. A more realistic solution of the Eastern Question would have recognised that the Ottoman Empire was beyond political redemption. Yet with all its defects, the Berlin Settlement freed the Balkans from major war for over a third of a century.[38]

When Anton Werner completed the official painting of the Congress he showed the German Chancellor shaking hands with Shuvalov, while Andrassy looked on, over Bismarck's right shoulder. To the left of the canvas, well behind Bismarck and Andrassy, was Gorchakov, the only first plenipotentiary shown sitting down, and depicted with Karolyi and Beaconsfield engaging him in conversation. The symbolism portrayed Bismarck's hopes for the immediate future. Gorchakov was one of yesterday's men; the German Chancellor took care to greet, as he thought, Russia's Foreign Minister of tomorrow, Peter Shuvalov. Now that the Great Eastern Crisis was resolved Bismarck was certain he could renew co-operation between the three empires. Stable diplomacy needed continuity and not change. Only gradually, over the winter of 1878–9, did Bismarck realise that Tsar Alexander II blamed him rather than Andrassy or Beaconsfield for Russia's failure to achieve all that the San Stefano Treaty had promised. Bismarck's belief that he had avoided the pitfalls which he had seen in congress diplomacy was not justified. He was losing his policy of free manoeuvre. Reluctantly he began to construct in its place a rigid alliance system of checks and balances across the European continent. The handshake Werner painted on his canvas was a gesture of farewell rather than of salutation.

12 Checks, Balances and Diversions, 1879–89

On 3 July 1878 the plenipotentiaries to the Berlin Congress were invited to a private banquet at a mansion in the Behrenstrasse. Shuvalov, Andrassy, Waddington, Beaconsfield, Salisbury and all the lesser envoys were present at what an Austrian diplomat considered 'the best dinner I have ever been to'. So impressed was the British Prime Minister with the occasion that he sent a long account of the evening to his queen, written in the style which enriched *Coningsby* and *Tancred*. His descriptive pen lingered over the mansion ('where it is not marble, it is gold'), the ballroom ('fit for a fairy tale'), the banqueting hall ('very vast and very lofty') and the music played throughout the dinner by an orchestra in the gallery ('Wagner, and only Wagner, which I was very glad of'). But what fascinated Dizzy most of all was his host. Presiding over this glittering feast was 'the great banker of Berlin . . . Mr Bleichröder'. The queen was told how once he had been 'penniless', and then 'Rothschild's agent'. Now, 'after the Prussian wars', he seemed 'almost to rival his former master'.[1]

To Beaconsfield, the social eminence of Baron Gerson von Bleichröder, personal banker to the Iron Chancellor for over thirty years, was a triumph of Jewish integration and assimilation. It is indeed interesting to compare Bleichröder's role as a munificent merchant-prince in 1878 with Metternich's condescension at the Aix Congress sixty years before, when he had gone so far as to entertain Carl and Solomon Rothschild to luncheon, unobtrusively. But the real significance of Bleichröder's banquet is his guest list. Nothing illustrates so vividly the extent to which statesmen and diplomats in the later 1870s already recognised the interplay of economic and financial forces in the shaping of foreign policy. Bleichröder and the great bankers in other cities figured prominently in the coming two decades as investors, as servicers of foreign government loans and as advisers on the feasibility of colonial enterprises. At first, however, their horizons were narrower and they were concerned chiefly with the immediate problems of trade and industry in their own lands. The general European recession, which deepened year by year from 1873 onwards, threw doubts on established economic principles, especially in Germany. Gradually the bankers came to accept the need for tariffs, Bleichröder more slowly than many others. Bismarck, sounding out opinion week by week as one unfamiliar with such problems, cautiously followed his personal banker towards an undoctrinaire Protectionism.

For the first seven years of the German Empire, the Chancellor had accepted the basic Free Trade doctrines of his National Liberal parliamentary allies. Even as late as 1877 he was still prepared to reduce the remaining duties on iron. But Protection had a particular political appeal for Bismarck. Tariffs would provide him with revenue from indirect taxation, not dependent on an annual vote in the Reichstag (parliament). He was far from displeased at the prospect of disconcerting the more doctrinaire Liberals by a change in policy. There was, too, a pressure group of Junker agriculturalists from eastern Prussia who had been angered by a sudden jump in Russia's protective tariffs announced in January 1877. Hence when, three months after the Congress of Berlin dispersed, 200 Reichstag deputies petitioned the Chancellor to impose duties on imported food and on manufactured goods, he gave the question sympathetic consideration. By the end of the year 1878 he had taken the great decision: Germany would change to Protection, although the tariff bill was not enacted until the following July. The gains made by the factory and mine owners of Silesia, Westphalia and Alsace-Lorraine, together with new techniques of production, enabled Germany to become the third industrial Power in the world by the turn of the century; and at the same time Protection safeguarded the grain producers east of the Elbe. Germany's change set the trend for the coming decade. Every continental government except the Belgian followed Bismarck's example and raised tariffs, a development ominous for the textiles and manufactured consumer goods of Free Trade Britain.

Within a few years intense commercial rivalry created new antagonism between Germany and 'England', throwing in doubt the value of purely political or strategic considerations in determining chancellery diplomacy. So long as Bismarck remained in the Wilhelmstrasse, however, little attempt was made to base diplomatic alignments on economic interests. Traditional principles and old habits of thought lingered on. Bismarck was surprised by the extent to which his change to Protection worsened relations between Berlin and St Petersburg, failing to perceive that no Power suffered so much as Russia from effective measures to safeguard Germany's economy, especially agriculture.

Yet Russo-German relations deteriorated even before tariffs began to bite. Bismarck had hoped to revive the old Three Emperors' League. To his dismay he found Alexander II prejudiced against himself and against Shuvalov, whom the Tsar held too ready to appease Germany and Austria-Hungary and too susceptible to 'Jewish intrigue', notably to the influence of Bleichröder. Alexander's attitude was hardened by Bismarck's behaviour, not so much through his actions during the Congress as from his folly in encouraging a Press campaign against Gorchakov throughout the second half of the year 1878. On 7 September the London *Times* published an interview with the German Chancellor which appeared to gloat over Gorchakov's discomfiture after the Congress of Berlin and 'the political defeat he has just experienced'. An article drafted by Bismarck for his newspaper, *Norddeutsche Allgemeine Zeitung*, three weeks later somewhat patronisingly placed the diplomatic skill of Shuvalov on a level with the bravery of the Tsar's army as a reason why Russia was entitled to her 'great gains' from the settlement, presumably in Bessarabia and Asia. It is hardly surprising that Alexander II resented this clumsy campaign. Gorchakov himself spent most of the five months after the Congress on sick leave in Switzerland, celebrating his eightieth birthday there; but on the first weekend in December he passed through Berlin on his way back to St Petersburg. He made it clear that he had no intention of retiring, delivered some sniping remarks against the Austrians and the Germans, praised his own merits in a private audience with Emperor William I, and was back in nominal charge of the Russian Foreign Ministry by the middle of the month. Not until the spring of 1882 did he formally resign office.[2]

The strained relations between Germany and Russia from the autumn of 1878 until January 1880 form what is sometimes called the 'Two Chancellors' War'. The phrase rightly emphasises the intense mutual antipathy between Bismarck and Gorchakov, but it exaggerates the control exercised by the Russian Chancellor over policy in these eighteen months. The day-to-day conduct of foreign affairs was managed by Jomini, and by Nikolai Giers, who had succeeded Stremoukhov as director of the Asiatic Department in December 1875. Giers, unlike most of the department's personnel, was not a Russian. His family came from Riga and were Swedish Lutheran in origin. He was a mild, self-effacing realist who considered the Tsar's empire too vulnerable militarily and economically for any forward policy in Europe. Left to himself, Giers would have worked for a German alliance, as he did throughout the 1880s, but he did not entirely possess Alexander II's confidence since he lacked 'a good Russian name'. He suffered from the nationalistic intrigues of the Panslav pressure group and from his own misfortune in having little standing with the old Russian aristocracy and no resources of personal wealth to combat his social isolation. His advancement owed much to his qualities of hard work and total reliability, but it owed something, also, to a family alliance with Gorchakov; for, as long ago as 1849, Giers had married Olga Cantacuzene, a favourite niece of the future Chancellor. Olga came from one of the best-known Moldavian princely families, whose traditions of service over the years were equally divided between the Sultans and the Tsars.[3] Yet this 'Romanian' marriage, too, made poor Giers suspect in St Petersburg society. Both Alexander II and his Chancellor were prepared to allow 'the Switzer' (Jomini) and 'the Swede' (Giers) to run the Foreign Ministry, but only so long as they initiated no startling change of policy and were content to leave titular control in the veteran's shaky hands.

Bismarck was kept well informed of what was happening in St Petersburg by carefully phrased dispatches from the embassy. General von Schweinitz, who spent in all some twenty-two years at the Russian court, was a shrewd ambassador. By the beginning of 1879 Bismarck thus knew that his Russian rival was little more than a pasteboard chancellor. Yet he thought it essential to remove Gorchakov's negative power of veto if he was to bring life and purpose to a revived Three Emperors' League, and he therefore waged the Two Chancellors' War relentlessly throughout the year. The German Press was to print anti-Russian articles but was, he insisted, to word them 'delicately without offending the person of the Tsar'. He even sent a respected senior officer, General Werder, on a mission to make certain that Alexander was aware of his Chancellor's enormities. At the same time, Bismarck hoped he might induce the Russians to feel a need for German support by increasing their sense of isolation. He was especially concerned at the risk of a Franco-Russian entente. This nightmare he tried to combat by encouraging the French to interest themselves in North Africa, where there was no reason for France and Russia to come together. During the three years after the Berlin Congress, Franco–German relations improved considerably, thanks largely to the tact of the Comte de St Vallier, whom Bismarck reckoned (as he told Odo Russell) 'the best ambassador that France has ever had in Berlin'.[4]

So long as Beaconsfield was in power, Anglo-German relations remained close, and there were soundings of a possible alliance, perhaps taken more seriously by the Prime Minister than by either Salisbury or Bismarck. The great merit of the Beaconsfield–Salisbury partnership in Bismarck's eyes was its opposition to Russia, notably in central Asia. But the situation was drastically changed by the victory of the Liberals in 1880 and the return of Gladstone to Downing Street and of Granville to the Foreign Office. Gladstone, misrepresented by the German ambassador as a Slavophile 'more Russian than the Russians themselves', ultimately replaced Gorchakov as the bane of Bismarck's highly personalised view of Europe. 'Herr Professor Gladstone', who had enunciated general principles of foreign policy in the Midlothian speeches before returning to office, denounced 'needless and entangling engagements' and sought to 'bring about the common accord of Europe, embodying in one organ the voice of civilized mankind'. Such phrases puzzled Bismarck. Gladstone, he confided to Schweinitz, was not simply 'anti-monarchical' like Palmerston; he was a 'revolutionary'. When, at the start of the Gladstone ministry, the British took the initiative in convening a conference at Madrid to discuss the problems of anarchy in Morocco, there was deep suspicion in Berlin. Bismarck supported France in insisting that the Great Powers had no natural obligation to impose reforms on a country outside Europe whose affairs were in chaos.[5] Gladstone's sense of mission – even, in this case, his sponsorship of the neutral capital in a Power no longer 'Great' as a meeting place – ran counter to Bismarck's assumption that the conduct of foreign affairs was concerned with what was tangible, worthwhile and attainable.

Occasionally Bismarck sought to benefit from Gladstone's flights of rhetoric. His denunciation of Austria-Hungary as 'the unflinching foe of freedom in every country of Europe' in the last great speech of the Midlothian Campaign (Edinburgh, 17 March 1880) was used by the Germans as a means of emphasising to Francis Joseph his empire's need of friendly backing from the most powerful state on the continent. Although diplomats both in Vienna and London tried to smooth over the incident once Gladstone had come to power, there remained a certain Austrian resentment against the new Prime Minister for his strangely irrelevant and injudicious remarks. The substitution of Gladstone and Granville for Beaconsfield and Salisbury inevitably strengthened the bonds linking Berlin and Vienna at a time when Francis Joseph and his ministers regarded them as no more than a temporary expedient.

A secret alliance between Germany and Austria-Hungary was the final achievement of the Bismarck–Andrassy partnership. The German Chancellor seems first to have considered an alliance in the spring of 1879 when he was alarmed by Russian troop movements in Poland and rumours of Russian contacts with the French, and by the angry response of Russian newspapers to his own Press campaign against Gorchakov. When, on 12 August 1879, he heard that Andrassy was about to resign in order to devote his later years to the improvement of his Hungarian estates, Bismarck at once sought to ensure continuity in Austrian foreign policy by concluding a formal treaty. Nine days later Bismarck was shown a personal letter from the Tsar to Emperor William in which Alexander complained of Bismarck's anti-Russian attitude and warned his 'dear uncle' of the 'sad consequences' of continued friction between the two empires. William's reaction to the letter was a hurriedly arranged meeting with his nephew at Alexandrovo, on the Russo–German frontier in Poland. Bismarck travelled to Gastein, where he found Andrassy prepared to stay in office long enough to conclude a formal agreement with Germany. The Chancellor would have liked to link Russia in a triple alliance at the same time, thus turning the Tsar's complaints to advantage, but Andrassy was disturbed by the continued Russian intrigues in the western Balkans and hostile to any revival of the Three Emperors' League. There was, indeed, little enough that the Austrians would give, apart from Andrassy's autograph on a secret treaty promising assistance in case of a Russian attack across the eastern frontiers of Germany in return for a similar pledge from Bismarck. The Germans refused to support Austria-Hungary in any forward policy in the Balkans, the Austrians rejected any commitment in Western Europe. Even this document, limited in validity to five years in the first instance, was at first rejected by Emperor William for its anti-Russian tone; it was, he wrote in a memorandum a few days after returning from Alexandrovo, a reflection on 'his conscience, his character and his honour'.[6] Nevertheless, faced by a threat of resignation from Bismarck and the whole of his government, William reluctantly agreed and authorised the conclusion of the treaty, which was signed in Vienna on 7 October 1879 by Andrassy and the German ambassador. Neither man could have imagined that so extemporised an agreement would survive, with modifications, until the disasters of November 1918.

The Russians did not know the nature of the Austro–German commitment – nor, indeed, for another six years, that there was any treaty at all. They had, however, been worried by the presence of Bismarck at Gastein and at Vienna for talks with Andrassy and his designated successor, the Russophobe Baron Haymerle. They therefore sent to Berlin as a special envoy from the Tsar the young diplomat Count Peter Saburov. So successful was Saburov at placating Bismarck that in January 1880 he was appointed to succeed the septuagenarian Oubril as ambassador. Saburov was a nephew of Gorchakov, but he was highly critical of his uncle's vanity and obstinacy in clinging to office. He found Bismarck agreeably accommodating: Germany's motive in improving relations with Vienna, the Chancellor explained, 'was to dig a ditch between Austria and the Western Powers'.[7] Alexander II was gratified by Bismarck's assurance and at once authorised Saburov to begin negotiations for a revival of the League of the Three Emperors, although this time the League was to be based upon a formal alliance and not merely on the goodwill of the sovereigns. Bismarck rightly interpreted the Russian change of policy as a sign that the Tsar was now ignoring Gorchakov and conducting foreign affairs himself, with Giers acting as his secretary much as had Nesselrode in earlier years. Ideally, of course, Bismarck would have preferred to work with Shuvalov rather than with Giers and Saburov. But Alexander II could never free his mind from the calumnies implanted there by Gorchakov, and the lionised second plenipotentiary at the Berlin Congress remained for another seven years a sardonic observer of distant events. Bismarck, for his part, may have had misgivings over the ultimate trend of policy in St Petersburg, but he was satisfied by the beginning of 1880 that Russia was returning to the fold.

Now it was the Austrians who proved tiresome. Andrassy had resigned as Foreign Minister less than twenty-four hours after signing the Austro-German alliance and his successor, Haymerle, was reluctant to commit the Dual Monarchy to any form of collaboration with Russia unless the Tsar was prepared to recognise Austria-Hungary's primacy in the western Balkans. It took fifteen months of negotiations before Haymerle approved a draft treaty which was also acceptable to Alexander II. A week later (13 March 1881) the Tsar was assassinated in St Petersburg; his successor was his son, Alexander III, a Russian nationalist in his habits of thought and, through the influence of his Danish wife, naturally anti-pathetic to Bismarck. Even so, it was still the Austrians rather than the Russians who found fault in the proposed agreement. At last, secretly in Berlin on 13 June 1881, the Three Emperors' Alliance was signed by Bismarck and by the ambassadors of Russia and Austria-Hungary. If one of the three empires was at war with a fourth Power (apart from Turkey) the other two signatories would observe benevolent neutrality. It was accepted that Austria-Hungary might eventually annex the two Turkish provinces occupied since 1878, Bosnia and Herzegovina; and it was agreed that the three Powers would recognise the union of Bulgaria and the artificial semi-autonomous province of Eastern Rumelia 'should this question arise from force of circumstances'. Basically the alliance seemed to give each signatory what was wanted: for Austria, supremacy in the western Balkans; for Russia, a free hand (so far as the British would allow it) in the eastern Balkans; for Germany, a semblance of security. As Bismarck told William I, he could now 'count on the peace of our two neighbours for some years to come'. 'The danger for Germany of a Franco-Russian combination is totally removed', the Chancellor added.[8]

This was an excessively optimistic conclusion. Confidential and un-official talks continued between successive French military attachés and Russian staff officers throughout the 1880s. They achieved little, how-ever, for the French reckoned it would take Russia some three months to mobilise for a war against Germany, by which time France would have been defeated. But the French had influential champions in St Petersburg. Katkov and the Russian nationalists favoured an understanding and so did General Mikhail Skobelev, whose exploits as a 34-year-old army com-mander in the Balkans in 1877–8 had made him Russia's most popular soldier since Kutuzov. General Nikolai Obruchev, chief of the Russian

General Staff from 1881 to 1897, was also, militarily, a Francophile and his opinions carried great weight with the new Tsar. Germany was still the chief supplier of capital to Russia, and Alexander III bestowed a coveted Order on Bleichröder in 1885 'for services rendered' just as Alexander I had honoured Solomon and James Rothschild in 1822. But Bleichröder repeatedly pointed out to Bismarck that, with a divergence of fiscal and commercial interests, Russia might well turn to the French money market; and it was regarded as significant that, as early as 1878, the Credit Lyonnais became the first foreign bank to open a branch in St Petersburg. Bismarck was not particularly disturbed by Bleichröder's warnings. 'Financial relations do not necessarily lead to political intimacies', the Chancellor once remarked to him, adding, 'If it were true, we would virtually be welded to Russia'.[9] There were moments when Bismarck was alarmed by a Russian political flirtation with the French – notably in February 1882 when Skobelev visited Paris and made a speech to students in which he denounced Germany as the natural enemy of Slavdom – but it seemed to him impossible for the Autocrat of All the Russias to make common cause with the radicals of the Third Republic. In old age the Chancellor exaggerated the ideological divisions of Europe, becoming to some extent a captive of his own newspaper campaigns. He failed, in particular, to comprehend the changing moods of official Russia.

He was slow, too, to respond to the colonial agitation which gripped so many Western European capitals in the 1880s. A small group of German traders, mainly from Bremen and Hamburg, had long been eager for overseas expansion. They had even asked Bismarck to add demands for the surrender of Napoleon III's colonial acquisitions around Saigon to the peace terms submitted to the French in 1870–1. The Chancellor was not interested, although he was sufficiently conscious of Germany's imperial dignity four years later to propose Anglo-German naval collaboration off the Philippines to protect traders menaced by the breakdown of Spanish colonial authority. Disraeli's acquisition for Britain of the largest single allocation of Suez Canal shares, in November 1875, may have fired the fiscal imagination of Bleichröder, but it left Bismarck unmoved. When in 1883 a Bremen merchant, Adolf Lüderitz, founded a trading station at the mouth of the Orange River and asked for 'the protection of the German flag' Bismarck was slow to take up his cause. He was prepared to use the colonial rivalry of other Powers as a diplomatic lever to improve Germany's standing within the European system, but it was only for some twenty months in 1884 to 1886 that he showed any enthusiasm whatsoever for the adventure of far-flung empire.[10]

There were two main areas where Germany profited from disputes between other colonial Powers: Tunisia and Egypt. In 1869 the Bey of Tunis, the local ruler of a region still technically under the suzerainty of Turkey, went bankrupt and was forced to accept joint financial control by the French, British and Italians. The British had little interest in Tunisia, and at the Congress of Berlin Salisbury suggested to Waddington that France might 'take Tunis', adding that 'England will raise no objections'. Bismarck, too, favoured a French seizure of Tunis: 'The Tunisian pear is ripe and it is time for you to gather it', he told the French ambassador in January 1879. Andrassy, however, had tried to distract Italy from the Balkans by mentioning the possible seizure of Tunisia as early as 1876; and the Italian delegation to the Congress received the impression that Bismarck thought Tunisia was 'a morsel' to which 'we might help ourselves'.[11] Between 1879 and 1881 there was fierce rivalry between France and Italy to secure commercial concessions from the Bey, the French promoting an ambitious project for a trans-Saharan railway. Resentment at French penetration of their homeland led some Arab tribes to mount raids across the Algerian frontier in March 1881. This growing lawlessness prompted Courcel, of the Quai d'Orsay, to urge the republican Prime Minister, Gambetta, to follow the advice of Salisbury and Bismarck and to occupy Tunisia. French troops crossed the border from Algeria, nominally in pursuit of the raiders, and in May 1881 the French consul in Tunis induced the Bey, under threat of deposition, to accept 'protection' of his lands.

The establishment of a French protectorate angered the Italians. Mounting criticism of his government's timidity led the Prime Minister, Agostino Depretis, to seek diplomatic support from Bismarck. The German Chancellor was at first unresponsive, but Skobelev's warlike posturing in France led him to change his mind. At the end of February 1882, Bismarck proposed that the Austrians should take the lead in creating a secret triple alliance binding Rome, Berlin and Vienna. By now, Haymerle was dead and Gustav Kálnoky – a German Count from Moravia, despite his Magyar name – had presided in the Ballhausplatz since early December. The new Foreign Minister was a devout clerical, very conscious of Francis Joseph's stature as leading Roman Catholic sovereign of the world. It says much for Kálnoky's commitment to the German alliance that he was prepared to meet Bismarck's wishes and offer Italy friendly support. By the Triple Alliance of 20 May 1882 Germany and Austria-Hungary guaranteed Italy against a French attack in return for an Italian pledge to assist the Germans and Austrians should they be attacked by Russia and another Great Power, other than Britain, while Italy would also aid Germany in case of an unprovoked attack by France alone. The alliance seemed strangely academic in the spring of 1882; even the Italians did not believe France would go to war in Europe and Bismarck's Skobelev bogey soon dissolved, with the young general's sudden death in June 1882. To Italy the secret Triple Alliance Treaty brought a certain standing in the European order, higher for example than Spain or Sweden or the Netherlands. Ironically, as part of the terms for the alliance, the Italians had to assure their partners they had no intention of seeking to wrest Tunisia from French protection.[12]

The Egyptian Question had a more lasting significance than the passing storm over Tunis. From the days of Mehemet Ali until Disraeli's purchase of the Canal shares in 1875 Egypt had served as a rich field of French investment. The Suez Canal itself was primarily a French concept, formally opened in November 1869 by the Empress Eugénie, a first cousin of Ferdinand de Lesseps, the diplomat turned engineer who masterminded the project. After 1875 the French at first collaborated closely with the British in seeking to establish order in the finances of the

Egyptian ruler, Khedive Ismail, a spendthrift deposed in favour of his hardly less profligate son, Tewfik, in June 1879. Anglo–French dual control of Egyptian finances provoked a strong xenophobic movement in Alexandria and Cairo. In July 1882 joint naval and military action was planned to protect the interests of foreign bondholders, but, with memories of the Mexican affair still vivid in French political life, the prospect of intervention was sufficient to bring down the government in Paris. A purely British naval force bombarded Alexandria, and it was British troops who routed the Egyptian nationalist army and entered Cairo.

Gladstone authorised the victorious British forces to occupy all the towns of Egypt, eventually permitting troops to be sent southwards into the rebellious Sudan, too. A legislative council and an assembly were established to administer the country under the guidance of a British resident agent and consul-general, Sir Evelyn Baring (who was raised to the peerage as Lord Cromer in 1892). Granville, the Foreign Secretary, delivered a circular note to the Great Powers on 3 January 1883 affirming that the British would withdraw 'as soon as the state of the country and the organization of proper means for the maintenance of the Khedive's authority will admit of it'. In fact, Baring remained virtual pro-consul of Egypt for twenty-four years, and the British army was on Egyptian soil until June 1956, although it was not until December 1914 that Egypt was declared a British protectorate and sovereign independence was recognised eight years later. The French, deeply angered by the extent of British intervention in 1882–3, led the united opposition of the Powers to the attempt 'to make a second India' of Egypt. Germany was not directly concerned with the Egyptian Question until 1885, when Bleichröder and the other bankers competed for a loan. Bismarck was content to use Egypt as a means of putting pressure on the British or, if he was alarmed at rumours of a Franco–Russian rapprochement, of pleasing London by some magnanimous gesture of goodwill.[13]

There was certainly no desire on Bismarck's part to curry favour with the British in the spring of 1884, when – somewhat dramatically – he began the German drive for colonies. Four years of Gladstonian high principle had not changed his views on English liberalism. Indeed he was particularly incensed by the alleged influence of Gladstonian ideals on the liberal and Anglophile circle around the German Crown Prince. A recent school of German historians claims that the principal motive behind Bismarck's colonialism was his desire to discredit the heir to the throne and his German liberal allies, trouncing them under a wave of German nationalist sentiment in the next Reichstag elections. But there was, too, a more positive reason for Bismarck's colonial diversion. His national pride was irritated by the clumsy treatment accorded to German traders in south-west Africa by the British authorities in Cape Colony. In April 1884 he informed the British that Lüderitz's settlement of Angra Pequena, on the Orange River, had been taken 'under the protection of the Reich'. Within six weeks the newspapers in London were reporting German commercial activity in the Cameroons, Fiji and New Guinea. Both Granville and Gladstone were cool-headed and conciliatory, the Prime

Minister suspecting that Bismarck's colonial enthusiasm was linked with Germany's domestic problems. But the Cape government bumbled, seeking at one time to annex the whole of the coastline as far as the British settlement of Walfisch Bay, some 160 miles north of Angra Pequena. The misunderstanding over colonies soured Anglo–German relations throughout the second half of the year 1884.[14]

By contrast, Franco–German collaboration was closer during the second ministry of Jules Ferry, from February 1883 to April 1885, than at any other time in the half century after Sedan.[15] Ferry, who had led the parliamentary opposition in the last years of the Second Empire, was a laicist lawyer who had recast the French educational system. He was a late convert to the colonialist cause, believing overseas possessions would supply France with markets rather than serve as a source of raw materials. Ferry, consistently unpopular with his countrymen, was a man of world vision. He was prepared to seek concessions in Madagascar, to support the pioneering work of De Brazza at the mouth of the Congo and to extend the earlier French settlements in Indo-China along the coast of the Gulf of Tonkin. His qualities won Ferry approbation in Berlin. Bismarck's anti-British outbursts coincided with a period of Anglo–French tension over Egypt, rival colonial claims in central and west Africa and a clash of interests in Asia, too. Ferry was interested in German suggestions of a joint naval force which would 'defend itself against the vexatious usurpations of the English fleet'. Germany supported France in opposing British attempts to settle Egypt's financial problems in round table discussions at London in the late autumn of 1884. To Ferry's satisfaction, Bismarck convened a conference on central and west African affairs in Berlin at the end of November 1884. It is interesting that the continental Powers should have treated British willingness to attend such a meeting in Germany's capital as proof that Britain's colonial paramountcy was on the wane.

The Berlin Conference was, however, far from being a diplomatic defeat for Gladstone and Granville. Indeed, in one sense it was a fillip to Gladstone's ideal of the Concert of Europe, the fifteen-week conference serving as a model of anticipatory diplomacy. No less than fourteen governments sent delegations. The British abandoned an earlier plan to support Portuguese claims in the Congo basin against the ambitious designs of the King of the Belgians, not least because their traders in west Africa made it clear they preferred King Leopold II's *Association Internationale du Congo* to Portuguese rule. Bismarck, too, favoured the king's claims, provided that the Congo was accepted as a 'neutralised' private possession of the ruler of Belgium rather than a Belgian colony and provided also that it remained a free trade zone. To Ferry's surprise the Berlin Conference was marked by Anglo–German collaboration against France, not only on the Congo but on the Niger, too. The British recognised Germany's protectorates over the Cameroons and Togoland as well as over south-west Africa. Tension remained over New Guinea, a region outside the competence of the Berlin Conference, but it began to seem as if British and German objectives in colonial policy had much in common. In fact, Bismarck was losing interest in colonial enterprise and soon reverted to his earlier, suspicious mood. By the spring of 1889 he was even prepared to suggest, not entirely as a wry aside, that Francesco Crispi, the Italian Prime Minister, might like to purchase from Germany all her colonial acquisitions.[16]

The frail Franco-German entente ended abruptly in the spring of 1885 with the fall of Ferry's government, the first since enactment of France's republican constitution to have lasted for more than two years. Ferry was ousted, technically, because Parisian newspapers picked up a misleading report that French troops fighting in Tonkin had suffered defeat at the hands of a Chinese and rebel Vietnamese force in a battle at Lang-Son. But what led a hostile mob to threaten Ferry with a lynching – or, at best, immersion in the Seine – was a speech by Georges Clemenceau, who was bitterly opposed to the Prime Minister for his willingness to collaborate with Bismarck's Germany. On 3 August 1885 one of the Chancellor's mouthpieces, the *Norddeutsche Allgemeine Zeitung*, carried an article which denounced the new militant mood of revenge popular with France's patriots. A few days later Bismarck received Kálnoky at his country home of Varzin and listened with interest as the Austro-Hungarian Foreign Minister explained how 'the long continued existence of a French Republic, recognised as a fully equal Power, is a dangerous matter for the monarchical principle'.[17] The old pattern of continental politics was beginning to show once more through the confused medley of colonial rivalries. When, sometime afterwards, the Saharan explorer Gustav Nachtigall sought to interest Bismarck in further colonial acquisitions, he found the Chancellor unresponsive: 'Your map of Africa is very fine', Bismarck told Nachtigall, 'but my map of Africa is here in Europe. There is Russia and there is France, and here we are in the middle. That is my map of Africa.'[18]

The Russians had observed what was happening in the 'dark continent' but took no part in the scramble for colonies. They continued to push southwards through Turkestan and closer to the frontiers of India. In March 1885 they gained a victory against an Afghan force at Pendjeh and seemed poised to establish a lasting influence over the government of Afghanistan. Momentarily there was alarm in London and talk of another Anglo-Russian war. For the Liberal government the Pendjeh crisis was the final straw: chronic Irish terrorism, uncertainty in Egypt and the Sudan culminating in the death of General Gordon at Khartoum, strained relations with Germany, and now the threat of war with Russia over Afghanistan. It was almost a relief for Gladstone to resign over so familiar a domestic issue as the budget; and on 25 June 1885 Lord Salisbury formed his first ministry, himself taking charge of foreign affairs. One of his earliest tasks was to ease the tension in central Asia by securing a compromise agreement early in September which settled Afghanistan's frontier.[19] However much Salisbury might wish to assert Britain's influence in the European Chancelleries, he was hampered by the political instability of the country. Seven months of a minority Conservative government were followed by five months of Liberal rule, in which Gladstone left foreign affairs to the comparatively young Lord Rosebery. Salisbury then returned as Prime Minister in July 1886, although the Earl of Iddesleigh was nominal Foreign Secretary until January 1887. Continuity in British foreign policy would normally have been assured during these rapid changes of management by the guiding hand of a permanent under-secretary, but Julian Pauncefote (who held that post from 1882 to 1889) was a colonialist, a lawyer and an administrator, not strong on European problems. The key British figure in the diplomatic exchanges of those eighteen months was the assistant under-secretary, Sir Philip Currie, a friend and confidant of both Salisbury and Rosebery. His influence has been much underrated.

Soon after becoming Prime Minister in June 1885 Salisbury had written to Bismarck expressing his hopes of 'restoring the good understanding between the two countries'. A month later Salisbury sent Currie to Germany on a personal mission. On 3 August Currie visited Bismarck's son, Herbert (his opposite number in the German Foreign Office), at Königstein, a resort in the Saxon highlands on the banks of the Elbe. The two men had met on several occasions, most recently when Herbert was a guest of Lord Rosebery in London five months before. Now, in holiday surroundings, Currie indulged in the 'secret diplomacy' which Salisbury's later critics were to condemn so self-righteously even when they did not know its details. Currie suggested to Herbert Bismarck that, were his father to mediate over the outstanding question in settling the Pendjeh crisis, 'he would be laying for himself the foundations of a closer and more intimate alliance' between Britain and Germany.[20] The Chancellor, though pleased that Salisbury was interested in associating himself with the Bismarckian states system in Europe, remained suspicious. Never again did he wish to be represented in St Petersburg as England's partner against Russia. The Three Emperors' Alliance seemed to be flourishing: Francis Joseph, Alexander III and William I had come together amiably at the Tsar's Polish hunting lodge of Skierniwice in the previous autumn; the Tsar and the Austrian emperor were about to meet at Kremsier, William having declined an invitation through poor health; and Bismarck was expecting Kálnoky at Varzin and Giers at Friedrichsruh, his favourite estate near Hamburg. The machinery of the alliance was running so smoothly that the Chancellor saw no need to tune it anew at England's request.

Six weeks after Currie's trip to Königstein and three weeks after the Kremsier meeting, the Chancelleries were faced once more by a crisis in the Balkans. The Treaty of Berlin had created the principality of Bulgaria, whose throne was accepted in 1879 by the German prince, Alexander of Battenberg, and the semi-autonomous province of Eastern Rumelia, administered by a governor appointed by the Turks. By 1885 Alexander of Battenberg was distrusted by Bismarck and by the Russians, not least because he never hid his resentment of the way in which Panslavs from Moscow and St Petersburg appropriated every command in the Bulgarian army higher than the rank of captain. ('All the scum of Russia has taken refuge here and tainted the whole country', he once wrote indignantly from Sofia.) On 18 September 1885 Bulgarian patriots in Philippopolis (Plovdiv) ousted the Sultan's governor and declared for union with Bulgaria under Prince Alexander. The coup took the Great Powers by surprise; the Three Emperors' Alliance had (as was noted above) recognised the possibility of union between the Bulgarias, but at a moment convenient to the European Chancelleries rather than through the precipitate action of local hotheads. Everyone suspected everyone else. The Austrians thought the Russians had reverted to the discarded 'Big Bulgaria' policy; the Russians and Germans noted the close dynastic links of the Battenbergs with Britain; and there was also the odd coincidence that the rulers of both Serbia and Greece were, at that moment, in Vienna and ready to seek Francis Joseph's patronage of their claims for 'compensation' now that the Balkan balance was overturned. At the beginning of October the Russians formally condemned the coup and ordered their officers to return home from serving in Prince Alexander's army. The Eastern Alliance and Britain convened an ambassadorial conference at Constantinople which, it was hoped, would find some way of keeping the Balkans quiet.

Meanwhile King Milan Obrenović of Serbia could not resist the prospect of marching on a Bulgaria whose army was deprived of senior officers. Within a week the Serbs were decisively defeated by the Bulgars at Slivnitza (17 November 1885) and Niš, the chief town in southern Serbia, was in Bulgar hands. Only the threat of intervention by the Austrians prevented Prince Alexander's army from marching northwards on Belgrade itself. A discreet naval blockade dissuaded the Greeks from military action; the ambassadorial conference hit upon the ingenious solution, first proposed by Salisbury and backed by Kálnoky, of suggesting to the Turks that Alexander of Battenberg should be appointed governor of Eastern Rumelia, thus making possible a personal union of the two Bulgarias. By February 1886 the crisis seemed over.[21]

It had hardly begun. Alexander of Battenberg (an uncle of Earl Mountbatten of Burma) was too strong a personality to satisfy the Russians. In August 1886 a conspiracy organised by the Russian military attaché in Sofia culminated in a palace revolution and three weeks of chaos. Prince Alexander was abducted, forced to abdicate and then allowed to return to Sofia and resume his rule under Russian restraint. He finally signed a second abdication and left the country on 9 September. Kálnoky and Giers agreed that a regency council in Sofia should, in consultation with the Turks, speedily elect a new ruler who would maintain the union of the Bulgarias. At this point, however, the Panslav militarists appear to have intrigued successfully against Giers at court, for the Tsar now began to act independently of his partners in the Three Emperors' Alliance. On 25 September General Kaulbars, his former aide-de-camp and currently military attaché in Vienna, arrived in Sofia with orders to prevent the disintegration of the country. Kaulbars imposed what was virtually a Russian military dictatorship in Bulgaria; the Panslavs were masters of Sofia.

It was clear to Austrian and British diplomats in St Petersburg that Giers was embarrassed by a shift in policy decided solely by the Tsar and his generals. Kálnoky was faced with formidable opposition from the Hungarians, notably from Andrassy, who argued that the Kaulbars mission had destroyed the balance of power in south-eastern Europe and justified Austrian military measures against Russia. Poor Kálnoky appealed to Bismarck, complaining that he feared the Russians wished to secure permanent control of the two Bulgarias. The German Chancellor was unsympathetic. He pointed out that Bulgaria had long been accepted as falling within the Russian sphere of influence in the Balkans just as Serbia lay within the Austrian sphere. A few weeks later Bismarck spoke about the Bulgarian crisis to the Reichstag, the German parliament: 'It is a matter of complete indifference to us who rules in Bulgaria, or what becomes of Bulgaria', he declared. 'No one is going to entangle us in conflict with Russia, for the friendship of Russia means more to us than that of Bulgaria.'[22] Kálnoky could only assume that the Three Emperors' Alliance was dead; and in Vienna the indefatigable Archduke Albrecht argued that all other engagements of the Dual Monarchy with Germany might as well be buried alongside it.

Yet Kálnoky could not risk total isolation. Although he had deplored Italy's colonial ambitions in east Africa and Tripoli when last he visited Bismarck, he recognised the continued value of the Italian connection to Austria-Hungary. It safeguarded the Dual Monarchy's south-western flank, and it also strengthened Austrian contact with the British. For in the autumn of 1886 the Italians had taken the initiative in seeking a Mediterranean entente. Intermittent talks continued in Rome and London until the opening weeks of 1887. At first Salisbury could see little point in the Italian proposals. He was worried in those winter months both by the dangers of a Russian descent on Constantinople in the spring and by the mounting tension between Germany and France over the aggressive nationalism of General Boulanger's movement. The German ambassador, Hatzfeldt, even told Salisbury in the fourth week of January 1887 that his country would have to launch a preventive war against France if the Boulangist threat did not soon recede.[23] Salisbury therefore toned down the anti-French aspects of the Italian proposals, turning the draft agreement into a vague pledge to co-operate in the maintenance of the *status quo* in the Mediterranean. An Anglo-Italian secret treaty was signed on 12 February 1887; the 'Mediterranean Agreement' was extended to include Austria-Hungary six weeks later, with specific reference on this occasion to the maintenance of the *status quo* in the Aegean and the Black Sea as well. The Triple Alliance between Austria-Hungary, Italy and Germany was duly renewed at the end of February, a separate Italo-German treaty committing the two Powers to closer collaboration against the pretensions of France.

This latest series of secret commitments severely strained Bismarck's convoluted system of checks and balances. The weakest point in the system remained the one to which the Chancellor attached greatest importance, the wire to St Petersburg. In January 1887 the almost forgotten Peter Shuvalov came to Berlin, where his brother Paul had been serving as ambassador for eighteen months; and there were serious conversations with the Bismarcks, father and son, on ways of replacing the Three Emperors' Alliance by a secret Russo-German understanding which would have given the Tsar a free hand in the eastern Balkans in return for an assurance of 'benevolent neutrality' in a Franco-German war. The

Tsar, however, thought that the Shuvalovs and Giers were pushing him too fast; Obruchev and others on the General Staff still had hopes of France. Only the suspicion of intrigues between Bismarck, Kálnoky and the British induced Alexander III to change his mind. A secret agreement was signed in Berlin on 18 June 1887 valid for three years: Russia and Germany pledged themselves to benevolent neutrality in the case of a war with a third Power unless Germany attacked France or Russia attacked Austria-Hungary; and the Germans recognised Russia's predominant right of influence in Bulgaria and Eastern Rumelia as well as promising moral support if Russia was forced to seize the entrance to the Bosphorus in order to keep foreign warships out of the Black Sea. In later years Bismarck dubbed this agreement the 'Reinsurance Treaty' and represented it as a masterly stroke of diplomatic ingenuity, Germany's safeguard against Franco-Russian encirclement. Its merits, as some of Bismarck's subordinates recognised at the time, were largely illusory; the treaty played for time, postponing issues rather than attempting to solve them. The one person apparently 'reassured' by its existence was the Chancellor himself – and even he seems to have been less confident of its value in the three years of its existence than he became amid the frustrations of enforced retirement.[24]

The Russo–German secret compact was soon put to the test, and found wanting. At midsummer in 1887 the curtain went up on the third act of the Bulgarian drama. The Bulgarian National Assembly defied Russian pressure and elected as prince a cavalry officer in Francis Joseph's army who was also a grandson of King Louis Philippe and a second cousin of Queen Victoria. Prince Ferdinand of Saxe-Coburg-Gotha, a valetudinarian aesthete who delighted in wearing glittering rings on his carefully manicured fingers, was a curious choice for the throne of a primitive Balkan principality; and the practical Queen Victoria gave him twelve months at the most. But the Russians were convinced they had been tricked: Ferdinand's election was condemned as 'an unworthy comedy staged by the most wretched rabble'. The Russians put pressure on the Sultan of Turkey, still technically the suzerain of both the Bulgarias, to raise objections to the election of Ferdinand, seizing on the point that he was a Roman Catholic. Kálnoky and Francis Joseph – both uneasy at Ferdinand's election, for they knew him too well – feared that Russian pressure on the Sultan would include some form of military or naval intimidation. In reality, the Turks were as incensed as the Russians by Ferdinand's election and the Sultan had no intention of giving it his approval. But the Austrians and the Italians used the alleged crisis at Constantinople as an opportunity to secure from Lord Salisbury a more precise British commitment than he had conceded in the Mediterranean agreements of the previous February and March. In the second week of December 1887 Britain, Italy and Austria-Hungary concluded the so-called second Mediterranean Agreement by which the three Powers pledged themselves to maintain the existing order in Asia Minor, on the Straits and in Bulgaria. Bismarck was prepared, despite the Reinsurance Treaty, to give this Mediterranean Agreement his 'moral support' – for what it was worth. Meanwhile, however much the Russians might protest at his election, Prince

Ferdinand installed himself in Sofia. There he remained for over thirty years, his devious statecraft, sharp eyes and long pointed nose soon winning him the soubriquet 'the Fox of the Balkans'. To a ruler of such political cunning it mattered little that the Powers denied him formal recognition until the spring of 1896.[25]

Bismarck's approval of the second Mediterranean agreement in December 1887 was a sign of the growing disenchantment with Russia in Berlin during the last two years of his chancellorship. Francis Joseph noticed that even Emperor William I had lost his old faith in Tsardom when the two sovereigns met (for the last time) at Gastein in August 1887. Three months later the German authorities forbade the official *Reichsbank* to accept Russian collateral securities for loans, a retaliatory action for alleged discrimination against German landholders in Russian Poland. The banking veto – generally known as the *Lombardverbot* – pleased the Prussian Junkers and the General Staff. It was said that good German money was being lent to Russia to build railways which transported grain (to the detriment of East Prussia's agriculture) and which also had an ominous significance for the planners of military strategy. General von Waldersee, the deputy Chief of the General Staff, was encouraging the Austrians to stand up to Russian intrigues during the last phase of the Bulgarian crisis because he favoured a German–Austrian preventive war; better a conflict now, he argued, than wait for the Tsar's generals to launch an offensive at a time of their own choosing. This irresponsible belligerency angered Bismarck who remained convinced that to wage war with Russia, while France waited to avenge the defeats of 1870, was to court disaster. Waldersee was reprimanded for permitting the military attaché in Vienna to make statements contrary to the government's declared intention of keeping peace within Europe.[26]

Yet Waldersee and his henchmen were, it seemed, the makers of to-morrow's policies. William I was in his ninety-first year and the Crown Prince was grievously ill with cancer of the throat. It was certain that the throne would soon pass to the Crown Prince's son, Prince William, a young man who delighted in exaggerating his soldierly qualities and who had little sympathy with the restraints which Bismarck still exercised over Germany's relations with her neighbours. Not the least of the Chancellor's concerns in the winter of 1887–8 was the prince's friendship with Waldersee. William I died on 9 March 1888; his son's tragic reign lasted for a mere ninety-nine days; and on 15 June 1888 the style and titles of Kaiser William II were proclaimed for the first time. His accession was greeted with enthusiasm by the younger generation in Germany and with misgiving abroad. Soon Queen Victoria was describing her German grandson to Lord Salisbury as 'a hot-headed, conceited and wrong-headed young man, devoid of all feeling'. But Waldersee noted in his journal, 'Everyone in the army is rejoicing over our new ruler'.[27]

Bismarck, assuming that his long experience was essential to a young emperor suddenly thrust into world affairs, concentrated on keeping his system of checks and balances unimpaired by the aggressive nationalist fervour now in favour at court. The Kaiser himself enjoyed travelling abroad in state, whether in the new imperial train or the imperial yacht

Hohenzollern or at the head of a naval squadron. During the first eighteen months of his reign he visited St Petersburg, Stockholm, Copenhagen, Vienna, Rome, Venice, Athens, Constantinople and his grandmother on the Isle of Wight. 'The emperor is like a balloon', Bismarck grumbled. 'If you don't hold fast to the string, you'll never know where he'll be off to'; but the Chancellor was not entirely displeased by the imperial diversions. They enabled him to give his mind to the real problems of the European system: to the neo-Bonapartist threat of General Boulanger's popularity in France; to the possibilities of an open alliance with 'England . . . the old traditional ally'; to the improvement of those financial relations with Russia on which Bleichröder continued to lay such stress. When in October 1889 Tsar Alexander III came on a three-day state visit to Berlin the Chancellor was determined to reassure the Russians. He was assiduous in courtesy, even breaking the habit of twenty years and accompanying his sovereign's guests to a gala performance at the Opera. And Alexander reciprocated by inviting him to be seated when he received him in private audience.[28]

This audience, though he could not have expected it, was Bismarck's moment of truth. He set about relieving his host's immediate worries. The Tsar need not be disconcerted by the army's sabre-rattling along Russia's Polish frontier or by the young Kaiser's interest in the affairs of Turkey. For, Bismarck insisted, he personally would never make any fundamental change in policy. It was the conversational mood which prompted one of his personal advisers to recall, a few years later: 'With Bismarck, it was always Me, Me, Me!' But Alexander III was not impressed. He was a coldly calculating realist, well accustomed to puncturing the puffs of egocentricity. Now, towering over his seated guest, he asked a simple question: was Bismarck confident he would remain chancellor in the years ahead? The old man was disconcerted. His health, he assured the Tsar, was perfectly sound. But Bismarck was too shrewd an interlocutor to miss the significance of Alexander's unanswered question. Six days later Bismarck left the Wilhelmstrasse for Friedrichsruh, insisting that if Kálnoky wanted to discuss the state of the alliance he might as well journey up to Hamburg as to Berlin. Bismarck did not return to the capital after the Tsar's visit until summoned there at the end of January 1890 by the crisis of confidence which led to his fall in the middle of March.[29]

13 World Policies, 1890–99

Although Bismarck's fall was precipitated by differences with the Kaiser over domestic politics rather than foreign affairs, it was seen at the time as an event of world significance, one of those occasions when the theatre of history brings down the curtain on an era with a grand flourish of finality. Later commentators, however, look upon Bismarck's departure from the Wilhelmstrasse in the early spring of 1890 as far less momentous. The foundations of his European system survived virtually unshaken. His successors may not have juggled so adroitly with alliances but they recognised, as he had done, that the surest way to preserve peace and stability was through a series of limited agreements linking potential rivals or groupings of powers. Yet there was certainly a distinction between the diplomacy of the 1880s and of the 1890s. Extra-European affairs were for Bismarck a digression, often enough an irrelevance; it could be argued that the twenty months of his colonial policy have received from students of history more attention than they merit simply because it was out of character for him to have had a colonial policy at all. But after 1890 the attention of every Great Power except Austria-Hungary was concentrated outside Europe, and the latent antagonisms of imperial rivalry came to dominate the international scene. Not until the turn of the new century did these antagonisms gradually harden into a dangerous confrontation of two – and only two – potentially hostile camps.

The quest for new markets, the need to relieve overpopulation by emigration, the search for food and raw materials, the advantages of improved communications, the benefit of wider medical knowledge, the lure of untapped mineral wealth, the availability of surplus capital, the desire for strategic bases to protect old-established settlements overseas, the identification of remote possessions with national prestige, the arrogant assumption that Europe enjoyed civilised values which should be bestowed on 'lesser breeds without the Law' – all these considerations, and others, caused imperialism to blossom in the closing years of the nineteenth century. The 'scramble for Africa', a phrase which appears to have been coined by *The Times* as early as September 1884, was encouraged by colonial leagues in London, Berlin and Paris and made effective by a succession of chartered companies. By the start of the 1890s the two peripheral European Powers – Great Britain and Russia – were poised to resume a 'scramble for China', held in check for more than thirty years. The foundation of the China Association in London in the spring of 1889 created a powerful pressure group of 'old China hands', rich in knowledge and financial resources; while two years later Alexander III's imperial rescript announcing the decision to build a trans-Siberian railway marked the beginning of a new phase of Russian interest in the Far East which stimulated a reaction from Germany, France and other Powers.

The unique characteristic of Russian imperialism was its construction of overland routes to support a widely scattered fleet. Other governments, studying the writings of the American naval captain, Alfred Mahan, convinced themselves that the prosperity of empire rested ultimately upon command of the seas; and then built up their navies accordingly. The naval expenditure of Britain, France, Russia and Germany soared during the 1890s, the British seeking to maintain a two-power standard by which the Royal Navy was 'at least equal to the naval strength of any two other countries'. The relative merits of battle-fleets or of cruiser warfare (as favoured by the *jeune école* of theorists in the second strongest naval Power, France) inevitably influenced the response of rulers, statesmen and ambassadors to the successive crises of the decade. 'Navalism' and 'Imperialism' were dominant themes throughout the politics of the 1890s.[1]

Neither held great appeal for the 58-year-old general whom the Kaiser surprisingly chose to succeed Bismarck as Chancellor. Count Leo von Caprivi had been Chief of the Admiralty on William II's accession, but resigned in protest at his sovereign's attempt to bring warship construction programmes under the royal prerogative; and though a strip of land on the Zambezi still commemorates Caprivi's moment of colonial acquisitiveness, he out-Bismarcked Bismarck with the dictum 'the less of Africa Germany has, so much the better for us'.[2] General Caprivi was a conscientious administrator well aware that he knew little of world affairs and content to raise the status of the State Secretary for Foreign Affairs, and so, as he thought, create a Foreign Minister for the Reich. Here, however, Caprivi ran into difficulties; for during the last four years of the old chancellorship the post of State Secretary was held by Bismarck's son, Herbert, who declined to stay in the Wilhelmstrasse after his father's fall. Herbert's successor, Baron Adolf Marschall von Bieberstein, was an expert on international law but no more than an outside observer of the Bismarckian diplomatic machine, having served in Berlin as envoy of the Grand Duke of Baden, his native state. Inevitably both Caprivi and Marschall were overshadowed by veteran ambassadors, such as Schweinitz and Hatzfeldt, and they looked for advice to the senior counsellor of the German Foreign Ministry, Baron Friedrich von Holstein, whom they had known for at least four or five years, dining occasionally with him at the restaurant he invariably frequented in the Französische Strasse.

Historians long regarded Baron Holstein as a soured and sinister political blackmailer whose spies in embassies abroad sent him material with which he moulded Germany's foreign policy throughout the 1890s and the turn of the century. Publication in the late 1950s of Holstein's journal and papers has modified this view; he appears in these four volumes (and in Professor Rich's biography) as a hard-working civil servant, with few outside interests, who allowed his opinions to be shaped by prejudice based on real or imaginary slights.[3] Had Bismarck trained a successor – apart from Herbert – Holstein would have stayed obscurely in the background, as much a silhouette as he appears in Werner's famous painting of the Berlin Congress. Under Caprivi, too, he crept naturally into the shadows, declining a responsible post and shunning social gatherings at court. 'I hear that I have an excellent official in the Foreign Office, Herr von Holstein', the Kaiser told a foreign diplomat in March 1893. 'I haven't yet succeeded in getting to make his acquaintance';[4] and, indeed, the sovereign and his alleged 'evil genius' met only once, and then not until November 1904. Yet during the first six or seven years after Bismarck's fall Holstein enjoyed an unrivalled sense of power in the Wilhelmstrasse, for he knew that he was the one person who could find his way unfalteringly through the files of the Foreign Ministry while, at the same time, carrying in his mind a clear picture of the general pattern formed by the chancellery diplomacy of all the Great Powers. With the passage of time, the image became less sharply defined and his authority hollower than he imagined; but in 1890 it was to Holstein that Caprivi and Marschall turned when their emperor proclaimed that Germany was 'sailing in perfect order upon a new course'.

Holstein was helmsman throughout the Caprivi era, and it was to his touch on the wheel that German policy responded. The Reinsurance Treaty with Russia was allowed to lapse when it had run its three-year term in June 1890. The Triple Alliance was tightened by commercial treaties benefiting German industry and the agricultural produce of Germany's partners. An agreement with Britain ceded to Germany the long-neglected North Sea island of Heligoland in exchange for African colonial concessions in Zanzibar. Good relations between Britain and Germany even survived the return of Gladstone and the Liberals in the summer of 1892, for when Salisbury left the Foreign Office he drafted an explanatory memorandum for the new Foreign Secretary, Lord Rosebery, in which he stressed the importance of friendly contacts with Berlin, Vienna and Rome. So long as Rosebery was at the Foreign Office he kept faith with Salisbury's precepts, not always successfully. Relations became strained after Rosebery succeeded Gladstone as Prime Minister in March 1894 and Kimberley went to the Foreign Office. For although Rosebery was more sympathetically inclined towards imperial Germany than any other British Prime Minister, he failed to understand the depth of feeling in Berlin, Bremen and Hamburg over African colonies. As during the previous Liberal ministry, there was mistrust of each others' intentions in the Congo and around the borders of what became Uganda and Kenya. And this time the colonialism of the Germans was backed enthusiastically by their emperor.[5]

There was a strange air of reluctant shadow-boxing about much of the diplomacy of the early 1890s. The Russian Foreign Minister, Giers, had shown no desire for alliance with France, fearing it would give France's Jewish financiers a considerable hold over Russia's internal administration. When a French naval squadron sailed up the Gulf of Finland to visit Kronstadt in July 1891, Giers even hoped the ostentatious display of friendship between Russia and France would frighten the naval-minded Kaiser into seeking an improvement in Russo-German relations and thereby render any alliance with Paris superfluous. But Holstein and Marschall convinced themselves that these maritime festivities were more likely to send the British cap-in-hand to the Triple Alliance. As always, they exaggerated the anti-Russian mood in London, paying too much attention to Press scares of Tsarist intrigue in central Asia, where the Russians were said to be infiltrating the Pamirs plateau, between China and Afghanistan. Alexander III, for his part was more concerned with Europe than Asia; he was especially worried by what he interpreted as German backing for Polish cultural nationalism. By the spring of 1892 Alexander was losing patience with Giers; 'We really must reach an agreement with the French,' he told him, 'and, if war comes between France and Germany, we must throw ourselves at once upon the Germans so as not to give them time to beat the French first of all, and then turn on us.'[6] A Franco-Russian military convention was drafted in August 1892, but fresh doubts over the internal stability of the republic made the Russians hesitate yet again. It was not until the turn of the year 1893–4 that the agreement was finally concluded. The precise nature of the alliance remained unknown, but no public figures in London, Berlin, Vienna, or Rome doubted thereafter that France and Russia were partners.

Rumours of the mounting collaboration between the Russian and French General Staffs caused alarm in Berlin. William II encouraged Caprivi to give up wooing the worthless English and strike a trade bargain with Russia as a preliminary to restoring the old Hohenzollern-Romanov dynastic friendship. The Chancellor dutifully concluded a commercial treaty with Russia in February 1894, only to find himself the butt of every splenetic east Elbian landowner capable of articulating his grievances. Thereupon the Kaiser despaired of Caprivi, his lack of confidence being soon reciprocated, and the Chancellor felt compelled to resign, over a domestic constitutional issue. On 26 October 1894 the Kaiser chose as his third Chancellor Prince Chlodwig zu Hohenlohe-Schillingsfürst, his cousin by marriage. It was another strange appointment. At 75 Hohenlohe was a few months older than Bismarck when he was dismissed. Had he been younger, Hohenlohe would have been the ideal choice for the Kaiser's new objective in foreign policy, the recovery of a 'free hand'; for he belonged to a cosmopolitan family, influential in Vienna, in papal Rome, in Moscow and in St Petersburg. He had tried to keep abreast of trends in government and served with courtesy and tact as ambassador in Paris during the closest years of Franco-German collaboration. But he was puzzled by the noisy nationalism of the younger generation. He did not doubt William II's 'free hand' policy was wise; but there was never any certainty that some sudden inspirational whim would not divert the Kaiser from the tasks agreed with his ministers into what Holstein soon sourly dubbed 'operetta government'.[7]

Hohenlohe's appointment was followed by a succession of changes in government outside Germany which drastically altered the list of possible recipients of Williams's 'free hand'. A week after Hohenlohe took office news reached Berlin that Alexander III had died at Livadia, in the Crimea. At once the Kaiser – who saw all foreign relations in personal terms – assumed the world picture was dramatically changed: if Alexander III had been Germany's natural enemy, Nicholas II would be Germany's natural friend; for had not William himself helped 'Nicky', just six months before, to win his bride, Princess Alix of Hesse, the Kaiser's first cousin? Within a week there began the famous exchange of letters, written mostly in English, between William II and Nicholas II which continued intermittently for eighteen years. What the ambassador in Vienna called 'His Majesty's family politics' alarmed and exasperated ministers too often left to speculate on the offers of support their imperial master may have given his brother sovereign without taking them into his confidence.[8]

Giers, too, had an instinctive mistrust of 'family politics', but his health was failing and he survived Alexander III by only a few months. Tsar Nicholas chose as Giers's successor Prince Lobanov-Rostovsky, ambassador at Vienna since 1882, a convinced believer in Austro-Russian collaboration. But, to Lobanov's dismay, no sooner had he returned to St Petersburg than Kálnoky, after more than thirteen years in the Ballhausplatz, found himself accused by the Hungarian Prime Minister of being pro-Romanian, and suddenly resigned (15 May 1895). Francis Joseph now confounded both the Russians and the Germans by appointing Count Goluchowski to succeed Kálnoky. There was nothing personally disagreeable about the count, a retired diplomat of 46; but in St Petersburg and Berlin he was suspect as a Pole, a nobleman with great estates around Lemberg (Lvov). Moreover, he was married to Princess Anne Murat, great-granddaughter both of the one-time King of Naples and of Marshal Berthier. To the satisfaction of successive French governments, Goluchowski continued his custom of lengthy summer visits to his wife's properties in the Val-de-Marne and the Vosges. Some two years elapsed before the Russians were convinced of Goluchowski's sincerity; and the foreign service in Berlin long remained uneasy at those sojourns in France. It is an interesting comment on the practice of diplomacy at the close of the old century that the Ballhausplatz staff should be sending telegrams to Austria-Hungary's Foreign Minister in Vittel just as a few years earlier Foreign Office messengers crossed the Channel to Dieppe with the latest state papers for Lord Salisbury at the Chalet Cecil, his Normandy seaside villa at Puys. Salisbury sold the Chalet Cecil in 1895 when, within a month of Goluchowski's appointment, he returned to office after Rosebery's government was defeated in the Commons in a snap vote on the provision of cordite for the army.[9]

Once again, in this third ministry, the Prime Minister took personal charge of foreign affairs. Uncertainty over Rosebery's intentions had left Britain isolated in Europe, and Salisbury's return was welcomed in most capitals. So elated was Kaiser William II with Salisbury's subsequent electoral victory that he telegraphed rapturous congratulations direct from Potsdam to Hatfield House. It was assumed Salisbury would once more incline his policy towards the Triple Alliance Powers. But problems, familiar in themselves, looked different after an interlude of three years. In the Far East the Japanese, with their westernised army and navy, were gaining swift victories over the Chinese in a war caused by Japan's imperial designs on Korea and watched anxiously by Russia. The old (Near) Eastern Question entered a new phase when the long anticipated risings of the Armenians against the Sultan in the summer of 1894 led to such brutal repression that humanitarian sympathisers in the West recalled the Bulgarian atrocities eighteen years before. At the same time, there was tension in southern Africa on the borders of Cape Colony and the Transvaal (where the Cape authorities resented the way in which President Kruger treated British immigrants working in the Rand mines), in West Africa (where French and British interests clashed in the hinterland of modern Ghana and Nigeria) and on the frontier of Venezuela and British Guiana, where President Cleveland and Secretary of State Olney made it clear – somewhat aggressively – that they believed British colonialism was trespassing on the Monroe Doctrine. It was hard for Salisbury to comprehend the global character of the Foreign Secretary's problems when the red dispatch boxes began to come to him again in the last week of June 1895. He decided that the most pressing of all these problems was the future of Turkey and the protection of British interests if, as he feared, the Ottoman Empire were to fall apart.[10]

Salisbury had been critical of Ottoman administration ever since his visit to Constantinople for the conference of 1876–7 and he returned to office convinced that Britain had 'backed the wrong horse' in supporting Turkey during the Palmerston era. He told the Turkish ambassador sharply that it was essential for the Armenians to receive good government under a man whom Europe could trust. 'If the Sultan will not move', Salisbury telegraphed to Currie (now ambassador in Constantinople), 'I must address myself in the next place to Russia.'[11] Unfortunately Salisbury had to break down not only the Anglophobe suspicions of Prince Lobanov but the strong prejudices of a neo-Panslav movement in St Petersburg which was closely associated with the Tsar's ambassador to the Sultan, Alexander Nelidov, once Ignatyev's right-hand man. In neither of these tasks was Salisbury successful. Lobanov had told Nicholas II shortly before Salisbury's return to Downing Street, 'Incontestably our principal and most dangerous enemy in Asia is England'.[12] Nothing made him change his mind.

It was Salisbury's intention to counter Britain's dangerous isolation, not by any formal and comprehensive alliance with a Power or a group of Powers but by limited agreements to collaborate with other governments in particular parts of the world. He was prepared throughout the autumn of 1895 to discuss with Courcel (French ambassador to London) means of settling Anglo-French differences in Siam, Tunisia and west Africa. The two men achieved an embryonic entente cordiale which could well have served, as Salisbury hoped, as a means of easing Russia's mistrust of London; but the Courcel–Salisbury understanding was weakened by British policy in Egypt and the Sudan and by the project of the Ministry of Colonies in Paris for asserting French influence over the Upper Nile, an enterprise soon to become famous as the 'Marchand Mission'. Salisbury was also prepared to modify and renew the Mediterranean Agreements with Austria-Hungary and Italy but they were allowed to lapse as he declined to commit Britain to a more precise treaty (virtually an alliance) as Goluchowski wished.[13] Foreign governments found it difficult to discover how far Salisbury would carry Britain into partnership with them, either in Europe or in more distant continents.

Private talks held by Salisbury with the German ambassador (Hatzfeldt) late in July 1895 led the Germans to believe that he wished to partition the Ottoman Empire and permit the Russians to occupy Constantinople and the Straits. So revolutionary a shift in British policy caused consternation in Berlin. A few days later the Kaiser was at Cowes for the annual regatta. He dined with his grandmother at Osborne on 5 August, and Hatzfeldt and Salisbury were among the guests. William was puzzled by Salisbury's failure to raise the question of partition in his after-dinner conversation; the next day he sent a request to the Prime Minister to come to his yacht that afternoon. There was, however, general confusion. Salisbury had an audience with the queen arranged for that very time and was delayed in Osborne House by a heavy rainstorm. He then left for a meeting in London, and sent a letter of apology to the German ambassador, assuming that the Kaiser's invitation was a personal one rather than a serious political initiative. William II was grieved by the episode, and Salisbury did not meet him again until the eve of Queen Victoria's funeral in 1901. Soon after the Cowes misunderstanding some articles in the *Standard*, a Conservative daily newspaper highly critical of Germany, were read by the Kaiser and attributed by him to the Prime Minister's malevolence, largely because Salisbury had, as a young man, contributed to the newspaper. Small wonder if Salisbury privately came to the conclusion there was a genuine risk of William 'going completely off his head'.[14]

Such an eventuality had certainly occurred to Marschall in Berlin, for these last years of the century were the peak period of William II's 'personal rule'. 'He interferes persistently in foreign policy', Marschall wrote in his diary. 'A monarch ought to have the last word, but H.M. always wants to have the first, and this is a cardinal error.'[15] The most disconcerting aspect of the Kaiser's interventions were their superficiality, the sudden interest he would take in the Far East, or southern Africa, or the fate of Constantinople – and the equal rapidity with which his mind would turn to another topic. A small group of favourites could cajole their master at times into pursuing the semblance of a consistent policy; chief among this inner circle in the 1890s were William's closest personal friend, Philip zu Eulenburg, and his protégé, the young Bernard von Bülow. Eulenburg was sent to Vienna as ambassador in 1894 and Bülow became ambassador in Rome in the same year. Occasionally both Hohenlohe and Holstein used Eulenburg as an intermediary who would coax William away from some act of folly, provided they could anticipate it. But Marschall had no influence whatsoever on the Kaiser's shifts of policy. Indeed, by the end of 1895 William had taken so marked a dislike to the State Secretary for Foreign Affairs that he could hardly bring himself to throw a word to the poor man on the rare occasions they met.

Yet curiously enough, Marschall was responsible for the most famous and disastrous of William's interventions. Three times in the closing months of 1895, the Kaiser treated the British military attaché in Berlin, Colonel Swaine, to personal lectures on the folly of Salisbury's policies and, in particular, on the stupidity of the English in not seeking a German alliance. The Prime Minister was unimpressed; he was too concerned with Lobanov and the Turkish problem to take the Kaiser's prediction that he was 'courting a crash' seriously. But on New Year's Eve reports reached London and Berlin of the abortive Jameson Raid, when a high official in the British South Africa Company led an English force of nearly 500 men from Bechuanaland into the Transvaal as part of a plot to overthrow the Boer leader, President Kruger. Some 20 per cent of the foreign capital invested in the Transvaal was German in 1895 and German firms had extensive commercial links there. The Kaiser (whose personal behaviour had been extremely odd throughout December) was indignant at Jameson's invasion. On 3 January 1896 he went in person to the Chancellery with plans for action in support of Kruger, including an offer of German 'protection' and the sending of warships and marines to south-west Africa. So dangerous were his proposals that Marschall, as an alternative, suggested that his sovereign might (as a first step) send a telegram congratulating Kruger on the capture of the raiders. Holstein, waiting in an antechamber, tried to dissuade Marschall, only to be told that all the other suggestions put forward by the Kaiser were even worse. A 53-word telegram was duly sent to Kruger, and its text was carried by the Berlin evening newspapers as a gesture of Germano-Boer solidarity against Britain.[16]

The Kruger telegram provoked the first anti-German demonstrations in London, or indeed in any British city. The country as a whole had not followed Palmerston in the last serious Anglo-German crisis, the Schleswig-Holstein dispute of 1864; but in 1896 public opinion boiled over, while the government was content to simmer indignantly. Salisbury – and Queen Victoria – recognised that what Baron Holstein called the Kaiser's 'prank' was fully in keeping with the ambivalent attitude he had shown towards 'England' over the preceding five months. William himself made use of the Germanophobe outbursts to justify his pleas for expanding the navy: 'To impress seafaring Powers, a fleet is needed', he told Chancellor Hohenlohe on 8 January. But eight weeks after sending the telegram, William visited the British embassy in Berlin and spent three and a half hours trying to convince the ambassador that 'Russia is your implacable enemy' and, by implication, Germany a natural ally.[17] It was several years before the Kaiser appreciated the harm inflicted by the Kruger telegram on Anglo-German relations.

Both the German and the British Admiralties responded to the Kruger telegram crisis: Germany for the first time prepared a naval contingency plan for operations against Great Britain; and in London it was announced, largely as a sop to public opinion, that the Royal Navy would establish a 'flying squadron' of warships capable of sailing to any trouble-spot in the world. The storm of indignation against Germany in Britain was accompanied by a Press campaign for more amicable relations with Russia, notably in the *Edinburgh Review* and the *Fortnightly Review*. The French and Russian ambassadors in London both reported back to their governments in the third week of February 1896, stressing the desire of Salisbury and other members of his Cabinet to ease the chronic suspicion of Britain in St Petersburg. But, as the British ambassador told Salisbury, Lobanov's 'general policy seemed to have for its key note almost a diseased mistrust of England and of British machinations, not only at Constantinople but well-nigh all over the world'.[18] Russia was more interested in the Far East than the government in London as yet appreciated. When the Greeks in Crete revolted against Turkish misrule in the spring of 1896, Nelidov in

Constantinople countenanced rumours that Britain was planning to establish a protectorate over the island, while Lobanov genuinely believed that what he called Britain's 'habitual obstruction' to a proposal from Goluchowski for a naval blockade of the Cretan coast was part of a British intrigue to magnify the crises in the eastern Mediterranean so as to prevent Russia from concentrating on a forward policy along the borders of China. In August 1896 Lobanov accompanied Nicholas II on a state visit to Vienna, where Goluchowski received the impression that Russia was playing for time, maintaining the *status quo* until the Trans-Siberian Railway was complete. Yet if Goluchowski was disappointed with Lobanov, it mattered little, for as the imperial train neared Kiev on 30 August the Russian Foreign Minister, returning to his compartment after dinner, collapsed and died from a heart attack.[19]

Three weeks later the Russian royal family arrived in Scotland to visit Queen Victoria at Balmoral. Lord Salisbury held two conversations with Nicholas II while he was at the castle. By now the massacre of Armenians had spread to the Turkish capital itself and the problem of Constantinople was uppermost in their minds. Salisbury argued that the Powers should intervene, deposing Sultan Abdul Hamid and jointly imposing administrative reforms. The Prime Minister also told the Tsar that, provided Russia did not precipitate the collapse of the Ottoman Empire, Great Britain would not attempt to prevent the Russians from taking control of Constantinople and the Straits if the other Powers of Europe favoured such a move. This was a major break in British policy, and though it is possible that Salisbury counted on Austrian objections to frustrate Russian hopes, he appeared to be offering the Tsar a significant concession in the hopes of winning Russian support for his general policy. Nicholas was nonplussed. He had with him no expert Foreign Ministry counsellor, only the ambassador, Baron de Staal, whom Lobanov had looked upon as an Anglophile. The Tsar wavered indecisively, unwilling to approve the deposition of the Sultan by a concert of European Powers but aware that Salisbury's proposal might provide Russia with a long-coveted prize.[20] When, at the end of the Balmoral visit, Nicholas travelled on to Paris he magnificently avoided committing himself – a trick of which he fast became a master. Salisbury, for his part, was left to propose that well-worn device, an ambassadorial conference in Constantinople, which duly opened on 22 December 1896. Six weeks later the ambassadors completed a reform programme, but they lacked authority to compel the Sultan to enact its admirable recommendations.

The Foreign Office, and the European Chancelleries, were intrigued throughout the closing months of 1896 by the Tsar's search for a new Foreign Minister. When Nelidov was summoned home from Constantinople in the second week of November, the British assumed he would be appointed to the post. But the real reason for his journey was the unresolved conflict in St Petersburg between the 'traditionalists', who wished to use the anarchy in Constantinople as an excuse for securing the Bosphorus, and the 'Easterners', who looked to China and Korea rather than to the Straits. Nelidov, who had first put forward the idea of seizing the Straits as long ago as December 1882, developed a detailed plan by which, on receipt of a code signal from his embassy, Russian warships and troop transports would sail from Odessa and Sebastopol for a surprise descent on the Bosphorus, which could soon 'be turned into a Russian Gibraltar', he said. The project was discussed at a Crown Council on 5 December 1896. The Easterners' case was presented by Serge Witte, Minister for Finance and Communications; but the Tsar was attracted by the thought of occupying the Bosphorus heights 'for ever', and Nelidov was able to return to Constantinople a week later convinced that his arguments had at last prevailed. But Witte would not accept defeat. He enlisted the support of the influential Procurator of the Holy Synod, Konstantin Pobedonostsev, who agreed with him that 'an occupation of the upper Bosphorus without prior agreement between the Great Powers' was 'full of risk and possibly fatal for Russia'. Once Nelidov had returned to his embassy, Witte and Pobedonostsev found it not difficult to persuade the Tsar to abandon the project. The troop transports remained at Odessa until the spring, a source of much interest to the resident British consul.[21]

Rumours of the Crown Council's deliberations were soon circulating abroad. Some details reached Berlin on 27 December, and a fortnight later the British ambassador in Constantinople telegraphed a remarkably accurate account to the Foreign Office, basing his report on facts provided by his Italian colleague. Salisbury certainly knew of the Crown Council before his important talks with the Austro-Hungarian ambassador at the end of January, when he rejected a proposal from Vienna that Britain should join the Triple Alliance Powers in meeting a Russian assault on the Bosphorus. Goluchowski thought Salisbury was renouncing Britain's traditional policies in the eastern Mediterranean; and he took the lead in promoting an Austro-Russian entente in the spring of 1897, based on a joint recognition of the need to maintain the *status quo* in the Balkans. But Goluchowski exaggerated the extent to which Salisbury was breaking the mould of tradition. When in May 1897 Greece was defeated in a thirty-day war with Turkey (caused partly by the Cretan rebellion and partly by frontier incidents in Thessaly) it was the British who insisted on maintaining the principle that a town previously freed from the Sultan's rule should not be retroceded to Turkey by a Christian state. So determined was Salisbury to uphold Britain's obligations as a Protecting Power of Greece that on 15 May 1897 he sent a remarkable telegram to the British ambassador in St Petersburg, Sir Nicholas O'Conor, proposing a joint naval demonstration at the heart of the Turkish empire. Britain, Russia 'and any other Powers who may wish to co-operate' would send warships through the Straits to anchor off the Sultan's palace and compel him to accept a settlement dictated by Europe in concert. The Russians, however, were uneasy at such a proposal, which seemed to them to smack of Palmerston, Nesselrode and the crisis of 1839–40. O'Conor was told that Russia was convinced Abdul Hamid would treat the Greeks generously without coercion from foreign warships; and, indeed, nothing more was heard of the Turkish army's ambition to recover Thessaly. The Salisbury Plan, like the Nelidov Plan, remained untested.[22]

This proposed naval accord places Salisbury's apparent change of policy in perspective. He was certainly less concerned than in earlier years about the future of the Straits and the integrity of the Ottoman Empire; but he was not abandoning Britain's responsibilities in the eastern Mediterranean, as Goluchowski feared. Salisbury's shift of emphasis was a strategic disengagement. He wished to transfer the defensive centre of Britain's Near Eastern interests away from the Dardanelles and Constantinople to Egypt, where the military authorities had embarked on their campaign to secure the valley of the Nile by destroying Dervish power in the Sudan. From Unkiar Skelessi to the Treaty of Berlin the British had seen the Mediterranean leading to the Black Sea; now it seemed to point to the Red Sea, and beyond.

Meanwhile, on 11 January 1897, Nicholas II had at last appointed a successor to Lobanov, Count Michael Muraviev. The new Foreign Minister was a man of limited experience. As envoy in Copenhagen, he was known 'to hold a firm faith in the Oriental mission of his country' – a creed causing little trouble to a diplomat whose windows looked out across the Sound to the Kattegat. It was assumed by foreign commentators that he would be a puppet of Witte and the financiers who backed a Russo-Chinese bank and a Chinese Eastern Railway as a subsidiary of the Trans-Siberian. Sir Nicholas O'Conor predicted that China rather than Turkey would dominate Anglo-Russian relations over the turn of the century, but as Sir Nicholas had just completed four years as minister in Peking, there was a feeling in the Foreign Office that he gave undue attention to the part of the world most familiar to him.[23] On the other hand, it was true that half the commercial enterprises in the Chinese Empire were British in 1897, that the Hong Kong and Shanghai Bank made Witte's financial interests seem puny, and that the Inspector General of China's Maritime Customs – responsible for tariffs on all imported goods – was the Ulsterman Sir Robert Hart, who had held this post of great influence for the last thirty years. O'Conor had good reason to emphasise the importance of the China Question.

It was, however, posed in its newest form by Germany rather than by Russia. In June 1897 Kaiser William II, conscious of disquiet in the German Press, decided to seek a spectacular success to thrill the imagination of his subjects. He began with two significant but unsensational changes in government: the replacement of Marschall by Bülow as State Secretary for Foreign Affairs; and the appointment of his favourite naval officer, Real Admiral Alfred Tirpitz, as State Secretary of the Navy Office, a post he was to hold for nineteen years. In the first week of August the imperial yacht *Hohenzollern* brought the Kaiser on a six-day visit to the Russian capital. During a pause in the succession of parades and galas William engaged Nicholas in casual conversation at Peterhof, asking if Russia would object should German warships winter at the anchorage of Kiaochow Bay, in the Gulf of Pechili. So informal was the conversation that Nicholas did not mention it to Muraviev or any other minister. It was, however, clear to Witte that Germany was taking a new interest in the Far East; and at the end of August Witte went out of his way to emphasise to O'Conor that Russia was determined to safeguard the *status quo* 'in China and Korea as elsewhere', adding that he saw no reason why

the British and Russian governments should not reach a political understanding. O'Conor then left St Petersburg for four months of home leave,
reporting Witte's remarks to the Foreign Office as he passed through
London.[24]

During O'Conor's leave, the break-up of China began in earnest. On
14 November 1897 German marines landed in Kiaochow Bay from a
cruiser squadron and seized the town and harbour in retaliation for the
murder by Chinese brigands of two German Catholic missionaries on All
Saints' Day. Tsar Nicholas was indignant at William's disingenuous
conduct. Muraviev argued that 'the time for maintaining the integrity of
China was gone' and recommended the occupation of the Kwangtung
peninsula, including the potential naval base of Port Arthur and the
commercial harbour of Talienwan (Darien), 23 miles farther up the coast.
Witte opposed drastic action of any kind, with much the same argument
as he had used against the Nelidov Plan; other governments would follow
Russia's example. But the Tsar, intensely angered by the German move,
ordered five Russian warships to enter the Gulf of Pechili and winter at
Port Arthur, where they arrived at the end of the third week in December
1897. As yet, no formal moves were made to annex or lease the
peninsula.[25]

The seizure of Kiaochow was presented in Berlin as an event of world-
shattering importance; and it is interesting that when, thirty years later,
Gooch and Temperley published the first volume of *British Documents on
the Origins of the War* they selected the crisis caused by the German action
as their starting-point. At the time, British newspapers and periodicals
took their cue from the tone of the German Press. After the Russian warships reached Port Arthur, *The Times* and the political monthlies (notably
the *Nineteenth Century*) mounted a sustained assault on the diplomatic
failings of the Salisbury government, which suffered a surprise by-
election defeat at Durham in the New Year.[26] The Prime Minister personally thought far too much fuss was being made of the whole affair.
Kiaochow had not surprised him; as early as December 1895 the Foreign
Office had heard that Baron Holstein was indicating, in private conversation, that Germany was looking for a coaling-station on the Chinese
coast. Salisbury argued that the German presence 'would act as an irritant
to the Russians'. He was, however, under pressure from the China
Association to uphold British interests; and he was constantly badgered
by long and able memoranda from his vigorous assistant under-secretary,
Francis Bertie, who was head of the African and Asian Departments and
unofficial spokesman for the China Association in the Foreign Office.
Reluctantly Salisbury acknowledged that the British public would
demand 'some territorial or cartographical consolation'. For the moment,
however, he calmed the hotheads in his Cabinet, sent two British
warships to anchor beside the Russians at Port Arthur, and sought to
pursue a double policy over Far Eastern affairs: the conclusion of a new
loan with China to strengthen the Peking government against foreign
(non-British) predators; and the achievement of a preliminary understanding with Russia, so as to prevent chronic friction from boiling
up to war.[27]

Salisbury's pursuit of an agreement with Russia 'covering the general area of our respective interests' in China and the Ottoman Empire well illustrates the problems of preventive chancellery diplomacy. Even with the advantage of electric telegraph, decisions still depended on the ability of the ambassador on the spot to decide whom to approach, when to do so and how far to modify London's instructions so as to meet local peculiarities in the conduct of business. Sir Nicholas O'Conor had to face not only the jealousy between the Foreign Ministry and the Finance Ministry in St Petersburg, but the long delay while proposals were passed on for assessment to rival special departments in the ministries, to the army and navy chiefs, and to Russia's diplomatic agents in Peking. As ever there was, too, uncertainty over the Tsar's attitude, for Nicholas suffered from the characteristic fault of ineffectual autocrats, the echoing of the most recent arguments he had heard, whether or not they were consistent with earlier points of view. On this occasion, after three weeks of talk, Nicholas imposed an absolute ban on the consideration of disputes in any region apart from the Far East; and reports sent by O'Conor to the Foreign Office only eight days apart show the Tsar (to use the ambassador's phrase) in a completely different 'humour' over the sincerity of British intentions.[28]

Ultimately Salisbury's parallel attempt to secure good political and economic terms from China in return for a loan vitiated the discussions in St Petersburg, for the Chinese were so accommodating that there seemed no reason for weakening Britain's prospects by a compromise with Russia. O'Conor's suggestion that a joint Anglo-Russian loan would increase the prospects for genuine collaboration elsewhere in Asia prompted Francis Bertie to draw up a powerful memorandum which reflected the views of the China Association and its fear that 'We shall let power slip out of our hands'. When, at the beginning of March 1898, the newspapers reported Russian demands for railway concessions from China as well as the lease of Talienwan and Port Arthur, Salisbury recognised there was no hope of a comprehensive agreement with the Tsar's ministers. Britain entered the scramble for ports, securing a lease on Wei-hai-wei which had been in Japanese hands since the 1895 war with China. It was an inferior anchorage between Port Arthur and Kiaochow, but Bertie maintained not only that it was likely to be seized by the Russians but that it was sheltered by an island which 'could be made a Gibraltar'. In fact, Wei-hai-wei was acquired as a consolation prize or, more precisely, as a sop to criticism of what *The Times* called 'Lord Salisbury's childlike faith' in Russian assurances.[29]

This failure to achieve an Anglo-Russian entente was followed by a sustained attempt by Joseph Chamberlain to settle differences in Africa and Oceania with Germany. The Prime Minister, however, mistrusted his Colonial Secretary's initiative. Salisbury assumed Germany really sought a formal alliance, which would have implied British acceptance of the frontiers established by the Treaty of Frankfurt, and he was not prepared to commit Britain to such obligations on the European continent as he feared that Germany wished to embroil Britain with France. Bülow, for his part, was no less convinced that open alignment with Great Britain in the Far East would make it difficult to paper over the cracks in Russo-German friendship, while William II frightened himself into believing that acceptance of Chamberlain's proffered hand would provoke three Russian armies to march into East Prussia. This was unlikely, but the existence of such fears made it clear that only proposals for local settlement of particular issues had any chance of success. A secret Anglo-German agreement in late August 1898 provided for collaboration should Portugal find it essential to dispose of her southern African colonies; and an Anglo-Russian agreement in April 1899 defined spheres of predominant interest for railway construction within China. Even so, there remained problems which aroused such unexpected antagonism that it seemed unlikely a settlement would ever be reached. Thus William's personal desire to acquire the island of Upolu in Samoa as a possible coaling-station for his fleet led to tense relations between Germany and Great Britain (and, to a lesser extent, the United States) in March and April 1899. William II threatened to recall his ambassador from London when he thought the British dilatory in meeting Germany's requests. Only pressure from his Cabinet colleagues persuaded Salisbury to conclude the Samoa Convention of November 1899, which permitted the establishment of a German protectorate over the four western islands of the archipelago.[30]

The French gave moral support to their Russian ally in the Far East and, as it were in passing, acquired the lease of Kuangchowan, an anchorage in southern China. But their principal colonial effort in the 1890s was concentrated on girdling Africa from the Congo to Somalia. Rumours of France's grand design had caused the British to warn off trespassers on the upper Nile as early as March 1895, two years before Jean-Baptiste Marchand set out from Brazzaville on his famous trans-continental expedition. It was on 10 July 1898 that Marchand reached Fashoda and occupied the ruined Egyptian fort beside the Nile. Ten weeks later Kitchener's Anglo-Egyptian flotilla arrived there from Khartoum, 390 miles downstream, where Dervish rule had just been broken in the Battle of Omdurman. For three weeks there was acute tension between the governments in Paris and London. France claimed the Fashoda region by right of prior occupation, Britain by right of conquest. Distant observers, including Kaiser William II, believed the two countries would go to war over their rival claims.[31]

Yet, in a sense, the Fashoda crisis was manufactured by the Press on both sides of the Channel, and beyond the Rhine too. Relations between Kitchener and Marchand were not unfriendly, the Frenchman even travelling down the Nile to Cairo on one of Thomas Cook's commandeered steamers before being peremptorily ordered back to his tricolour flagstaff by telegraph from Paris. There was little risk of war. France was weakened by the Dreyfus Case, unsure of Russian support and conscious that the navy had fallen back from the high standard of ten years before. Theophile Delcassé, a republican with national vision who had become Foreign Minister in June, favoured a dignified retreat and found that Salisbury was anxious to save France from humiliation. On 11 December the tricolour was lowered at Fashoda; Marchand's force – six whites and

120 Senegalese – set out eastwards for Addis Ababa, French Djibuti and, at least for the white officers, a triumphant return to metropolitan France. Talks continued quietly through the winter at the Quai d'Orsay and led in March 1899 to a French renunciation of any claim on the Nile valley. The principal French colonial pressure group, Eugène Etienne's *Comité de l'Afrique Française*, was disappointed by Delcassé's willingness to appease the English but accepted, readily enough, the principal lesson that Fashoda taught Europe's chancellery strategists – that far-flung imperial power was effective only through naval mastery over the intervening sea routes. So powerful was the Royal Navy in October and November 1898 that, without mobilisation, the concentration of warships at Portland, Malta and Gibraltar effectively paralysed the French fleet and, as the House of Commons was later assured, at an additional cost to the taxpayer of a mere £13,600.[32] At almost the same time American victories in the brief war of 1898 with Spain emphasised the value of a modern efficient fleet. Salisbury and Commodore Dewey between them had vindicated the historical teachings of Captain Mahan.

The point was well taken in Germany. In March of that year the Reichstag approved Tirpitz's first programme of warship construction, and by the autumn the newly founded German Navy League was gaining enthusiastic members at a rate above 3,000 a week. A directive from the Foreign Ministry to newspaper editors in November indicated that the Kaiser wished them to comment on the role of warships in the Spanish-American War and to present France's 'retreat before England' as evidence that there could be 'no successful overseas policy without a strong fleet'.[33] Germany, it was assumed, could afford a large navy and still maintain the most powerful army in Europe. But less efficient and less industrialised economies found the expense of new weapons at sea and on land dangerously burdensome. The cost of keeping up with the armaments of Russia's European neighbours (and of Japan) especially worried the Tsar's recently appointed Minister of War, General Kuropatkin, an 'Easterner' who wished eventually to annex northern Manchuria. In the second week of March 1898, when Russia was settling the final terms for leasing the Port Arthur area, Kuropatkin wrote to Muraviev stressing the need of Europe's political leaders to call a halt to the arms race. His arguments were taken up both by the Foreign Ministry and by the Ministry of Finance in St Petersburg. So rare an instance of harmony among his ministers seems to have stimulated the Romanov strain of Messianic idealism in Nicholas II's character. At the same time the Tsar may have been indirectly influenced by the publication of a detailed multi-volume study on the horror and social dislocation of war by the Jewish railway tycoon Jan Bloch. It is most unlikely that Nicholas read Bloch (who was, however, an old friend and colleague of Witte) but the study certainly impressed some of the officials in the Foreign Ministry, notably Mikhail Basily, one of Muraviev's right-hand men. Basily may have prepared for the Tsar a résumé of Bloch's arguments, which seem to be echoed in the famous 'peace manifesto' circulated to the envoys in St Petersburg on 24 August 1898. In the manifesto Nicholas urged the summoning of a conference which would seek ways of lifting 'the crushing burden' of 'massed war material'.[34]

The response to the Tsar's initiative recalls the mingled embarrassment and derision with which his great-great-uncle's draft proposal for a Holy Alliance was received in 1815. William II, in his calmer moments, thought the idea 'dangerously Utopian', while the Prince of Wales considered it 'the greatest nonsense and rubbish I ever heard of' and Lord Salisbury was inclined to dismiss it as 'not serious'. Public opinion, however, was intrigued and a number of humanitarian campaigners, by no means sympathetic to Tsarism, welcomed the manifesto. In the last months of 1898 Muraviev toured the continental capitals seeking support and, indeed, during a tense week in the Fashoda crisis, the Russian ministers of Foreign Affairs, of Finance and of War all came in quick succession to Paris to sell their sovereign's ideas to his suspicious and resentful ally. But, as both Goluchowski and Baron Holstein commented, no public figures wished to displease the young Tsar; even the Kaiser felt bound to telegraph to 'Nicky' that 'henceforth honour will be lavished upon you by the whole world', though he pointed out that 'the practical part may fail through difficulties in detail.'[35]

The peace conference opened at The Hague on 18 May 1899, a date chosen to honour the Tsar, for it was his thirty-first birthday. It was fitting that in a decade of 'world policies' delegations from the United States, Japan, China, Siam and Mexico should have joined the representatives of twenty-one European powers. The conference itself attracted less attention than the manifesto had done; it was said the only Dutchmen interested in what was taking place at The Hague were the hall porters of the two best hotels. Little was heard of the original Russian plea to halt the arms race for, when it was seen that the delegations were being packed with naval and military experts, Kuropatkin was reluctant to risk revelation of Russia's weaknesses. The chief Russian delegate, Baron de Staal (ambassador in London), was unanimously voted president of the conference, but he was an octogenarian with no knowledge of modern weapons, although proud of a diplomatic experience which went back to the Metternich era. Passage of a pious resolution that 'the limitation of military budgets . . . is highly desirable' stretched Staal's range of ideas to their fullest extent. The conference agreed on formal conventions to lessen the horrors of war. Goluchowski insisted that the Austrian delegation should persuade their German colleagues to accept the establishment of a Court of International Arbitration, but even this modest innovation so shocked Baron Holstein's faith in the free play of diplomatic forces that he momentarily considered resigning from the German foreign service. When, after seven weeks, the peace conference held its final session, Goluchowski told his ambassador in Berlin how relieved he felt that nothing settled at The Hague would impose genuine restrictions on the conduct of future policy.[36] Most statesmen of his day agreed with him and turned back to the familiar reality of decision-making in the Chancelleries of the five Great Powers. Only in later years was it appreciated that The Hague Conference, despite the air of distilled scepticism which pervaded its sessions, was a milestone in the pursuit of peace. By 1907 it was seen to have held promise of an international organisation more cohesive than the improvised states system of the dying century.

14 The Diplomatic Revolution, 1899–1906

Fashoda was soon recognised as the climax of Salisbury's years as Foreign Secretary, a quiet victory for calmly reasoned diplomacy through strength in the tradition not of the Don Pacifico affair but of Palmerston's triumph of 1840–1 over the Straits. To some extent, the ease of the Prime Minister's success surprised his Cabinet colleagues; they thought him out of touch with the mood of politics and ageing rapidly. He seemed to them a rheumy-eyed bronchial patriarch, more decrepit than his 68 years warranted and hampered by the girth of a crumpled Falstaff. Soon, they felt, he must hand over his twin responsibilities as Prime Minister and Foreign Secretary to his nephew Balfour (who deputised for him at the Foreign Office when he was forced to recuperate in the south of France) or the most dynamic member of his government, the Colonial Secretary, Joseph Chamberlain, Yet Salisbury, who had cultivated the image of a reluctant office-holder, exaggerated his weariness and social isolation from force of habit. He might affect contempt for the new journalism, complain that 'the rows of cameras' outside Westminster Abbey robbed Gladstone's funeral of dignity, or deplore the noisy patriotism which was soon 'to maffick' in the streets of London. He might show puckish absent-mindedness over colleagues' names and prod himself with a wooden paper-knife to fight off the torpor of listening to visiting ambassadors. But when a problem engaged his attention his mind remained acutely logical. He could still read a dispatch and sift fact from embassy gossip; and when other members of the government sought to slant British policy towards the Triple Alliance Powers, they found their efforts blocked by dispassionate arguments marshalled by a veteran statesman still intent on guiding his country into an unfamiliar century.

The South African Question clouded Salisbury's closing years as it did those of his sovereign, too. In the second week of October 1899 the Boers of the Transvaal and the Orange Free State launched their attack on Natal and Cape Colony, a response to the provocative forward policies of Chamberlain and the High Commissioner in Cape Colony, Sir Alfred Milner. Salisbury himself tended to call the conflict 'Joe's War', not because he wished to disclaim responsibility but because he regarded it primarily as an imperial concern, a matter for the Colonial Office in the first instance. But the embarrassment of the early defeats, together with the unpopularity of the British cause in almost every European country, posed problems for the Foreign Office. Would the French seek to avenge Fashoda by a precipitate move when British resources were under strain? Would Germany send something more than a telegram to Kruger this time? Where would the Russians pounce next? It seemed inconceivable that Britain would be allowed to destroy the Boer republics without intervention.

Russia was the great bogey in London. Reports from embassies and legations abroad spoke of Russian intrigue in Korea, Manchuria and even in the horn of Africa. More than once the Viceroy of India, Lord Curzon, returned to a theme which had obsessed him before his departure from England, his fear that the Persian Gulf would 'turn into a sort of mid-Asian Gulf of Pechili, with the danger of another Kiaochau or Talienwan'. Three days after the Boer War began the Director of Military Intelligence, Sir John Ardagh, circulated the first of several directives recommending a careful watch on Russian movements, since he considered a Russian flank attack on India probable.[1] When twelve days later it was learnt in London that the Russian Foreign Minister, Muraviev, had travelled to Paris and on to San Sebastian for conversations with the Foreign Ministers of France and Spain, Whitehall was convinced that he was seeking to organise a common front against Britain. Muraviev's subsequent stop-over in Berlin, when he was received in audience by the Kaiser, did not ease suspicions in London; an inspired article in the *Fortnightly Review* by 'Diplomaticus' (Lucien Wolf) gave alleged details of Muraviev's activities, much to his indignation. 'I was amazed at finding myself portrayed as an arch-conspirator of a somewhat silly type', he told the British ambassador in St Petersburg in mid-December.[2] Nevertheless, the sources of the Foreign Office information were sufficiently reliable for Salisbury to attach some importance to the tales of Muraviev's 'indiscretions'. It was assumed that the French would not support Russia unless Germany came into line and that Muraviev had been cold-shouldered in Berlin, for his visit came shortly before the final discussion on the Samoa Convention and thus at a time when Germany wished to cultivate good relations with Great Britain. Salisbury remained slightly sceptical about the whole affair. He did not rate highly Russia's naval or military effectiveness. When Sir John Ardagh suggested that Russia 'is willing to wound but yet afraid to strike', the Prime Minister endorsed his assessment of the situation.[3]

There were, nevertheless, intermittent discussions on ways of taking advantage of the Boer War in St Petersburg throughout January and February 1900. Muraviev and the Minister of Finance and Communications, Witte, thought little could be done, although the Foreign Minister was unwisely induced to approach Germany yet again in the hope of creating a continental league against Britain – an initiative at once revealed by the Kaiser to the Prince of Wales in a bid to court favour in London. Both Muraviev and Witte were upstaged by Kuropatkin, who urged the Tsar to authorise action in central Asia or at the Straits. The Minister of War even appears to have taken another look at the Nelidov Plan of 1896–7, which had been abandoned before Kuropatkin's appointment to office: occupation of the Bosphorus heights, Kuropatkin declared, was 'Russia's most important task for the opening of the twentieth century'. Once again there was for several months considerable military and naval activity round Odessa and Sebastopol, and on 1 June Sir Nicholas O'Conor (now ambassador at Constantinople) telegraphed a request to London for the Mediterranean fleet to cruise nearer the approaches to the Straits in case the Russians made a sudden descent on the Turkish capital. But Salisbury was not impressed: 'What is the use of our fleet being nearer when it dare not pass the Dardanelles?', he minuted on O'Conor's telegram.[4] Salisbury's patience was strained, too, by the India Office. In March the British military attaché reported a conversation with Kuropatkin in which the minister recommended the division of Afghanistan into British and Russian spheres of influence. At the same time, he admitted that Russian troops had been moved from the Caucasus to Kushk on the Russo-Afghan border and he added, disarmingly, that they would return to Tbilisi 'as soon as peace is declared in the Transvaal'. While the Foreign Office was intrigued by this conversation, the India Office and the viceroy himself regarded it as proof of their darkest fears and were irritated by Salisbury's refusal to share their alarm. Curzon, with his penchant for drawing not quite parallels, was afraid that Afghanistan would become a second Transvaal, but Salisbury seems to have been impressed by suggestions from the ambassador in St Petersburg that the Russians were encouraging rumours and reports which exaggerated the movement of troops to central Asia in order to pin down British forces in India. Nevertheless there was, within the Cabinet, a feeling that the Prime Minister was over-indulgent to the Russians.[5] His ministers did not appreciate that pessimism over the future of the Straits and of Afghanistan had clouded Salisbury's professional reading matter for much of the last thirty years – and yet there was still no Russian garrison within sight of the Golden Horn or the Khyber Pass.

The most likely region for a Russian diversionary move was the Far East. When Russian vessels arrived at the Korean port of Masampo in March 1900, *The Times* gloomily reminded its readers of events at Port Arthur, but Salisbury was prepared to leave such problems to the Japanese, who were already seeking to make Korea a sure foothold on the Asian mainland. At first, too, he wished to minimise the xenophobic threat from the 'Boxer Rising' in China, maintaining in private conversation as late as the second week of June that 'it would not come to much'. He did, however, acknowledge that Russia might use the excuse of Boxer unrest to strengthen her grip on Manchuria and the north. 'Of the many possible dangers', he telegraphed to Sir Claude MacDonald, the British minister in China, on 7 June, 'the most serious is that Russia should be moved to occupy the whole or part of Peking'.[6] This was a misjudgement on the part of Salisbury. Within a week the foreign legations were cut off by Boxer fanatics, and the newspapers in London, Berlin, Paris and St Petersburg were full of alarming stories of 'the siege at Peking'.

The Boxer Rising was accepted in Russia as evidence that China was falling apart even more rapidly than the experts in the Asiatic Department had predicted. Kuropatkin at once wished to seize Manchuria so as to safeguard the Russian-financed Chinese Eastern Railway. Witte was opposed to any move which might increase Chinese hostility to Russia, while Muraviev believed that Russia should concentrate on Peking. So heated were the disagreements between the three ministers that on 21 June Muraviev (like his predecessor, Lobanov) suffered a heart-attack and was dead before doctors could reach him. Nicholas II hurriedly appointed a Foreign Ministry official, Count Lamsdorff, to take over Muraviev's work, confirming his appointment as minister early in the following year. Lamsdorff, a naturally cautious and conservative bureaucrat, was (in Witte's words) 'a walking archive' of the Foreign Ministry, where he had spent his entire career. He was also more interested in Europe than the Far East. If forced to choose between the policies of Kuropatkin and Witte, Lamsdorff would support the Minister of Finance, provided this did not bring him into conflict with the Tsar. He was, however, so fastidious an epicene that he deplored argument and controversy, and this was an unfortunate trait in the Foreign Minister of a weak-willed autocrat.[7]

The assassination by the Boxers of the German minister and the First Secretary of the Japanese legation were followed by wild rumours that other diplomats had been butchered, including MacDonald and his family. While the European Chancelleries exchanged telegrams over the problems of fitting out an international relief force, local contingents in the Gulf of Pechili mounted their own independent rescue operation. British officers subordinated themselves without any difficulty to the command of a Russian admiral, Alexander Alexeyev, reputedly an illegitimate son of Tsar Alexander II. With a nice touch of historical irony, the first contingent from Alexeyev's force to enter the legation area of Peking was an Indian detachment under General Sir Alfred Gaselee. By the end of the second week in August it was known in the European capitals that the legations were relieved and most foreign residents in Peking safe and secure. Within three weeks the British minister could look back almost nostalgically on the siege: 'On the whole, very good fun', MacDonald told Sir Francis Bertie in a letter to the Foreign Office at the beginning of September.[8] That was not the view held in Berlin.

The Kaiser took the murder of his envoy as both a personal affront and an insult to the German nation. He planned to send a massive punitive expeditionary force, commanded by the newly promoted Field Marshal von Waldersee, who would have under his command token contingents from other nations. Since Waldersee's force was still in Europe when the legations were relieved, it was difficult for outsiders to understand German intentions; and old mistrust was easily rekindled. 'Lord Salisbury suspects William II of having big designs on China', an ambassador on leave noted in his diary after a conversation with the Prime Minister on 20 August.[9] Yet there were others in the Cabinet who saw German indignation over the Boxer murders as a means for promoting the Anglo-German understanding which they had long sought. Joseph Chamberlain consistently championed an Anglo-German alliance from March 1898 onwards, although rebuffed by both Bülow and his own Prime Minister. Remarks made by William II to the British ambassador, Sir Frank Lascelles, at Wilhelmshöhe in favour of a joint Anglo-German 'Open Door' policy in China revived Chamberlain's enthusiasm for an agreement with Berlin, even though Salisbury insisted that any bargain struck with Germany would be to the disadvantage of British traders. Chamberlain, however, was supported by at least five other members of the Cabinet, who argued that collaboration with Germany, and possibly Japan, would block Russian ambitions in Manchuria and the provinces around Peking. Reluctantly Salisbury gave way; and on 16 October 1900 an Anglo-German agreement was concluded which affirmed the desire of the two governments to uphold freedom of trade in China 'as far as they can exercise influence' and to preserve the integrity of the Chinese Empire. This extraordinarily vague agreement – 'unnecessary, but innocuous' was Salisbury's considered verdict on it – was misinterpreted from the start: the Germans called it the 'Yangtse Valley Agreement'; the British assumed it applied to China as a whole. The Russians may at first have been deterred by the fact that Britain and Germany were collaborating at all. But within six months Bülow had publicly declared in the Reichstag that the agreement 'was in no sense concerned with Manchuria', thus relieving Russia's fears of a hostile Great Power combination in the Far East.[10]

The Anglo-German agreement was the last achievement of Chancellor Hohenlohe's administration. The old prince, by now in his eighty-second year, complained that he had not been consulted over the Waldersee expedition and that everything was being settled by the Kaiser and Bülow without considering his views at all. William II duly appointed Bülow to succeed Höhenlohe on 17 October, assuming that he would be a Chancellor in the mould of Bismarck although more compliant to the imperial will. Bülow at once suggested that Holstein should become State Secretary for Foreign Affairs, a post which both the Kaiser and the new head of government intended to make once more subordinate to the chancellorship, denying it full ministerial status. Holstein declined the offer: he disliked the official public duties which a State Secretary was expected to perform; and he believed that he could continue to exercise greater influence as a confidential adviser with an inner door between his room and the office of the State Secretary, a privilege he had enjoyed for twenty years. Baron Oswald von Richthofen, Bülow's deputy since the closing months of 1897, took over as State Secretary, content to go on echoing his master's opinions although now from behind a bigger desk and to more eminent visitors. Richthofen was a tidy-minded bureaucrat who detested Holstein and deplored his habit of unceremoniously intruding on his working hours; but he lacked the courage to lock that famous connecting door. Better the counsellor's looming presence over his shoulder than the machination and intrigue which would follow any attempt to curb Holstein's opportunities for tendering unsolicited advice.[11]

The change from Hohenlohe-Bülow to Bülow-Richthofen caused hardly a ripple of comment in the European Press. It was otherwise with Salisbury's decision, announced a few days later, to hand over the Foreign Office to the fifth Marquess of Lansdowne. There were three main reasons for the widespread interest: Salisbury's Cabinet had remained unchanged for five and a quarter years, a record of continuity unsurpassed in British administrative history; Lansdowne, as Secretary for War, had been much criticised after the initial failures against the Boers in South Africa; and, a topic of more limited appeal, the new Foreign Secretary was the first incumbent of the office to be descended from an eminent continental statesman – Lansdowne's grandfather was the Comte de Flahaut, an aide-de-camp to Napoleon I and a natural son of Talleyrand. Most of all, it was recognised that with Salisbury's departure from the Foreign Office, the last of the gifted amateurs in statecraft had retired.

It is true that Salisbury remained Prime Minister for another twenty months, and at first foreign envoys and the general public in Britain assumed he would continue to guide policy along familiar lines. Queen Victoria even told Salisbury that, as Foreign Secretary, Lansdowne 'must be entirely under his personal supervision . . . and no telegram or despatch should be sent without first being submitted to him'. Salisbury, however, was too wise and experienced to treat Lansdowne as Bülow treated Richthofen, and Lansdowne would never have submitted to such behaviour, for he was a man of strong personality. The queen's death, thirteen weeks after Lansdowne went to the Foreign Office, freed Salisbury from any obligation to keep close watch on outgoing dispatches; and during the last eighteen months of his premiership Salisbury only intervened on two occasions in top-level diplomatic decision-making, each time seeking to counter what he regarded as dangerous proposals for a foreign alliance.[12]

Lansdowne began his term of office by seeking further agreements with Germany in the Far East. His principal objective was joint action to resist Russian encroachment southwards through Manchuria. Bülow refused to risk incurring Russian hostility along the indefensible borders in East Prussia and Poland because of some clash of distant interests in the Orient. Germany wanted a precise British commitment in Europe, preferably by transforming the Triple Alliance into a Quadruple Alliance of Britain, Germany, Austria-Hungary and Italy. It was this proposal which induced Salisbury, on 29 May 1901, to draft the most concise and cogent of all his masterly memoranda, a thousand-word document arguing that it was against Britain's interests to take on responsibilities for safeguarding more than 2,000 miles of frontier in Europe in order to gain allies who would counter the perils of 'isolation', 'a danger (wrote Salisbury) in whose existence we have no historical reason for believing'.[13] Sporadic exchanges between British and German statesmen continued until the autumn, but the basic contradiction between the British desire for partnership in China and German hopes of a 'European' agreement ruled out any real prospect of success. Lansdowne did not limit his approach to the Germans. He was prepared to seek an understanding with Russia; and at the end of October 1901 he telegraphed to the ambassador in St Petersburg requesting him to propose to Lamsdorff a series of talks which might settle Anglo-Russian differences in Persia and Manchuria. But Lamsdorff was not interested: it was assumed by the Russian council of ministers that time and interior lines of improved railway communication were on Russia's side both in central Asia and the Far East. Lamsdorff's rebuff – his rejection of the proposed talks reaching London only ten days after Lansdowne first suggested them – intensified the Foreign Secretary's determination to make a complete break in diplomatic tradition and seek alliance, not with one of the European Great Powers but with Japan, whose military leaders had already made it clear they would welcome links with the British.[14]

Salisbury was uneasy over the prospect of a Japanese alliance. He feared Japan would push Great Britain into war with Russia and France; and he stated his objections roundly in one final memorandum. His son-in-law, the Earl of Selborne (who was the First Lord of the Admiralty), favoured the alliance as a means of adding 'materially to the naval strength of this country all over the world', for he thought that the combination of the Royal Navy and the new Japanese fleet would 'effectively diminish the probability of a naval war with France or Russia'. Lansdowne himself was driven into support of the alliance by the assistant under-secretary, Sir Francis Bertie, who had already tried to shape policy in 1897–8 and now had a wider field of action, with the removal of Salisbury's restraining hand. Baron Hermann von Eckardstein, First Secretary at the German embassy and an inveterate intriguer himself, suggested that Bertie was the real power in the Foreign Office during the opening years of the century, a Germanophobe Baron Holstein. This is an exaggeration, but there is no doubt that the influence of a small professional élite in the Foreign Office increased during the Lansdowne era and that Bertie was a persuasive advocate of an Anglo-Japanese entente. Ultimately it was Bertie who drafted the treaty of alliance, signed on 30 January 1902; Great Britain recognised Japan's special interest in the fate of Korea and undertook to ensure that France remained neutral in a Russo-Japanese war while Japan would fight alongside the British should they find themselves at war with more than one other Power in the Far East.[15] The treaty, which was made public at once, was a warning to Russia and France and, though the Kaiser failed to see it, to Germany too – for it offered Britain an alternative ally. Even without the mounting concern over German naval expansion, it is unlikely there would have been any further talk in London of joining the Triple Alliance.

Austria-Hungary and Italy, Germany's two partners in the alliance, took little part in the Far Eastern imbroglio. The Austro-Hungarian Foreign Minister, Count Goluchowski, gradually and patiently improved relations with Russia, establishing the principle that Vienna and St Petersburg would work in harmony in the Balkans rather than seek to take advantage of each other's problems to disturb the *status quo*. There were occasional moments of friction, notably over Serbia where King Alexander Obrenović seemed throughout 1901 to be courted by Panslav Russian diplomats: 'Should anything serious happen in the Balkans and the Serbs follow a line of policy we do not like, we shall simply strangle Serbia', Goluchowski told the German ambassador ominously in the first week of the new century.[16] When Serbian radical army officers butchered Alexander Obrenović and his consort in the Belgrade coup d'état of June 1903, Goluchowski and Lamsdorff collaborated closely and recognised the accession of Peter Karadjordjević as 'the relatively lesser evil'. In early October 1903 Francis Joseph, Nicholas II, Goluchowski, Lamsdorff and the Austro-Hungarian ambassador to the Tsar, Baron von Aehrenthal, all gathered for some happy days of hunting at Mürzsteg in Styria, sparing the stags long enough to conclude the 'Mürzsteg Punctation', an agreement to seek the maintenance of the Ottoman Empire in the Balkans by requiring the Sultan to introduce reforms which, it was hoped, would reconcile his Christian subjects in Macedonia (Serbs, Greeks and Bulgarians) to Turkish rule. A 'Mürzsteg euphoria' sustained Austro-Russian relations for some two and a half years after the meeting. Both Great

Powers resented the new interest which Germany was taking in the Near East and, in particular, the patronage given by Berlin to the Baghdad Railway project. It seemed as if Goluchowski was turning his back on the Triple Alliance: German policy, he complained privately to the ambassador in Berlin, was marked by arrogance, lack of consideration and 'the desire to play the schoolmaster everywhere'.[17] Although the Triple Alliance was revised and renewed on 28 June 1902, the bonds linking Berlin, Vienna and Rome were wearing thin.

Italy, the junior among the Great Powers, seemed at the start of the century the most prone to revolution. The governments of Francesco Crispi, from July 1887 to January 1891, and from December 1893 to March 1896, had held promise of a great colonial empire in Africa. He colonised Eritrea, established a foothold in Somalia and sought to annex Ethiopia. But when Italian troops were cut to pieces by Emperor Menelik's Abyssinians at Adowa on 1 March 1896, Crispi was driven from power by an angry people who thought his flamboyant imperialism imposed additional burdens on a nation suffering deep social distress. The last four years of the old century were marred in Italy by anarchy, repression and terrorism which culminated in the assassination of King Humbert at Monza in July 1900 and the accession of Victor Emmanuel III (who was sovereign throughout both World Wars). These internal disorders lessened Italy's effectiveness as a Great Power: in February 1899 the Foreign Minister, Admiral Canevaro, even suffered the humiliation of having a claim to lease a segment of Chinese territory in Chekiang rejected by the government in Peking because Italy had no real commercial interests in China nor a significant naval presence in the China Sea. Victor Emmanuel III began his reign determined to improve his kingdom's standing abroad: his queen – a Montenegrin princess educated at the Russian court – had valuable contacts in St Petersburg, where the Italian royal couple were welcomed in great state in July 1902; but Lamsdorff suspected that Italy wished to stir up the Russians against Austria-Hungary in the Balkans, and rather than risk a major shift in policy, he ensured that the royal visit was not politically productive. More sensational was the mounting friendship between Italy and France which began, in standard form, with Prince Tomasso of Savoy taking the Italian fleet on a courtesy call to Toulon in April 1901 and continued with some hard bargaining at the Consulta, the Foreign Ministry in Rome. From 1902 to 1912 the vision of creating an Italian 'Algeria' out of the nominally Turkish provinces of Tripolitania and Cyrenaica loomed large in the conduct of Italy's external relations. Britain and Austria-Hungary raised no objection and in June 1902 an understanding was reached between the French and Italian Foreign Ministers by which, in return for financial assistance and a free hand in seeking the acquisition of Tripoli, the Italians pledged themselves to neutrality in any Franco-German conflict provoked by Germany.[18]

French policy, too, was concentrated on North Africa, much to the irritation of their Russian ally, whose sovereign and statesmen still looked to the Far East. The leaders of the *Comité de l'Afrique Française*, the most powerful colonialist pressure group in France, had urged Delcassé ever since Fashoda to renounce ambitions in the Nile valley and the eastern

Mediterranean in favour of the gradual absorption of Morocco. Egypt, they maintained, was an unnatural Bonapartist dream; the Third Republic should seek the creation of a Greater France, across the Mediterranean from Marseilles and extending from the Atlas Mountains to Tunisia.[19] Delcassé was slow to follow their lead but he agreed to talks about Morocco with the Spanish and Italian authorities in the summer of 1902. At this point, however, Morocco gave one of its frequent violent lurches towards civil war. Spain and Britain became alarmed, not so much because of Morocco's economic value as because of its strategic position; the British Admiralty in particular was determined to keep the coastline opposite Gibraltar neutralised. Although Bülow assured the French ambassador in January 1903 that German concerns in Morocco were 'trifling and insignificant', the foundation in Berlin of a Morocco Association seemed ominous. For the moment, however, the real obstacle remained Great Britain, as the colonial pressure group frequently reminded Delcassé. An offer, first put forward in August 1902, that France would collaborate with the British over Egyptian affairs in return for approval of a plan to partition Morocco between France and Spain, aroused no enthusiasm in London. Balfour, who had succeeded his uncle, Salisbury, as Prime Minister in July, warned the French in November that Morocco could well become a threat to Europe's peace. By the following spring Delcassé was anxiously looking around for means of placating the British. Fortunately, on May Day 1903 King Edward VII arrived in Paris for the first state visit of a British sovereign since 1855. It was a city he already knew and loved.

Contemporaries, especially in Germany and France, attributed deep significance to Edward VII's role in shaping British policy.[20] His nephew, Kaiser William II, was so convinced of his hatred for Germany that, thirty years after the king's death, he could read of Hitler's army marching into Paris and exclaim, 'Thus is the pernicious entente cordiale of Uncle Edward VII brought to nought'.[21] But this picture of a devious schemer does not stand up to close scrutiny. The king combined charm, irascibility and strong prejudice with a better knowledge of European high society than any of his predecessors. He was, however, not gifted with any shrewd intelligence and could no more have plotted the 'encirclement' of Germany than have emulated M. Blériot and flown the Channel. Nevertheless, on this one occasion in May 1903, he helped turn a page of history; for the king's goodwill, tact and obvious delight in being in Paris convinced Delcassé that he might persevere and seek from the British an assurance about Morocco and the settlement of other outstanding difficulties. Even so, it is doubtful if the British would have responded to Delcassé's renewed approach had not Lord Cromer, Britain's pro-consul in Cairo, urgently requested the government in London to seek agreement with France. Cromer needed French backing for his plans to reform Egypt's finances, an undertaking which might well have encountered opposition from the bankers of Paris. Paul Cambon, the French ambassador in London, soon perceived the importance of Cromer's influence. At a sticky moment in the negotiations, he saw to it that the French chargé d'affaires in Cairo enlisted Cromer's aid to encourage

Lansdowne to make a concession over the 200-year-old dispute concerning fishing rights off Newfoundland. If any single individual shaped the form of the new Entente Cordiale, it was Paul Cambon.[22]

The negotiations, which began in earnest in October 1903, ranged over problems concerning West Africa, Siam, Madagascar and the New Hebrides as well as the Newfoundland fisheries and North Africa. The Anglo-French treaties, signed in London on 8 April 1904, sought primarily to heal old wounds and their character was symbolised by Lord Cromer's decision to change the name of Fashoda to Kodok so as to ease French susceptibilities. Recognition by France of British supremacy in Egypt was balanced by British recognition of France's right to take any suitable action 'to preserve order in Morocco', provided that the coast opposite Gibraltar remained unfortified and that Spanish rights in northern Morocco were respected should the Sultan's power collapse entirely. The treaties did not in any way commit Britain to follow a predetermined policy within Europe. Only in offering France an almost free hand over Morocco did the agreement look to the future rather than to the past. 'We are liquidating all our old quarrels', Delcassé told his principal assistant at the Quai d'Orsay, Maurice Paléologue, on 1 February; but he added: 'I shall not stop at that. It must lead to a political alliance with England. What fine prospects would then open up for us! If we could lean on both Russia and England how strong we should be in dealing with Germany!'[23]

Yet, in that first week of February 1904, Delcassé and Paléologue were less immediately concerned with the German problem or Morocco than with a mounting crisis which threatened war in the Far East. For Russian policy over the preceding twenty months was marked by more than the usual show of chaos and confusion. Captain Bezobrazov, a retired Guards officer, and his cousin Captain Abaza, of the Russian navy, had persuaded prominent figures at court, including Nicholas himself, to invest heavily in two imperialistic companies which they had founded to secure commercial concessions in Manchuria and Korea. This irresponsibly adventurous clique challenged the authority of both Witte and Kuropatkin in Russia's most easterly provinces and acted in total independence of Lamsdorff and the Foreign Ministry. In July 1903 the Tsar seems at last to have perceived that Bezobrazov was a charlatan and had no further personal contact with him. At the same time, Nicholas turned against Witte whom he dismissed from all his posts. Subsequently, he appointed Admiral Alexeyev his viceroy in the Far East and, to the intense chagrin of the Asiatic Department in the Foreign Ministry, he also established a Far Eastern Committee, with Captain Abaza as its secretary general. The inconsistencies of Russian policy puzzled the Japanese. Abortive diplomatic exchanges continued between Tokyo and St Petersburg from August 1903 to January 1904, and it is possible that an agreement which assigned Korea to Japan and Manchuria to Russia would have checked the drift to war. But there were groups in both capitals spoiling for a fight and confident of victory. Japan's admirals thought little of Russia's outdated fleet while the army preferred war now rather than when the last gaps along the Trans-Siberian Railway were closed. By contrast there was, in St Petersburg, a group which believed that only new battle honours and tales of heroism would rally a backward people behind their Tsar. 'Russia needs a nice little victorious war to stem the revolutionary tide', Vyacheslav Plehve, the Minister of the Interior, told Kuropatkin. On the night of 8 February 1904 the Japanese gave the Russians their 'little war' by a surprise attack on the fleet as it lay anchored at Port Arthur. But the eighteen months' fighting which followed the Japanese attack brought Russia not the victories for which Plehve had hoped but defeat in the Far East and disintegration at home.[24]

War between their respective allies posed an immediate problem for Lansdowne and Delcassé, challenging the durability of the entente cordiale as soon as it was concluded. The tragic blunders which led Russia's Baltic fleet to fire on English trawlers fishing on the Dogger Bank in mistake for Japanese torpedo boats aroused such indignation in London that it seemed as if Russia and Britain would be plunged into war during the closing days of October 1904. Mediation by Paléologue and by Delcassé led both Lansdowne and Nicholas II to suggest that an international commission should examine the evidence on the Dogger Bank incident, a procedure envisaged by the Hague Peace Conference. By the middle of November this dangerous crisis was over, its peaceful outcome showing the reluctance of Britain and Russia to go to war with each other despite the antagonism shown by the Press in London and St Petersburg. Momentarily, Holstein and Bülow hoped to benefit from the crisis, and the Kaiser sent a personal message to the Tsar which encouraged Nicholas to hope once more for a continental league of Russia, Germany and France which, in William II's words, would make Britain and Japan 'think twice before acting'. Delcassé protested strongly in St Petersburg at this flirtation with Germany; he also let Lansdowne know of the German initiative. This cumbersome move by the Germans coincided with the first serious signs of alarm in Britain at the growth of Tirpitz's fleet; and the closing weeks of 1904 saw not only a redeployment of Britain's capital ships so as to increase naval power in home waters, but also a violently Germanophobe tone coming into the periodical Press as well as the more popular dailies.[25]

The decision of Kaiser William II to land at Tangier while on a Mediterranean cruise at the end of March 1905 and affirm Germany's concern for Morocco's independence was one of the most inept master-strokes ever essayed by the German Foreign Ministry. Bülow and Holstein recommended the Tangier visit, first proposed to them by the young and ambitious chargé d'affaires in Morocco, Richard von Kühlmann. It was assumed in Berlin that an assertion of Germany's interest in the Moroccan Question would make it possible to summon an international conference at which France would see how valueless was the Entente Cordiale and how ineffectual the support of a weakened Russia. The Tangier visit was thus planned as the start of a campaign which would inflict a rebuff on French diplomacy at least as great as Fashoda. The Kaiser's instinct told him that the Tangier visit was folly; he sought to cancel it and was ill at ease for the few hours he spent on shore. It was only when his ship put into Gibraltar on the resumption of his cruise that William was able to see for himself the consternation of the British at his presence in Tangier.[26] The nightmare of a Moroccan Kiaochow, a German naval base in the most strategically sensitive waters of the world, alarmed the British for the next seven years, pushing them closer and closer towards the French.

At first German policy seemed successful. There was no doubt Germany had a genuine commercial interest in Morocco and it was difficult for other Powers to oppose Berlin's request for an international conference to settle the country's future, however much the French might deny the need for such a gathering. The single-mindedness of German policy caused divisions in the radical-republican coalition governing France and on 6 June Delcassé felt bound to resign in protest at the appeasement policies pursued by the Prime Minister, Maurice Rouvier. Delcassé's fall was reckoned by Bülow and Holstein as a major victory: he had been Foreign Minister for seven years, longer than any other politician under the Third Republic, and over the second half of this period he had identified himself closely with the betterment of Anglo-French relations; and it was believed he was about to win kudos as a world statesman by mediating between Russia and Japan to end the war in the Far East. The immediate effect of Delcassé's fall was agreement by Rouvier to support Germany's plea for a conference on Morocco. In the Wilhelmstrasse it was still hoped that a new turn in French policy would enable Germany to create the continental league which had flickered like a will-o'-the-wisp through the diplomacy of the past six years.

The Kaiser had high hopes of winning support from the Tsar by the vigorous exercise of his compulsive personality. It was a bad time for Russia: in the first six months of the year Port Arthur had fallen to Japan, the army had suffered defeat at Mukden and the navy at Tsushima, and Nicholas II's empire was wracked by strikes, terrorism and mutiny. When, in July, Tsar Nicholas invited William II to interrupt a Baltic cruise for a rendezvous of imperial yachts off the coast of Finland, the Kaiser optimistically telegraphed to Bülow for a copy of the draft Russo-German treaty prepared in the previous November after the Dogger Bank crisis. William assumed that Russia in defeat would need Germany's patronage just as Prussia, a century before, had received chivalrous protection from Alexander I. It was in a mood of benign self-confidence that William set off in the launch of the *Hohenzollern* to be greeted by Nicholas aboard the *Polar Star* as the two yachts lay in the bay of Björkö on 24 July 1905. In his pocket William carried the draft treaty by which each empire undertook to help the other if attacked by a third Power, the Kaiser himself adding to the original proposals a clause limiting the treaty to Europe. 'That is quite excellent, I agree', said Nicholas in English, after he had read the treaty; and with no government ministers in attendance, the two sovereigns signed the alliance there and then, in the little cabin of the Russian imperial yacht.[27]

The secret Björkö Treaty was the final gesture of dynastic diplomacy. Bülow was furious. He emphasised to the Kaiser the folly of limiting the effectiveness of the treaty to Europe, but his real grievance was against the Kaiser's independent initiative, an autocratic stroke which made the Chancellor and his ministers mere clerks in the administration. Holstein, curiously enough, thought the treaty ridiculous and its manner of conclusion anachronistic in the modern world; but he recommended that Germany should wait on events rather than disown the pact as soon as possible. Bülow followed this advice, and as the Tsar did not tell Lamsdorff the full details of his meeting with the Kaiser after he returned to St Petersburg, there was a lull of some three months when 'Willy' and 'Nicky' could delude themselves into believing they had made history on that July morning off the Finnish shore. Lamsdorff's attention was concentrated in those late summer weeks on events in Washington and in Portsmouth, New Hampshire, for President Theodore Roosevelt had stepped forward as mediator between Russia and Japan, and Witte had travelled to America as the Tsar's emissary, seeking a settlement which would preserve Russia's empire in the Far East. It was not until after the conclusion of the Treaty of Portsmouth that Nicholas II, almost as an afterthought at the end of an evening audience with his Foreign Minister, showed the text of the Björkö agreement to Lamsdorff. Three more weeks elapsed before Lamsdorff, Witte and the Grand Duke Nicholas Nicolayevich travelled out to Peterhof and convinced a reluctant Tsar that the Björkö pact was incompatible with Russia's commitments to France.[28] As Holstein anticipated, the Russians were thus left with the embarrassment of wriggling out of the treaty which their sovereign had signed; and the Kaiser continued until the end of his reign, and even in exile, to deplore Nicholas's fatal weakness of character and to look upon Björkö as the greatest of his lost opportunities.

During this winter of 1905–6 Russia needed France more than ever before. It is true that Witte had achieved considerable success in the peace negotiations, keeping a Russian hold on northern Manchuria and frustrating Japanese efforts to impose a war indemnity even if Russia had to see Port Arthur and Talienwan pass under Japanese rule. But the real problems of Russia lay in the very nature of Tsardom. Gradually Nicholas was coming to accept the need for reform from above. But both Witte and Lamsdorff knew that Russia could only stave off radical revolution and recover the authority of a Great Power with the aid of French loans and French investment. Small wonder that when the conference of Morocco opened at Algeciras in the middle of January 1906 the Russian delegates gave total support to their French ally.[29]

So, indeed, did Italy and Great Britain. The German delegates found themselves isolated, with only Morocco and Austria-Hungary prepared to support their attempts to check the spread of French colonial influence. The Final Act of the Algeciras Conference, signed on 7 April 1906, duly asserted the independence of Morocco and proposed the establishment of a Moroccan Bank, which would be an international institution, as the Germans had wished. But the vital question of internal order was decided in favour of France and Spain who were left to control the police force, although under the nominal supervision of a Swiss inspector-general. Even though the Final Act recognised the need for Morocco to keep an open door for foreign trade, the conference virtually accorded France a vote of confidence.

The Kaiser and Bülow acknowledged that Algeciras was a double defeat for German diplomacy: their Moroccan policy was in shreds and they had failed to disrupt the Anglo-French Entente. So closely had Britain worked with France that the Russians were beginning to consider the value of an understanding with the new Liberal government which had come to power in London during the last weeks of the old year. Many commentators, both in 1906 and in more recent years, believed that William II looked for a scapegoat for the Algeciras disaster and placed the blame for Germany's failure on Baron Holstein, who was prised from his sanctum in the Foreign Ministry within a few days of the conference's final session. The immediate cause of his political demise was, however, an inability to work with Heinrich von Tschirschky, who had taken over as State Secretary in the Wilhelmstrasse on the sudden death of Richthofen in the third week of January. On several occasions in earlier years Holstein had sent in his resignation when thwarted over petty details and each time he was coaxed to stay in office. But at the end of March 1906 he made the irreparable blunder of tendering his resignation when Bülow was away from Berlin, recovering from a heart attack, and when the Kaiser was angry with the Foreign Ministry in general and its most formidable counsellor in particular. The bankruptcy of Germany's Moroccan policy did not in itself cause Holstein's fall, but the opportunity for William to rid himself of the mystery man he had come to distrust was too good to be missed. An imperial counter-signature approving the letter of resignation ended thirty years of service; and poor Holstein was left with another three years of life in which to seek vengeance on those who he believed had encouraged the Kaiser to dismiss him, never realising he was his own worst enemy.

Yet, all in all, it was a fitting moment for Holstein to fade finally into the shadows from which he was always so reluctant to emerge. For Algeciras marked the completion of a diplomatic revolution which was in the end to destroy the chancellery system as he had known it. His style of statecraft depended on fluidity in international politics, unconfined by tightly knit power groups in confrontation. Although the European governments might come together to form opposing alignments in different parts of the world, they retained sufficient freedom of movement to adjust their loyalties when interests elsewhere impelled a change of policy. By standing outside Bismarck's alliance system and accepting only limited local commitments, successive British statesmen had encouraged this flexibility. Even the Anglo-Japanese alliance seemed at first to fall within a familiar pattern of diplomacy since its obligations applied to a particular region, remote from vital interests in Europe. But by the spring of 1906 all these considerations had changed. Defeat and revolution paralysed Russia, thus impairing the effectiveness of one of the traditional Great Powers in Europe as well as Asia. At the same time suspicion of the Kaiser's navy hardened the hostility towards Germany felt intermittently in Britain over the past ten years. From 1905 onwards France and Russia had to emphasise the reality of their alliance in order to ensure the continuance of any balance of power within Europe; and the British, without fully perceiving the implications of their action, tentatively strengthened the Franco-Russian partnership until Bülow himself began to fear isolation and encirclement. 'Who is Europe?', Bismarck had scornfully asked a British diplomat in 1863, the year Holstein passed the final examination to qualify for the foreign service. 'Several great nations', the diplomat replied. Had the question been posed in the year of Holstein's dismissal it is hard to see how there could have been any reply other than 'Two armed camps'.[30]

15 Failure of a System, 1906–14

Sir Edward Grey, who succeeded Lansdowne as Foreign Secretary when the Liberals returned to power under Campbell-Bannerman in December 1905, was the first Foreign Secretary to sit in the House of Commons for thirty-seven years; and it is significant that before Grey finally accepted the post, Campbell-Bannerman offered it to two peers, Lord Elgin (a former Viceroy of India) and Lord Cromer, who preferred the powers of a pro-consul in Cairo.[1] Grey was a high principled patrician with an astute political mind, a combination which exasperated radicals on his back-benches and led later commentators to accuse him of hypocrisy and bad faith. He was acutely conscious of divisions in his own party and of doubts in Europe over the willingness of the Liberals to maintain policies begun by Lansdowne. The last Liberal Prime Minister, Rosebery, was an out-standing critic of the Entente Cordiale, and in his first months of office Grey took pains to emphasise the continuity of British policy. Curiously enough, the outgoing Foreign Secretary's brother, Lord Edmund Fitz-maurice, was appointed Grey's parliamentary under-secretary, although he was subsequently given little chance to help formulate policy. It was to reassure the French ambassador, Paul Cambon, that Grey took the momentous step of according his approval to unofficial Anglo-French military and naval conversations in the second week of January 1906, a week before the Algeciras Conference opened. He does not seem to have appreciated the extent to which the talks were morally committing Britain to support of France in the event of a German attack, and it was another five and a quarter years before the Cabinet as a whole was informed that the conversations were taking place from time to time. Grey believed that, provided he did not give France a categorical assurance Britain would participate in a European war, he was retaining the freedom of choice which he thought essential to a democratic community. But he saw more clearly than Lansdowne that the acute phase of rivalry in world policies was over, to be succeeded by a dangerous confrontation of Powers in Europe itself.

Grey's arrival at the Foreign Office coincided, fortuitously, with a major change at the top of the diplomatic service. Lord Sanderson, permanent under-secretary since 1894, left the Foreign Office in February 1906 after forty-six years spent entirely in Whitehall. He had served as a mine of information for Rosebery, Salisbury and Lansdowne, fussing over the detailed workings of the Office, whimsically concerned that junior clerks should 'observe the use and abuse of red tape', insisting almost playfully that they know 'the sizes of the various islands of the Samoan archipelago and whether the various inhabitants do or do not wear trousers';[2] and it was fitting he should retire to write good, uplifting children's stories. His successor, Sir Charles Hardinge, was the first experienced ambassador to head the foreign service – a significant change in administrative procedure. Hardinge came direct from St Petersburg, eager for close association between Britain, France and Russia, highly suspicious of the German navy and confident of backing from Edward VII, for the king had long treated him as a personal friend and Lady Hardinge was a lady-in-waiting to Queen Alexandra. Despite occasional friction over minor issues, Hardinge was supported in his determination to bring the foreign service into the twentieth century by Sir Francis Bertie, the former assistant under-secretary, who was ambassador to Paris from 1905 to 1918, and another member of the king's dining circle. Hardinge was largely responsible for the advancement of the new Foreign Secretary's closest personal advisers: Louis Mallet became Grey's private secretary; and William Tyrrell was Grey's précis-writer and eventually his chief confidant. All four men – Hardinge, Bertie, Mallet and Tyrrell – knew, disliked and distrusted Germany, a country which Grey was never to visit. No previous Foreign Secretary, coming to office in the middle of a crisis concerned with German affairs, was so exposed to the collected wisdom of the experts. The tragic death of Lady Grey in a riding accident seven weeks after her husband became Foreign Secretary weakened his decisiveness, increasing a dependence on the strong personalities within the Foreign Office at such a time of personal grief.

A fifth Foreign Office mandarin, still in his early 40s, soon achieved magisterial authority as a specialist on German affairs. Technically Eyre Crowe was senior clerk in the Western Department of the Foreign Office in 1906, but his interests and background gave him greater influence than was merited by his ranking in the official hierarchy. He had been born in Leipzig at a time when his father, Sir Joseph Crowe, was beginning a career in the consular service which was to make him the most knowledgeable observer of German political life in Bismarck's heyday. Eyre Crowe was educated in Germany and France; his wife and mother were German, his maternal grandmother a member of the Ribbentrop family. He had personal contact with prominent figures in the German establishment, and for many years Germany's naval attaché in Paris was his brother-in-law. No one could describe Eyre Crowe as conventionally anti-German, for he was himself naturally Germanic in habits and cultural tastes, but he was also exceptionally responsive to what he regarded as anti-English trends in German policy. In a famous 15,000-word memorandum, dated 1 January 1907, Eyre Crowe surveyed British relations with the countries in which he had been educated.[3] He emphasised the extent to which the Moroccan crisis had transformed the friendly accords with France into a more positive acceptance of resistance to a common danger. Great Britain, he argued, should not oppose legitimate expansion of German interests, even the growth of the fleet so long as it was not obviously designed for a war against the British Empire; but 'the action of Germany towards this country since 1890 might be likened not inappropriately to that of a professional blackmailer, whose extortions are wrung from his victims by the threat of some vague and dreadful consequences in case of refusal'; and he insisted that the best 'way to win the respect of the German government and of the German nation' was to avoid any 'one-sided bargains or arrangements' which might be regarded in Berlin as a sign of weakness. Lord Sanderson, from retirement, answered many of Crowe's points and Grey did not accept all his senior clerk's premises, but Crowe's long and logical survey – an exposition without precedent in the Foreign Office records – strengthened Grey's inclination to believe in a German threat to Britain's interests. In later years, and especially in the crisis weeks of 1914, Grey shaped his own policy, frequently overriding his permanent officials. But at first, as a newcomer to the Foreign Office, he turned to them for advice and allowed their prejudices to determine his predilections. Unlike Palmerston or Salisbury, Grey held professional expertise in high regard – a sign, perhaps, of the twentieth century taking over from the nineteenth.

An understanding with Russia was a natural complement to the entente with France and it is probable Lansdowne would have concluded an agreement in St Petersburg had the Conservative-Unionists stayed in power longer. The risk of a European war over Morocco encouraged Grey to seek a *rapprochement* with Russia: 'An entente between Russia, France and ourselves would be absolutely secure', Grey wrote in the first general survey which he circulated in the Foreign Office after returning from his wife's funeral. 'If it is necessary to check Germany it could then be done.'[4] But the convention concluded in St Petersburg eighteen months later (31 August 1907) totally ignored the German problem. Like the Anglo-French agreements of 1904, it was a settlement of old disputes; the convention defined spheres of influence in Persia and regulated the relations of the two governments with Afghanistan and Tibet. Grey, however, intended it to be something more than a truce in the 'Great Game' for mastery of central Asia. In his eyes it was a potential weapon in the struggle to limit Germany's mounting world power. He was prepared to accept that the convention had a significance for Europe's problems if the Franco-Russian allies continued to co-operate with Britain. The Russians made it clear that they wanted to modify the rules concerning the Bosphorus and the Dardanelles so that their Black Sea fleet could have access to the Mediterranean, and Grey was willing to discuss a change in the status of the Straits with the other Great Powers. Privately he let senior members of the diplomatic service know that he was treating the convention as a touchstone of Russia's goodwill: 'If Asian things are settled favourably the Russians will not have trouble with us about the entrance to the Black Sea', he told Sir Arthur Nicolson, who had gone to St Petersburg as ambassador after his success in heading the British delegation to the Algeciras Conference.[5]

Yet Grey and Nicolson were puzzled over the objectives of Russian policy. In May 1906 Nicholas II appointed Alexander Izvolsky, his envoy at Copenhagen, to succeed Lamsdorff as Foreign Minister. There was no doubt about Izvolsky's intentions in the Far East. He had served in Tokyo before going to Copenhagen and had never approved of the disastrous forward policies which had provoked the Japanese attack on Port Arthur. His first task as Foreign Minister was reconciliation with Japan, and an agreement reached in July 1906 began nine years of co-operation in a region where the two Powers had long treated each other as enemies.

Izvolsky, however, was vain and ambitious, a career diplomat eager for a triumph to gratify Russian public opinion but conscious of the need to attract investors from Britain, France and Germany. He therefore sought collaboration with the governments in London, Paris and Berlin; and he looked for cheap diplomatic success at the expense of Russia's old rival in the Balkans, Austria-Hungary. At the end of October 1906 he spent a few days in Berlin where he held friendly talks with Chancellor Bülow, whom he had known some twenty years before in St Petersburg. Momentarily, Izvolsky seems to have hoped he might isolate Austria-Hungary. To foreign observers he gave the impression of a would-be statesman in a hurry, desperately looking for a policy in which to display shrewd subtlety.[6]

If there was uncertainty in Izvolsky's behaviour, the fault did not lie entirely with the Russian Foreign Ministry. Before meeting Bülow he had visited Paris. There he found political doubt and chaos. For, after two short-lived ministries, President Fallières had at last plucked up the courage to invite Georges Clemenceau, an Anglophile and Germanophobe anti-clerical, to form a government; and Clemenceau was choosing his ministers while Izvolsky was in Paris. To the Quai d'Orsay Clemenceau sent his one-time associate in radical journalism, Stephen Pichon, newly elected to the Senate after thirteen years as a diplomat, mainly in Peking and North Africa. Ultimately the Clemenceau–Pichon partnership proved a stable political force; the government was in power for fully thirty-three months, and Pichon was Foreign Minister until June 1911. But at the time no one could tell whether Clemenceau would pursue an aggressive foreign policy or plunge into combat with the Church, and Izvolsky was unsure if the new government would uphold an alliance with autocratic Russia. Nor was France his only worry. Hardly had Izvolsky returned to St Petersburg than he learned that Francis Joseph had accepted Goluchowski's resignation. As the Dual Monarchy's new Foreign Minister, Francis Joseph had chosen Baron von Aehrenthal, ambassador at St Petersburg for the last seven years. Izvolsky knew him as a former friend and confidant of Kálnoky, and in his own right an efficient and knowledgeable diplomat. Time was to show he had a taste for grand designs and an authoritarian disinclination to delegate responsibility.[7]

Aehrenthal came to the Ballhausplatz hoping to bring new life to the Triple Alliance and check Italy's inclination towards the Anglo-French camp. He even thought it might be possible to detach Russia from France and create another League of the Three Emperors. Like Izvolsky he began with a success, an amicable agreement with the Italians concluded at Desio in July 1907 and providing for collaboration over Balkan problems. For the first year he was in office he worked well with the Russians too, and as late as December 1907 the two Powers offered common resistance to proposals by Grey for international action against terrorist bandits in Turkish-held Macedonia. But only a month later Izvolsky reacted violently to a plan announced by Aehrenthal for the building of a railway through the Sanjak of Novibazar from Sarajevo to Mitrovica. The project made good sense in Vienna and Budapest. The line would link the Austro-Hungarian and Turkish networks and provide a direct route to the port of

Salonika outside the territory of Serbia, with whom the Austrians had been on bad terms for the past two years. Izvolsky, however, feared that the Sanjak railway would boost Austrian influence in the Balkans in much the same way as the concession given by the Sultan to Germany for a Baghdad railway in 1899 had brought German financial interests into Asia Minor. On 3 February 1908 Izvolsky proposed to his fellow ministers in St Petersburg that Russia should test the value of the entente with Britain by suggesting that Grey join him in putting pressure on the Sultan to refuse to co-operate with Austria over the Sanjak railway project. If the Sultan proved obdurate Izvolsky hoped Britain and Russia would take joint military and naval action against Turkey. This wild scheme, which would never have been condoned in Whitehall, was rejected out of hand by Stolypin, the Tsar's Prime Minister. The Russian brouhaha, as echoed in what was by now an almost uncensored Press, induced Aehrenthal to drop the Sanjak railway project entirely. From April to July 1909 there were exchanges between Aehrenthal and Izvolsky which sought once more to find a common Austro-Russian approach to Balkan problems.[8]

Ultimately this short-lived Sanjak crisis had a greater effect on the British attitude to European problems than on Austro-Russian relations. For eighty years Britain had backed Austria rather than Russia in any dispute raised by the Eastern Question. There was no direct Austro-British antagonism in the winter of 1907–8; Edward VII treated Francis Joseph with friendly respect, which was indeed shown in the highly enjoyable meeting of the two monarchs at Ischl in August 1908; and the Austro-Hungarian ambassador, Count Mensdorff-Pouilly (a son of the earlier Foreign Minister), enjoyed great popularity in London society at a pinnacle of eminence appropriate to a rich and cultured second cousin of the King. But the Sanjak railway project convinced the Foreign Office that Austria-Hungary had become a mere tool of German policy. German commercial interests were said to lie behind Aehrenthal's initiative; the Machiavellis in the Wilhelmstrasse were now reaching out to grab the Balkans. The heavy sarcasm which Germany's delegates poured on every proposal for disarmament made at the Second Hague Peace Conference in the late summer of 1907 intensified Grey's suspicion of Germany – 'Bülow has now come into the open, and we know where we are', he told Nicolson in St Petersburg; and reports that Tirpitz's latest naval construction programme would give Germany more dreadnoughts at sea than Britain by the autumn of 1911 speedily destroyed any good achieved by the Kaiser's state visit to Windsor and his protracted private sojourn near Bournemouth in the closing weeks of 1907. There were some grounds for Aehrenthal's complaint that the English 'had Germany on the brain'.[9] The international situation was already deteriorating before the events which constituted the Bosnian crisis of 1908–9 exacerbated the latent unrest in the Balkans.

At the end of July 1908 the young military leaders of the Turkish 'Committee of Union and Progress' seized power in Constantinople and induced Sultan Abdul Hamid to implement the abortive Turkish Constitution of 1876 as a first stage towards the political modernisation of the Ottoman Empire. The action of these 'Young Turks' – Enver, Talaat and Jemal – alarmed the government in Vienna as restoring Turkish authority in Bosnia-Herzegovina, provinces which the Austrians had treated as a virtual colony since the Treaty of Berlin. Aehrenthal persuaded a ministerial council in Vienna on 19 August that his recent exchanges with Izvolsky suggested Russia would not object to an Austro-Hungarian annexation of the provinces in return for Austrian support over Russia's desire to change the status of the Straits.[10] He did not, Aehrenthal told the council, anticipate trouble with Austria's German and Italian allies, and he assured the Austro-Hungarian Chief of the General Staff, Conrad von Hotzendorf, that 'England desires good relations with us' – an optimistic pronouncement apparently based on talks with Sir Charles Hardinge at Ischl during Edward VII's visit to Francis Joseph in the previous week.

On 15 September Aehrenthal met Izvolsky at Buchlau, a Moravian shooting-lodge belonging to the Austro-Hungarian ambassador in St Petersburg, Count Berchtold. No written agreement was concluded and there are discrepancies between the accounts given by the two main participants, but the general pattern of the talks is clear enough.[11] Aehrenthal took up an earlier proposal made by Izvolsky that Austria-Hungary should annex Bosnia-Herzegovina and, in return, look with sympathy on Russian plans to revise the Straits Convention. It was assumed by Izvolsky that Aehrenthal would not act before he had prepared the ground with France and Britain and that the Powers would meet in conference to settle the final form of any new system in south-eastern Europe. But Aehrenthal was playing an over subtle game. Soon after the Buchlau meeting he held talks with Prince Ferdinand of Bulgaria, who had come to Budapest as a guest of Francis Joseph. The Bulgars, alarmed by assertions of the Young Turks that Bulgaria remained a vassal state in the Sultan's empire, were eager to attain full independence; and Aehrenthal encouraged the prince to proclaim himself king, a move which would distract the Powers from the Bosnian problem and also make Bulgaria more dependent on the Dual Monarchy. Aehrenthal's squib misfired. Ferdinand, newly returned from Budapest, proclaimed Bulgaria an independent kingdom on the day after Aehrenthal had denied to a British diplomat all knowledge of any imminent move in Sofia and on the day before the official announcement of Bosnia-Herzegovina's annexation. Not since Napoleon III's intrigues over Italy in 1859–60 had there been such deep mistrust and suspicion within the Chancelleries.

Izvolsky insisted he had been duped. Neither Tsar Nicholas nor his other ministers as yet knew of the Buchlau agreement, and Izvolsky was still touring the European capitals rallying support for his plans over the Straits. But he was not the only public figure angered by the course of events. Grey and Hardinge complained that Aehrenthal had deceived them over Bulgaria; Kaiser William II was deeply offended at Austria's failure to let him know in advance of the intention to annex Bosnia-Herzegovina; and Clemenceau and Pichon were disinclined to assist Izvolsky to extricate himself from a crisis caused by his over-cleverness in seeking a bargain with the Austrians. Most ominously, the powerful Radical Party in Belgrade called for a war against Austria-Hungary unless the two annexed provinces were granted autonomy, or Serbia given compensation; and the Serbian heir-apparent even accompanied the leader of the Serb Radicals, Nikola Pašić, to St Petersburg to win support from Russia's Panslavs.

Aehrenthal possessed three great advantages which saw Austria-Hungary safely through the crisis: the two provinces were already occupied by Francis Joseph's army; the forward party in Vienna (headed by the Chief of Staff, Conrad von Hotzendorf) would have welcomed a brief campaign to discipline Serbia, while Russia by contrast could not risk a war; and, whatever the feelings of Kaiser William might be, his Chancellor was prepared from the start of the crisis to back Austria-Hungary up to the hilt in order to strengthen the alliance between Berlin and Vienna. The most that Grey and Pichon would offer Izvolsky was support for the idea of an international conference to discuss Balkan problems in general, including the fate of the annexed provinces and the future of the Straits Convention. But neither Aehrenthal nor Bülow was prepared to accept a conference, not least because Germany was still smarting from her defeat at Algeciras, and round table diplomacy was far from popular in the Wilhelmstrasse. The six-month crisis over Bosnia-Herzegovina ended in victory for the two Central Powers, but at a price. In March 1909 Russia was brought to heel by a peremptory demand from Berlin that the annexation be recognised in St Petersburg. The discredited Izvolsky was left eager for revenge; and so, too, were Serbia and the Panslavs. A promise to live on good neighbourly relations with Austria-Hungary given in Belgrade, under pressure from London and St Petersburg, rang singularly hollow.

The Bosnian crisis did not lead to any fatal polarisation within the alliance system. On 9 February 1909 France and Germany concluded an agreement over Morocco: Germany recognised French political primacy there; France undertook to respect Germany's commercial interests in the Sultanate. There was also a flicker of Anglo-German goodwill. The 'interview' with William II published by the *Daily Telegraph* at the end of October was a well-intentioned attempt by the Kaiser to show English readers the sweet reasonableness of German policy towards their country since the outbreak of the Boer War, but what might be said in confidential jocularity on a country walk through Hampshire lanes looked tactlessly abrasive in the small print of a newspaper column, and William's comments ruffled sensitivities in London and Berlin.[12] A state visit by Edward VII to Germany in February 1909 was intended by the king to convince his nephew that neither he nor his government wished to encircle Germany and that they were eager not to be drawn into a Balkan conflict caused by the impetuosity of others. Grey complained that the state visit did not lead to Anglo-German diplomatic collaboration in ending the crisis. This was true enough; but it revived the Kaiser's waning faith in the bonds of dynastic sentiment as a cohesive force standing above the friction caused by the rivalries of the peoples. It was no doubt as a sign of monarchical solidarity that Edward VII was entrusted with one particular confidence by his nephew. Bülow had failed to defend his sovereign from attacks in the Reichstag by deputies who criticised the Kaiser's intervention in foreign affairs; and William told his uncle that he felt he could no longer trust the Chancellor who he had once hoped would be the Bismarck of his reign. Already, at the end of the previous year, the British ambassador had shrewdly predicted to Grey that he thought the days of Bülow's chancellorship were numbered.[13] But it was anyone's guess who would replace him.

The change of Chancellor was delayed until July 1909. By then Bülow's attempts to raise the funds to build up the German fleet had led him to propose death duties on the Junker estates, a move which cost him all conservative support in the Reichstag. Technically he fell over a domestic issue and his successor, Theobald von Bethmann-Hollweg, was a cautious reformer whose political interests and experience derived from internal administration in Prussia. But Bethmann was not without ideas on foreign policy. He wanted to cut the prohibitive cost of Tirpitz's High Seas Fleet, an economy possible only through the ending of the naval arms race; and for the first two years of his chancellorship Bethmann sincerely sought an Anglo-German understanding. He was supported by the Kaiser, partly because of William's strangely ambivalent attitude to his mother's homeland, but also because he was sensitive to complaints that the competition in dreadnoughts was depriving the German army of funds which were essential if it were to remain the most powerful in Europe. On 21 August 1909 Bethmann proposed that Britain and Germany should begin negotiations aimed at securing a political and naval agreement.

Bethmann's initiative, which followed tentative suggestions from the Foreign Ministry to the British ambassador in the spring, posed a dilemma for Grey.[14] Britain had sought naval disarmament at the Second Hague Peace Conference in 1907 but Germany was unreceptive. Now that a new German Chancellor held out a promise of concessions, Grey felt inclined to respond but he found his permanent officials highly suspicious. Crowe, for example, while respecting Bethmann's integrity, maintained that the German Foreign Ministry was trying to drive a wedge into the ententes with France and Russia by seeking a public declaration from Grey that Britain favoured maintenance of the *status quo* in Europe – including, that is, Germany's possession of Alsace-Lorraine and the closing of the Straits to the Black Sea fleet. Grey was prepared to assure Germany that her isolation 'is not our aim and our understandings with France and Russia have no such object', but this was hardly a basis for a political agreement.[15] Conversely, Bethmann could extract from Tirpitz only an offer to slow down the rate of naval construction, not to abandon the attempt to build up a formidable High Seas Fleet in its entirety. It is a mistake to assume that the antagonism between Britain and Germany deepened more and more with the passage of each month which separated the Algeciras Conference from the invasion of Belgium. Personal contact between leaders of industry, as well as attachments of dynastic sentiment, held promise of agreement on several occasions, and the possibility of slowing down the naval arms race persisted in exchanges between the two governments until the autumn of 1913. What was lacking after the

Bosnian crisis was any real trust in the machinery of negotiation among the Great Powers themselves.

The German attempt to reach agreement with Britain was matched by similar moves intended to improve relations between Berlin and St Petersburg, and more deviously even between Berlin and Paris. Izvolsky never recovered his standing at the Russian court after the Buchlau débâcle and in September 1910 he accepted an offer of the Paris embassy. The Tsar appointed as his successor Serge Sazonov, a relative by marriage of the ablest of Russia's Prime Ministers, Stolypin. A few weeks after taking office Sazonov accompanied Nicholas II on a visit to Potsdam for a meeting with the Kaiser. Also present there were Bethmann-Hollweg and Kiderlen-Waechter, whom William II had made State Secretary for Foreign Affairs in the previous June. The 'Potsdam agreement', concluded by Sazonov and Kiderlen in the first week of November 1910, withdrew Russian objections to German development of the Baghdad railway in return for German assistance in opening up the Russian sphere of influence in Persia. Russo-German relations became outwardly friendlier than at any time in the past five years and remained free of stress until the next crisis in the Balkans forced Berlin once more to make common cause with Vienna. [16]

Bethmann hoped a demonstration of Russo-German friendship would serve 'as a springboard for an understanding with Britain'; but he misread the signs. The Potsdam agreement almost caused Grey's resignation, for it unleashed a fresh outburst of criticism from the radical wing of the Liberal Party against a Foreign Secretary who seemed a tool of Tsarist Russian imperialism. Attacks on Grey, in the Commons and the periodical Press, intensified with the realisation that the new permanent under-secretary at the Foreign Office was himself heavily committed to the Anglo-Russian entente. For at the beginning of October 1910 Hardinge became Viceroy of India and Sir Arthur Nicolson was brought home from the St Petersburg embassy to take his place in London. 'Nicolson', as his son was to write some twenty years later, 'believed profoundly in "The German Menace"' and 'pressed continuously for the strengthening of the fragile bond that united us with Russia'. [17] He found that his ideas naturally complemented those of Eyre Crowe. Nicolson and Crowe working in tandem were intellectually persuasive enough to give Grey the strength to defy his radical critics. Moreover, neither of them was likely to respond to the 'Be my brother or I will bash your head in' attitude of the Wilhelmstrasse in its cruder moments of diplomacy.

This, unfortunately, was the approach favoured by Kiderlen-Waechter in his dealings with France. Some twenty-five years previously, Kiderlen had seemed one of the liveliest horses in Bismarck's diplomatic stable. Now, in his late 50s, Kiderlen was a brash bully, remembering how to make Bismarckian noises but failing to have in hand an alternative policy ready for dignified retreat. Kiderlen proposed that Germany should put on a show of strength in protest at the French decision to send a military expedition to Fez, the Moroccan capital, in the spring of 1911, allegedly to safeguard European residents against a rebel force. He hoped it would be possible to bring to power in Paris a government favourably inclined to German commercial interests and prepared to cede French colonial territory in Africa to Germany as compensation for the setting up of a French protectorate in Morocco. The Kaiser from the start disliked any new enterprise over Morocco, and urged Bethmann-Hollweg 'to stand firmly against sending warships', as Kiderlen wished.[18] But, with a weakness he would not have shown in earlier years, William II allowed himself to be convinced by a memorandum which Kiderlen drew up recommending the dispatch of German warships to the Atlantic ports of Mogador and Agadir ('where there are large German firms') and arguing that, since both ports were some 'distance from the Mediterranean, England would scarcely raise difficulties'. Even so, the Kaiser withheld final approval until he had sounded out opinion in London, for he was about to make the twelfth – and, as it happened, final – visit to Great Britain since his accession.

William was much gratified by the warmth of his reception in London, where he attended the unveiling of the statue to his grandmother, outside Buckingham Palace, on 16 May. He raised the Moroccan Question to King George V in very general terms on the eve of his departure, apparently mentioning a warship but not specifically the port of Agadir. From these confused exchanges, and even more from the cheers with which he was received in the streets, William convinced himself that Kiderlen was right after all, and there would be no trouble from 'England'. At noon on 1 July the signatories of the Algeciras pact were solemnly informed by the Kaiser's envoys that Germany had sent a warship to Agadir to protect the interests of her nationals there. The news caused mild surprise in Paris and intense excitement in Berlin and London. The warship, SMS *Panther*, was not the menacing cruiser of so many newspaper articles. She was a gunboat of 1,700 tons displacement with a top speed of 14 knots, two 4-inch guns, no wireless communication, and standards of seaworthiness so uncertain that within two years of being in the headlines she was towed to the scrapyard. But her presence at a port close to the trade routes to South America and southern Africa revived all the old fears in London of a Moroccan Kiaochow; and an extraordinary oversight on the part of Kiderlen, who left the ambassador in London without clear instructions for the first three weeks of July, convinced the officials in the Foreign Office that the German State Secretary was determined to let the crisis worsen in the hopes of weakening the Entente. Grey stood out against the 'anti-Germans' in the diplomatic service, reminding Bertie in Paris that Britain would not go to war to give France Morocco or to chase Germany out of Agadir. But the stern speech of Lloyd George, the allegedly pacific Chancellor of the Exchequer, at the Mansion House on 21 July was interpreted by Kiderlen, and even more by the German Press, as evidence of deep-rooted hostility towards Germany's claims.[19]

The more responsible British newspapers – and, of course, Grey and the Cabinet – realised that the chief motive behind the 'Panther's leap' was a desire to strike some sort of bargain with France: and within a few days the British government's fear of a German fortified port began to recede. Grey was particularly concerned throughout the crisis that the new French

Prime Minister, Joseph Caillaux, would reach such a comprehensive settlement with Germany that Britain might be forced into a far-from-splendid isolation. To succeed Pichon Caillaux chose as Foreign Minister Jean de Selves, who had no experience of diplomacy and was subsequently made a scapegoat for the government's failure to satisfy its critics at home. But on 2 July (the day after the crisis broke) de Selves left Paris to accompany President Fallières on a state visit to the Netherlands, and Caillaux himself took charge at the Quai d'Orsay until 8 July. Kiderlen's original demand that France should cede the whole of her colonial territory on the Congo in return for German acquiescence in the establishment of a protectorate in Morocco was gradually modified until, by a treaty concluded in the first week of November, Germany was ceded an extensive segment of the French Congo, but situated in a region which was totally undeveloped and, for the most part, undevelopable.

Agadir remains the most puzzling of prewar crises. Essentially it was an unreal confrontation of bogeys, never seriously endangering peace. France's ally, Russia, showed no interest in the crisis, finally settling the details of the Potsdam agreement on the Middle East in direct negotiations with Germany while it was at its height. Germany's allies, Austria-Hungary and Italy, refused to meddle in Moroccan affairs. Kaiser William II, who spent the early weeks of the crisis cruising in the Norwegian fjords, was constantly critical of Kiderlen-Waechter's rash behaviour. Kiderlen himself, though willing to 'thump the table' (as he said), never thought Morocco worth a war; like Bethmann, he was surprised by the reaction in London. Yet there is no doubt that Agadir hardened opinion in France and in Britain. The French threw out the Caillaux ministry as unduly sympathetic to Germany. In January 1912 French politics swung sharply to the right, with the conservative republican senator, Raymond Poincaré, who formed a government in which he was his own Foreign Minister. In London resentment at what was called 'Prussian bullying' (although Kiderlen was in fact a Swabian, from Stuttgart) won over to the side of Grey and Asquith two Cabinet ministers who had consistently played down the threat from Germany, Lloyd George and Churchill. For the first time joint planning by the British General Staff and the Admiralty faced the probability of fighting beside France's army and ships against the Germans in a continental war. In Berlin, too, there was a change of political mood after Agadir, with right-wing nationalist complaints in the Reichstag at Bethmann's failure to answer Britain's 'humiliating challenge' winning much publicised applause from the Crown Prince, as he sat in the gallery. The Kaiser, as if reacting to the suspicion that he favoured his English friends and relations, spent the remainder of the winter and much of the following year peppering marginalia and personal letters with appropriately anti-British sentiments. If privately he hoped his dynastic contacts with Windsor and Tsarskoe Selo would check the drift towards war, he effectively concealed his inner convictions from those around him.[20]

A war did indeed break out in the later stages of the Agadir crisis. On 27 September 1911 the Italians delivered a totally unacceptable ultimatum to the Sultan of Turkey demanding the right to occupy the two Libyan provinces, Tripolitania and Cyrenaica, because of persistent Turkish maltreatment of Italian subjects. War followed twenty-four hours later, the Italian fleet and marine detachments preparing the way for landings at Tripoli, Tobruk, Derna and Benghazi. The Italian move was partly a response to the new wave of French colonial activity in Morocco; businessmen in Rome and Milan were afraid that if Libya was not taken soon it would fall into French hands. But the war was also caused by what the Italian Foreign Minister, Antonio di San Giuliano, called 'a general vague desire to do something' among his compatriots, a nationalistic hysteria which he personally detested but felt bound to appease. Contrary to expectation the war dragged on for thirteen months; for the Arabs in Libya joined the Turkish regular forces in resisting the invaders, sometimes fighting with a savage religious fanaticism. Most foreign governments condemned Italy's decision to resort to arms: Austria-Hungary was alarmed by Italian naval action against Albania, still a Turkish possession and in an area of acute concern to Aehrenthal in Vienna; France was angered by the Italian seizure of two French steamers with Turks on board; Britain formally, and rather quaintly, complained that Italy's aggression 'was very embarrassing to the Powers'; and Kaiser William II, while claiming that England was behind the whole affair, was worried in case the action of his Italian ally marked 'the start of a world war with all its terrors'.[21] He feared an Italo-Turkish war, beginning in Libya, would overflow into the Asian and European possessions of the Sultan, thus serving as a bridge to link the colonial crises in North Africa with the latent tension of the Eastern Question.

Other governments, too, were concerned at the risk of war spreading to so sensitive a region. What if an Italian naval force entered the Dardanelles and attacked the heart of the Ottoman Empire? Sazonov discussed the problem at length with the French ambassador in St Petersburg, but he was incapable of deciding on a consistent line of policy. That, indeed, was his great failing once his brother-in-law, Stolypin, was removed from the political leadership of Russia by an assassin's bullet in September 1911. There was astonishing weakness and confusion in the Russian foreign service during the years immediately preceding the First World War; Sazonov was overshadowed in St Petersburg by his influential deputy, Neratov, and both men were treated with scant respect by some of the Tsar's envoys abroad – Izvolsky at the Paris embassy, Charykov in Constantinople and the Panslavs in Belgrade and Sofia, Hartwig and Nekliudov. Charykov, on his own initiative, now proposed an updated version of Unkiar Skelessi, a guarantee to Turkey of the *status quo* in return for opening the Straits to Russian warships with the prospect of a Russian-sponsored Balkan League (Turkey, Bulgaria, Serbia, Greece and Romania) to check Austro-Hungarian penetration of south-eastern Europe. Izvolsky supported Charykov, but the peremptory tone of the Russians forced the Turks to seek reinsurance from Germany; and Sazonov hurriedly re-pudiated the 'Charykov kite'.[22] Italy's allies dissuaded her from extensive naval operations in the Aegean, but had to acquiesce in the occupation (and eventual annexation) of the islands of the Dodecanese. In mid-April 1912 an Italian squadron at last entered the Dardanelles. For the first time in history shore batteries on the Gallipoli peninsula and at Chanak exchanged fire with battleships, but after a couple of hours the Italians withdrew. This episode, and a night raid by a torpedo-boat flotilla three months later, led the Turks temporarily to close the Straits to all vessels, thus severing a vital artery of Russian trade. By midsummer in 1912 Russia was more than ever anxious to control the means of entering and leaving the Black Sea.

The Italo-Turkish War encouraged the Balkan States to come together under Russian auspices and take advantage of Turkey's preoccupation with other problems. The possibility of a Balkan League had concerned Aehrenthal since early in 1910, but it worried him less than it disturbed Conrad and the military expansionists in the capital, for he thought the hatred of Serb for Bulgar too deep for any effective collaboration between them. Aehrenthal was already by then suffering from the leukaemia from which he died in February 1912. His influence on policy in these last two years of his life was fitful, for he remained so jealously possessive of nominal authority that the departmental chiefs in the Ballhausplatz were afraid to voice an opinion in his absence, and when he was well enough to attend to the business of the day, he preferred – like so many sick men – to do nothing, and wait upon events. His successor, Count Berchtold, came to the Ballhausplatz direct from the embassy at St Petersburg, as Kálnoky and Aehrenthal himself had done; but Berchtold was in character and habits of work like Goluchowski, though more conscientious. He was a charming aristocrat, with estates in both Bohemia and Hungary; and when he was puzzled by the problems left unresolved by poor Aehrenthal, he looked for advice to those around him. It was said that his chief innovation in Metternich's old study at the Foreign Ministry was a bell-push system which, at the press of a button, ensured that the appropriate departmental official would scurry to his desk and supply Berchtold with the words to answer any question with which he might be faced.[23]

But what, indeed, was the answer to the newest twist of the Eastern Question? Within a month of taking office it was clear to Berchtold that two years of preparation by Hartwig and Nekliudov had brought a striking success for Russian diplomacy, a reconciliation between Serbia and Bulgaria. No one, however, realised that the two Balkan states had already concluded a secret alliance, providing for the eventual partition of Macedonia after a victorious war against Turkey. Hartwig and Nekliudov were themselves aware that their treaty, settled in Belgrade in mid-March, left a 'disputed zone' in Macedonia which would be referred to the Tsar for arbitration and that this ingenious device could hardly keep Serbo-Bulgar rivalry on ice for more than a few months. But in Sofia, Belgrade and Athens it was recognised that, whatever their own differences might be, a determined thrust by the Balkan peoples might now expel the Ottoman Turks from Europe after five and a half centuries. Further negotiations were carried on between Bulgaria and Greece, and by the autumn, tenuous links bound Serbs, Montenegrins, Greeks and Bulgars in an anti-Turkish Balkan League. Unrest and mutinies in Albania, Thrace and Macedonia in the autumn of 1912 provided the Balkan states with the excuse for declaring war on Turkey in the second week of October, seven days before the preliminaries of the Treaty of Ouchy brought a ceasefire in the Italo-Turkish conflict.[24]

Active operations in the first phase of the Balkan Wars lasted a mere seven weeks, the Turks suffering defeat in five separate theatres of war on land as well as humiliating rebuffs from the Greek navy in the Aegean. The most serious threat to the Sultan's authority came from the eight Bulgarian divisions who broke through the frontier outposts in Thrace and headed for Constantinople, less than a hundred miles away; but the most startling military successes were the victories of the Serbs at Kumanovo and the Greek thrust for the vital port of Salonika, which they reached and seized twenty-four hours ahead of the Bulgarians. None of the European Great Powers welcomed the war, not even Russia despite the role of Hartwig and Nekliudov in encouraging the formation of a Balkan League.[25] The imminent collapse of Turkey posed problems which cut across the recent policies of the Powers; thus the Triple Alliance was weakened by Austro-Italian rivalry over Albania and by the firm support offered by Berlin to the Young Turk faction in Constantinople; while the Entente suffered from marked suspicion of Russian ambitions in Asiatic Turkey on the part of Grey and, to a lesser extent, of the experts in the Quai d'Orsay too. So divisive were the Balkan Wars that they even resurrected that almost forgotten concept, the Concert of Europe. An armistice was agreed in the first week of December, and delegates from Turkey and the Balkan states came to London where peace negotiations began in St James's Palace on 16 December. On the following day a parallel conference of ambassadors opened under the chairmanship of Sir Edward Grey, with little formality. The two conferences between them were to seek a final settlement of the Balkan problem.

Nothing in Grey's career stands so highly to his credit as the skill and patience with which he presided over the ambassadors' conference. 'We made the proceedings as informal as those of a committee of friends', he later recalled. 'We met in the afternoons, generally about four o'clock, and, with a short adjournment to an adjoining room for tea, we continued till six or seven.'[26] The delegates were the ambassadors of the five Great Powers chiefly concerned: from France, Paul Cambon (whose brother, Jules, had been ambassador in Berlin since April 1907); Russia, Count Alexander Benckendorff; Austria-Hungary, Count Mensdorff-Pouilly; Italy, the Marchese Guglielmo Imperiali; and Germany, Prince Karl Max Lichnowsky. Four of these ambassadors knew each other, and their chairman, well. Cambon had been at the London embassy for nearly fifteen years, Benckendorff and Mensdorff for nearly ten, and Imperiali since George V's accession. Although Lichnowsky had only emerged from retirement to take up his post in London a few weeks earlier, he was respected for his probity and experience. He was the last of the cosmopolitan grand seigneurs in diplomacy, related to great families in the Habsburg and Romanov empires, concerned to preserve huge estates in Silesia, and convinced of the need to save the Europe he knew from the devastation of war. It is hardly surprising that men of this calibre – colleagues rather than rivals – were able to thrash out the highly confused problem of Turkey-in-Europe without threatening a war between each other's countries.

It was, at times, a difficult task: 'We shall be six skeletons before our work is done', Cambon remarked, as the ambassadors began their sixth month of deliberation. Their work was hampered by a resumption of hostilities early in February 1913, by the persistence of the Montenegrins in seeking to capture the fortress of Scutari in Turkish-held Albania and the insistence of the Austrians in backing the creation of an Albanian national state and preventing the Serbs from establishing themselves on the Adriatic coast. The future of Macedonia, claimed by Serbs, Greeks and Bulgarians, received less attention, largely because it was in practice already virtually divided by Serbian and Greek armies of occupation. A preliminary peace was signed in London on 30 May 1913, recognising an Albanian state (although leaving its boundaries ill-defined and its princely throne unfilled) and confining Turkey-in-Europe to the hinterland of Constantinople. But the ambassadors' conference continued to meet until 11 August, patiently trying to prevent Bulgaria's thwarted ambitions from ruining hopes of a lasting settlement. In this, the conference failed. The Bulgarians ordered their army in Macedonia forward on the night of 29–30 June 1913, a move seen by their former allies as an attack. Within six days the Bulgarians were broken. Defeat by the Serbs and Greeks in this Second Balkan War was followed by a southward advance of a Romanian army and by a successful Turkish thrust which recaptured the historic city of Adrianople (Edirne). Final peace between the Balkan states was signed in the second week of August at Bucharest, with scant reference to any conference in London. One in five of the soldiers in the Bulgarian army of 1912 perished in the Balkan Wars and half of the survivors were wounded; but for these losses Bulgaria gained only a single valley in Macedonia, a strip of the Aegean coast including the harbour of Dedeagatch and a segment of eastern Thrace, while losing the southern Dobrudja to Romania. By contrast Serbia and Macedonia doubled their size, while Greece gained western Thrace, southern Macedonia, much of Epirus and mastery over the Aegean, including the cession of Crete. It was inevitable that Bulgaria should become a bitter revisionist Power. Within six months of the Treaty of Bucharest King Ferdinand was seeking an alliance with Francis Joseph or with William II (who, as it happened, disliked and distrusted him intensely).[27] Balkan resentments overspilled the peninsula.

After war engulfed Europe in 1914 both Grey and Lichnowsky looked back to the ambassadors' conference as evidence that the diplomatic procedure instituted a century before could still preserve stability on the continent when it was permitted to function normally.[28] Neither statesman seems to have appreciated that the Concert of Europe was revived in 1912–13 because the Great Powers were not prepared for a war forced upon them by the precipitate action of the smaller Powers, unofficially encouraged though they may have been by individual diplomatic agents. On Sunday 8 December 1912 William II had summoned Tirpitz, two of his admirals and the younger Moltke, Chief of the Greater German General Staff, to an informal council meeting at his palace in Potsdam to discuss the possibility of war spreading from the Balkans to Europe as a whole. Moltke thought war between the rival power blocs inevitable; so far as the army was concerned, 'the sooner the better'. The navy needed at least another eighteen months of peace, and the Kaiser himself resolved to continue efforts to keep Britain neutral in a continental war, relying partly on dynastic links – his brother, Prince Henry, had visited George V at Sandringham two days before the informal council – and partly on the mounting tension in the Middle East between Britain and her Entente partner, Russia.[29]

Three days after the ambassadors' conference opened in London, Kiderlen-Waechter collapsed and died from a heart attack in Berlin. The natural successor was Lichnowsky, but he had only recently returned to the diplomatic service, and it was felt in the Wilhelmstrasse that Kiderlen's deputy, Arthur Zimmermann, would make a good State Secretary. Zimmermann, however, declined the post: his health was poor; his command of French weak; and, above all, he was 'a man of the people' who was as ill at ease as Holstein in Berlin society. Lichnowsky suggested Gottlieb von Jagow, the ambassador in Paris, as State Secretary even though he had only been a diplomat for seventeen years, most of which he had spent in Rome. Jagow accepted the appointment on 5 January 1913 and proved a sound partner for Chancellor Bethmann-Hollweg. Soon he was earning somewhat patronising praise from the Kaiser, on the ominous grounds that 'the little man says he will be the first to recommend war . . . if anyone tries to dispute Germany's rights in Asia Minor'.[30]

The map of Asia Minor was frequently in the Kaiser's mind during 1913 for it was in this year that long-term German plans for the economic and political domination of the Turkish heartland reached their climax. William II first visited Constantinople in 1889, but it was his ostentatious 'expedition to the Orient' in October 1898, with its ceremonial entries into Jerusalem and Damascus, which marked the start of German commercial infiltration into the Middle East, a source of constant friction with Britain and with Russia. In the summer of 1913 the British at last made it clear that they would waive their objections to German railway penetration of Asia Minor, provided neither the Germans nor their Turkish clients posed any threat to Britain's growing interests in the Persian Gulf. In Berlin this gesture was interpreted as a sign of a British desire to use Turkey and Germany as barriers against the Russian southward thrust in central Asia. There was also a group of German specialists on the Orient who believed that the British naval mission, stationed at Constantinople since 1909 to strengthen Turkey's fleet, was an anti-Russian rather than an anti-German undertaking. Such, indeed, was the view of Sazonov, too; and the Russians were much disturbed in October 1913 when a British consortium was given the right to modernise Turkey's naval dockyards and orders were placed for two dreadnoughts and ten other warships to be built in British yards. The Admiralty and the Foreign Office insisted that Britain was only rearming Turkey to check the spread of German influence, but neither Sazonov nor ambassador Benckendorff was wholly convinced.[31]

In December 1913 the Kaiser dispatched General Otto Liman von Sanders to Constantinople with a group of more than forty officers. They were, William told them, to create in Turkey 'a new strong army which obeys my orders' and serve as 'a counter balance for Russia's aggressive intentions'. He also thought a German presence on the Straits would coax Britain away from the Ententes, providing support against Russian encroachment in an area so long a major concern of successive Foreign Secretaries. William deceived himself. The Russians responded fiercely to the Liman von Sanders mission; Moltke, faced by the prospect of a sudden winter war with Russia, urged his sovereign and Jagow to moderate their policies. Liman was seconded from the German army to the Sultan's service, created a Turkish Field-Marshal and appointed Inspector-General of the Turkish army. The change from pickelhaube to fez seems, rather oddly, to have taken the steam out of Russia's indignation. The British remained determined to avoid a breach with St Petersburg: 'I do not believe that the whole thing is worth all the fuss that Sazonov is making about it', Grey said, 'but so long as he does make a fuss it will be important and embarrassing to us, for we cannot turn our backs on Russia.'[32]

Neither Kaiser William nor his ministers could understand the nature of the Anglo-Russian commitment. At times it puzzled Grey, too. Nicolson, Crowe and Bertie favoured closer links with Russia, including military and naval talks. Grey was more cautious. He distinguished between the Anglo-French connection and the more limited understanding with Russia. Grey knew that many members of his own party criticised Tsarist repression in home affairs and especially the persecution of the Jews. He was also aware that at least one of his Cabinet colleagues – Lewis Harcourt, the Colonial Secretary – preferred co-operation with Germany to a Russian entente. Moreover, Grey and his Prime Minister, Asquith, responded to the goodwill shown by Lichnowsky and the peaceful assurances given by both Bethmann-Hollweg and Jagow. Throughout the twelve months preceding the Sarajevo murders, there was thus a thaw in Anglo-German relations.[33] Lichnowsky became the first German ambassador to receive an honorary degree at Oxford, early in June 1914. Until the last moment he hoped Britain would not simply stay neutral but mediate between the rival alliances and so ensure the maintenance of peace.

In later years Grey blamed himself for having concentrated so much on Berlin, St Petersburg and Paris that he neglected Vienna.[34] At the time, as he explained to the British ambassador in St Petersburg, he thought Germany would restrain Austria-Hungary 'in essential matters of policy that were really important'. Britain and France sensed danger in the chronic Austro-Serb conflict, but could see no direct political or strategic reason for intervening in western Balkan affairs. Both countries (France especially) had commercial and financial interests in maintaining the existing order throughout the Balkans and the Near East; and they therefore favoured stability. When on two occasions in 1913 the Austrians threatened punitive measures against Montenegro and Serbia for encroaching on the northern boundaries of the new Albania, it was generally accepted that the Dual Monarchy was entitled to impose the collective will of Europe on dissident and anarchic peoples. This had been Palmerston's way in the Aegean and the Levant, and in the later 1890s the Great Powers had jointly maintained international law and order in

Crete and other trouble spots of the Sultan's empire. Only the specialists of the Quai d'Orsay seem to have appreciated the centrifugal pull of Belgrade and Bucharest on nationalities within the Habsburg lands. Even Berlin tended to look on the Serbs as an external threat and minimised the significance of any South Slav agitation, seeing it as the clumsy work of Russia's agents.

Yet there was a general feeling in the Wilhelmstrasse and the Ballhausplatz that Germany and Austria-Hungary needed to emphasise their alliance so as to counter the apparent successes of Russia. Military collaboration between France and her Russian ally was thought in Berlin to have become closer and there was genuine alarm at the speed of Russian rearmament. A Turkish delegation was received by Nicholas II at Livadia, his palace in the Crimea, in May 1914; and in the second weekend of June the Russian royal family was entertained by the King of Romania at Constanta, their visit coinciding with a less publicised journey of Kaiser William II to Konopischt in Bohemia, where he was a guest of Archduke Francis Ferdinand, the heir to the Austro-Hungarian thrones. It was widely believed that the Tsar was seeking to marry off one daughter to Prince Carol of Romania and another to Prince Alexander of Serbia, a marriage project which would have raised Romanov influence in the Balkans considerably. But of more immediate concern than these dynastic manoeuvres was a motor-car trip undertaken by the Romanian Prime Minister and the Russian Foreign Minister together. On 15 June they crossed the Hungarian frontier and drove for several hours through villages and small towns in Transylvania, where the population was overwhelmingly Romanian. Berchtold saw this tactless excursion as yet another attempt by Entente diplomacy to destroy Habsburg primacy over the Danubian basin. With Francis Joseph's approval, he ordered Baron Matscheko, the head of the Balkan Department in the Austro-Hungarian Foreign Ministry, to prepare a memorandum which would remind Francis Ferdinand's recent guest and his ministers in Berlin that joint diplomatic action was essential if the Dual Monarchy was to avoid 'encirclement' by the entente Powers. Matscheko's memorandum was completed and awaiting Berchtold's comments by the final weekend in June.[35] That Sunday – 28 June, Serbia's National Day – Archduke Francis Ferdinand and his wife were murdered by the Bosnian Serb student, Gavrilo Princip, as their car carried them along the Appel Quay at Sarajevo. Berchtold amended Matscheko's memorandum so as to take account of the 'wicked murder'; something stronger than diplomatic action was needed if the Monarchy was to free itself from 'the threads which its opponents are seeking to form into a net above its head'.

Kaiser William II heard the news of Francis Ferdinand's death while at Kiel for the annual regatta week. He hurried back to Potsdam and began consultations with the Foreign Ministry and with his naval and military advisers. His mood was angry, not least because he was distressed at the murder of a personal friend. No one doubted the Serbian government was behind the conspiracy. Only the French diplomats seem to have realised that there was a power struggle in Belgrade, and that what had happened in Sarajevo was the work of Pan-Serb militarists opposed to the ruling

Serbian Radical Party and Prime Minister Pašić. The tone of recent speeches by Serbian politicians made distinctions in anti-Austrian feeling imperceptive to foreign observers. 'The Serbs must be disposed of, and that very soon', the Kaiser commented in the margin of a dispatch from Vienna four days after the assassination; and, as if in antiphon, Francis Joseph wrote to him, 'Serbia must be eliminated as a political power-factor in the Balkans'.[36] Not everyone in the two capitals favoured war: Tirpitz now wanted another six years before risking battle with the Royal Navy, although he thought the German fleet was ready for a conflict in which Britain remained neutral; and there were several diplomats uneasy at the 'full support' which William was offering Francis Joseph. In Vienna the Hungarian Prime Minister, Tisza, continued to urge Berchtold to find a purely diplomatic solution of the crisis for at least a fortnight after the assassination; but a combination of persuasive argument from the German ambassador and indignation at Serbian newspaper presentation of Princip as a hero and patriot led Tisza to modify his views.[37] By 8 July it was decided in Berlin and Vienna that Serbia must be crushed by war; 'the sooner the Austrians make their move against Serbia, the better', noted the Kaiser's principal military aide-de-camp in his diary. William II convinced himself that Russia would not come to the aid of a nation 'which had stained itself by assassination' and that France would hardly seek to spread the war at a time when the French army was awaiting new artillery. 'We should desire under all circumstances a localisation of the conflict', the German Foreign Ministry informed the ambassador in London at the end of the first week in July, urging him to influence the Press so that public opinion helps 'the various Governments to look on while Austria and Serbia decide their difference, without taking sides'. Privately William was assured his army and navy were ready for a con-tinental conflict should Russia and France risk a general war.[38]

Churchill later recalled that in the high summer of 1914 there was an air of 'exceptional tranquillity' in Europe. Most public figures in Germany and Austria continued their annual holidays as if nothing unusual was going to happen. Lichnowsky, who had been at Kiel for the regatta and subsequently spoken to Bethmann Hollweg in Berlin, was alarmed by the mood of his countrymen. On his own initiative, he visited Grey at the Foreign Office on 6 July and asked him to seek a peaceful settlement of the crisis. Grey saw the Russian and French ambassadors and three days later tried to reassure Lichnowsky: 'I would continue the same policy as I had pursued through the Balkan crisis', Grey said, looking back apparently to the conference diplomacy of the previous year.[39] In retrospect, it seems strange that Grey did not raise the European problem in full Cabinet until the afternoon of Friday 24 July, despite the concern of his permanent officials. But the government was preoccupied with a grave crisis in Ulster, where civil war threatened to wrack northern Ireland; and it was only on the evening of 21 July that the tone of the Press, and the state of the Bourse, made the Entente envoys in Berlin seriously uneasy at rumours of a strong Austrian note being prepared for delivery in Belgrade. Their fears were justified. At six o'clock on the evening of Thursday 23 July, a 48-hour ultimatum, which would have virtually reduced Serbia to an Austro-Hungarian dependency, was handed over to the senior Serbian government minister in Belgrade, Pašić himself being absent on his election campaign.[40] London, Paris and St Petersburg were officially informed of the ultimatum only on the Friday morning

The timing of the ultimatum's delivery was significant. Almost four weeks had elapsed since the Sarajevo crime, long enough for the Austrians to begin their military preparations and gather in the harvest, but also long enough for a widespread revulsion against Serbia to give way to consternation at the harsh terms of the Austrian note. Nicholas II told his ministers that he was convinced Russia would have to support Serbia 'even should it prove necessary to proclaim mobilisation and open hostilities'. Grey and Jagow, independently, continued to distinguish between the Austro-Serbian and an Austro-Russian conflict, both men still seeking to localise the crisis. But Entente reaction was hampered by three curious circumstances: the sudden death of Hartwig, the influential Russian envoy to Serbia; the continued political disunity in Belgrade; and, above all, by uncertainty in Paris. For Austria's note coincided with the departure from St Petersburg of President Poincaré and René Viviani (who had held the combined offices of Prime Minister and Foreign Minister since mid-June). The French heads of state and government, returning from a ceremonial visit to Russia, were at sea aboard the battleship *France* for five crucial days, not reaching Paris until the early afternoon of Wednesday 29 July. In their absence the diplomats and officials of the Quai d'Orsay concentrated on holding France to her alliance with Russia and on seeking closer naval links with the Entente partner, Britain; but Paris was unable to give the European Chancelleries a lead in this gravest of crises. It was left to General Joffre to assure the Russian military attaché of their ally's 'full and active readiness' for war.[41]

Relations between Serbia and Austria-Hungary were broken off on 25 July. But Vienna would not declare war until Francis Joseph's armies were fully ready and deployed for action. In this breathing space Grey put forward his key proposal. On Sunday 26 July he invited Germany, Italy and France to send delegates to a conference in London which would decide on a constructive form of mediation. But the proposal was rejected by Bethmann Hollweg even before it was officially handed to him: 'We would not be able to summon Austria before a European court in her case with Serbia', he wrote to Lichnowsky at midday on Monday.[42] That afternoon the Kaiser arrived back from his Norwegian cruise. He still thought there was a reasonable prospect of keeping the general peace; he was exchanging messages with Tsar Nicholas; and his brother, Prince Henry, had visited Buckingham Palace on Sunday morning to sound out their cousin, George V. When early on Tuesday the Kaiser read Serbia's moderate and co-operative reply to the Austrian ultimatum, he considered it so reasonable that there was no longer a pretext for even a localised war. About ten o'clock that morning he instructed Jagow to ensure that his ambassador in Vienna put pressure on Berchtold to reply to the Serbs in conciliatory terms.

It was at this moment – the forenoon and afternoon of Tuesday 28 July – that the old safeguards of chancellery diplomacy failed to function.

A quarter of a century later the Kaiser himself declared, 'the machine . . . ran away with me'.[43] In Vienna it was decided that the Serbian reply merely repeated promises of good behaviour already given and broken; and a declaration of war was sent to Belgrade within the hour. Meanwhile the Kaiser's message to Jagow was still in the Wilhelmstrasse. No instructions were sent to the German ambassador in Vienna until the late evening. They were then drafted by Chancellor Bethmann, not by Jagow; and they bore even less resemblance to William II's proposals than the edited Ems telegram of 1870 to William I's verbal exchanges with Benedetti. In particular, Bethmann said nothing of the Kaiser's assertion that all pretext for war had disappeared. The general tone of Bethmann's telegram did, indeed, urge moderation but the ambassador was to avoid 'any impression that we wish to hold Austria back'.[44] By the time the telegram was deciphered in Vienna, two monitors from the Austro-Hungarian flotilla on the Danube had begun to bombard Belgrade.

William II and Bethmann-Hollweg had toyed with the possibility, even at this late hour, of proposing that Austria should call 'a halt in Belgrade'. But the suggestion was impracticable, not least because the Austrians never intended any move so rash as a frontal assault on the Serbian capital. But by 29 July the needs of the General Staff precluded diplomatic improvisation. In St Petersburg, Berlin and Vienna war plans, long prepared and kept updated, awaited implementation, circumscribing policies to an extent which Germany's 'Supreme War Lord' seems never to have anticipated in all the war games and manoeuvres of the past twenty years. The vastness of Russia's empire had always delayed the concentration of the Tsar's armies. As soon as news reached St Petersburg of the Austrian bombardment, the War Ministry ordered partial mobilisation, and Russia's southern armies took up their war positions on that same Wednesday, 29 July. Early on Friday 31 July the crucial decision was taken to placard the streets with the announcement of full mobilisation. The Russian move was followed in Berlin by a proclamation of 'imminent war' and a call to Russia to halt all military preparations. When this demand was refused, Germany formally declared war on Russia on Saturday 1 August. So swift was the march of events that a final appeal from the Kaiser to the Tsar to demobilise and 'avoid endless misery' was sent by telegram at half-past ten that Saturday night, three and a half hours after the declaration of war had been handed to Sazonov. On that same evening the Kaiser had found, to his dismay, that the General Staff insisted on an invasion of Luxemburg and Belgium as soon as war with Russia became certain. Military plans, perfected by Count Schlieffen in December 1905, assumed that in any continental war Germany would strike first against Russia's ally, France, and would drive back the Tsar's armies only when Paris had fallen. For some five hours William II succeeded in delaying the march into Luxemburg in the hopes of British, and even French, neutrality. But by eleven o'clock at night he knew there was no possibility of avoiding war in the West. 'Now you can do what you like', he told the Chief of the General Staff.[45] War was declared on France on 3 August, and German troops entered Belgium and Luxemburg that night.

The Belgian issue resolved the doubts within Asquith's Cabinet. Grey's permanent officials – Nicolson and Crowe, in particular – had urged him to make a public declaration of military and naval support to Russia and to France as soon as his proposal for a four-power conference was brushed aside. But Grey still hoped that Bethmann-Hollweg would triumph over the 'militarists' in Berlin and he was determined not to encourage Russia, whose leaders in 1914 he regarded as more irresponsible than the German Chancellor or Jagow. The semi-paralysis of the French government, caused by the absence of Poincaré and Viviani, left Anglo-French relations more confused than in either of the Moroccan crises. At one time Paul Cambon was even forced to leave the London embassy and hurry to Paris in order to help the permanent officials in the Quai d'Orsay explain to the leaderless council of ministers what precisely were France's obligations. To Cambon, on his return, it seemed as if the British Cabinet was in no better shape, hesitating between intervention and neutrality which would have given France naval protection of her Channel coast, but no more. Grey knew that the thoughts of many of his colleagues were still with Irish affairs, a point of view which Cambon, Nicolson and Crowe could not appreciate. The Belgian issue, a traditional concern of Britain over the centuries, was the catalyst which enabled the Cabinet to find resolution. Even had King Albert allowed free passage to the German army and not appealed to his kingdom's sponsors for assistance against the invader, it is probable the House of Commons would have been asked to back intervention for the mere *principle* of Belgian neutrality. But an appeal to arms seemed to bring a touch of nobility to a cause, fighting 'for' Belgium rather than 'against' Germany.[46] At eleven o'clock at night on 4 August – midnight in Berlin – Great Britain entered an armed conflict in Western Europe for the first time in ninety-nine years. By doing so, Britain completed the transformation of an Austro-Serbian dispute over a cast-off Turkish province into the occasion of a world war.

16 The Passing of Chancellery Diplomacy, 1914–18

The four and a quarter years which followed the shelling of Belgrade by the Danubian flotilla marked the end of the old European order and with it the passing of chancellery diplomacy. By the close of the year 1918 ambassadors had become suspect members of a privileged élite in most of Europe's major capitals. Their method of business was discredited, for secret negotiation was seen as a denial of democratic control, and they were themselves scorned for respecting the conventions of a more leisurely world which their skills in statecraft had failed to save from destruction. When the British Prime Minister at the end of the war roundly declared that 'Diplomats were invented simply to waste time', he was, as so often, compounding the prejudices of the mass electorate which had borne the strain of the conflict. Yet it would be misleading to antedate the mood of supposedly enlightened revulsion. There was a protracted epilogue to the theatrical diplomacy in which peace had come to an end. While it was thought the fighting would 'be all over by Christmas', with Moltke and Joffre in the West and Hindenburg in the East seeking a rapid decision, the foreign ministries assumed that the postwar world would in essentials resemble its predecessor. There would be an adjustment of frontiers here and there, some transfer of colonies and payment of an indemnity by the vanquished to the victors. No one anticipated the war dragging on so long that the continent would become a jigsaw of fragmented monarchies. When the American envoy, Colonel House, came to Europe early in 1916 he found Kaiser William II still clinging to his faith in dynastic diplomacy: 'I and my cousins George and Nicholas shall make peace when the proper time has come', the American ambassador informed House that William had told him.[1] It was only after cousin Nicholas's autocracy fell in ruins and House's President promised new ideals to a shattered world that the merits of a peace based upon moral principles began to triumph over narrow thoughts of national interest in the public mind.

At first, therefore, the wartime diplomacy of both the Entente governments and the Central Powers followed a familiar pattern. Each side looked for allies. More significantly, each side sought to exploit the nuisance value of dissident groups in the other camp, treating internal disruption as a political weapon much as had Napoleon I and Bismarck in earlier years. Russians, Germans and Austrians all made bids for Polish support. Sazonov encouraged the Czechs to rise in rebellion while Izvolsky (Russia's ambassador in France) sent the Croatian emigré Frano Supilo to plead the cause of his fellow Yugoslavs within the Dual Monarchy before Grey and other allied leaders.[2] German agents were ordered to raise the Finns against Tsarist rule, encourage Ukrainian separatism and, as William II wrote, 'inflame the whole Mohammedan world to wild revolt' against the joint imperialisms of Britain and Russia. 'If we are to be bled to death, then at least the English shall lose India', he declared; and the German Foreign Ministry had hopes of Roger Casement's plans for an Irish rising. Later in the war Berlin gave support to the proponents of violent revolutionary upheaval and not simply to disruptive nationalist elements, but that was a rash political decision taken primarily by the army leaders rather than by advisers in the Wilhelmstrasse, and its consequences were disastrous for both sides of belligerents.[3]

In the first week of September 1914 Britain, France and Russia bound themselves in a solemn alliance, pledging each other to continue the war side by side until a satisfactory peace could be obtained. This 'Pact of London' was a diplomatic success of a sort, a sign of unity not attained in the last great war until Castlereagh reached Chaumont as the campaign against Napoleon entered its final stage. But the September treaty was a curb rather than an encouragement to diplomatic initiative. All negotiations thereafter had theoretically to be conducted on a tripartite basis; Grey and Delcassé (who was at the Quai d'Orsay once more from August 1914 to October 1915) thought it essential for the three Foreign Ministries to work together; Sazonov allowed himself more latitude. It was largely through the mistrust shown by Russia for neo-Byzantine sentiment in Athens that Grey declined the proposal made by the Greek Prime Minister, Venizelos, in the third week of the war that Greece's navy and army should assist the kingdom's three Protecting Powers (Britain, France, Russia) against their enemies. On the other hand, Sazonov had a habit of offering inducements to Romania for which he assured the Romanian leader Bratianu he would subsequently gain the backing of his allies. There were differences of approach, too, to the Bulgarian problem and to Turkey, where the Entente vainly sought to counter German offers in the first ten weeks of the war.[4] The flight of the German warships *Goeben* and *Breslau* up the Dardanelles and their transfer to the Sultan's fleet resolved Turkey's dilemma, and by the first week in November Great Britain, France and Russia were at war with the Sultan. The other Balkan states remained on the sidelines, waiting for news of striking victories before deciding to accept inducements to enter the war. Undignified haggling continued, notably in Sofia and Bucharest. At one point Pašić, the Serbian Prime Minister, was so alarmed at reports of Austro-Hungarian territory in which there was a Serbian minority being promised to non-belligerent Romania by France and Russia that he complained angrily, 'The Allies are disposing of the Serbs as if they were African tribes'.[5] None of these improvised arrangements, often incompatible with each other, could tempt the Balkan neutrals to risk suffering invasion without firm hope of military assistance.

Germany formulated a peace programme earlier than any other Power, although its nature remained a secret hidden in the archives until discovered by Professor Fritz Fischer in 1961.[6] Bismarck in 1870 had peace terms ready immediately after Sedan. Forty-four years later Bethmann-Hollweg and Jagow outpaced him. They spent most of the first week of September at field headquarters in Coblenz and Luxemburg drafting 'provisional notes on the direction of our policy on the conclusion of peace', for after four weeks of war it was confidently assumed that Moltke's modified Schlieffen Plan was about to bring the French to their knees. Bethmann's programme was completed by the morning of 9 September, which proved to be the decisive day in the first battle of the Marne. Had Joffre's armies suffered defeat that Wednesday and sought an armistice, the Chancellor would have recommended a peace which included the annexation of considerable areas of France and Belgium, the establishment of an enlarged Luxemburg within the German federal structure and the creation of a central European economic association 'in practice under German leadership'. Retreat to the River Aisne ruled out any sudden decision in the West that autumn, but the 'September Programme' remained the blueprint of Bethmann's war aims until the end of his chancellorship in July 1917.

The Entente allies did not attempt to produce a precise programme of this nature until later in the war. The French assumed they would recover Alsace-Lorraine; they also hoped for concessions in Africa and a buffer state on the left bank of the Rhine. Grey told the Americans in September 1914 that he would welcome attempts at mediation by the United States, provided Germany declared her terms first and that there was total agreement among the allies, compensation for Belgium and safeguards to prevent a great military power forcing another war on Europe. Privately the Prime Minister minuted on a dispatch from the ambassador in Washington that he expected the enemy to withdraw from all occupied territory in Belgium, France, Russia and Serbia before peace talks could begin, and that German warships on the high seas and in Turkish ports should be handed over to Great Britain. Sazonov's conversation shows that Russian objectives, too, were vague: a Romanov satrapy in Poland and a 'Greater Serbia' which would include Bosnia and Herzegovina and an outlet to the Adriatic. Turkey's entry into the war helped decide some war aims. Grey promised Russia an amicable settlement of the problems of Constantinople and the Straits in the second week of November, and George V specifically told cousin Nicholas's ambassador that after the war 'it is clear Constantinople must be yours'.[7] Thereafter the cartographic dismemberment of the Ottoman Empire became a favourite occupation at the Foreign Office, and in the Quai d'Orsay too.

Partitioning Turkey was a venerable pastime, antedating championship cricket and Rugby football. It was harder to think of ways to contain Germany; and, at least in Whitehall, there was a marked repugnance to accept emigré pleas for the dissection of the Habsburg Monarchy. Grey, in particular, disliked the 'Greater Serbia' agitation, no doubt influenced by the horror felt in London at the Sarajevo murders and earlier acts of terrorism. An astringent note from Grey to the British minister to Serbia in July 1915 found its way to Sazonov's desk and to the Russian archives, as no doubt it was intended to do: 'Before August 1914', Grey wrote, 'the people of Great Britain knew nothing of Serbian aspirations, the concept of Yugoslavia was one which had entered the minds of none but a dozen students, the electorate of Great Britain was unaware that any national movement of a serious character existed involving the extension of Serbia into the heart of Austria-Hungary'.[8] The Russian ambassador,

Benckendorff, had already commented with surprise on the persistence with which both the Liberal and the Conservative-Unionist leaders in London treated Austria-Hungary as a 'victim of Germany'.[9] From Petrograd (as St Petersburg was renamed on the tide of anti-German patriotism) the power structure of central Europe looked totally different. Historically it was tempting to see the Habsburg Monarchy as a buffer created by Castlereagh and Metternich to keep the present allies, France and Russia, apart; and the alleged British sympathy for the Habsburgs caused almost as much suspicion in Petrograd as did reports of Russo-German peace feelers in London.

Grey was convinced that in war the foreign service automatically became 'handmaid of the necessities of the War Office and the Admiralty', as he was to write in his memoirs.[10] As soon as fighting broke out in Europe he assumed that Clausewitz's notorious dictum was inverted, diplomacy becoming no more than the continuation of war by other means. This diminution of departmental status, a phenomenon by no means confined to Britain, necessarily weakened the power of the Chancelleries to shape events. Yet the entry of Turkey into the war provided the Foreign Office, War Office and Admiralty with the opportunity of an integrated strategy which, it was predicted, would counter the deadlock on the Western Front and offer a short cut to final victory. The Cabinet convinced itself in London that if the Royal Navy forced the Dardanelles and broke through into the Sea of Marmara, a military coup in Constantinople would oust Enver and his pro-Germans, the Balkan neutrals and Italy would leap aboard the allies' Orient Express, and Russia's vital trade route from the Black Sea to the Mediterranean would be opened up once more.

Only one of these desiderata was attained, the adhesion of Italy to the allied cause. When the naval assault was halted and half a million men failed to secure the commanding heights of Gallipoli, the remaining Balkan states preferred to keep their neutrality. Proposals by Lloyd George, Churchill and other soldiers and statesmen in Britain and France for supporting the Gallipoli operation by a diplomatic initiative in the Balkans and the sending of an army to Salonika were rejected. No more troops or guns could be spared for Eastern 'sideshows'. The chief consequence of the attempt to force the Dardanelles was to arouse Russian suspicion – the Western allies seeking to steal a march over the Eastern Question. In the first week of March 1915 Russia asked her two principal allies for an assurance that Constantinople and the Straits should be included in the Tsar's empire after the war. Grey agreed, provided Russia accepted a wider sphere of British influence in Persia and undertook not to oppose Greece's entry into the allied camp. Delcassé responded more slowly: the French insisted Sazonov accorded them a free hand in Syria, Palestine and other regions in the Levant where France had considerable commercial interests. But by the second week of April 1915 the secret 'Constantinople Agreement' had been accepted in both London and Paris.[11]

The Italian Foreign Minister, Sidney Sonnino, had conducted desultory talks with the Austrians ever since taking office in November 1914. Italy maintained that the Triple Alliance had bound her to support Germany and Austria-Hungary only if these empires were the victims of aggression themselves and that this circumstance had not arisen. Berchtold and Baron Stephen Burian (the Hungarian who succeeded Berchtold in the Ballhausplatz on 1 January 1915) were inclined to treat Italy with contempt for having chosen neutrality. The Germans, however, made some attempt to heal the breach with their former ally; Bülow, who had been ambassador in Rome from 1893 to 1897, was sent back to his old embassy early in 1915 because it was felt in Berlin that his contacts with Italian society could influence the behaviour of the Consulta.[12] But Sonnino was more impressed by the naval and military measures being taken by the Entente allies against Italy's recent enemy, Turkey. Sonnino recommended serious alliance negotiations to start in London and Paris on the day news reached Rome of the successful naval bombardment of the outer forts of the Dardanelles. Sazonov cut down Italy's demands, for the sake of the southern Slavs who easily outnumbered the Italian minority in Dalmatia. Even so, Italy struck a hard bargain. The secret Treaty of London (signed on 26 April 1915) promised Italy the eventual annexation of South Tyrol, Trieste, Istria, the northern Dalmatian coastline and most of the larger Adriatic islands, a protectorate over Albania, and enclaves in Asia Minor and Africa as well.[13] The promise of these rewards – a conspiratorial bargain which dwarfed in magnitude anything agreed at Plombières – tempted Italy to declare war on Austria-Hungary on 25 May 1915.

Although the treaty was concluded in secrecy, Sazonov let Supilo know its general nature within a week of its signature. From Petrograd Supilo rallied the champions of national self-determination in Britain and France, notably those indomitable critics of the Habsburg Monarchy, Wickham Steed (foreign editor of *The Times*) and R. W. Seton-Watson, a friend of the Czechoslovak philosopher and political spokesman Tomáš Masaryk. Grey received Seton-Watson on 4 May and sought to reassure him about the bargain with Italy, but Seton-Watson – a sound Gladstonian Liberal at heart – remained uneasy. Similarly in Paris, in that same first week of May, Wickham Steed visited the Quai d'Orsay and made clear his hostility to the secret deal. Delcassé, less ingenuous than Grey, conceded 'we may have been wrong'. But he held out to Steed the hope that the treaty would open up two new fronts for striking at the enemy. He confidently expected the Latin nation in the Balkans, Romania, to follow Italy's example and join the allies. 'Think what it means', Delcassé told Steed. 'Within a month there will be a million Italian bayonets in the field, and shortly afterwards 600,000 Roumanians'.[14] Negotiations with Romania had, in fact, opened in London in the last days of March; and the Austrians were convinced that, once Italy came into the war, they would be faced by a Romanian incursion into Hungary within forty-eight hours.

Had the hopes of Grey and Delcassé been realised, it is possible the Foreign Office and the Quai d'Orsay might have retained their prewar primacy over the service ministries in London and Paris. But the diplomatic coup of bringing Italy into the war came, like the Gallipoli landings, too late. Until the first week of April 1915 the Russians were attacking along the Carpathian sector of their front. By the first week in May General von Mackensen had begun his great Germano-Austrian offensive, which smashed through the Russian defences and sent a broken army reeling back eastwards. The 'million Italian bayonets' did not emulate Bonaparte and Bernadotte in 1797 and strike through Laibach and the Semmering Pass to the Danubian plain. Instead, the Italian army suffered on the rocky plateau around Gorizia as grievously as the British imperial forces on the Gallipoli peninsula. Wisely Romania (and Greece) stayed out of the war. To some extent, Grey, Delcassé and their advisers became scapegoats for the failure of the admirals and generals to lift public morale with news of victories. The British Press complained of the 'bungling of our diplomats'; and in France Clemenceau, president of the Senate committee on foreign affairs and editor of *L'Homme Enchaîné*, pulled no punches in ridiculing the folly of French initiatives abroad. Delcassé would have nothing more to do with plans for overseas enterprises. Rather than 'see France's soldiers sent across the seas while the enemy was on French soil', he resigned from the government on 13 October 1915.[15] The former socialist Aristide Briand succeeded him. Meanwhile, in London, a sense of duty carried Grey into his tenth year at the Foreign Office.

In Petrograd the influence of the Foreign Ministry had already substantially fallen. Indeed, some of the difficulties of both Grey and Delcassé sprang from Sazonov's subservience to the demands of Russia's military leaders, both over the Straits and over the timing of Italian intervention. In August 1915 Nicholas II personally became commander-in-chief in the field, a move opposed by most of his ministers as potentially disastrous. Sazonov was highly critical of the Tsar's decision, and Nicholas thereafter waited for an opportunity to rid himself of his Foreign Minister. But Sazonov, who was regarded as weak by foreign diplomats before the war, had increased his prestige with the Entente ambassadors, and the Tsar characteristically prevaricated. When, in July 1916, Sazonov clashed with the Tsar over concessions to the Poles, he finally fell from grace, despite efforts by both the French and British ambassadors to keep him in office. The low ranking of the Foreign Ministry was emphasised by the Tsar's appointment of Boris Stürmer as Sazonov's successor. For Stürmer, who had been a court functionary (Master of Ceremonies) until the previous February, was already Prime Minister and was known as a tool of Rasputin and the Empress Alexandra. With good reason, Stürmer was suspected of being pro-German. In May, independently of the Foreign Ministry, he met a Russian liberal living in Stockholm, Joseph Kolyshko, who made contact with the German coal and shipping magnate Hugo Stinnes and put out feelers for a separate peace. Kolyshko, once Witte's secretary at the Ministry of Finance, was married to a German, and may have misrepresented Stürmer to Stinnes, but rumours of the confusion in Russian policy reached the newspapers in Sweden and Switzerland. London and Paris noted these reports with foreboding.[16]

Almost inevitably war eroded the authority of Germany's Chancellor. Even Bismarck might have experienced difficulty in facing up to Falkenhayn's predominance as Chief of the General Staff in succession to Moltke or the more formidable Hindenburg-Ludendorff combination on the Eastern Front. Bethmann-Hollweg had no illusions of power. He was at first content to subordinate political gestures to military exigency, seeing the wartime role of a Chancellor much as Grey saw his tasks as Foreign Secretary. Jagow was frequently in attendance at headquarters as State Secretary but no one heeded him and he remained a puzzled rabbit among the heel-clicking Excellencies. The Kaiser, though nominally Supreme War Lord, was upstaged by his generals and he had little influence on the conduct of military operations. William retained, however, direct authority over the disposition of the fleet in time of war; and he was not prepared to relax his prerogatives at the prompting of Grand Admiral Tirpitz. The Kaiser shrank from the risks of a major battle between dreadnoughts in the North Sea. He was, moreover, opposed to unrestricted submarine attacks on merchant vessels. Over this question the Chancellor and the State Secretary were in full agreement with their sovereign. Indeed it was the U-boat issue which made Bethmann-Hollweg assert himself and, at least for a few months, recover some of the peacetime authority of the chancellorship.[17]

Bethmann-Hollweg and Jagow were convinced that unrestricted submarine warfare would bring America into the war against Germany. Throughout the summer of 1915 Falkenhayn shared their gloomy predictions and there was a united front of Kaiser, Chief of the General Staff, Chancellor and State Secretary against Tirpitz and the Chief of the Admiralty Staff, Admiral Bachman. But the Chancellor found Falkenhayn an uncertain ally who became increasingly unpopular as victory eluded him in the West. The prospect of Falkenhayn joining the U-boat pressure group tempted Bethmann to play the kingmaker. He had heard from Zimmermann, under-secretary at the Foreign Ministry since 1911, that the twin titans of the Eastern Front, Hindenburg and Ludendorff, were in full agreement with his views. Bethmann therefore joined the Kaiser's military secretariat and members of the imperial family in urging William to replace Falkenhayn with Hindenburg. The change took place on 29 August 1916, Hindenburg becoming Chief of the General Staff while Ludendorff became First Quartermaster-General.

Neither Bethmann-Hollweg nor the Kaiser realised the consequences of Hindenburg's elevation. The Field Marshal was idolised by the German people. In making themselves indispensable for the prosecution of the war, Hindenburg and Ludendorff became Germany's real rulers, the first military dictatorship in Europe since 1852. Jagow was soon jettisoned in favour of Zimmermann. Bethmann remained Chancellor long enough to see his warnings cast aside and the United States brought into the war within ten weeks of the resumption of unrestricted U-boat attacks. When, in July 1917, Bethmann was thought to favour a negotiated peace, he was ousted for George Michaelis, an obscure civil servant whom the Kaiser had never even met when he was induced to appoint him Chancellor. Less than four months later he was replaced by another nominee of the Hindenburg-Ludendorff combination, Count Hertling, a Bavarian Roman Catholic more adept at handling the Reichstag. Until the dark days of October 1918 Hindenburg and Ludendorff regarded the Imperial

Chancellery as a rubber stamp of approval for the decisions of the Supreme Command.[18]

The crisis which ensured Hindenburg and Ludendorff's elevation was caused by a rare success of Entente policy in the Balkans. On 27 August 1916 Romania declared war on Austria-Hungary. At last the invasion of Transylvania which Delcassé had anticipated fifteen months before was in progress. Curiously enough, the Romanians would never have risked entering the war had it not been for the very episode which induced Delcassé to resign office. For when, in the autumn of 1915, Bulgaria finally decided to join the Central Powers and attacked Serbia, the British and French sent an expeditionary force to Salonika under the French general, Maurice Sarrail, with the double intention of assisting the Serbs and encouraging Greece to renew the alliance of the Second Balkan War. All the ingenuity of allied diplomacy could not, however, persuade King Constantine I to bring his country into the war.[19] The muddle was too much for Delcassé's precise sense of responsibilities and was the principal reason why he had made way for Briand. There were others, too, who found embarrassment in retaining 150,000 British and French soldiers garrisoning the second city of a nominally neutral state. For the first twelve weeks after the landing, Germany, Turkey, Bulgaria and Austria-Hungary even maintained consulates in Salonika, able to report directly on Sarrail's movements. But in July 1916 Sarrail had a chance to justify his presence in the Balkans. General Brussilov's summer offensive had un-expectedly pushed the Austrians back from the River Dniester to the foothills of the Carpathians; and Bratianu let Briand and Grey know that Romania was again contemplating intervention. He needed assurance that Sarrail's army in Macedonia would launch a major attack at least three days ahead of Romania's declaration of war so as to relieve pressure on a kingdom hemmed in on three sides by the Central Powers. He insisted, too, on the promise of territorial gains in Austria-Hungary which would more than double the extent of Romania. A convention embodying these terms was signed in Bucharest on 17 August. Remarkably, within ten days the Romanian army was on a war footing and poised to march into Transylvania. It was the suddenness of Romania's intervention that alarmed the Kaiser and finally made him promote Hindenburg and Ludendorff, for Falkenhayn had told his sovereign Bratianu would never allow Romania's generals to march before the harvest was in. But the Romanian action did not ruffle Falkenhayn's successor: 'The last man that can be spared from the East and the West must be sent against Roumania', Hindenburg declared on the day he became Chief of the General Staff. With the Germany army heavily committed simultaneously at Verdun and the Somme, this comment is in itself testimony to the importance attached by the Germans to Romania.[20]

Ultimately the Bucharest Convention proved another hollow victory for Entente diplomacy. Sarrail's 'Army of the Orient', reinforced by Russian and Italian brigades as well as by a reconstituted Serbian army, might look impressive on war maps in Bucharest, but it was given no chance to prove its quality as an attacking force. On the day after the convention was signed, the Central Powers launched a surprise offensive in Macedonia. By 12 September, when Sarrail could at last counter attack, Romania was already in difficulties. Brussilov's army was a spent force and Russia brought her new ally little aid. Most seriously of all, a mainly Bulgarian thrust northwards along the Black Sea coast captured the Danubian bridgehead at Silistria. The Romanians were thus forced to send their reserve divisions not westwards against the gathering Germano-Austrian armies in Transylvania, but south-eastwards so as to ward off the enemy upper cuts. Worse followed. Within ten weeks most of Romania was overrun, German troops entering Bucharest on 6 December. The whole of the Danube was under German control.[21]

All in all, 1916 seemed as it drew to a close to have been a year of wasteful slaughter: 300 days of battle at Verdun; a million casualties in the opposing armies during twenty weeks of fighting on the Somme; an inconclusive encounter of the grand fleets at Jutland; and the mounting toll of U-boat warfare. By comparison, the Balkan débâcle was of small significance to the public in Britain and France, however it might appear in Berlin. Yet there was no disguising the fact that in two years of negotiations the Entente's diplomats had failed to create an effective grand alliance linking London, Paris, Petrograd and the Balkan governments. Turkey and Bulgaria, on the other hand, had chosen to join the Central Powers and were then able to contribute to the common cause rather than seek rescue from disaster. Grey's skill in having improved relations with the United States was not generally apparent. It was easier to criticise his Balkan failures. Seton-Watson complained of his 'growing tendency towards secret diplomacy' and the more left-wing 'Union of Democratic Control' blamed him for not taking 'the people' into his confidence and seeking a negotiated peace, with their backing.[22] Like Bethmann-Hollweg in Germany, Grey was considered, even by earlier admirers, to be tired and stale. No Foreign Secretary had ever held continuous office so long and, since Grey's time, only Ernest Bevin has reached even half his span.

On 11 December 1916 Grey at last left the Foreign Office, eleven years to the day since he first received his seals of office from Edward VII. Arthur Balfour, the former Prime Minister, succeeded him – but with a significant change of status. Six days earlier Asquith had resigned the premiership and George V, after sounding out the party leaders, invited Lloyd George to form a government. The Welshman's ideas of a wartime executive bore little resemblance to Asquith's cumbersome coalition ministry, with its Cabinet of twenty-four. Lloyd George preferred a War Cabinet of five, of whom only the Chancellor of the Exchequer (Bonar Law, the Conservative-Unionist leader) held departmental responsibilities. For the first time since the creation of the office in 1782 the Foreign Secretary was excluded from the Cabinet, and remained so until 1919. Balfour was invited to attend and seems to have been present at about three in every five War Cabinet sessions. He came, however, purely in a consultative and advisory capacity. Foreign policy was determined solely by the five (later, seven) members of the War Cabinet.[23] In British terms, Lloyd George had altered the character of government as drastically as the Hindenburg-Ludendorff takeover bid in Germany four months earlier.

To some extent, Balfour's exclusion from the War Cabinet reflected Lloyd George's antipathy to the Foreign Office; during the Second World War, the Foreign Secretary was always a member of Churchill's War Cabinet. But the influence and prestige of the Foreign Office had declined considerably in the two years preceding Balfour's appointment. The power of the permanent officials fell soon after the outbreak of war, partly because of virulent Press attacks on several of them for their marriage links and former social contacts with German families. Routine work increased as the Foreign Office became what Bertie described as a ' "pass-on" department' for Admiralty and War Office Intelligence and for other ministries, too.[24] A curious situation arose in the summer of 1916 when Sir Arthur Nicolson's poor health forced him to retire as permanent under-secretary and he was replaced by his immediate predecessor, Lord Hardinge, who returned to Whitehall after six years as Viceroy of India. Unfortunately Hardinge was no longer the assertive ex-ambassador who brought such detailed knowledge of Europe's Chancelleries to the Foreign Office in 1906; a narrow escape from assassination on his state entry into New Delhi in 1912 and concern at the failure of the Mesopotamian expedition which he had encouraged in 1915 had weakened his confidence. The rapid reversion from potentate of a sub-continent to civil servant was made no easier by the strange structure of the wartime Foreign Office. It was puzzling to find Lord Robert Cecil (the great Lord Salisbury's third son) serving there as parliamentary under-secretary, while also being Minister of Blockade, a Privy Councillor and, from February to December 1916, a member of the coalition Cabinet.[25] There was, too, at Wellington House a propaganda agency, designed to influence opinion in the neutral capitals of Europe and America, but under the control of the Chancellor of the Duchy of Lancaster, not the Foreign Secretary. It was Wellington House which, in distributing pamphlets by Masaryk, G. M. Trevelyan, Ernest Barker and Lewis Namier, frequently went beyond the limits of approved government policy.[26] At times it seemed as if the new Prime Minister, finding the Foreign Office stultified by the confusion of war, preferred an institution like Wellington House because it was seeking to win public support and gain the backing of the Americans for nationalities denied self-determination by Europe's decaying empires.

Churchill likened Balfour as Foreign Secretary to 'a powerful, graceful cat walking delicately and unsoiled across a rather muddy street'.[27] A politician of less equable temperament would have resented Lloyd George's treatment of his department of state. Crowe, Tyrrell and Mallet were allowed to work with Cecil on a British response to the Peace Note which President Wilson sent to the belligerent governments in Christmas week, and this distinguished group of public servants continued to promote and assess projects for a League of Nations during the remainder of the war. In April 1917 Balfour became the first Foreign Secretary to visit Washington, but increasingly Lloyd George looked outside the foreign service for the high-speed diplomacy which was intended to suck the dust from the old Chancelleries. The War Cabinet secretariat, a 'garden suburb' of huts in St James's Park, became the power-house of government policy over the next two years. Sir Francis Hopwood, a civil servant who had worked closely with Lloyd George at the Board of Trade, and Philip Kerr, the Prime Minister's political secretary, were entrusted with special missions to Scandinavia and Switzerland which might more profitably have been left to the diplomats. Lloyd George revelled in intrigue; two armament manufacturers, Zaharoff and Caillard, were employed to contact a Turkish emissary in Lucerne who claimed that, for 10 million dollars, he could induce Enver to open the Straits as a preliminary to Turkey's staged withdrawal from the war – an unprofitable episode for the British, and one in which the government was aptly code-named 'moneybags'.[28] More exasperating to the diplomats was the Prime Minister's handling of a secret peace offer from the new Austrian Emperor, Charles, who had succeeded his great-uncle, Francis Joseph, in November 1916. Lloyd George did not inform the Foreign Office of his first meeting with the French Prime Minister to discuss Emperor Charles's overture, and he did not invite any representative from the Foreign Office to accompany him when, at the end of April 1917, he travelled to St Jean-de-Maurienne for discussions with the French and Italian Prime Ministers. This was the kind of treatment meted out by Napoleon III to Walewski. Lloyd George had no liking for the familiar forms of conference diplomacy. He delighted in administrative iconoclasm.

It was, however, events in Russia which gave the deathblow to the chancellery system. The February Revolution, which led to the abdication of Nicholas II and the establishment of a provisional government, at first raised hopes of democratic reform and national liberation. The American people had consistently opposed Tsarist tyranny, and even with the folly of Zimmermann's intercepted telegram calling for an anti-American alliance with Mexico, they would hardly have accepted President Wilson's call for entry into the war had it been necessary to fight alongside Tsar Nicholas's army. But however much the new leaders of Russia, Prince Lvov and Kerensky, might appeal to democratic sentiment in the West, they could not satisfy the immediate need of the Russian people for food and an end to the 'imperialist' war. Lenin's promise of 'Bread and Peace' ensured the success of his October revolution within Russia, and he had ready a proclamation to the peoples of all the belligerent countries, offering peace on a basis of 'no annexations, no indemnities, and the right of self-determination of the peoples'. The practical application of the 'Decree of Peace' he left to the ingenuity of a more cosmopolitan socialist than himself, Lev Bronstein, alias Leon Trotsky, who had spent many years in Vienna.[29]

When on 10 November Trotsky formally took possession of the old Foreign Ministry building in the crescent facing the Winter Palace, 600 officials walked out in disgust, leaving the first Commissar for Foreign Affairs to create his own embryonic foreign service. Trotsky skilfully combined the practice of revolutionary propaganda with manipulation of conventional methods of diplomacy. While sending an assistant to search for the texts of secret treaties so that they might be published and thus discredit the bourgeois governments, he notified foreign ambassadors that authority in Russia's capital had passed into Soviet hands and drew their attention to the Decree of Peace. When the ambassadors declined to recognise the new Commissariat, he formally applied to the German High Command for an armistice.

Peace talks opened in the citadel of Brest-Litovsk on 20 December. There were five delegations present, military and civilian, between 300 and 400 people. Technically the president of the conference was Field Marshal Prince Leopold of Bavaria, brother of the King of Bavaria, son-in-law of Emperor Francis Joseph, and titular commander-in-chief of Germany's armies on the Eastern Front. Effective management of the conference was left to his Chief of Staff, General Max Hoffmann, whose tactical brilliance had decided the battle of Tannenberg in 1914. There were Bulgarian and Turkish representatives present, tolerated rather than consulted. The principal spokesman for the German government was Richard von Kühlmann, a career diplomat who had welcomed the Kaiser to Tangier in 1905, served as counsellor of the London embassy for five years and taken over as State Secretary at the Foreign Ministry from the discredited Zimmermann in August 1917. Emperor Charles's choice as Foreign Minister, Count Ottokar Czernin, headed the Austro-Hungarian delegation, an old style diplomat who saw himself in his more optimistic moments as a latterday Metternich saving Austria for Charles as the old Chancellor had saved her for Emperor Francis. But it was the Soviet delegation which attracted attention. Trotsky himself did not come until the second week of January 1918 and the first leader of the delegation was Adolf Joffe, an archetypal revolutionary intellectual, complete with pince-nez: 'I hope we may yet be able to raise the revolution in your country, too', he genially remarked to a horrified Count Czernin when they met after dining together at Prince Leopold's table on their first evening at Brest-Litovsk.[30] With Joffe were advisers from the former Tsarist army and navy, two of Trotsky's closest confidants, and Anastasia Bizenko, who had murdered a Russian general in 1905 and was recently released from Siberia, the first woman delegate to an international political conference. There were, too, in these early days at Brest-Litovsk three symbolic spokesmen for the people, a sailor and a labourer, who were sound Bolsheviks, and a peasant gathered haphazardly from the Petrograd streets as the original armistice delegation set out for the railway station.

Czernin and Kühlmann were inclined to make use of Bolshevik propaganda, accepting in principle the idea of a general peace and placing the onus for continuing the war on the Entente Powers. Kühlmann thought moderation would tempt war-weary politicians in the West to press their leaders for a complete peace. But Hoffman, and the Supreme Commanders, would not trim their annexationist programmes. Over the New Year the conference adjourned for twelve days so that each side might consider its position. When the delegates met again on 8 January, the mood had hardened. There was no more dining and wining at Prince Leopold's table. A Ukrainian separatist delegation had arrived, and the Bulgarian Prime Minister and the Turkish Grand Vizier came to add weight to their governments' representation. They need hardly have made the journey. The second session was dominated by long debates between Trotsky and Kühlmann. Both men played for time, Trotsky because he hoped the fuse of revolution would fire Berlin and Vienna, Kühlmann because he believed long discussions would embarrass Hoffmann and induce the Supreme Command to leave the last word to the diplomats. For a month the conference heard digressions on the meaning of self-determination and the validity of international law as Trotsky and Kühlmann enjoyed verbal confrontations as irrelevant as any procedural wrangling devised by Talleyrand at the Vienna Congress. But both men miscalculated. There was no murmur of revolution, only a ban on fraternisation so as to curb Bolshevik propaganda among troops at the Front, and the Supreme Command had no intention of allowing the most fertile regions of western Russia to slip through their hands for the sake of alleged moderates who would negotiate a general peace short of total victory. Rather than tolerate the argument and expediency of chancellery diplomacy any longer, Hoffmann decided the Russians should be given 'another taste of the whip'. The talks were broken off, and the war technically renewed on 18 February. The German and Austro–Hungarian armies met little resistance and, as soon as they came within 50 miles of Petrograd, the Soviet Republic sued for peace. There was no more conference bargaining. A treaty was presented, signed at Brest-Litovsk on 3 March and, so far as Russia and Germany were concerned, ratified on 29 March. It was a hard, 'annexationist' peace. Never before had a defeated European Great Power lost such vast territories: Poland, the Baltic provinces, Finland, Bessarabia, the Ukraine and the Caucasus among them. Virtually every conquest made by the Tsars since the days of Peter the Great was surrendered. Terms of this nature did not improve the prospects for a negotiated settlement in the West.

To the government in London the Brest-Litovsk Treaty seemed so severe that both the Prime Minister and the War Minister expressed fears of a German bid to dominate central Asia and take over Russia's traditional role as the principal threat to British supremacy in India.[31] Yet in the allied capitals as a whole the main impact of the Russian Revolution was on the way people thought about the great issues of war and peace. Very few were converted to socialism, but many more began to seek an ideal of some kind which would 'make the world safe for democracy'. By publishing recent treaties found in the archives of the old Foreign Ministry, the Bolsheviks exposed the bargains struck by Grey, Delcassé, Sazonov and Sonnino. 'Secret diplomacy', attacked by radical writers ever since the Moroccan crises, was now finally discredited among liberal democrats, too. In Paris the Jacobin patriotism of Clemenceau, who became Prime Minister a week after Lenin issued his Decree of Peace, discouraged speculation on war aims: *Père-la-Victoire* imposed his will on the nation so that defeat of the Boche and recovery of Alsace-Lorraine were seen in themselves as prizes worthy of suffering and sacrifice. But in London Lloyd George was more sensitive to the public mood.[32] He established the Press baron Lord Northcliffe at Crewe House as director of propaganda to enemy countries; and Lord Beaverbrook, who had purchased the *Daily Express* in the month Lloyd George formed his government, was made Minister of Information. Both men trespassed on what had been Foreign Office preserves and there were sharp exchanges between Balfour and Northcliffe in the summer of 1918. Lloyd George's inclination was to support the Press barons rather than a department of government which he had long distrusted. When, on 13 June 1918, Beaverbrook could boast to Lloyd George that his ministry had 'its own diplomacy, a popular diplomacy', he was certain the great Welsh opportunist would approve.[33]

The real answer to the simplistic appeal of Bolshevik peace propaganda came from Washington.[34] An inter-allied conference on peace terms had met in Paris on 30 November 1917 and failed to produce a coherent programme. President Woodrow Wilson, a liberal idealist who kept a portrait of Gladstone on his desk in the White House, had no sympathy for such prevarication. On 8 January 1918, the same Tuesday on which Trotsky was to make his first appearance at a plenary session of the Brest-Litovsk Conference, President Wilson addressed Congress, setting out Fourteen Points as 'the only possible program' on which to base the world's peace. The President's lofty aphorisms combined a set of general moral principles with specific proposals for a just settlement in Belgium, France, northern Italy, the Balkans, Poland, the Ottoman Empire and Russia, guidelines lacking in Lenin's bid for world opinion. In London, Paris and Rome there was disquiet over the detailed application of the Fourteen Points, but recognition that the New World was at least offering the Old World nobler ideals than a Concert of Europe maintained by a balance of power. 'Open covenants openly arrived at' sounded a trust-worthy antidote to the old and discredited diplomacy; and 'a general association of nations' to guarantee 'political independence and territorial integrity to great and small states alike' was an effective counter for those who believed France, Britain, Italy and Japan were fighting 'for imperial aggrandisement and domination'. With the war swinging in Germany's favour throughout the first six months of 1918, the allies needed inspiration from across the Atlantic to sustain their will to battle. By the spring Woodrow Wilson had assumed the mantle of visionary prophet borne in 1814–15 by the Christian conqueror from St Petersburg. A century of chancellery diplomacy was ending where it had begun, with the emergence of a liberator saviour.

It is, however, misleading to seek too close a parallel between Woodrow Wilson and Alexander I. The full revelation of his providential mission came to the Tsar only when the Napoleonic Wars were ended. Ten more months of battle elapsed between Wilson's address to Congress and the request from Prince Max of Baden, last Chancellor of imperial Germany, that the fighting should cease pending a peace settlement based on the Fourteen Points. By then the 'Army of the Orient' had broken Bulgarian resistance, Turkish power was crumbling and the allies were preparing to march up the Danube to Budapest and Vienna from a liber-ated Belgrade. Yet whatever might be gained from these 'sideshows' – and, for Britain, France and Italy, the prizes were attractive – the decisive theatre of war remained the Western Front.[35] Here final victory was impossible without American aid, and the promise of more to come if the war dragged on through another winter. Any threat by Wilson to his co-belligerents to conclude a separate peace was therefore enough to induce them to accept his leadership. In Vienna, Berlin and Sofia too, Wilson's Olympian detachment from the intrigues of chancellery diplomacy seemed the surest guarantee of a just settlement. Wilson never doubted that, through the patronage he was giving to a League of Nations, he possessed unique qualities which would ensure the Europeanised world a permanent peace. This sense of mission compelled him to break with tradition. Within a month of the armistice, he became the first President of the United States to leave America's shores in his term of office.

On 13 December 1918 – a Friday, as the superstitious noted – the liner *George Washington* steamed into the French port of Brest, with Woodrow Wilson and several hundred expert advisers aboard.[36] Wilson was greeted as rapturously as the Tsar in 1814, but he was in a far stronger moral and material position. He had never compromised with the enemy, and behind him was a nation of growing military and naval strength whose industrial and agricultural reserves had not suffered from the dislocation of the war. America's banks could offer the postwar world what the City of London had provided in the last years of the struggle against Napoleon. Europe needed the United States in 1919 much as the continent needed Great Britain in 1815. The parallel is less with the Tsar than with Castlereagh, on whose skill at keeping his country in Europe Metternich had set such store during the early years of chancellery diplomacy. In a sense, the *George Washington* was the successor to HMS *Erebus*, which had brought a British Foreign Secretary to continental Europe for the first time. Roundshot had greeted poor Castlereagh as his frigate pulled into Hellevoetsluis. President Wilson fared better at Brest: the salute of two navies boomed a welcome to the era of open diplomacy, token gunfire amplified by an echo from the ramparted boulevard. Perhaps it was an appropriate beginning.

Notes

I have used the following abbreviations in these notes:

AHR   *American Historical Review* (Washington, DC)
APP   *Die Auswartige Politik Preussens, 1859–71* (Berlin, 1932–58)
BD   G. P. Gooch and H. Temperley (eds), *British Documents on the Origins of the War, 1898–1914* (London, 1926–38)
BIHR   *Bulletin of the Institute of Historical Research* (London)
DDF   *Documents diplomatiques français, 1871–1914* (Paris, 1930–53)
EHR   *English Historical Review* (London)
FO   Foreign Office papers in the Public Record Office, London
GD   Karl Kautsky, *Outbreak of the World War, German Documents* (New York, 1924)
GP   J. Lepsius, A. Mendelssohn-Bartholdy and F. Thimme, *Die Grosse Politik der Europaischen Kabinette, 1871–1914* (Berlin, 1922–7)
GW   Otto von Bismarck, *Die Gesammelten Werke* (Berlin, 1924–35)
HJ   *Historical Journal* (Cambridge)
JCEA   *Journal of Central European Affairs* (Boulder, Colo)
JCH   *Journal of Contemporary History* (London)
JMH   *Journal of Modern History* (Chicago)
KA   *Krasny Arkhiv* (Moscow)
L   published in London
MO   *Mezhdunarodnye otnosheniya v Epokhu Imperializma* (Moscow, 1930 ff.)
NY   published in New York
O   published in Oxford
ODG   *Les Origines diplomatiques de la guerre de 1870–71* (Paris, 1910 ff.)
P   published in Paris
PRO   Public Record Office, London
QVL   *Letters of Queen Victoria:* First Series, 1837–61 (London, 1907); Second Series, 1862–85 (London, 1926); Third Series, 1886–1901 (London, 1930)
SP   published in St Petersburg
SEER   *The Slavonic and East European Review* (London)
SIRIO   *Sbornik Imperatorskogo russkogo istoricheskogo obshchestva* (St Petersburg)
TRHS   *Transactions of the Royal Historical Society (London)*

References

Chapter 1: Innocent Abroad, 1814

1   For Castlereagh's journey see: Emma, Countess Brownlow, *Slight Reminiscences of a Septuagenarian* (L, 1867), pp. 30–1; *The Times*, 28, 29 December 1813 and 3 January 1814; A. Aspinall (ed.), *Letters of George IV* (Cambridge, 1938), Vol. I, pp. 370–1. The best biographies are by C. J. Bartlett (L, 1966) and by Wendy Hinde (L, 1981). Background material on the Foreign Office in C. K. Webster, *The Foreign Policy of Castlereagh, 1812–1815* (L, 1931), Vol. I, pp. 44–53, and Sir John Tilley and Stephen Gaselee, *The Foreign Office* (revised edn, L, 1933).

2   Robinson's recollections are printed in Lord Londonderry (ed.), *Memoirs and Correspondence of Viscount Castlereagh* (L, 1848), Vol. I, pp. 125–9. See also Webster, Vol. I, pp. 193–210. For the extracts from Castlereagh's letters on the journey, ibid., pp. 503–4.

3   Metternich to the Duchess of Sagan, 21 January 1814, M. Ullrichova, *Clemens Metternich, Wilhelmine von Sagan; Ein Briefwechsel* (Graz-Cologne, 1966), p. 183; Alan Palmer, *Metternich* (L, 1972), p. 110.

4   H. Ritter von Srbik, *Metternich, der Staatsmann und der Mensch* (Munich, 1925), Vol. I, pp. 171–2; E. E. Kraehe, *Metternich's German Policy, 1799–1814* (Princeton, NJ, 1963), pp. 288–90.

5   Webster, Vol. I, pp. 229–30.

6   ibid., cf. footnote 2 on p. 198 and footnote 1 on p. 265. Webster also gives the fullest account of Castlereagh's sojourn in Paris, ibid., pp. 264–5.

7   Brownlow, pp. 93–5.

8   ibid., pp. 95–7; H. Nicolson, *Congress of Vienna* (L, 1946), p. 113.

Chapter 2: The Christian Conqueror, 1814–15

1   Jane Austen to Cassandra Austen, 23 June 1814, R. W. Chapman, *Jane Austen's Letters* (O, 1932), no. 97, p. 390; M. S. Anderson, *Britain's Discovery of Russia* (L, 1958), pp. 222–3; Alan Palmer, *Alexander I* (L, 1974), pp. 291–301.

2   The best survey of Nesselrode's early career is in P. K. Grimsted, *The Foreign Ministers of Alexander I* (Berkeley, Calif., 1969), pp. 196–210. But Nesselrode wrote an autobiographical fragment covering the years from 1780 to 1815 which forms a section of the second volume of A. de Nesselrode, *Lettres et Papiers du Chancelier Comte de Nesselrode* (P, 1908–12). His religious beliefs, Vol. II, p. 17; 'summoned . . . when needed', Vol. IV, p. 43.

3   On Czartoryski, Grimsted, pp. 107–9, 122–3, 221–5, and Palmer, *Alexander I*, pp. 188–9, 291, 300 and 304–5.

4   H. Nicolson, *Congress of Vienna* (L, 1946), pp. 156–8; Henry Kissinger, *A World Restored* (NY, 1964), pp. 147–9.

5   Palmer, *Alexander I*, pp. 310–12.

6   Gordon A. Craig, *The Politics of the Prussian Army* (revised paperback edn, NY, 1964), pp. 65–75; Gerhard Ritter, *The Sword and the Sceptre* (L, 1972), Vol. I, pp. 73 and 81.

7   M. H. Weil, *Les Dessous du Congrès de Vienne* (P, 1917), Vol. II, p. 32. On Capodistria at Vienna, see Grimsted, pp. 227–56, and C. M. Woodhouse, *Capodistria* (O, 1973), pp. 109–30.

8   Palmer, *Alexander I*, pp. 316–19; Francis Ley, *Alexandre I et sa Sainte Alliance* (P, 1975), pp. 63–84.

9   Elizabeth Longford, *Wellington, the Years of the Sword* (L, 1969), pp. 381–9 and 395.

10   ibid., p. 451; Alan Palmer, *Metternich* (L, 1972), pp. 148–9, and *Alexander I*, p. 327.

11   Countess Brownlow, *Slight Reminiscences of a Septuagenarian* (L, 1867), p. 126; R. Metternich (ed.), *Mémoires, Documents et Écrits par le Prince de Metternich* (P, 1880–4), Vol. II, pp. 523–5); Palmer, *Metternich*, pp. 150–4.

12   Alexander's letter to Julie von Krüdener was first printed by H. L. Empaytaz, *Notice sur Alexandre, Empéreur de Russe* (Geneva, 1840), p. 40. All earlier studies of the ceremony on the Plain de Vertus and the origin of the Holy Alliance have been outdated by Francis Ley's *Alexandre I et sa Sainte Alliance*, pp. 107–60.
13   ibid., pp. 149–53 and 160–3.
14   ibid., pp. 164–5; N. K. Shilder, *Imperator Aleksander I, ego zhiyn' i Tsarstovanie* (SP, 1897), Vol. III, p. 348.

Chapter 3: Congress Diplomacy, 1816–22

1   Castlereagh's speech, 19 February 1815, Hansard, *Parliamentary Debates*. New Series, Vol. XXXII, pp. 793–800. Other speeches in the debate, ibid., pp. 350–74, 673–737 and 748–93. C. J. Bartlett, *Castlereagh* (L, 1966), pp. 159–60. A. J. P. Taylor, *The Troublemakers* (L, 1957), pp. 35–9.
2   Alan Palmer, *Alexander I* (L, 1974), pp. 354–5; C. K. Webster, *The Foreign Policy of Castlereagh, 1815–1822* (L, 1925), Vol. II, pp. 97–9 and 103.
3   J. Capodistria, 'Aperçu de ma carrière publiqué depuis 1798 jusqu'à 1822', SIRIO, Vol. III (1868), p. 213; C. M. Woodhouse, *Capodistria* (O, 1973), pp. 158–9 summarises the exchanges between the Tsar and Capodistria.
4   P. K. Grimsted, *The Foreign Ministers of Alexander I* (Berkeley, Calif., 1969), pp. 244, 266–7 and 281–4.
5   G. de Bertier de Sauvigny, *Metternich et la France après le Congrès de Vienne* (P, 1968–74), Vol. I, pp. 91–6.
6   Alan Palmer, *Metternich* (L, 1972), pp. 172–8; Woodhouse, pp. 177–92; Grimsted, p. 14; E. C. Corti, *Metternich und die Frauen* (Vienna, 1949), Vol. II, pp. 81–3; Capodistria, SIRIO, Vol. III, pp. 230–3.
7   Webster, Vol. II, pp. 150–2.
8   ibid., p. 203; Paul Schroeder, *Metternich's Diplomacy at its Zenith* (Austin, Texas, 1962), p. 27.
9   For French policy in general, B. de Sauvigny, *Metternich et la France*, Vol. I, pp. 315–415. On Rayneval, Webster, Vol. II, pp. 133, 229–30 and 424.
10   On Troppau: ibid., Vol. II, pp. 285–311; Palmer, *Metternich*, pp. 192–5; Schroeder, *Metternich's Diplomacy*, pp. 47–69; Henry Kissinger, *A World Restored* (NY, 1964), pp. 259–69. See also the article by Paul Schroeder, 'Austrian policy at the Congresses of Troppau and Laibach', JCEA, vol. 22, no. 2 (1962), pp. 139–52.
11   R. Metternich (ed.), *Mémoires, Documents et Écrits par le Prince de Metternich* (P, 1880–4), Vol. III, p. 449; Schroeder, *Metternich's Diplomacy*, pp. 104–6; Woodhouse, pp. 247–51 and 253–4; B. de Sauvigny, *Metternich et la France*, Vol. I, pp. 417–71.
12   Woodhouse, pp. 254–61; M. S. Anderson, *The Eastern Question* (L, 1966), pp. 53–7; John Campbell and Philip Sherrard, *Modern Greece* (L, 1968), pp. 60–6.
13   Capodistria, SIRIO, Vol. III, pp. 266–85.
14   Metternich to Castlereagh, 6 June 1822, Webster, Vol. II, pp. 542–3; Castlereagh's reply on 29 July, ibid., Vol. II, pp. 548–9.
15   ibid., Vol. II, pp. 486–8; Bartlett, pp. 262–3. See also H. Montgomery Hyde, *The Strange Death of Lord Castlereagh* (L, 1959).
16   Canning to J. H. Frere, 7 August 1823, G. Festing, *John Hookham Frere and his Friends* (L, 1899), p. 259; H. W. V. Temperley, *The Foreign Policy of Canning, 1822–27* (L, 1925), pp. 63–4; Irby C. Nichols Jr, 'The Eastern Question and the Vienna Conference, September 1822', JCEA, vol. 21, no. 1 (1961), pp. 53–66.
17   B. de Sauvigny, *Metternich et la France*, Vol. II, pp. 610–59; Schroeder, *Metternich's Diplomacy*, pp. 211–36; Palmer, *Metternich*, pp. 216–19; Elizabeth Longford, *Wellington, Pillar of State* (L, 1972), pp. 99–105.

Chapter 4: Dutch Bottoms and an Untoward Event, 1823–30

1   The best biography of Canning is by Wendy Hinde (L, 1973). The analytical study by P. J. V. Rolo, *George Canning* (L, 1965). Canning and the king, see C. Hibbert, *George IV, Regent and King* (L, 1975), pp. 235–300. For his Blue book policy, H. W. V. Temperley and L. M. Penson, *A Century of Diplomatic Bluebooks* (Cambridge, 1938), pp. 30–7.

2 C. R. Middleton, *The Administration of British Foreign Policy, 1782–1846* (Durham, NC, 1977), pp. 110–11 and 177–8; H. W. V. Temperley, *The Foreign Policy of Canning, 1822–27* (L, 1925), pp. 258–86.

3 Canning to Wynn, 9 October 1826, FO 60/29, as cited by David Gillard, *The Struggle for Asia, 1828–1914* (L, 1977), p. 21.

4 There are several versions of the rhyming dispatch; see Temperley, *For. Pol. Canning*, pp. 294–6, from which this version is taken.

5 ibid., pp. 75–99; G. de Bertier de Sauvigny, *Metternich et la France après le Congrès de Vienne* (P, 1868–74), Vol. III, pp. 743–800; and, in general, G. Grandmaison, *L'Expédition française en Espagne* (P, 1929). On Canning and the Tagus squadron, C. J. Bartlett, *Great Britain and Sea Power, 1815–1853* (O, 1963), pp. 74–9.

6 Rolo, pp. 205–7 and 210; D. C. M. Platt, *Finance, Trade and Politics in British Foreign Policy* (O, 1968), pp. 312–16.

7 C. K. Webster, *Britain and the Independence of Latin America* (L, 1938), Vol. I, pp. 46–8; Rolo, pp. 227–30; Temperley, *For. Pol. Canning*, pp. 131–67.

8 Canning's speech of 12 December 1826, Hansard, New Series, Vol. XVI, pp. 395–8; Kenneth Bourne, *The Foreign Policy of Victorian England* (O, 1970), pp. 17–18 and 207–10.

9 Canning to Granville, 11 March 1825, E. J. Stapleton, *Political Correspondence of George Canning* (L, 1888), Vol. I, p. 258; B. de Sauvigny, Vol. III, pp. 953–87.

10 On Princess Lieven: H. W. V. Temperley, *The Unpublished Diary and Political Sketches of Princess Lieven* (L, 1925); H. Montgomery Hyde, *Princess Lieven* (L, 1938); P. Zamoyska, *Arch Intriguer* (L, 1957); L. B. Namier, *Vanished Supremacies* (L, 1958).

11 Temperley, *For. Pol. Canning*, pp. 344–51, and *Diary . . . Lieven*, pp. 85–100.

12 G. Canning to S. Canning, 9 January 1826, S. Lane-Poole, *Life of Stratford Canning* (L, 1888), p. 396.

13 Temperley, *For. Pol. Canning*, p. 355.

14 ibid., pp. 397–406. Canning to George IV, 22 September 1826, A. Aspinall (ed.), *Letters of George IV* (Cambridge, 1938), Vol. III, no. 1253, pp. 158–61. Professor Aspinall includes four other letters from Canning in Paris, nos 1254, 1256, 1258 and 1260.

15 Dudley to Aberdeen, 23 April 1827, cited from the Aberdeen papers by Middleton, p. 113. For Navarino and its historical setting see C. M. Woodhouse, *The Battle of Navarino* (L, 1965), and C. W. Crawley, *The Question of Greek Independence* (L, 1930), pp. 90–112.

16 Elizabeth Longford, *Wellington, Pillar of State* (L, 1972), pp. 147–51 and 156–7.

17 Crawley, pp. 150–1 and 168.

18 Nesselrode to Lieven, 29 April 1828, A. Fadeev, *Rossiya i Vostoknyi Krizis 20-X Godov. XIX Veka* (Moscow, 1948), p. 184.

19 Metternich to Emperor Francis, 9 October 1829, R. Metternich (ed.), *Mémoires, Documents et Écrits par le Prince de Metternich* (P, 1880–4), Vol. IV, pp. 602–10; Alan Palmer, *Metternich* (L, 1972), p. 243.

20 N. Shilder, *Imperator Nikolas I* (P, 1903), Vol. II, pp. 250–1; F. Martens, *Traités conclus par la Russie* (SP, 1878), Vol. IV, pp. 437–41.

21 A. Stern, 'Der grosse Plan des Herzogs von Polignac vom Jahre 1829', *Historische Vierteljahrschrift* (1900), pp. 49–77; B. de Sauvigny, Vol. III, pp. 1310–11.

22 Palmer, *Metternich*, p. 246; L. Madelin, *Talleyrand* (L, 1948), p. 282; Duc de Broglie, *Personal Recollections* (L, 1887), Vol. II, p. 193.

Chapter 5: Contest for Leadership, 1830–41

1 H. Ritter von Srbik, *Metternich, der Staatsmann und der Mensch* (Munich, 1925), Vol. I, p. 781; Alan Palmer, *Metternich* (L, 1972), p. 247; E. Molden, *Die Orientpolitik Metternichs* (Vienna, 1913), pp. 5–12.

2 J. A. Betley, *Belgium and Poland in International Relations, 1830–31* (The Hague, 1960), pp. 40–3; R. F. Leslie, *Polish Politics and the Revolution of 1830* (L, 1956), especially pp. 134–69; E. H. Kossmann, *The Low Countries* (O, 1978), pp. 151–60; W. Bruce Lincoln, *Nicholas I* (L, 1978), pp. 130–45; C. M. Woodhouse, *Capodistria* (O, 1973), pp. 488–507.

3   Wessenberg to Metternich, 13 January 1831, quoted in Sir Charles Webster, *The Foreign Policy of Palmerston* (L, 1951), Vol. I, p. 33; C. R. Middleton, *The Administration of British Foreign Policy, 1782–1846* (Durham, NC, 1977), pp. 117–18. For Palmerston's early life, see Jasper Ridley, *Lord Palmerston* (L, 1970), pp. 1–106.

4   Sir Charles Webster, *The Art and Practice of Diplomacy* (L, 1961), p. 193.

5   Lamb to Palmerston, 26 May 1832, Webster, *For. Pol. Palm.,* Vol. I, p. 57. On the Austrian Foreign Ministry in this period see the two studies by J. K. Mayr, *Geschichte der Oesterreichischen Staatskanzlei im Zeitalter des Fürsten Metternich* and *Metternichs Geheimer Briefdienst, Postlogen und Postkurse,* both published in Vienna in 1935.

6   Armand Baschet, *Histoire du Dépôt des Archives des Affaires Étrangères* (P, 1875). pp. 436–81. H. d'Ideville, *Émile Desages et sa correspondance* was published in Paris in 1876, but I have not seen a copy in English libraries. Webster printed some of Désages's letters in *For. Pol. Palm,* Vol. II, pp. 886–901.

7   L. Naud, *Histoire de la télégraphie en France* (P, 1890), pp. 54–8; J. H. Clapham, *Economic Development of France and Germany* (Cambridge, 1936), pp. 156–7.

8   Prince von Bülow, *Memoirs, 1849–1897* (L, 1932), pp. 304–5; A. Vagts, *The Military Attaché* (Princeton, NJ, 1967), p. 16; GW, Vol. XV, pp. 7–8; B. de Sauvigny, *Metternich and his Times* (L, 1962), p. 175.

9   Lincoln, pp. 151–80. On Benckendorff and Metternich, see two articles by P. S. Squires, SEER, vol. 45 (1967), no. 104, pp. 135–63, and no. 105, pp. 368–91. For Orlov's flattery of Metternich, see B. de Sauvigny, *Metternich and his Times,* p. 16.

10   Palmer, *Metternich,* pp. 247–52.

11   Webster, *For. Pol. Palm.,* Vol. I, pp. 89–103.

12   ibid., Vol. I, pp. 119–76 and 514–21; Kossmann, pp. 151–60.

13   Sir Charles Webster, 'Palmerston, Metternich and the European System', the Raleigh Lecture for 1934, appeared as a brochure and in *Proceedings of the British Academy,* Vol. XX (L, 1934); and it is reprinted in his *Art and Practice of Diplomacy,* pp. 152–80.

14   R. Bullen, *Palmerston, Guizot and the Collapse of the Entente Cordiale* (L, 1974), pp. 7–16.

15   For this paragraph see Webster, *For. Pol. Palm.,* Vol. I, pp. 278–84, and C. J. Bartlett, *Great Britain and Sea Power, 1815–1853* (O, 1963), pp. 144–7.

16   P. E. Moseley, *Russian Diplomacy and the Opening of the Eastern Question in 1838 and 1839* (Cambridge, Mass., 1934), p. 21; M. S. Anderson, *The Eastern Question* (L, 1966), pp. 81–6.

17   Palmer, *Metternich,* pp. 259–61; T. Schiemann, *Geschichte Russlands unter Kaiser Nicholas I* (Berlin, 1908–9), Vol. III, pp. 234–5.

18   Palmerston to W. Temple, 21 April 1834, H. Bulwer, *Life of Henry John Temple, Lord Palmerston* (L, 1872), Vol. II, pp. 180–1. A long extract from this letter is printed in Kenneth Bourne, *The Foreign Policy of Victorian England* (O, 1970), pp. 233–4.

19   Elizabeth Longford, *Wellington, Pillar of State* (L, 1972), pp. 306–8.

20   Middleton, p. 90; see J. H. Gleason, *The Genesis of Russophobia in Great Britain* (Cambridge, Mass., 1950), especially chs 5 and 6; A. J. P. Taylor, *The Troublemakers* (L, 1957), pp. 43–7.

21   J. A. Norris, *The First Afghan War* (Cambridge, 1967), pp. 214–16.

22   H. W. V. Temperley, *Britain and the Near East, The Crimea* (L, 1936), pp. 41–2 and 103–7; Palmer, *Metternich,* pp. 279–81.

23   Palmerston to Lamb, 28 June 1839, Webster's Raleigh Lecture, *Art and Practice of Diplomacy,* p. 173.

24   R. Metternich (ed.), *Mémoires, Documents et Écrits par le Prince de Metternich* (P, 1880–4), Vol. VI, pp. 327–30; B. de Sainte Aulaire, *Souvenirs, Vienne 1832–41* (P, 1926), pp. 256–62.

25   Ridley, *Palmerston,* pp. 208–24.

26   Temperley, *The Crimea,* p. 111; Anderson, pp. 98–9; Bulwer, Vol. II, pp. 299–303.

27   Webster, *For. Pol. Palm.,* Vol. II, pp. 644–737.

28   ibid., Vol. II, pp. 770–6.

Chapter 6: Ministers of Peace, 1841–48

1   Aberdeen to D. Lieven, 22 November 1834, *Correspondence of Lord Aberdeen and Princess Lieven,* Part I, Camden Society Third Series (L, 1938), Vol. LX, p. 21.

2 Grenville's journal, 18 March 1846, reports conversation with Clarendon: L. Strachey and R. Fulford, *Greville Memoirs* (L, 1938), Vol. V, p. 307.
3 Minute by Palmerston, cited from FO 96/19 by C. R. Middleton, *The Administration of British Foreign Policy, 1782–1846* (Durham, NC, 1977), p. 93; for 'inexperienced girl' comment, ibid., p. 92.
4 ibid., pp. 226 and 229.
5 Guizot wrote nine long and entertaining letters to Dorothea Lieven during the Eu visit. They are printed in Jacques Naville (ed.), *Lettres de François Guizot et la Princesse de Lieven* (P, 1964), Vol. III, pp. 76–108. The quotation given here is from a letter of 2 September 1843, pp. 91–2. Aberdeen's comments on meeting Guizot are in a letter from him at Haddo House to Dorothea Lieven, 16 October, *Aberdeen-Lieven Corr.*, pp. 216–17. See also E. Jones Parry, *The Spanish Marriages, 1841–1846* (L, 1936), pp. 117–21.
6 R. Bullen, *Palmerston, Guizot and the Collapse of the Entente Cordiale* (L, 1974), p. 38; A. B. Cunningham, 'Peel, Aberdeen and the Entente Cordiale', BIHR, vol. XXX (1957), pp. 189–206.
7 Jones Parry, pp. 236–7.
8 G. H. Bolsover, 'Nicholas I and the Partition of Turkey', SEER, Vol. XXVII (1948–9), pp. 115–25; M. S. Anderson, *The Eastern Question* (L, 1966), p. 111.
9 Bolsover, SEER, Vol. XXVII, pp. 128–30.
10 ibid., p. 132; C. Woodham-Smith, *Queen Victoria, Her Life and Times, 1819–1861* (L, paperback edn, 1972), pp. 316–17; three letters from Queen Victoria to King Leopold I, 4 June, 11 June, 18 June 1844, QVL, First Series, Vol. 2, pp. 12–17; *The Times*, 3 June 1844; H. W. V. Temperley, *Britain and the Near East, The Crimea* (L, 1936), p. 254.
11 Nesselrode memorandum, ibid., pp. 254–7 and 459; A. M. Zaionchkovskii, *Vostochnaya Voina, 1853–1856* (SP, 1908), Vol. I, pp. 132–9; G. B. Henderson, *Crimean War Diplomacy* (Glasgow, 1947), pp. 1–5 and 13–14; Alan Palmer, *Metternich* (L, 1972), pp. 290–1; T. Schiemann, *Geschichte Russlands unter Kaiser Nicholas I* (Berlin, 1908–9), Vol. IV, p. 377.
12 C. A. Macartney, *The Habsburg Empire, 1760–1918* (L, 1968), pp. 307–9.
13 Guizot to D. Lieven, 8 August 1846, Naville (ed.), Vol. III, p. 246.
14 Bullen, pp. 122–6; B. Connell, *Regina v. Palmerston* (L, 1962), pp. 38–42; J. Ridley, *Lord Palmerston* (L, 1970), pp. 308–14.
15 ibid., p. 316; K. Bourne, *The Foreign Policy of Victorian England* (O, 1970), pp. 62 and 274; R. Bullen, 'Guizot and the Sonderbund crisis', EHR, Vol. LXXXVI (1971), pp. 505–6.
16 A. J. P. Taylor, *The Italian Problem in European Diplomacy* (Manchester, 1934), pp. 44–5; Palmer, *Metternich*, pp. 300–1; E. L. Woodward, *Three Studies in European Conservatism* (L, 1929), pp. 178–200.
17 Taylor, *Italian Problem*, pp. 45–7.
18 Ann Imlah, *Britain and Switzerland* (L, 1961), chs 2 and 3; R. Bullen, EHR, Vol. LXXXVI, pp. 497–526.
19 ibid., pp. 523–4.
20 A. de Nesselrode, *Lettres et Papiers du Chancelier Comte de Nesselrode* (P, 1908–12), Vol. IX, p. 54.
21 A. de Tocqueville, *Souvenirs* (new edn, P, 1942), pp. 33–4.

Chapter 7: Europe in Disarray, 1848–51

1 J. A. Hübner, *Une Année de ma vie* (P, 1981), p. 12. For the Austrian Chancellor's 'political horoscope', R. Metternich (ed.), *Mémoires, Documents et Écrits par le Prince de Metternich* (P, 1880–4), Vol. VII, pp. 569–72.
2 Alan Palmer, *Metternich* (L, 1972), pp. 204–8.
3 W. Bruce Lincoln, *Nicholas I* (L, 1978), pp. 278–80.
4 E. Ashley, *Life of Henry John Temple, Viscount Palmerston* (L, 1877), Vol. I, p. 81; L. Jennings, *France and England in 1848* (O, 1973), pp. 7–8.
5 Palmerston's speech of 1 March 1848, Hansard, Third Series, Vol. XLVII, pp. 120–3. Extracts in Kenneth Bourne, *The Foreign Policy of Victorian England* (O, 1970), pp. 291–2, and J. Joll, *Britain and Europe, Pitt to Churchill* (L, 1953), pp. 109–11.

6   Jennings, pp. 10–20.
7   H. Ritter von Srbik, *Metternich, der Staatsmann und der Mensch* (Munich, 1925), Vol. II, pp. 276–7.
8   1848 revolutions in Hungary, C. A. Macartney, *The Habsburg Empire, 1760–1918* (L, 1968), pp. 389–432; and in Moldavia-Wallachia, H. W. V. Temperley, *Britain and the Near East, The Crimea* (L, 1936), pp. 258–9.
9   Palmerston to Ponsonby, 30 June 1848, quoted in J. Ridley, *Lord Palmerston* (L, 1970), p. 344.
10 A. J. P. Taylor, *The Italian Problem in European Diplomacy* (Manchester, 1934), pp. 91–3 and 137–74.
11 Nesselrode to Meyendorff, 8 May 1848, A. de Nesselrode, *Lettres et Papiers du Chancelier Comte de Nesselrode* (P, 1908–12), Vol. IX, p. 93; W. E. Mosse, *The European Powers and the German Question* (Cambridge, 1958), pp. 19–20.
12 ibid., p. 25. For Palmerston and the London Conference, see Ridley, pp. 356–7, and Bourne, pp. 67–8.
13 Macartney, pp. 428–9.
14 Nicholas I to Paskievič, 7 May 1849, Prince A. Scherbatov, *General-feld-marshal kniaz' Paskevich* (SP, 1900), Vol. VI, p. 281.
15 Palmerston's speech, 21 July 1849, Hansard, Third Series, Vol. CVII, pp. 808–10.
16 T. Schiemann, *Geschichte Russlands unter Kaiser Nikolaus I* (Berlin, 1908–9), Vol. IV, pp. 202–6; W. Heindl, *Graf Buol-Schauenstein in St Petersburg und London* (Vienna, 1970), pp. 44–52.
17 ibid., pp. 71–9.
18 Bismarck to O. Manteuffel, 26 May and 29 June 1851, GW, Vol. I, nos 4 and 9, pp. 3 and 17.
19 Le Flô (in St Petersburg) to Bastide, 11 November 1848, cited from the French Foreign Ministry archives by Jennings, p. 221.
20 J. Ridley, *Napoleon III and Eugénie* (L, 1978), pp. 248–53.
21 Napoleon III to Vieillard, 4 June 1849, cited by Ridley, ibid., p. 257.
22 Ridley, *Palmerston*, pp. 381–7. There is a refreshingly different insight into the Don Pacifico affair in L. M. Case, *Edouard Thouvenel et la aiplomatie du Second Empire* (P, 1976), pp. 34–51. Thouvenel was French Minister in Athens at the time.
23 Ridley, *Nap. and Eugénie*, pp. 275–6.
24 Bourne, pp. 301–9, prints extensive extracts from the Don Pacifico debate, reported in Hansard, Third Series, Vol. CXII, pp. 440–590, *passim*.
25 Lord John Russell to Queen Victoria, 27 June 1850, QVL, First Series, Vol. II, p. 252; Queen Victoria to King Leopold, 2 July 1850, ibid., p. 253.

Chapter 8: The Primacy of France, 1852–56

1   P. W. Schroeder, *Austria, Great Britain and the Crimean War* (Ithaca, NY, 1972), pp. 1–3; on Schwarzenberg the biographies by Adolf Schwarzenberg (NY, 1946) and by Rudolf Kiszling (Graz, 1956). For his last days, A. F. Berger, *Felix Fürst zu Schwarzenberg* (Leipzig, 1857), pp. 480–90. Karl von Czoernig, *Oesterreichs Neugesaltung, 1848–58* (Stuttgart, 1858) anatomises the Habsburg monarchy's decade of recovery and includes much statistical information.
2   Carl J. Burckhardt, *Briefe des Staatskanzlers Fürsten Metternich-Winneburg an Grafen Buol-Schauenstein, 1852–59* (Munich and Berlin, 1934), pp. 1–49.
3   R. Metternich (ed.), *Mémoires, Documents et Écrits par le Prince de Metternich* (P, 1880–4), Vol. VIII, pp. 589–90.
4   H. W. V. Temperley, *Britain and the Near East, The Crimea* (L, 1936), pp. 292–4; quotation from Rose to Malmesbury, FO 78/895/170, 28 December 1852, cited ibid., p. 295.
5   Nesselrode memorandum, 20 December 1852, A. M. Zaionchkovskii, *Vostochnaya Voina, 1853–1856* (SP, 1908), Vol. I, pp. 354–7.
6   G. B. H. Henderson 'The Seymour Conversations 1853' originally appeared in *History* (vol. L, October 1933) but was reprinted in his posthumous *Crimean War Diplomacy* (Glasgow, 1947), pp. 1–14. On the Grand Duchess, see W. Bruce Lincoln, 'The circle of Grand Duchess Elena Pavlovna', SEER, vol. 48, no. 112 (1970), pp. 373–87; Temperley, *The Crimea*, pp. 270–9.

7   Tsar's illness, S. W. Jackman, *Romanov Relations* (L, 1969), p. 336. 'Between gentle-men', Temperley, *The Crimea*, p. 277.
8   The best source on the Menschikov mission remains the appendixes to Volume I of Zaionchkovski, with many documents printed in the original French. See also J. K. Herkless, 'Stratford, the Cabinet and the outbreak of the Crimean War', HJ, vol. XVIII, no. 3 (1975), especially pp. 503–9.
9   Nicholas I to Anna, Queen-Mother of the Netherlands, 1 June 1853, Jackman, p. 338.
10 On Austrian policy, Schroeder, *Crimean War*, pp. 23–40; Herkless, HJ, vol. XVIII, no. 3, p. 509.
11 Vienna Note, Schroeder, *Crimean War*, pp. 41–66; Anderson, *Eastern Question*, pp. 126–7. For Stratford's role, Herkless, HJ, vol. XVIII, no. 3, pp. 510–21.
12 Schroeder, *Crimean War*, pp. 75–8.
13 Russell to Clarendon, 4–5 October 1853, cited ibid., p. 81.
14 ibid., pp. 256–63; Henderson, p. 41; Temperley, *The Crimea*, pp. 356–65.
15 J. Ridley, *Napoleon III and Eugénie* (L, 1978), pp. 359–65; Temperley, *The Crimea*, pp. 366–84.
16 See, in particular, Herkless's article, HJ, vol. XVIII, no. 3, pp. 497–8 and 519–23; and Brison D. Gooch, 'A century of historiography on the origins of the Crimean War', AHR, vol. 62 (1956), pp. 33–59.
17 Speech of Napoleon, 2 March 1856, *Oeuvres de Napoléon III* (Paris, 1858), Vol. III, p. 385.
18 Schroeder, *Crimean War*, pp. 193–6, 218–29, 232–6, 242–4, 303–7.
19 Alexander II's letter is printed in J. Redlich, *Emperor Francis Joseph* (L, 1929), p. 159. An extract is in Edward Crankshaw's *The Fall of the House of Habsburg* (L, 1963), p. 128. Chapter 8 of Crankshaw's book provides a clear account of Austrian policy between 1853 and 1856.
20 Clarendon to Westmoreland, 24 April 1855, cited by Schroeder, *Crimean War*, p. 273.
21 Ridley, *Nap. and Eugénie*, pp. 383–5.
22 Schroeder, *Crimean War*, pp. 311–46; W. E. Mosse, *The Rise and Fall of the Crimean System* (L, 1963), pp. 15–31.
23 A. Decaux, *La Castiglione* (P, 1953), pp. 78–107; Ridley, *Nap. and Eugénie*, pp. 386–7; K. Bourne, *The Foreign Policy of Victorian England* (O, 1970), pp. 362–7; A. J. Whyte, *Political Life and Letters of Cavour* (O, 1930), p. 206.
24 Mosse, *Rise and Fall*, p. 2.
25 The most detailed study of Napoleon III's plans for Poland is in an article (in German) by Henderson included in his *Crimean War Diplomacy*, pp. 15–32. On the Congress of Paris in general see H. W. V. Temperley, 'The Treaty of Paris of 1856 and its execution', JMH, vol. 4, nos 3 and 4 (1932), especially pp. 387–90; and A. J. P. Taylor, *The Struggle for Mastery in Europe* (O, 1954), pp. 83–95.
26 Whyte, pp. 213–20.

Chapter 9: Subverting the System, 1857–61

1   J. Morley, *Life of Gladstone* (L, 1903), Vol. I, pp. 550–1; W. E. Mosse, *The Rise and Fall of the Crimean System* (L, 1963), pp. 2–5; F. H. Hinsley, *Power and the Pursuit of Peace* (Cambridge, 1967), pp. 233–4.
2   A. J. P. Taylor, 'John Bright and the Crimean War', *Bulletin of the John Rylands Library* (Manchester, 1954), vol. 36, no. 2, pp. 501–22; A. J. P. Taylor, *The Troublemakers* (L, 1957), pp. 62–6.
3   Gorchakov's circular of 3 September is printed in S. S. Tatischev, *Imperator Aleksandr II* (SP, 1903), Vol. I, pp. 229–30. For the change of Foreign Ministers see W. E. Mosse, *The European Powers and the German Question* (Cambridge, 1958), pp. 70–6.
4   Mosse, *Rise and Fall*, pp. 107–11 and 122–4; Wodehouse (later first Lord Kimberley) to Malmesbury, 27 March 1858, FO 65/517/29, cited ibid., p. 123.
5   Bismarck's memorandum of March 1858, GW, Vol. II, no. 343, pp. 302–22. On Schleinitz, see Otto Pflanze, *Bismarck and the Development of Germany* (Princeton, NJ, 1963), pp. 130–3, and Mosse, *European Powers*, pp. 76–7.
6   Mosse, *Rise and Fall*, pp. 105–26.
7   The Orsini plot and its consequences are considered by J. Ridley, *Napoleon III and*

Eugénie (L, 1978), pp. 422–32; A. Hübner, *Neuf ans de souvenirs d'un ambassadeur d'Autriche à Paris* (P, 1904), Vol. II, pp. 87–93.

8   K. Bourne, *The Foreign Policy of Victorian England* (O, 1970), p. 99, and 336–40; D. Beales, *England and Italy, 1859–60* (L, 1961), pp. 39–40.

9   Ridley, *Nap. and Eugénie*, pp. 435–8; A. J. P. Taylor, *The Struggle for Mastery in Europe* (O, 1954), pp. 103–4.

10   B. H. Sumner, 'The secret Franco-Russian treaty of March 1859', EHR, vol. XLVIII (1933), pp. 65–83; Mosse, *European Powers*, pp. 82–4.

11   Ridley, *Nap. and Eugénie*, pp. 443–4; Alan Palmer, *Metternich* (L, 1972), pp. 61 and 337; SIRIO, vol. 89, p. 644.

12   E. Crankshaw, *The Rise and Fall of the Crimean System* (L, 1963), pp. 146 and 420–1.

13   E. C. Corti, *Mensch und Herrscher* (Graz, 1952), pp. 230–8; Ridley, *Nap. and Eugénie*, pp. 454–5.

14   Bourne, p. 100.

15   P. Guedalla, *Palmerston* (L, 1937 edn), p. 355.

16   A. J. Whyte, *Political Life and Letters of Cavour* (O, 1930), pp. 346–9; Beales, pp. 95–110.

17   Nigra to Cavour, 17 June 1860, Whyte, p. 466. There is an excellent study of Thouvenel by L. M. Case, *Edouard Thouvenel et la diplomatie du Second Empire* (P, 1976): see especially for this paragraph pp. 150–74.

18   The classic account remains G. M. Trevelyan's *Garibaldi and the Thousand* (L, 1909), but see also D. Mack Smith, *Cavour and Garibaldi 1860* (Cambridge, 1954), especially pp. 150–74. See also G. P. Gooch (ed.), *The Later Correspondence of Lord John Russell* (L, 1930), Vol. II, p. 234.

19   Queen Victoria to Palmerston, 25 October 1861, QVL, First Series, Vol. III, p. 462. Captain Macdonald's arrest was first raised in the Commons by Lord Robert Cecil (the future Prime Minister, Salisbury) on 26 April 1861, Hansard, Third Series, Vol. CLXII, pp. 1175–83. See, too, pp. 1206–7 and Vol. CLXIII, p. 29.

20   A. J. P. Taylor, *The Struggle for Mastery in Europe* (O, 1954), p. 120; Case, pp. 209–12; Ridley, *Nap. and Eugénie*, pp. 463–4.

21   ibid., p. 464. The fate of the Algiers cable provided *The Times* with a running story in the second half of September 1860.

22   Thouvenel's policy, Case, pp. 228–30. Taylor, *Struggle for Mastery*, p. 123, gives the impression that 'Thouvenel evaded the invitation'. Case's detailed study does not mention an 'invitation'. Mosse (*European Powers*, p. 91) says that Gorchakov 'expressed a wish that Thouvenel should join the discussions'.

23   Russell to Hudson, 27 October 1860, printed in Bourne, pp. 359–61.

24   Bismarck to Schleinitz, 10 December 1860, GW, Vol. III, no. 127, pp. 147–8.

Chapter 10: Prussia Triumphant, 1862–70

1   W. E. Mosse, *The European Powers and the German Question* (Cambridge, 1958), p. 105. For William I's coronation: Crown Princess to Queen Victoria, 19 October 1861, F. Ponsonby, *Letters of the Empress Frederick* (L, 1928), pp. 31–3; T. Aronson, *The Kaisers* (L, 1971), pp. 52–3.

2   Lothar Gall, *Bismarck, der Weisse Revolutionar* (Frankfurt, 1980), pp. 240–7; Alan Palmer, *Bismarck* (L, 1976), pp. 68–78.

3   See L. M. Case and W. F. Spencer, *The United States and France* (Philadelphia, Pa, 1970), and L. A. C. Schefer, *La Grande Pensée de Napoléon III* (P, 1939).

4   For the following paragraph: D. Gillard, *The Struggle for Asia, 1828–1914* (L, 1977), pp. 110–30; J. F. Cady, *The Roots of French Imperialism in Eastern Asia* (Ithaca, NY, 1954); M. S. Anderson, *The Eastern Question* (L, 1966), pp. 150–5; J. Campbell and P. Sherrard, *Modern Greece* (L, 1968), pp. 94–5.

5   L. M. Case, *Edouard Thouvenel et la diplomatie du Second Empire* (P, 1976), pp. 312–28.

6   Karolyi to Rechberg, 5 December 1862, APP, Vol. III, no. 60, p. 100; Gall, p. 267; F. Stern, *Gold and Iron* (L, 1977), p. 29.

7   *The Times*, 21 February 1862, cited by K. S. Pasieka in his article, 'The British Press and the Polish insurrection of 1863', SEER, vol. 42 (1963–4), pp. 17–18.

8   R. H. Lord, 'Bismarck and Russia in 1863', AHR, vol. 29 (1923–4), pp. 34–42.

9   Gall, pp. 286–92; Palmer, *Bismarck*, pp. 85–7.
10 J. Ridley, *Napoleon and Eugénie* (L, 1978), pp. 484–5.
11 ibid., pp. 485–6; Mosse, *European Powers*, pp. 138–43.
12 Fleury to Napoleon III, 24 December 1863, ODG, Vol. I, p. 3.
13 M. Busch, *Bismarck, Some Secret Pages of his History* (L, 1898), Vol. II, p. 337. The best study of the problem of the Duchies remains L. D. Steefel, *The Schleswig-Holstein Question* (Cambridge, Mass., 1932). But the evidence is given a fresh assessment in great detail by Gall, pp. 293–313.
14 ibid., p. 315; H. Ritter von Srbik, 'Die Schönbrunner Konferenzen von August 1864', *Historische Zeitschrift* (Berlin and Munich, 1935–6), pp. 43–88.
15 H. Friedjung, *The Struggle for Supremacy in Germany, 1859–66* (L, 1935), pp. 64–8.
16 Palmer, *Bismarck*, pp. 102–5.
17 Karolyi to Mensdorff, 21 March 1866, H. Srbik (ed.), *Quellen zur Deutschen Politik Oesterreichs, 1859–66* (Vienna, 1938), Vol. V(i), no. 2418, pp. 336–7; Gall, p. 359.
18 Derby's speech of 9 July 1866 printed from Hansard in K. Bourne, *The Foreign Policy of Victorian England* (O, 1970), p. 388; see, also, Bourne's editorial comments, ibid., pp. 111–13.
19 Palmer, *Bismarck*, p. 100.
20 For Biarritz and its aftermath: Bismarck, GW, Vol. V, nos 188 and 190, pp. 306–11; Paul Bernstein, 'Les entrevues de Biarritz et de Saint-Cloud', *Revue d'Histoire Diplomatique*, vol. 78 (P, 1964), pp. 330–9.
21 Lothar Gall (pp. 340–65) covers the immediate origins of the war in great detail, as he regards the year 1866, rather than 1870, as the climax of Bismarck's career. See, also, Palmer, *Bismarck*, pp. 108–18. C. W. Clark, *Franz Joseph and Bismarck* (Cambridge, Mass., 1934), has much valuable material, especially on the Gablenz plan, pp. 568–70.
22 The best account of the campaign in English is in Gordon A. Craig, *The Battle of Koniggratz* (L, 1965), pp. 99–175. For the peace settlement see Craig's *Germany, 1866–1945* (O, 1978), pp. 3–10; Palmer, *Bismarck*, pp. 118–24; and Gall, pp. 365–81.
23 Mosse, *European Powers*, pp. 243–4.
24 Bismarck to Goltz (Paris), 5 and 8 August 1866, GW, Vol. VI, no. 530, p. 101, and no. 538, pp. 106–10.
25 On Rouher, see the biography by R. Schnerb, *Rouher et le Second Empire* (P, 1946), especially for this episode, pp. 190–96.
26 O. Pflanze, *Bismarck and the Development of Germany* (Princeton, NJ, 1963), pp. 380–1; M. R. D. Foot, 'Great Britain and Luxembourg, 1867', EHR, vol. 67 (1952), pp. 352–79.
27 H. Potthoff, *Die Deutsche Politik Beusts* (Bonn, 1968), p. 46. On Beust's background and appointment, see C. A. Macartney, *The Habsburg Empire, 1760–1918* (L, 1968), p. 549, and, in particular, F. R. Bridge, *From Sadowa to Sarajevo* (L, 1972) pp. 33–7.
28 E. C. Corti, *Mensch und Herrscher*, p. 386.
29 Bridge, *From Sadowa to Saravejo*, pp. 37 and 391.
30 ibid., pp. 43–4; M. Howard, *The Franco-Prussian War* (L, 1960), pp. 46–7.
31 For differing views of these events, see: A. J. P. Taylor, *Bismarck, the Man and the Statesman* (L, 1955), pp. 116–22; W. L. Langer, 'Bismarck as a dramatist', in A. O. Sarkissian (ed.), *Studies in Diplomatic History* (L, 1961), pp. 202–8; Howard, ch. 2; Palmer, *Bismarck*, pp. 138–46; Lynn Case, *French Opinion on War and Diplomacy in the Second Empire* (Philadelphia, 1954), pp. 244–51; L. D. Steefel, *Bismarck, the Hohenzollern Candidacy and the Origins of the Franco-German War of 1870* (Cambridge, Mass., 1962); G. Bonnin, *Bismarck and the Hohenzollern Candidature for the Throne of Spain* (L, 1957); and, most recently, Gall, pp. 421–35.
32 Gorchakov to Alexander II, 13 July 1870, C. W. Clark, 'Bismarck, Russia and the War of 1870', JMH, vol. 14, no. 2 (1942), pp. 201–2.
33 Howard, pp. 56–7; Case, *French Opinion*, pp. 254–65; Steefel, pp. 208–9 and 216.
34 A. R. Allinson (ed.), *War Diary of the Emperor Frederick III, 1870–71* (L, 1927), pp. 265–74; Bismarck, GW, Vol. XV, pp. 327–9, and GW, Vol. XIV(ii), p. 810.

Chapter 11: The Three Emperors, 1871–79

1   Buchanan to Granville, 16 November 1870, FO 65/805/466, W. E. Mosse, *The European Powers and the German Question* (Cambridge, 1958), pp. 342–3.

2   R. Millman, *British Policy and the Coming of the Franco-Prussian War* (O, 1965), pp. 120–4.

3   Cited from the records of the ministerial conference by F. R. Bridge, *From Sadowa to Sarajevo* (L, 1972), p. 51.

4   This point is emphasised by Professor Mosse both in his *European Powers*, pp. 333–58, and his *The Rise and Fall of the Crimean System* (L, 1963), pp. 162–83.

5   ibid., p. 178, citing Rumbold to Granville, 19 March 1871, FO 65/820/28.

6   W. R. Fryer, 'The Republic and the Iron Chancellor; the Pattern of Franco-German Relations, 1871–1890', TRHS, Series 5, Vol. 29 (1979), pp. 168–73. For Bismarck's recognition of the inevitability of French resentment, see Lothar Gall, *Bismarck, der Weisse Revolutionar* (Frankfurt, 1980), pp. 436–40, 454 and 503.

7   Bismarck to Arnim, 20 December 1872, GP, Vol. I, no. 95, pp. 157–62. On the Arnim affair, G. O. Kent, *Arnim and Bismarck* (O, 1968), pp. 59–185; and N. Rich, 'Holstein and the Arnim Affair', JMH, Vol. 28, no. 1 (1956), pp. 35–54.

8   Gordon A. Craig, *Politics of the Prussian Army* (O, 1955), pp. 204–16 and 266–8.

9   F. Stern, *Gold and Iron* (L, 1977), pp. 304–50.

10 See, for example, the remarkable analysis of the South Slav problem sent from Belgrade by Engelhardt (a consul, not an ambassador!), 4 February 1872, DDF, Series I, Vol. I, pp. 127–30; the reports of Courcel from London on the change from Liberal to Unionist rule in 1895, DDF, Series I, Vol. XII, nos 69, 88, 144, 306; the similar assessments by Paul Cambon when Balfour succeeded Salisbury, DDF, Series II, Vol. II, nos 369 and 373; and many reports by Jules Cambon from Berlin in Series III.

11 Bridge, *From Sadowa to Sarajevo*, pp. 22–9 and 108; and L. Cecil, *The German Diplomatic Service 1871–1914* (Princeton, NJ, 1976), p. 69.

12 B. H. Sumner, *Russia and the Balkans, 1870–80* (O, 1937), pp. 28–32.

13 Sir Horace Rumbold, *Recollections of a Diplomatist* (L, 1901), Vol. I, p. 109. There is a brief and entertaining historical survey of the 'physical structure of the Foreign Office' in Zara Steiner, *The Foreign Office and Foreign Policy, 1898–1914* (Cambridge, 1969), pp. 9–10.

14 ibid., pp. 6–9 and 21–2; W. Roger Louis, 'Sir Percy Anderson's Grand African Strategy, 1883–1896', EHR, Vol. LXXXI (1966), pp. 292–314.

15 R. Blake, *Disraeli* (L, 1966), pp. 590–1: Sumner, p. 33.

16 For White, see Colin L. Smith, *The Embassy of Sir William White at Constantinople* (O, 1957).

17 Mountague Bernard, *Four Lectures on Subjects Connected with Diplomacy* (L, 1868), pp. 160–1.

18 W. F. Monypenny and G. E. Buckle, *The Life of Benjamin Disraeli, Earl of Beaconsfield* (L, 1910–20), Vol. VI, p. 316. Lytton to Granville, 23 November 1871, FO 7/791/76, a beautifully written character sketch of some 600 words, partly quoted by A. J. May, *The Hapsburg Monarchy, 1867–1914* (Cambridge, Mass., 1965), pp. 112–13. See also E. Wertheimer, *Andrassy* (Stuttgart, 1911), Vol. 2, especially pp. 242–3.

19 Bridge, *From Sadowa to Sarajevo*, pp. 60–3; K. Bourne, *The Foreign Policy of Victorian England* (O, 1970), p. 124.

20 Sumner, p. 89; Alan Palmer, *Bismarck* (L, 1976), p. 173.

21 George F. Kennan, *The Decline of Bismarck's European Order, Franco-Russian Relations 1875–1890* (Princeton, NJ, 1979), pp. 14–15.

22 See the biography of Gontaut-Biron by the Duc de Broglie, *An Ambassador of the Vanquished* (L, 1896), p. 9. On the War in Sight crisis: Gontaut-Biron to Decazes, 21 April 1875, DDF, Series I, Vol. I, no. 395; Fryer's article, TRHS, Series 5, Vol. 29 (1979), pp. 73–7; W. Taffs, *Ambassador to Bismarck, Lord Odo Russell* (L, 1938), pp. 85–6; Kennan, pp. 11–23; and the contribution by Andreas Hillgrüber to E. Schulin, *Gedenkschrift Martin Göhring* (Wiesbaden, 1968), pp. 239–53.

23 Bruce Waller, *Bismarck at the Crossroads* (L, 1974), pp. 69–71.

24 Sumner, pp. 138–9. See, for later material, W. N. Medlicott, 'The Near Eastern Crisis of 1875–78 reconsidered', *Middle Eastern Studies* (L, 1971), Vol. VII, pp. 105–9.

25 The most detailed treatment of the opening phase of the crisis is D. Harris, *Diplomatic History of the Balkan Crisis of 1875–78, the First Year* (Stanford, Calif., 1936), but on the outbreak of the revolts in 1875 see R. Millman, *Britain and the Eastern Question, 1875–1878* (O, 1979), pp. 13–26.

26 Sumner, p. 187; R. W. Seton-Watson, *Disraeli, Gladstone and the Eastern Question* (L, 1935), pp. 51–101, needs to be supplemented both by Millman's book and by

R. T. Shannon, *Gladstone and the Bulgarian Agitation* (Hassocks, 1975), an interesting study of the part played by the campaign in restoring Gladstone's political primacy.

27 Odo Russell to Derby, 29 November 1875, Taffs, pp. 112–15.

28 Andrassy to Francis Joseph, 27 August 1875, cited from the Vienna archives by Bridge, p. 394.

29 Sumner, pp. 142–5, 151–6, 162, 164 and 235–51. Text of Alexander II's Moscow speech, 11 November 1876, ibid., p. 227.

30 Seton-Watson, chs 7 and 8.

31 Bismarck to Bülow, 14 August 1876, GP, Vol. II, no. 228, pp. 31–2. For Bismarck's patronage of Waddington, see DDF, Series I, Vol. II, p. 279.

32 I have based the following paragraph mainly on Sumner and on W. N. Medlicott, *The Congress of Berlin and After* (L, 1938), supplemented by M. S. Anderson, *The Eastern Question* (L, 1966), pp. 203–18.

33 Layard to Derby, 13 March 1878, FO 195/1176/343. For criticisms of Layard in general, see Seton-Watson, pp. 203–13 and 404–8.

34 Bridge, *From Sadowa to Sarajevo*, p. 89; Sumner, pp. 444–56.

35 ibid., p. 501.

36 W. N. Medlicott, 'Bismarck and Beaconsfield', in A. O. Sarkissian (ed.), *Studies in Diplomatic History* (L, 1961), p. 250.

37 Sumner, pp. 522–3.

38 It is interesting to compare: Seton-Watson, pp. 460–89; Medlicott, *Congress of Berlin*, pp. 126–36; and A. J. P. Taylor, *The Struggle for Mastery in Europe* (O, 1954), pp. 253–4.

Chapter 12: Checks, Balances and Diversions, 1879–89

1 Beaconsfield to Queen Victoria, 3 July 1878, cited from Monypenny and Buckle by F. Stern, *Gold and Iron* (L, 1977), pp. 378 and 478. See, in addition to Stern's detailed study, the article by H. Böhme, 'Big business pressure groups and Bismarck's turn to Protection', HJ, Vol. X (1967), pp. 218–36.

2 B. Waller, *Bismarck at the Crossroads* (L, 1974), pp. 75–83.

3 C. Jelavich, *Tsarist Russia and Balkan Nationalism* (Westport, Conn., 1978), pp. 16–17.

4 Stern, pp. 328–9.

5 See on Bismarck and Gladstone, Paul Kennedy, *The Rise of the Anglo-German Antagonism* (L, 1980), pp. 157–66; W. N. Medlicott, *Bismarck, Gladstone and the Concert of Europe* (L, 1956), pp. 123–4, 126, 129–30; W. Windelband, *Bismarck und die Europäischen Grossmächte, 1879–85* (Essen, 1942), pp. 139–40. On Morocco and the Franco-German rapprochement see P. Guillen, *L'Allemagne et le Maroc de 1870 à 1905* (P, 1967), pp. 97–114.

6 Memorandum by William I, 9 September 1879, GP, Vol. III, no. 465, pp. 62–4.

7 J. Y. Simpson, *Saburov Memoirs* (Cambridge, 1929), pp. 70–92; W. N. Medlicott, *The Congress of Berlin and After* (L, 1938), pp. 390–2; and see his 'Bismarck and the Three Emperors' Alliance', TRHS, Fourth Series, Vol. 27 (1945), pp. 66–70.

8 Bismarck to William I, 15 June 1881, GP, Vol. III, no. 531, pp. 173–6.

9 Stern, p. 441.

10 Kennedy, *Antagonism*, pp. 167–83; A. J. P. Taylor, *Germany's First Bid for Colonies, 1884–5* (L, 1938); and see three articles in *Past and Present* (Oxford): Hartmut Pogge von Strandmann, 'The domestic origins of Germany's colonial expansion under Bismarck', no. 42 (1969), pp. 140–59; Hans-Ulrich Wehler, 'Bismarck's imperialism, 1862–90', no. 48 (1970), pp. 119–55; Paul Kennedy, 'German colonial expansion; Has the "manipulated Social Imperialism" been ante-dated?', no. 54 (1972), pp. 134–41.

11 W. L. Langer, 'The European Powers and the French occupation of Tunis', AHR, vol. 31 (1928), pp. 58–73; L. Albertini, *The Origins of the War of 1914* (O, 1952), Vol I, pp. 28–30. These earlier studies may be supplemented by L. Ganiage, *Les Origines du protectorat français en Tunisie, 1880–81* (P, 1959), and by A. Marsden, *British Diplomacy and Tunis, 1875–1902* (NY, 1971), especially pp. 50–66.

12 C. J. Lowe and F. Marzari, *Italian Foreign Policy, 1870–1940* (L, 1975), pp. 21–7; F. R. Bridge, *From Sadowa to Sarajevo* (L, 1972), pp. 130–3, and text of the Triple Alliance treaty, ibid., pp. 406–8.

13 For this paragraph: K. Bourne, *The Foreign Policy of Victorian England* (O, 1970), pp. 139

and 422; G. N. Sanderson, *England, Europe and the Upper Nile* (Edinburgh, 1965), pp. 3–25; J. Gallagher and R. Robinson, *Africa and the Victorians* (O, 1961), pp. 89–121; J. Ganiage, *L'Expansion coloniale de la France sous la 3ᵉ République* (P, 1968), pp. 94–101.

14   Kennedy, *Antagonism*, pp. 180–1.
15   Alan Palmer, *Bismarck* (L, 1976), pp. 227–8.
16   S. E. Crowe, *The Berlin West African Conference* (NY, 1942).
17   Fall of Ferry: Ganiage, *L'expansion coloniale*, pp. 120–39; David Robin Watson, *Georges Clemenceau* (L, 1974), pp. 107–9. Kalnoky's comment: Bridge, p. 151.
18   G. A. Craig, *Germany, 1866–1945* (O, 1978), pp. 116–170.
19   D. Gillard, *The Struggle for Asia, 1828–1914* (L, 1977), pp. 146–7.
20   Bourne, pp. 145 and 423–5.
21   Jelavich, pp. 215–43.
22   Bismarck's speech of 11 January 1887, GW, Vol. XIII, pp. 212–13. See also Bridge, *From Sadowa to Sarajevo*, pp. 163–7.
23   Salisbury to Queen Victoria, 24 January 1887, QVL, Third Series, Vol. I, pp. 261–3; C. J. Lowe, *Salisbury and the Mediterranean, 1886–1896* (L, 1965), pp. 12–25.
24   N. Rich, *Friedrich von Holstein* (Cambridge, 1965), Vol. I, pp. 210–11. For a recent reassessment of the Reinsurance Treaty, Lothar Gall, *Bismarck der Weisse Revolutionar* (Frankfurt, 1980), pp. 633–5.
25   Stephen Constant, *Foxy Ferdinand* (L, 1979), pp. 91–129.
26   G. A. Craig, *Politics of the Prussian Army* (O, 1955), pp. 268–70.
27   A. von Waldersee, *Denkwurdigkeiten* (Berlin and Stuttgart, 1922–3), Vol. I, p. 405; Alan Palmer, *The Kaiser* (L, 1978), pp. 34 and 39.
28   Alan Palmer, *Bismarck* (L, 1976), pp. 249–50.
29   On Bismarck's fall: Rich, *Holstein*, Vol. I, pp. 250–68; Gall, pp. 695–708; Palmer, *The Kaiser*, pp. 43–9; J. C. G. Röhl (ed.), *Philipp Eulenburgs Politische Korrespondenz* (Boppard, 1976), Vol. I, pp. 393–498.

Chapter 13: World Policies, 1890–99

1   The basic study of the two themes of imperialism and navalism remains W. L. Langer, *The Diplomacy of Imperialism* (rev. edn, NY 1951), especially pp. 67–100 and 415–44. There is much dispute over the nature and the starting date of the imperialist phenomenon in the nineteenth century; and Langer must be supplemented by: R. Robinson and J. A. Gallagher, *Africa and the Victorians* (L, 1961); H.-U. Wehler, *Bismarck und der Imperialismus* (Cologne, 1969); D. K. Fieldhouse, *Economics and Empire, 1830–1914* (L, 1973); and Paul Kennedy, *The Rise of the Anglo-German Antagonism* (L, 1980), ch. 10, with a valuable guide to further reading on p. 498. For 'navalism' A. J. Marder's great work, *British Naval Policy 1880–1905* (L, 1940) may be supplemented by P. Kennedy (ed.), *War Plans of the Great Powers 1880–1914* (L, 1979), pp. 171–98, and Holger Herwig, *Luxury Fleet: The Imperial German Navy, 1888–1918* (L, 1980), especially pp. 17–110, with a comprehensive bibliography.
2   The best study of Caprivi is J. Alden Nichols, *Germany after Bismarck, the Caprivi Era* (Cambridge, Mass., 1958). For the Africa comment, see L. Cecil, *The German Diplomatic Service* (Princeton, NJ, 1976), p. 259.
3   In addition to the two-volume life of Holstein by Norman Rich, *Friedrich von Holstein* (Cambridge, 1965), his memoirs, diaries and correspondence have been published by N. Rich and M. H. Fisher, *The Holstein Papers* (Cambridge, 1955–63, 4 vols). See also the stimulating review article on Holstein by J. C. G. Röhl, HJ, vol. 9, no. 3 (1966), pp. 379–88.
4   The Austro-Hungarian ambassador to Kalnoky, 22 March 1893, cited by Cecil, p. 263.
5   Kennedy, *Antagonism*, pp. 214–15.
6   Diary entry for 25 February 1892, V. N. Lamsdorff, *Dnevnik 1891–2* (Moscow, 1934), p. 299.
7   Holstein to Eulenburg, 11 November 1894, Rich, *Holstein*, Vol. II, p. 486. On this period in general, J. C. G. Röhl, *Germany without Bismarck* (L, 1967), pp. 118–240.
8   Rich, *Holstein*, Vol. II, pp. 484–8.
9   On Goluchowski, F. R. Bridge, *From Sadowa to Sarajevo* (L, 1972), pp. 211–12: Salisbury and the Chalet Cecil, Kenneth Rose, *The Later Cecils* (L, 1975), pp. 42–3.

10   J. A. S. Grenville, *Lord Salisbury and Foreign Policy* (L, 1964), especially chs 2 and 3.

11   Salisbury to Currie, 10 July 1895, FO 195/1862/109.

12   Lobanov to Nicholas II, 6 April 1895, A. Popov, 'First steps of Russian imperialism in the Far East' (in Russian), KA, vol. LII (1932), p. 74.

13   On Salisbury and Goluchowski, J. A. S. Grenville, 'Goluchowski, Salisbury and the Mediterranean agreements 1895–97', SEER, vol. XXXVI (1958), pp. 363–9. On Salisbury and Courcel, Grenville, pp. 107–13, and J. D. Hargreaves, '*Entente Manqué*, Anglo-French relations 1895–1896', *Cambridge Historical Journal*, vol. XI (1953), pp. 65–92.

14   G. Ebel (ed.), *Botschafter Paul Graf von Hatzfeldt Nachgelassene Papiere, 1883–1901* (Boppard, 1976), Vol. II, pp. 1048–51; Grenville, pp. 37–9; QVL, Third Series, Vol. II, pp. 544–8; Alan Palmer, *The Kaiser* (L, 1978), pp. 71–2.

15   Marschall's journal, 25 December 1895, cited Röhl, p. 161.

16   Rich, *Holstein*, Vol. II, pp. 466–8; Palmer, *The Kaiser*, pp. 76–8; Kennedy, *Antagonism*, pp. 220–1 and 407–8.

17   Lascelles to Salisbury, 4 March 1896, FO 64/1376/59; cf. Grenville, p. 106.

18   O'Conor to Salisbury, 7 September 1896, FO 65/1515/194.

19   Bridge, pp. 223–4; Montebello (French ambassador in Russia) to Hanotaux, 31 August 1896, DDF, Series I, Vol. 12, no. 449, pp. 738–40.

20   Grenville, pp. 78–80; Hanotaux memorandum after conversation with Nicholas II, 12 October 1896, DDF, Series I, Vol. 12, no. 472, pp. 782–3.

21   The Nelidov plan was first given detailed treatment by Langer, pp. 330–1 and 337–40, based principally upon the documents edited by V. Khvostov in KA, vol. I (1922), pp. 152–61, and on Khvostov's article in KA, vol. XLVII (1931), pp. 50–70. But an article by E. J. Dillon in the periodical *National Review* for February 1909 (pp. 908–18) is surprisingly well informed.

22   Rumours of Nelidov plan: Currie to Salisbury, 11 January 1897, FO 78/4813/7; Mackie to Salisbury, 5 February 1897, FO 65/1540/10. The Austrian approach of 20 January 1897, BD, Vol. IX, Appendix 2; and see two articles by E. Walters, 'Austro-Russian relations under Goluchowski, 1895–1906', SEER, vol. XXXl (1952–3), pp. 212–32 and 503–27. On Salisbury's planned naval demonstration see: Salisbury to O'Conor, 15 May 1897, FO 65/1535/244, and O'Conor to Salisbury, 17 May 1897, FO 65/1536/39 and FO 65/1532/112.

23   'Oriental mission of his country', Scott to Salisbury, 14 January 1897, FO 22/549/4. A series of dispatches from O'Conor to the Foreign Office emphasising the importance of the China Question and sent in April–May 1897 are filed in FO 65/1514.

24   O'Conor to Salisbury, 31 August 1897, FO 65/1533/219.

25   The fullest account of the Russian reaction is in B. Romanov, *Rossiia v Manchkhurii* (Leningrad, 1928), pp. 186–8. A translation of Romanov's book was published in Madison, Wisconsin, in 1952 but the transliteration is odd at times and the method of indexing exasperating. On the other hand, the summary of Romanov in English by J. J. Grapanovich in *The Chinese Social and Political Science Review* (Peking, 1934) is good and clear.

26   *The Times*, 4 and 14 February 1898; *The Nineteenth Century*, January 1898, pp. 164 ff. and 181 ff.

27   N. Pelcovits, *Old China Hands and the Foreign Office* (NY, 1948), pp. 211–12; Bertie memorandum, 29 December 1897, FO 17/1330.

28   A. W. Palmer, 'Lord Salisbury's approach to Russia, 1898', *Oxford Slavonic Papers* (O, 1955), vol. VI, pp. 102–14.

29   Pelcovits, p. 213; Bertie's memorandum reflecting China Association views, 8 February 1898, FO 17/1330; his memorandum on Wei-hai-wei as another Gibraltar, 23 March 1898, FO 17/1357; Press criticisms, FO 17/1359.

30   P. M. Kennedy, *The Samoan Tangle* (Dublin, 1974), especially pp. 228–38; and the same author's *Antagonism*, pp. 238–9.

31   Earlier studies of Fashoda (e.g. Langer, pp. 537–80, Marder, pp. 320–40, and A. J. P. Taylor, *The Struggle for Mastery in Europe* (O, 1954), pp. 380–2, as well as M. B. Giffen's slightly disappointing *Fashoda*, Chicago, 1930) need to be supplemented by C. Andrew, *Théophile Delcassé and the Making of the Entente Cordiale* (L, 1968), pp. 91–119, chapter X of Grenville, and the last chapters of G. N. Sanderson's *England, Europe and the Upper Nile* (Edinburgh, 1965).

32 Marder, p. 322.
33 Bülow's directive of 22 November 1898 is printed in translation by Kennedy, *Antagonism*, p. 237.
34 Langer, pp. 581–91; A. C. F. Beales, *The History of Peace* (L, 1931), pp. 230–47.
35 William II to Nicholas II, 29 August 1898, GP, Vol. XV, no. 4217.
36 Bridge, p. 247.

Chapter 14: The Diplomatic Revolution, 1899–1906

1   Memorandum by Sir John Ardagh, 15 October 1899, FO 106/2; Curzon's comments are in his memorandum of 19 November 1898, FO 78/4947.
2   Scott to Salisbury, 14 December 1899, FO 65/1580/369; cf. Max Beloff, *Lucien Wolf and the Anglo-Russian Entente* (L, 1951), and Diplomaticus, 'Count Muraviev's indiscretion', *Fortnightly Review*, December 1899, pp. 1036 ff.
3   Memorandum by Sir John Ardagh, 9 December 1899, FO 106/2.
4   O'Conor's telegram to Salisbury, 1 June 1900, FO 78/5248/43, with a minute in Salisbury's hand.
5   Kuropatkin's remarks are reported in Scott to Salisbury, 7 March 1900, FO 65/1598/63.
6   Salisbury to Macdonald, 7 June 1900, FO 17/1417/64. For Salisbury's private views on the Boxer rising see the journal of Sir Ernest Satow, 12 June 1900, PRO 30/33/16/3.
7   Scott to Salisbury, 22 August 1900, FO 65/1600/272, and a private letter from Scott to Bertie, 6 September 1900, FO 65/1601. On Lamsdorff, see Prince von Bülow, *Memoirs, 1897–1903* (L, 1931), p. 407, and R. R. Rosen, *Forty Years of Diplomacy* (NY, 1922), Vol. I, p. 175.
8   For events in China, see Peter Fleming, *The Siege at Peking* (L, 1959), and for an analysis of the Boxer movement, V. Purcell, *The Boxer Uprising* (L, 1963).
9   Satow journal, 20 and 24 August 1900, PRO 30/33/16/3.
10 Julian Amery, *Life of Joseph Chamberlain* (L, 1951), pp. 138–40; G. L. Monger, *The End of Isolation* (L, 1963), pp. 15–20; J. D. Hargreaves, 'Lord Salisbury, British isolation and the Yangtse valley', BIHR, vol. 30 (1957), pp. 62–75.
11 L. Cecil, *The German Diplomatic Service, 1871–1914* (Princeton, NJ, 1976), pp. 290–4.
12 J. A. S. Grenville, *Lord Salisbury and Foreign Policy* (L, 1964), pp. 321–5.
13 Salisbury memorandum, 29 May 1901, BD. Vol. II, pp. 68–9; printed also in K. Bourne, *The Foreign Policy of Victorian England* (O, 1970), pp. 462–4, and J. Joll, *Britain and Europe, Pitt to Churchill* (L, 1953), pp. 198–200.
14 Lansdowne to Hardinge, 29 October 1901, telegram, FO 65/1624; Hardinge to Lansdowne, 4 November 1901, FO 65/1623; Grenville, pp. 401–2.
15 Z. S. Steiner, 'Great Britain and the creation of the Anglo-Japanese Alliance', JMH, vol. XXXI (1959), pp. 27–36; I. Nish, *The Anglo-Japanese Alliance* (L, 1966), pp. 153–226. On Bertie, see Z. Steiner, *The Foreign Office and Foreign Policy, 1898–1914* (Cambridge, 1969), pp. 60–6 and 369–70.
16 Eulenburg to Bülow, 6 January 1901, GP, Vol. XVIII (i), no 3443, pp. 115–16.
17 Goluchowski to Szögyeny, 17 January 1902, cited from the Vienna archives, by F. R. Bridge, *From Sadowa to Sarajevo* (L, 1972), p. 427.
18 C. J. Lowe and F. Marzari, *Italian Foreign Policy, 1870–1940* (L, 1975), pp. 69–89.
19 C. M. Andrew and A. S. Kanya-Forstner, 'The French Colonial Party; its composition, aims and influence 1885–1914', HJ, vol. XIV (1971), pp. 99–128; C. Andrew, *Theophile Delcassé and the Making of the Entente Cordiale* (L, 1968), pp. 180–201.
20 Compare the assessments of Crowe (BD, Vol. III, p. 398) and Balfour (Lord Newton, *Lord Lansdowne*, L, 1929, p. 293); and see, in general, G. B. Shepherd, *Uncle of Europe* (L, 1975); Steiner, pp. 202–5; and Paul Kennedy, *The Rise of the Anglo-German Antagonism* (L, 1980), p. 402.
21 The Kaiser's letter to his daughter, the Duchess of Brunswick, in late June 1940, Princess Viktoria Luise, *Im Strom der Zeit* (Göttingen, 1975), p. 286.
22 'Un Diplomate', *Paul Cambon* (P, 1937), pp. 211–16; Andrew, pp. 201–15.
23 Paléologue's journal, 1 February 1904, M. Paléologue, *Un Grand Tournant de la politique mondiale* (P, 1934), p. 12.
24 B. H. Sumner's famous Raleigh Lecture of May 1940, 'Tsardom and Imperialism in the Far East and the Middle East, 1880–1914', was printed as a brochure and in *Proceedings*

of the British Academy, vol. XXVII. Bezobrazov is covered in the brochure, pp. 5–14. But Sumner's study must be supplemented by A. Malozemoff, *Russian Far Eastern Policy, 1881–1904* (Berkeley, Calif., 1958), pp. 179–86 and 208–23. For Plehve's remark, A. Yarmolinsky (ed.), *The Memoirs of Count Witte* (L, 1921), p. 250.

25 Monger, pp. 206–11; A. J. Marder, *British Naval Policy 1880–1905* (L, 1940), pp. 501–8.
26 Alan Palmer, *The Kaiser* (L, 1978), pp. 111–12 and 118; Andrew, pp. 268–301.
27 William II to Bülow, 25 July 1905, GP, Vol. XIX (ii), no. 6220, pp. 458–60.
28 Yarmolinsky (ed.), pp. 425–9.
29 Monger, ch. 8; H. Nicolson, *Lord Carnock* (L, 1930), pp. 170–202; Hardinge to Grey, 10 January 1906, BD, Vol. IV, no. 206, p. 220; B. F. Oppel, 'The waning of a traditional alliance, Russia and Germany after the Portsmouth Peace Conference', *Central European History* (Atlanta, Ga, 1972), vol. 5, pp. 318–29.
30 On Holstein's fall, N. Rich, *Friedrich von Holstein* (Cambridge, 1965), Vol. II, pp. 736–52; Cecil, pp. 290–4.

Chapter 15: Failure of a System, 1906–14

1 K. Robbins, *Sir Edward Grey* (L, 1971), pp. 125–6; T. Boyle, 'The formation of the Campbell-Bannerman government in December 1905', BIHR, vol. LXV (1972), pp. 283–302.
2 Quoted from Sanderson's 'Observations on the use and abuse of red tape' by Zara Steiner, *The Foreign Office and Foreign Policy, 1898–1914* (Cambridge, 1969), p. 35. Dr Steiner's book is an invaluable source of information on the personnel of the Foreign Office.
3 Memorandum by Eyre Crowe, 1 January 1907, BD, Vol. III, Appendix A, pp. 397–420. Sanderson's comments, annotated by Crowe and others, form Appendix B, pp. 420–33. On Crowe, see Steiner, pp. 108–18.
4 Memorandum by Grey, 20 February 1906, BD, Vol. III, no. 299, p. 267.
5 Grey to Nicolson, 1 April 1907, cited from the Nicolson MSS. by Beryl Williams in her contribution to F. H. Hinsley (ed.), *British Foreign Policy under Sir Edward Grey* (Cambridge, 1977), p. 146.
6 Prince von Bülow, *Memoirs, 1903–1909* (L, 1931), pp. 284–6; R. P. Churchill, *The Anglo-Russian Convention of 1907* (Cedar Rapids, Iowa, 1939), pp. 117–21. For a vivid and not unsympathetic sketch of Izvolsky, see H. Nicolson, *Lord Carnock* (L, 1930), p. 216. The Kaiser, reading *Carnock* in Doorn, commended this passage; a German edition, with many marginal comments by the Kaiser, is in my possession.
7 F. R. Bridge, *From Sadowa to Sarajevo* (L, 1972), pp. 289–92; C. A. Macartney, *The Habsburg Empire, 1760–1918* (L, 1968), pp. 779–80; E. Crankshaw, *The Fall of the House of Habsburg* (L, 1963) gives a refreshingly fair assessment of the often maligned Aehrenthal, pp. 328–33.
8 Bridge, *From Sadowa to Sarajevo*, pp. 297–9; A. J. May, 'The Novibazar railway project', JMH, Vol. X (1938), pp. 496–527.
9 F. R. Bridge, *Great Britain and Austria-Hungary, 1906–1914* (L, 1972), especially pp. 49–91; Bülow 'into the open', Grey to Nicolson, 1 May 1907, BD, Vol. VIII, no. 195, p. 228. For the Kaiser's visit to England and his residence at Highcliffe Castle see Alan Palmer, *The Kaiser* (L, 1978), pp. 128–31, using the Stuart-Wortley papers.
10 Conrad von Hötzendorf, *Aus Meiner Dienstzeit* (Vienna, 1921), Vol. I, p. 104; Bridge, *From Sadowa to Sarajevo*, p. 303.
11 A. J. P. Taylor, *The Struggle for Mastery in Europe* (O, 1954), pp. 451–2; L. Albertini, *The Origins of the War of 1914* (O, 1952), Vol. I, pp. 206–210; N. V. Charykov, *Glimpses of High Politics* (L, 1931), p. 269. The standard work by Bernadotte Schmitt, *The Annexation of Bosnia* (Cambridge, 1937) may be supplemented by D. W. Sweet's study of aspects of the crisis in Hinsley (ed.), pp. 178–92.
12 Palmer, *The Kaiser*, pp. 133–4; Paul Kennedy, *The Rise of the Anglo-German Antagonism, 1860–1914* (L, 1980), pp. 367 and 344.
13 Goschen to Grey, 13 November 1908, BD, Vol. VI, no. 136, pp. 217–18.
14 Konrad H. Jarausch, *The Enigmatic Chancellor, Bethmann Hollweg and the Hubris of Imperial Germany* (L, 1973), pp. 64–8; D. W. Sweet, 'Great Britain and Germany 1905–1911', in Hinsley (ed.), pp. 229–31.

15 Kennedy, *Antagonism*, pp. 446–7; Crowe comment on Goschen to Grey, 4 November 1909, BD, Vol. VI, no. 204, pp. 309–10.
16 F. Fischer, *War of Illusions* (L, 1975), pp. 67–8.
17 Nicolson, *Carnock*, p. 330.
18 William II to Bethmann Hollweg, 22 April 1911, GP, Vol. XXIX, no. 10538, p. 89; Palmer, *The Kaiser*, pp. 142–7; Kennedy, *Antagonism*, pp. 447–508. I. C. Barlow's *The Agadir Crisis* (Durham, NC, 1940) may be supplemented by Fischer, pp. 71–94, by Joanne Mortimer, 'Commercial interests and German diplomacy in the Agadir crisis', HJ, vol. 10, no. 3 (1967), pp. 440–56, and by the contribution of M. L. Dockrill to Hinsley (ed.), pp. 271–87.
19 Richard Cosgrove, 'Lloyd George's speech at the Mansion House', HJ, vol. 12, no. 4 (1967), pp. 698–701; K. Wilson, 'The Agadir crisis, the Mansion House speech and the double-edgedness of agreements', HJ, vol. 15, no. 4 (1972), pp. 513–32.
20 J. Caillaux, *Agadir, ma politique extérieure* (P, 1919); J. Ganiage, *L'Expansion coloniale de la France sous la 3ᵉ République* (P, 1968), pp. 266–72; V. R. Berghahn, *Germany and the Approach of War in 1914* (L, 1973), pp. 94–103; Walter Görlitz (ed.), *Der Kaiser. Aufzeichnungen des Chefs des Marinekabinetts Admiral Georg Alexander von Müller* (Göttingen, 1965), pp. 88–92.
21 Albertini, *Origins of the War*, Vol. I, pp. 340–63, remains the best account of the war diplomacy in 1911–12. See also C. J. Lowe and F. Marzari, *Italian Foreign Policy, 1870–1940* (L, 1975), pp. 114–19, and the interesting contribution by C. J. Lowe to Hinsley (ed.), pp. 315–23.
22 For the Charykov Kite see Taylor, *Struggle for Mastery*, pp. 474–5. The complicated diplomatic activity may best be followed in the pages of DDF, Third Series, Vol. I, notably nos 18, 54, 94, 106, 114, 322, 326, 332 and 344.
23 Bridge, *From Sadowa to Sarajevo*, pp. 20–1 and 339–42; H. Hantsch, *Leopold Graf Berchtold* (Graz, 1963), Vol. I, pp. 235–310.
24 E. C. Helmreich, *The Diplomacy of the Balkan Wars* (Cambridge, Mass, 1938), chs 1 to 4, may be supplemented by E. C. Thaden, *Russia and the Balkan Alliance of 1912* (University Park, Pa, 1965), pp. 43–125.
25 Görlitz (ed.), pp. 121–2; Albertini, Vol. I, pp. 376–7.
26 Grey of Fallodon, *Twenty-Five Years* (L, 1925), Vol. I, p. 265; Fischer, pp. 174–6. For a recent assessment of the conference, see R. J. Crampton in Hinsley (ed.), pp. 262–4.
27 Hantsch, Vol. II, pp. 506–7. Berchtold résumé of conversation with William II, 28 October 1913, L. Bittner, A. Pribram, H. Srbik and H. Uebersberger (eds), *Oesterreich-Ungarns Aussenpolitik* (Vienna, 1930), Vol. VII, no. 8934.
28 Grey, Vol. I, pp. 276–7; Lichnowsky memorandum of January 1915 printed in J. C. G. Röhl, *1914, Delusion or Design?* (L, 1973), pp. 88 and 97–8.
29 Fischer, pp. 161–4; cf. Röhl, pp. 29–30; Görlitz (ed.), pp. 124–6, but cf. J. C. G. Röhl, 'Admiral von Müller and the approach of War', HJ, vol. 12 (1969), pp. 661–3. See also the criticisms of Wolfgang J. Mommsen, 'The debate on German war aims', JCH, vol. I (1966), pp. 47–9.
30 L. Cecil, *The German Diplomatic Service* (Princeton, NJ, 1976), pp. 317–18.
31 M. K. Chapman, *Great Britain and the Bagdad Railway* (Northampton, Mass., 1948) supplements two well-known studies, E. M. Earle, *Turkey, the Great Powers and the Baghdad Railway* (NY, 1923), and J. B. Wolf, *The Diplomatic History of the Baghdad Railway* (Columbia, Miss., 1936), but Chapman relies heavily on the German documents. Chapters 7 and 11 of Hinsley (ed.) are a useful corrective. On the naval mission see the contribution by Crampton, ibid., pp. 269–70.
32 Grey to Goschen, 15 December 1913, BD, Vol. X (i), no. 431, pp. 383–4.
33 Lichnowsky memorandum printed in Röhl, pp. 98–9; Prince Karl Max Lichnowsky, *Heading for the Abyss* (L, 1928), pp. 33–9; Kennedy, *Antagonism*, p. 390.
34 G. M. Trevelyan, *Grey of Fallodon* (L, 1937), pp. 250–1; Grey, Vol. II, pp. 32–3.
35 Matscheko's undated memorandum (*Oesterreich-Ungarns Aussenpolitik*, Vol. VIII, no. 9918) is printed in an English translation by F. R. Bridge in *From Sadowa to Sarajevo*, pp. 443–8, with summarised excisions. See also ibid., pp. 368–9.
36 William II's comments on Tschirschky to Bethmann Hollweg, 30 June 1914, GD, no. 7; Francis Joseph to William II, 3 July 1914, Immanuel Geiss (ed.), *Julikrise und Kriegsausbruch 1914* (Hanover, 1963–4), Vol. I, no. 9. On Sarajevo there is a vast literature: Vladimir Dedijer, *The Road to Sarajevo* (L, 1966), uses material not

available to earlier writers; J. Remak, *Sarajevo* (L, 1959), is sympathetic to the Austrian version of events.

37 N. Stone, 'Hungary and the Crisis of July 1914', JCH, vol. I (1966), pp. 153–70; Bridge, *From Sadowa to Sarajevo*, pp. 373–6.
38 Jagow to Lichnowsky, 7 July (sent 12 July) 1914, GD, no. 36; Palmer, *The Kaiser*, pp. 167–8.
39 Michael G. Ekstein and Zara Steiner, 'The Sarajevo crisis', in Hinsley (ed.), pp. 398–9.
40 The text of the ultimatum is printed in English in I. Geiss (ed.), *July 1914* (L, 1967), pp. 143–6; and an account of the handing over of the ultimatum to the acting Serbian Prime Minister is also printed ibid., pp. 169–70.
41 ibid., pp. 93, 101, 225.
42 Ekstein and Steiner, in Hinsley (ed.), pp. 401–2; Bethmann Hollweg to Lichnowsky, 27 July 1914, GD, no. 248 (also printed in Geiss, ed., pp. 237–8).
43 J. W. Wheeler-Bennett, *A Wreath to Clio* (L, 1967), p. 181.
44 William II to Jagow, 28 July 1914, GD, no. 293 (Geiss, ed., p. 256); Bethmann Hollweg to Tschirschky, 28 July 1914, GD, no. 323 (Geiss, ed., p. 259).
45 ibid., pp. 336–7; H. von Moltke, *Erinnerungen, Briefe, Dokumente, 1877–1916* (Berlin, 1922), pp. 18–21.
46 J. E. Helmreich, 'Belgian concern over neutrality and British intentions, 1906–1914', JMH, vol. XXXVI, no. 4 (1964), pp. 416–27; Ekstein and Steiner, in Hinsley (ed.), p. 407.

Chapter 16: The Passing of Chancellery Diplomacy, 1914–18

1 C. Seymour, *The Intimate Papers of Colonel House* (L, 1928), Vol. II, p. 139.
2 A. Popov, 'The Czechoslovak Question and Tsarist diplomacy' (in Russian), KA, vol. 33 (1929), pp. 3–33, and vol. 34 (1929), pp. 31–8; Izvolsky to Sazonov, 13 October 1914, MO, Series 3, Vol. 6, no. 386; Josip Horvat, *Supilo* (Zagreb, 1922), pp. 354–8; C. A. Macartney and A. W. Palmer, *Independent Eastern Europe* (L, 1962), pp. 52–3.
3 F. Fischer, *Germany's Aims in the First World War* (L, 1967), ch. 4, with the two remarks of the Kaiser cited from GD, Vol. II, pp. 130 ff. by Fischer on p. 121.
4 On Romania, see Zoltan Szasz, 'The Transylvanian Question, Roumania and the Belligerents, July to October, 1914', JCEA, vol. 13, no. 4 (1954), pp. 409–35. See also chs 24 and 25 of F. H. Hinsley (ed.), *British Foreign Policy under Sir Edward Grey* (Cambridge, 1977).
5 Trubecki (Russian Minister to Serbia) to Sazonov, 16 August 1915, MO, Series 3, Vol. 8 (ii), no. 522.
6 Fischer, *Germany's Aims*, pp. 103–6. See also Fischer's *War of Illusions* (L, 1975), pp. 534–41, and his *World Power or Decline* (L, 1974), pp. 32–45.
7 George V's remark is cited from a dispatch of Benckendorff of 13 November 1914 by Michael G. Ekstein in 'Russia, Constantinople and the Straits 1914–15', chapter 25 of Hinsley (ed.), p. 429, the fullest treatment of the question; but see also A. J. P. Taylor, *The Struggle for Mastery in Europe* (O, 1954), pp. 540–1. C. M. Mason's chapter on Anglo-American relations in Hinsley (ed.) covers early attempts at mediation, pp. 468–9. For Sazonov's views, see Paléologue to Delcassé, 14 September 1914, MO, Series 3, Vol. 6 (i), p. 256, and Macartney and Palmer, p. 42.
8 Demidov to Sazonov, 8 July 1915 (enclosing a dispatch from Grey to the British Minister to Serbia), MO, Series 3, Vol. 8, no. 423, p. 304.
9 See, in particular, Kenneth J. Calder, *Britain and the Origins of the New Europe* (Cambridge, 1976), pp. 14–15 and 44–6.
10 Grey of Fallodon, *Twenty-Five Years* (L, 1925), Vol. II, p. 166.
11 Ekstein, in Hinsley (ed.), pp. 423–35.
12 C. J. Lowe and F. Marzari, *Italian Foreign Policy, 1870–1940* (L, 1975), pp. 133–46.
13 ibid., pp. 150–6; Hinsley (ed.), pp. 415, 421, 519 and 543; G. M. Trevelyan, *Grey of Fallodon* (L, 1937), pp. 295–9; W. W. Gottlieb, *Studies in Secret Diplomacy* (L, 1957), pt 2, *passim*.
14 H. Wickham Steed, *Through Thirty Years* (L, 1924), Vol. II, p. 66; Harry Hanak, *Great Britain and Austria-Hungary during the First World War* (O, 1962), pp. 84–6; Hugh and Christopher Seton-Watson, *The Making of a New Europe* (L, 1981), p. 130.

15 For Delcassé's speech, see Georges Bonnefous, *Histoire politique de la Troisième République* (P, 1957), Vol. II, pp. 145–50. On Clemenceau's attitude, David Robin Watson, *Georges Clemenceau* (L, 1974), pp. 249–58.

16 On Russia in general, George Katkov, *Russia 1917* (L, 1967), pp. 133–52; and on Kolyshkov in particular, ibid., pp. 66, 68, 99 and 193–4.

17 There is a good general survey of Bethmann's activities at this time in Gordon A. Craig, *Germany, 1866–1914* (O, 1978), pp. 366–73, a more charitable judgement than that of Fischer (cf. his *Germany's Aims*, pt 2, *passim*).

18 Craig, p. 374; J. W. Wheeler-Bennett, *Hindenburg, the Wooden Titan*, (L, rev. edn, 1967), pp. 70–1; Alan Palmer, *The Kaiser* (L, 1978), pp. 189–91.

19 Alan Palmer, *The Gardeners of Salonika* (L, 1965), pp. 11–50; John Campbell and Philip Sherrard, *Modern Greece* (L, 1968), pp. 117–21.

20 Norman Stone, *The Eastern Front, 1914–17* (L, 1975), pp. 247–57 for Brussilov; Palmer, *The Kaiser*, pp. 190–2; Macartney and Palmer, pp. 55–60.

21 Stone, pp. 264–81, for the best treatment of the Romanian campaign; for Sarrail's attack, Palmer, *Gardeners of Salonika*, pp. 71–91.

22 Hanak, p. 94; H. and C. Seton-Watson, p. 154.

23 Roberta Warman, 'The erosion of Foreign Office influence, 1916–18', HJ, vol. 15, no. 1 (1972), p. 133–59; Zara Steiner, 'The Foreign Office and the war', ch. 30 of Hinsley (ed.), pp. 530–1.

24 Warman. HJ, vol. 15, no. 1, p. 133.

25 Zara Steiner, *The Foreign Office and Foreign Policy, 1898–1914* (Cambridge, 1969), pp. 166 and 171; K. Rose, *The Later Cecils* (L, 1975), pp. 149–54.

26 Calder, pp. 53–8; M. L. Sanders, 'Wellington House and British propaganda in the First World War', HJ, vol. 18 (1975), pp. 117–46.

27 W. S. Churchill, *Great Contemporaries* (rev. edn, L, 1941), p. 211.

28 Warman, HJ, vol. 15, no. 1, pp. 143–4.

29 J. W. Wheeler-Bennett, *Brest Litovsk, the Forgotten Peace* (rev. edn, L, 1966), pp. 63–96.

30 Ottokar Czernin, *In the World War* (L, 1919), p. 221 (journal entry for 20 December 1917). Wheeler-Bennett's account of the conference (cited above) may be supplemented by a study in some 200 pages by Wolfdieter Bihl, *Oesterreich-Ungarn und die Friedenschlusse von Brest-Litovsk* (Vienna, 1970).

31 See the interesting points raised by Paul Kennedy in ch. 4 of his *The Realities behind Diplomacy* (paperback edn, L, 1981).

32 Watson, *Clemenceau*, p. 277; D. Collins, *Aspects of British Politics 1904–19* (O, 1965), pp. 268–95.

33 Warman, HJ, vol. 15, no. 1, p. 140.

34 V. S. Mamatey, *The United States and East Central Europe* (O, 1958), supplements older studies of this question.

35 Palmer, *Gardeners of Salonika*, pp. 197–236; Paul Kennedy, *Realities*, pp. 207–11.

36 Diary entry of 13 December 1918, T. T. Shotwell, *At the Paris Peace Conference* (NY, 1937), pp. 79–83.

I have found four works, not noted above, of particular general value:

F. R. Bridge and Roger Bullen, *The Great Powers and the European States System, 1815–1914* (L, 1980)

Harold Nicolson, *The Evolution of Diplomatic Method* (L, 1954)

P. Renouvin, *Histoire des relations internationales* (P, 1954), Vols V and VI

Hugh Seton-Watson, *The Russian Empire 1801–1917* (O, 1967).

Index

Compiled by Veronica Palmer

There are general collective headings for 'Alliances', 'Conferences', 'Congresses', 'Conversations', 'Crises', 'Ententes', 'Foreign Ministries', 'Treaties, Agreements and Conventions' and 'Wars'. For quick reference, subdivisions under these headings are arranged alphabetically rather than chronologically. The use of these general headings cuts the length of entries under the individual Great Powers.

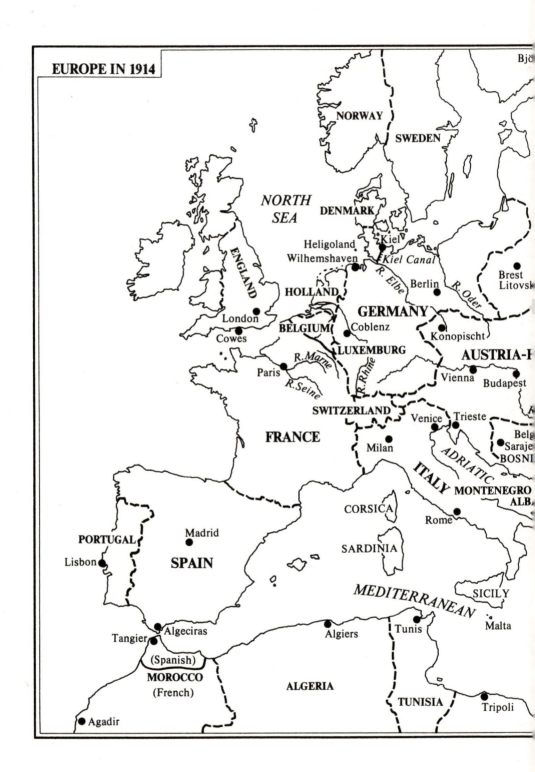

EUROPE IN 1914

NORWAY

SWEDEN

Bjö

NORTH
SEA

DENMARK

Kiel

Heligoland
Wilhemshaven

Kiel Canal

Berlin

R. Elbe

R. Oder

Brest
Litovsk

HOLLAND

GERMANY

Coblenz

Konopischt

AUSTRIA-H

BELGIUM

London

LUXEMBURG

Vienna

Budapest

Cowes

R. Marne

Paris

R. Seine

R. Rhine

SWITZERLAND

Venice

Trieste

Belg

FRANCE

Milan

Saraje

BOSNI

ADRIATIC

ITALY

MONTENEGRO

CORSICA

Rome

ALB.

PORTUGAL

Madrid

SARDINIA

Lisbon

SPAIN

SICILY

MEDITERRANEAN

Tangier

Algeciras

Algiers

Tunis

Malta

(Spanish)

MOROCCO
(French)

ALGERIA

TUNISIA

Tripoli

Agadir